TAIL CODE

PATRICK MARTIN
TAIL CODE
THE COMPLETE HISTORY OF USAF TACTICAL AIRCRAFT TAIL CODE MARKINGS

Schiffer Military/Aviation History
Atglen, PA

Dedication

To Doug Remington

I first met Doug Remington on July 9th, 1983 while shooting Kodachrome at McChord AFB open house. We traded aircraft slides in the hundreds over the years. There was no way to keep up with the overwhelming number of slides Doug sent out. Doug had two main consuming aviation interests, the Tail Codes and the F-4 Phantom. Doug was never short of interesting stories. Each visit to the family abode was a scene of kids, grandchildren, various indecipherable relations, stamps, dogs, cats, and yellow slide boxes. Among the deluge of activity was the ongoing battle for space at the kitchen table to answer correspondence and stamp slides with data.

While I was working in my modelling dungeon, Doug called and asked me to dispose of "the slide collection" on his passing away. While knowing of his ill-health, I thought this rather peculiar as he was in a recovery mode. A few weeks later the request became a reality. In the process of sorting and selling, I set aside from the tens of thousands of slides, the best of the USAF tail coded slides in case somebody wanted to do a book. In spite of informing several potentially interested parties from Doug's mailing list, nobody came forward offering to do the book.

My own early unexpected retirement allowed the "luxury" of seriously considering the project. After conferring with Bernie Remington (*if there ever was a living saint*), the go decision was made. This work would not have been possible without Doug's research. The following pages are the result of a year and a half of collating, phoning, sorting, and writing.

Acknowledgements

Many people have contributed to this book through correspondence with Doug Remington and myself. Several Tail Code code-ologists and *non-coders* have put in many hours contributing to and editing this work. Also thanks to the numerous USAF Historians and Public Affairs Air Force personnel who took the time out to answer hundreds of enquiring letters. A special thanks also goes to the writings of Charles A. Ravenstein whose books provided a great deal of assistance. A special thanks also goes to Marty Isham, Charles Mayer, and William Peak. The biggest thanks goes to my wife Irene, for providing not only editing and patience but the enumerable brews and meals while I *flew* the keyboard. My thanks also to the following people: Captain Kevin Baggett, Lt Col Harold H Barton 77 TFS, Peter Bergagini, 1 Lt Peter D Bird 81 TFS, Nancy J. Bissett 121 TFW, Tom Brewer, Rob Brown, Kenneth Buchanan, MSgt Rolf Carter 831 AD, Fredrick D Claypool 4 TFW, Major Michael R. Cook 69 TFS, Sgt Susan Cooper 108 TFW, Captain P.B. Cranium 57 FIS, Captain George Culley USAFHRC, Major Constance A Custer 51 TFW, SrA Sharon L. Davis 33 TFW, Lt Col George DeFilippi 23 TASS, 2 Lt Robert J Diantonio 4 TFS, Captain G.W. Doe (CAF), Robert Dorr, Sgt Michael Dorset 1 TFW, SSgt Michael Dugre 432 TFW, Leislie Dyson, Sgt Raymond East 10 TFW, William Elliott PhD 16 AF, Kevin Folsom 52 TFW, Rene Francillon, TSgt Joann W Galindo 103 TFG, 1Lt Petra M Gallert 33 TFW, MSgt Christopher J Garland 27 TFW, 2 Lt Tammie D Grevin 924 TFG, Cheryl Gumm AFFTC, Grant Hales TAC, Lt James A. Hallman 7 TFS, TSgt Carey P Hendrix 23 TFW, Betty J. Hoeper 71 FTW, Major John E. Hoffmaster Air Attache Canada, MSgt Micheal J. Hrivnak 363 TFW, 2 Lt Christopher P Jester 38 TRS, Kansau, Sean Keating, TSgt John P Kamelamela 26 TRW, Ben Knowles, John Kuborn PACAF, Don Larsen, 2Lt Michael P. Liechty, Della Lindley OCALC, Captain Robert R. McCarty 313 AD, Jack McKillop, Pat Martin Sr., Julie Massoni AFSC, Gerry A Mauss, TSgt Susan Miller 12 FTW, Kurt Miska, MSgt Terry R Mitchell 48 FIS, 2Lt Lance T Murray 335 TFS, SMSgt. Harold P. Myers, Charles F. O'Connell HQ AFRES, 1Lt Edwin L O'Rourke 435 TFTS, Peter Oakley, 1Lt Mark Philips 2TFTS, 2Lt Lisa M. Potter 12 TRS, Lt Col John P Pope 44 TFS, SSgt Hugh S. Porter 836 AD, SSgt John Roberts 112 TFRG, TSgt Rick Roffer 162 TFG, 1Lt Richard P Roth 23 TFW, Abraham Scherr, PhD 56 TTW, Peter A. Schinkelshoek, D.F. Sherman 66 ECW, Marilyn S Silcox ADWC, Harold J Smarkola USAFE, Dorthy K Spiegelberg AFFTC, Margaret M. Stanek TAC, Joe D Stettler 160 TRS, Paul Stevens, Robert C. Sullivan 832 AD, Lt Col Charles O. Sylling 67 TFS, Norman Taylor, SSgt Doyle Tillman 316 AD, Captain James F Tynan 831 AD, 1Lt J Brian White 35 TFW, Wally Van Winkle, Gusta Vinas 832 AD and Major Charles G Whitley 140 TFW, plus all those who traded slides with Doug and myself and didn't complain when their slides were used.

Copyright © 1994 by Patrick Martin.
Library of Congress Catalog Number: 93-84496

All rights reserved. No part of this work may be reproduced or used in any forms or by any means – graphic, electronic or mechanical, including photocopying or information storage and retrieval systems – without written permission from the copyright holder.

Printed in China.
ISBN: 0-88740-513-4

We are interested in hearing from authors with book ideas on related topics.

Published by Schiffer Publishing Ltd.
77 Lower Valley Road
Atglen, PA 19310
Please write for a free catalog.
This book may be purchased from the publisher.
Please include $2.95 postage.
Try your bookstore first.

Contents

Dedication & Acknowledgements	4
Introduction	6
Glossary	6
Abbreviations	7
History of Tail Codes	8
Tail Code Usage	11
Pacific Air Forces (PACAF)	17
Wing Summary	18
Squadron/Code Summary	25
Alaskan Air Command	65
Wing Summary	66
Squadron/Code Summary	67
Tactical Air Command Continental United States (TAC - CONUS)	69
Wing Summary	71
Squadron/Code Summary	81
Air Force Reserve (AFRES)	156
Air National Guard (ANG)	166
United States Air Forces Europe (USAFE)	181
Wing Summary	182
Squadron/Code Summary	183
Air Training Command	201
Air Force Logistics Command	204
Air Force Systems Command	205
Conclusion	209
Appendix A: Tail Code Summary	215
Appendix B: Tail Code Unit - Base Lists	230
Appendix C: Tail Code Aircraft Types	232
Appendix D: T.O. 1-1-4	233
Appendix E: USAF Tail Codes, 31 December 1990	241

Introduction

Tail codes are a series of two-letter sequences that provide unit identification of tactical aircraft operated by United States Air Force. The purpose of this book is to provide a complete historical record of Tail Codes usage. The history, evolution and presentation of all known tail codes are presented by major Air Force theatre and commands, followed by appendix.

The first published Tail Code list appeared in the February 1970 issue of Air Britain journal– Air Pictorial. The list was far from complete and contained numerous understandable omissions. Shortly thereafter, the International Plastic Modellers Society - Tidewater Branch (*Langley, Virginia*), printed a far more accurate picture by Tom Brewer. A third published work by Frederick W. Roos appeared in the American Aviation Historical Society Journal in the spring 1971 issue and updated in summer of 1972.

Several people started producing tail code lists. By far the most comprehensive effort was by Doug Remington (*Associate editor of IPMS Tidewater*) and Tom Brewer. Nearly two dozen updated full lists were produced up until 1973. Doug Remington's work continued, with the aim of producing a Tail Code book. Doug's work further appeared as an appendix in the back "United States Military Aviation: The Air Force" (*Midland Counties Publications 1980*). Jack McKillop produced 24 very well presented current lists between March 1983 and March 1987, information coming from Doug Remington. In all, I have seen over 120 different tail code lists from 65 sources. Often information was not available, classified, or too "paint fresh" to produce accurate results at the time. One interesting facet in comparing different authors' lists is the transcribing of inaccurate or unconfirmed information.

This book is not written for the novice aviation enthusiast. It is for those who have a specialized interest in USAF tactical aircraft markings. It provides a history based solely on tail code usage. All entries, listings and appendix are focused on units that carried tail codes. The intent is to provide a reference manual to identify tail coded aircraft.

It should be noted that aircraft are not always assigned to individual flying squadrons, as *ownership* maybe to a designated aircraft maintenance unit, organisational maintenance squadron or the wing itself. In the interest of clarity, this text singles out the operator rather than the *owner* of tail coded aircraft. A further qualification to the text is, USAF units, in proper title, should be written as 334*th* TFS or 363*d* TRW. Aircraft types are noted by designation such as C-130 or RF-101 rather than nomenclature such as Hercules or Voodoo in text. Such names are used in photo captions only. All photographs are taken at unit home bases unless otherwise noted. Many of the squadron reassignments were in fact a renumbering process.

To identify a tail code user, or identify a photograph, either use the command section (*if known*), or the quick reference appendix and look up the tail code alphabetically. Summaries are provided for controlling units, such as wings, for Pacific Air Forces (PACAF), Tactical Air Command — Continental United States (TAC-CONUS), Alaska Air Command (AAC) and the United States Air Forces Europe (USAFE). Units maintaining the same tail codes post 1972, due to AFM66-1 (*see section*) have separate entries under the parent wing.

The bulk and aim of this book is to document the history of USAF use of Tail Codes from their inception to the end of 1990. The main problem for the study of aircraft markings is setting out a big enough net to catch all possible users in a given time period. This is only possible after the passage of time to document their use.

Perhaps twenty years from now someone else (another tail code-ologist) will pick up from this point and produce a work covering the post Cold War-Gulf War years. This period in the early 1990s looks to be as fluid as the Vietnam years were. Now for the United States Navy . . .

Glossary

Activate:	To bring an establishment into existence by assigning personnel to it's headquarters unit.
AFM66-1:	Concept that changed tail code assignment to wing level from squadron level.
Assign:	To place a unit within an establishment so that the unit becomes an element or component of a larger organization.
Attach:	To place a unit temporarily under the control of another unit or establishment. The attachment of a unit does not make the unit formally an element or component of the organization to which it is attached.
Battle Creek:	Complex transfer of wings and squadrons within USAFE 1972-73.
Consolidate:	To combine two or more units merging their lineage into a single line.
Designation:	The name of a unit or establishment.
Detach:	To relinquish control of an assigned component, usually for a specific purpose and period of time.
Inactivate:	To withdraw all personnel from an active listed unit, terminating the units existence (*albeit some times temporarily*).
Linebacker:	Series of air operations against North Vietnam.
Parent Unit:	A unit that directly administers and controls subordinate units and establishments.
Provisional Unit:	A temporary unit established to perform a specific task (*ie deployment*).
Ready Switch:	Complex switch of F-111A, D and F-4D between 474, 366 and 48 TFW in 1977.

Abbreviations

AAC	Alaskan Air Command	SOF	Special Operations Flight
AB	Air Base	SOS	Special Operations Squadron
ABG	Air Base Group	SOTG	Special Operations Training Group
ABW	Air Base Wing		
ACCS	Airborne Command & Control Squadron	SOTS	Special Operations Training Squadron
ACS	Air Commando Squadron	SOW	Special Operations Wing
ACW	Air Commando Wing	S/RS	Strike/Reconnaissance Squadron
AD	Air Division	SS(SPA)	Support Squadron (Special Projects Activity)
ADCOM	Aerospace Defense Command		
ADTAC	Air Defense - Tactical Air Command	SVAF	South Vietnamese Air Force
		TAC	Tactical Air Command
ADTC	Air Armament Development Center	TACW/TAIRCW*	Tactical Air Control Wing
		TAG	Tactical Airlift Group
AF	Air Force	TAS	Tactical Airlift Squadron
AFB	Air Force Base	TASS	Tactical Air Support Squadron
AFLC	Air Force Logistics Command	TASG	Tactical Air Support Group
AFSC	Air Force Systems Command	TASW	Tactical Air Support Wing
ALC	Air Logistics Center	TASTG	Tactical Air Support Training Group
AMU	Aircraft Maintenance Unit		
ANG	Air National Guard	TASTS	Tactical Air Support Training Squadron
ANGB	Air National Guard Base		
ARRS	Aerospace Rescue & Recovery Squadron	TATS	Tactical Airlift Training Squadron
		TAW	Tactical Airlift Wing
ARS	Aerial Refuelling Squadron	TAWC	Tactical Air Warfare Center
AS	Attack Squadron (pre 1970)	TDS	Tactical Drone Squadron
AS	Aggressor Squadron (post 1973)	TDG	Tactical Drone Group
ATC	Air Training Command	TECG	Tactical Electronic Combat Group
ATD	Adversary Threat Division		
ATS	Air Transport Squadron	TES	Test & Evaluation Squadron
AEW & CW	Airborne Early Warning and Control Wing	TESTS	Test Squadron
		TESTW	Test Wing
BS	Bombardment Squadron	TEWG	Tactical Electronic Warfare Group
CCTS	Combat Crew Training Squadron		
CFB	Canadian Forces Base	TEWS	Tactical Electronic Warfare Squadron
CCTW	Combat Crew Training Wing		
CONUS	Continental United States	TEWTS	Tactical Electronic Warfare Training Squadron
CSS	Combat Support Squadron		
CSW	Combat Support Wing	TFAS	Tactical Fighter Aggressor Squadron
CW	Control Wing		
CW	Composite Wing	TFG	Tactical Fighter Group
Det	Detachment	TFRS	Tactical Fighter Replacement Squadron
DSES	Defense Systems Evaluation Squadron		
		TFS	Tactical Fighter Squadron
ECS	Electronic Combat Squadron/ Countermeasures Squadron	TFTG	Tactical Fighter Training Group
		TFTS	Tactical Fighter Training Squadron
ECW	Electronic Combat Wing/Counter measures Squadron		
		TFTW	Tactical Fighter Training Wing
FAC	Forward Air Control	TFW	Tactical Fighter Wing
FIS	Fighter Interceptor Squadron	TG	Tactical Group
FIW	Fighter Interceptor Wing	TRG	Tactical Reconnaissance Group
FTS	Flying Training Squadron	TRS	Tactical Reconnaissance Squadron
FTW	Flying Training Wing		
FW	Fighter Wing	TRW	Tactical Reconnaissance Wing
FWS	Fighter Weapons Squadron	TRTS	Tactical Reconnaissance Training Squadron
FWW	Fighter Weapons Wing		
HQ	Headquarters	TS	Test Squadron
IAP	International Airport	TTS(T)	Tactical Training Squadron (Test)
MAC	Military Airlift Command	TTW	Tactical Training Wing
MAG	Military Airlift Group	US	United States
MAP	Military Assistance Plan	USAF	United States Air Force
MAP	Municipal Airport	USAFE	United States Air Forces Europe
MAS	Military Airlift Squadron	USS	United States Ship
MASDC	Military Aircraft Storage & Disposition Center	WRALC	Warner-Robins Air Logistics Center
MCAS	Marine Corps Air Station	WWS	Wild Weasel Squadron
NAS	Naval Air Station		
OMS	Organisational Maintenance Squadron		
PACAF	Pacific Air Forces		
RAF	Royal Air Force		
ROK	Republic of Korea		
RS	Reconnaissance Squadron		
RTU	Replacement Training Unit		
RSVN	Republic of South Vietnam		
RTAFB	Royal Thailand Air Force Base		
SAC	Strategic Air Command		

Abbreviation Dates*
1966* - 1968: Initial tail code dates within PACAF
"10/7/68*": Initial tail code assignment date CONUS
"1972*": AFM66-1 generic wing tail code date
"1/12/74+": MAC control of TAC airlift assets

United States Air Force
Distinctive Unit Aircraft Markings

During the late 1960s, United States Air Force tactical aircraft flew in a natural metal finish marked with fuselage letters and numbers, known as "Buzz Numbers." These identified the aircraft types with two letters along with the last three numbers of the aircraft serial number. In addition, a variety of colour markings emblazoned aircraft providing squadron identification in both air and ground operations. Tactical fighter operations in Southeast Asia adopted a toned down appearance starting in 1964. This appearance spread to other commands and theatres shortly thereafter. Topside colours consist of two greens and one brown, with a light grey underside, as set out by Technical Order 1-1-4 (*Federal Standard Colour; FS.595a 34079, 34102, 30219 and 36622*). This scheme is commonly referred to as the *Southeast Asia* or *SEA* scheme. Fixed patterns for all camouflaged types application are noted in T.O. 1-1-4. This document, with regular updates, to the present day, provides a very authoritative view of USAF paint schemes.

F-100D Super Sabre 56-3318, 50 TFW, Hahn AB, displaying blue, yellow and red tail bands. Photo: Bill Stranberg, over Germany, in the late 1960's.

This uniformity of aircraft appearance hindered unit identification of individual squadrons in air and ground operations. "Tail Codes", or the official name, "Distinctive Unit Aircraft Identification Markings", provided the solution. This identification concept, first introduced in the Southeast Asian theatre, consists of two alphabet letters placed on the tails of tactical camouflaged aircraft. Tail Codes were applied in both lustreless white and light grey (*36622 and 37875*), although light grey very much the principal until the early seventies. The fleet wide substitution to lustreless white took years to complete. By May 1970 Appendix D of T.O.1-1-4 laid out size, placement and exact specification for tail code application, on all USAF tail coded types.

The various changes to camouflage schemes affected tail code application. An additional scheme, known as *Asia Minor*, utilized tan, green, and brown (*20400, 30140 and 34079*) for application on C-47, C-54, C-130, F-4, F-5, F-84 and F-86. Although approved, not all of these types carried the variation. All schemes utilized light grey (*36622*) underside. The PACAF (*also* SAC) deviated, on approval, from specification requirements and painted underside black (*17038*) on some types. This supplemented grey on tactical types, such as B-57, C-47, C-130 and F-4.

On inception of tail codes, two lettering systems were initiated during 1966 and 1967 in PACAF. One system used the first letter to represent the squadron, the second an individual aircraft within the squadron. The second system, adopted a common first letter within the wing, followed by a second varying letter allocated to different component squadrons. The latter system was later adopted as the standard.

Along with tail codes, tactical aircraft continued to carry squadron colours as a single six inch wide stripe across the upper tail, or the thicker fin cap form. Unless otherwise noted, squadron colours were carried as checkered pattern. Any wider horizontal tail markings, are referred as bands. Both forms of markings were also noted as fin caps. Many units added colour to title blocks, canopy rails and tank trim. Beyond the scope of this work are the specialized squadron markings applied for special occasions, such as weapons meets, commanders and special event aircraft.

F-105F Thunderchief 63-8326, 49 TFW Spangdahlem AB, alongside a KC-135A, with red, yellow and blue markings on tail and nose with Buzz number "FH-326." Photo: Richard Kierbow, over the Atlantic, December 1965.

HISTORY OF TAIL CODES

Several USAF bases have tail coded display aircraft painted in former markings. Many have erroneous codes applied representing current base occupants or abbreviations of guarded location. Many non-flying airframes assigned to the BDR (*Battle Damage Repair, non-flying*) role have been painted in schemes representing current or past history. Several aircraft have had erroneous tail codes applied by intent or accident. The 17 TFS 363 TFW painted three F-16C with the **DS** (*Desert Shield*) tail codes when aircraft were temporally assigned from the 50 TFW (**HR**) at the end of 1990.

F-105D Thunderchief 61-0100 **RU**, 357 TFS, 62-4353 **RM**, 354 TFS 355 TFW, Takhli RTAFB, enroute north from base. Photo: Les Sundt.

In the mid-1970s, the standard Southeast Asia scheme changed with the extension the topside colours underside and omitting the underside grey. With this amendment, tail code letter application switched to black in colour as part of a general toning down of aircraft eliminating high visible markings. This toned down look also included items such as national insignia, rescue markings, and serial numbers. In time, European One camouflage colours of two green and charcoal (*34092, 34102 and 36118 [or 36081]*) in wrap-a-round form became standard. There were many exceptions, variations and combinations of schemes, including temporary colours. Many "special" aircraft such as representative, demonstration, or squadron, wing and Air Division commander's aircraft had a shadow effect added to the tail code letters and serials. A few squadrons such as the 18 TFS in Alaska added the shadow effect to all aircraft.

While beyond the scope of this work, the various paint schemes adopted since tail code assignment to tactical types have affected application and colour of tail codes. The introduction of the F-15 and F-16 aircraft inaugurated a series of air to air schemes. The F-15 utilized an initial Air Superiority Blue scheme (*35450 topside and 15450 gloss underside*) with white tail codes, before adopting a standard two tone grey (*Compass Ghost 36320 and 36375*) with black tail codes. The F-16 applied a further all grey scheme (*36118, 36270 and 36375*), maintaining black tail codes. Tail codes on F-4 grey schemes (*Hill I 36118, 36270 topside and 36375 underside, Hill II 36118 topside, 36270 on topside and underside*), utilized gunship grey (*36118*) for tail code presentation. The overall gunship grey scheme used on AC-130 and adopted by the F-15E with black tail codes after several experimental schemes evaluated at Nellis AFB, on F-15C.

The initial two tone light grey scheme (*close to 34672 and 36463*) on the A-10A changed, to 'European One', starting in late 1979. The A-7 and A-37 progressed through various low visibility schemes. A green and grey scheme (*34079 and 36081*) noted until A-7 adopted a two grey scheme (*36118 and 36270*) in the late eighties. Both schemes applying black codes. The F-117 applied grey tail codes over a special black coloured surface.

AFM66-1

On 1 April, 1972 the basic USAF maintenance concept changed from squadron to wing level. As a result of this concept, a single two-letter tail code designated the entire wing, rather than an individual squadron. This tail code was usually in prior usage within wings as a single squadron code. The AFM66-1 document does not mention tail codes, as the wing common tail code is a consequence of the restructuring. The wing level single tail code concept had prior usage within Combat Crew Training Wings at Davis-Monthan AFB, Luke AFB and Sewart AFB (**DM, LA** *and* **TS**). The sole Fighter Weapons Wing at Nellis AFB had a common code (**WA**) for detachments before adopting the code for all components in late 1969.

All text noted "1972*" indicates an AFM66-1 affected date of change to wing common tail code, usually mid 1972. Dates of actual tail code change vary throughout 1972, though rarely before June. This system embraced all PACAF, USAFE and US based units. It was some time before fleet wide utilization became reality. In some cases, especially in Southeast Asia the older squadron tail code system lasted until 1973.

Pacific Air Forces (PACAF)

Visual identification based on large colour patches, was not advisable in the combat zones of Southeast Asia. To aid both aerial and surface identification a system of unit identification was developed based on two letters of the alphabet. There has been a long running debate on which wing within PACAF started placing tail codes on aircraft.

TAIL CODE

The first theory concerns the 8 Tactical Fighter Wing based at Ubon RTAFB. In this system the wing adopted a common first letter **F**, followed by a second varying letter allocated to squadrons. While late in 1966 is generally accepted as the starting period of tail codes, the first documented 8 TFW sighting is in January 1967, on an F-4C of the 433 TFS. The initial 8 TFW coded units noted flying the F-4C were:

FG	433 TFS	F-4C (*F-4D arrived 7/67; re 4 TFS 33 TFW*)
FP	497 TFS	F-4C
FY	555 TFS	F-4C (*F-4D arrived 5/67; re 40 TFS 33 TFW*)

The second claim is the 366 TFW based at Da Nang AB, RSVN with F-4C, by spring 1967. The first letter represented the squadron, and the second an individual aircraft. This system continued through conversion to F-4D in early 1968. Late in 1969 the 390 TFS recoded **LF** while the 480 and 389 TFS transferring to the 37 TFW at Phu Cat AB, RSVN and adopted **HB** and **HK** tail codes in June and April 1969, ending the system. This allowed for 26 different tail codes per squadron, or 78 within a three squadron wing. Thus possible tail codes:

AA to **AZ**	389 TFS
BA to **BZ**	390 TFS
CA to **CZ**	480 TFS

The third claim is the 12 TFW at Cam Ranh Bay AB, with the same system adopted as the 8 TFW. Codes were applied to at least some F-4C by December 1966. Initial coded within the 12 TFW units:

XC	557 TFS	F-4C
XD	558 TFS	F-4C
XN	559 TFS	F-4C
XT	391 TFS	F-4C

Units controlled by PACAF applied tail codes on most tactical aircraft by 1968. Tail codes were assigned to bases using the 8/12 TFW method of common wing letter first, followed by a varying second letter, indicating the individual squadron. Taking some time to reach all wings, the general commencement of codes in early July 1968 within PACAF noted as:

		A_, B_, C_	389, 390, 480 TFS	366 TFW	Da Nang, RSVN
A	-	AC, AE, AH, AJ, AL, AN	12, 16, 45 TRS, 360, 361, 362 TEWS	460 TRW	Tan Son Nhut AB, RSVN
B	-	BO, BP	390, 127 TFS (*CONUS assigned*)	354 TFW	Kunsan AB, ROK
C	-	CB, CE, CK, CP	90, 510 TFS, 604 ACS, 531 TFS	3 TFW	Bien Hoa AB, RSVN
D	-	DE, DH, DL	50, 345, 776 TAS	314 TAW	Ching Chuan Kang AB, Taiwan
E	-	EC, EL, EN, EO, ER, ET	1, 3, 4, 5, 9, 6 ACS	14 ACW	Phan Rang AB, RSVN
F	-	FA, FG, FO, FP, FY	25, 433, 435, 497, 555 TFS	8 TFW	Ubon RTAFB
G	-	GG, GL, GR, GT	35, 36, 80 TFS, 556 RS	347 TFW	Yokota AB, Japan
H	-	HA, HE, HP, HS	174, 416, 355, 612 TFS	37 TFW	Phu Cat AB, RSVN
J	-	JE, JJ, JV	44, 34, 469 TFS	388 TFW	Korat RTAFB
K	-	KA, KC, KE, KH, KL, KN	457, 458, 459, 535, 536 537 TAS	483 TAW	Phu Cat/Vung Tau AB, RSVN
M	-	MA	815 TAS	315 AD	Tachikawa AB, Japan
N	-	NV	82 FIS	51 FIW	Naha AB, Okinawa
O	-	OC, OO, OY, OZ	13, 11 TRS, 555 TFS, 14 TRS	432 TRW	Udorn RTAFB
P	-	PE, PK, PN, PQ, PV	64, 509 FIS, 523 TFS, 8, 13 BS	405 FW	Clark AFB, Philippines
Q	-	QB, QF, QG, QW	29, 772, 773, 773, 774 TAS	463 TAW	Clark AFB, Philippines
R	-	RC, RH, RK, RM, RU	41, 42 TEWS, 333, 354, 357 TFS	355 TFW	Takhli RTAFB
S	-	SD, SG, SK, SM, SS	306, 136, 188, 308, 309 TFS	31 TFW	Hoa AB, RSVN
T	-	TA, TC, TO, TT	609, 1, 606, 602 ACS	56 ACW	Nakhon Phanom RTAFB
U	-	UD, UK, UP	391, 356, 67 TFS	475 TFW	Misawa AB, Japan
V	-	VM, VP, VS	352, 614, 120 TFS	35 TFW	Phan Rang AB, RSVN
W	-	WE, WH, WM, WV	19, 309, 310, 311 ACS	315 ACW	Phan Rang AB, RSVN
X	-	XC, XD, XN, XT	557, 558, 559, 391 TFS	12 TFW	Cam Rang AB, RSVN
Y	-	YD, YJ, YP, YU	21, 35, 41, 817 TAS	374 TAW	Naha AB, Okinawa
Z	-	ZA, ZZ	12 TFS, 15 TRS	18 TFW	Kadena AB, Okinawa

A few of these could not exist at the same time (*such as 1 ACS* **EC**, *recoded to* **TC** *in December 1967*). The B-57 units 35 TFW/405 FW, tail coded **PQ** and **PV**, rotated from Clark AFB. The 14 and 315 ACW, 3 TFW, and elements of 460 TRW were noted with tail codes in 1967. The 355 TFW may have also received tail codes in early 1968. Tactical fighter squadrons and wings deployed to Southeast Asia maintained CONUS codes when temporarily attached. Units with a permanent change of station adopted in-theatre codes. Several tactical fighter units maintained tail codes for short periods on return to CONUS. The South Vietnam based wings (*3, 12, 31, 35, 37, 366 TFW, 460 TRW*) and Thailand based (*8, 355, 388 TFW, 432 TRW*) fighter and reconnaissance wings provided an abundant variation of different tail codes. Dates in text between 1967 and 1968, and marked with "*" indicate the initial coding period within PACAF.

As the USAF commitment in Southeast Asia expanded so did the number of units with assigned tail codes. There were numerous transfers between wings, as well as wing movement. Due to the fluid situation, numerous deployments, attachments and reassignments may go unrecorded. Many of these movements are still classified.

HISTORY OF TAIL CODES

A-1E Skyraider 53-9577 **TC**, 1 SOS 56 SOW, Nakhon Phanom RTAFB. Photo: Don Larsen, Udorn RTAFB, 19 December 1971.

Tactical airlift squadrons in the Pacific theatre also applied tail codes during 1968. The main airlift assets were assigned to four (*314, 374, 463 and 483*) Tactical Airlift Wings. There were several basing methods for tactical airlift capacity in Southeast Asia. Several medium sized transports, such as C-7 and C-123 were based in theatre. The C-130 wings based out of country deployed large detachments in theatre. These detachments would vary in size depending on requirements of the conflict. The three PACAF C-130 wings (*314, 374, and 463 TAW*) maintained permanent detachments, rotating crews and aircraft in country. Aircraft returned to wing bases for major maintenance. Squadron colours rarely applied to exterior of aircraft.

The 14, 56, and 315 Air Commando Wings and later retitled as Special Operations Wings, provided the largest variety of unit movements is Southeast Asia. Air Commando units applied tail codes between April and December 1967. Many units flew types that remained uncoded throughout the conflict, such as CH-3, O-1, O-2 and OV-10A. The number of units assigned to Special Operations Wings diminished as US forces withdrew from the conflict. The wing common tail codes introduced under the AFM66-1 concept, did not fully catch on within PACAF tactical units until the conflict diminished. The following wings adopted common tail codes at different times:

Code	Wing	Squadrons	Date	Base
HG	347 TFW	428, 429 TFS	July 1973	Takhli RTAFB
OS	51 ABW	19 TASS, 36, TFS	October 1971	Osan AB, ROK
PN	405 FW	1 TS, 523 TFS	1972	Clark AB, Philippines
UD	432 TRW	4, 13, 421, 555 TFS, 14 TRS	August 1973	Udorn RTAFB
UP	3 TFW	35, 36, 80 TFS	not implemented	Kunsan AB, ROK
WP	8 TFW	25, 433, 435, 497 TFS	January 1973	Ubon RTAFB
ZZ	18 TFW	25, 44, 67 TFS, 15 TRS	late or confirmed 1973	Kadena AB, Okinawa

Tactical Air Command
Continental United States (TAC CONUS)

A six page message distributed on 10 July 1968, lists initial CONUS tail codes. It also refers to TACR 66-12, dated 8 February 1968, which contains the initial application instructions. All dates marked "10/7/68*" within the text are in reference to CONUS initial tail code date. Considerable time passed before application fleet wide was implemented.

Air National Guard and Air Force Reserve followed suit and by late 1971, tail codes were universally applied on most tactical USAF units. As tail codes were assigned to individual squadrons, the variation was rather large. The conforming first letters usually coincided with the initial letter of base name or proximate centres of population. The second letter assigned to components, usually alphabetically, was dependent on prior usage in other theatres and commands. The initial TAC CONUS assigned codes were:

Letter	Codes	Squadrons	Wing	Base
A	- AD, AO, AP, AQ	4407, 4408, 4409, 4410 CCTS	4410 CCTW	Hurlburt Field
B	- BA, BB, BC	91, 4, 9 TRS	67 TRW	Bergstrom AFB
C	- CA, CC, CD	481, 522, 524 TFS	27 TFW	Cannon AFB
D	- DB, DY, DZ,	346, 347, 348 TAS	516 TAW	Dyess AFB
DM		4454, 4455, 4456, 4472 CCTS	4453 CCTW	Davis-Monthan AFB
E	- EB, ED, EE, EG	4, 16, 40 TFS, 4533 TTS	33 TFW	Eglin AFB
F	- FB, FC, FD, FE, FF*	43, 45, 46, 47 TFS, 4530 TTS	15 TFW	MacDill AFB
F	- FB	47 TAS	313 TAW	Forbes AFB
G	- GA, GB, GC, GD*, GE	68, 431, 434, 476 TFS, 4452 CCTS	479 TFW	George AFB
H	- HB+, HC+, HD+	7, 8, 9 TFS	49 TFW	Holloman AFB
I	- IA, IB, IC, ID, IE, IF, IG, IH, II	Det 1, 2, 71 TAS, 317, 319, 603 ACS, 4412, 4413, 4532 CCTS 1 ACW		England AFB
J	- JK, JL, JM*, JN, JO	4414, 4415, 4416 TES, 4417 CCTS, 29 TRS	363 TRW	Shaw AFB
K	- KB+, KR, KS, KT	417 TFS, 10, 22, 7 TRS	67 TRW	Mountain Home AFB
LA		4511, 4514, 4515, 4517 CCTS	4510 CCTW	Luke AFB
L	- LM, LN, LO	36, 37, 38 TAS	316 TAW	Little Rock AFB
LZ		4441 CCTS	4510 CCTW	William AFB
M	- MC, MD, ME, MF, MG	560, 561, 562, 563 TFS, 4519 CCTS	23 TFW	McConnell AFB
N	- NA, NB, NC, ND	428, 429, 430 TFS, 4527 CCTS	474 TFW	Nellis AFB

TAIL CODE

O	-	OA, OB	39, 40 TAS	317 TAW	Lockbourne AFB
P	-	PB, PG, PR	777, 778, 779 TAS	464 TAW	Pope AFB
S	-	SA, SB, SC	334, 335, 336 TFS	4 TFW	Seymour-Johnson AFB
S	-	SR, ST,	62, 61 TAS	64 TAW	Sewart AFB
TS			4446, 4447, 4449 CCTS	4442 CCTW	Sewart AFB
WA			Det 1	4525 FWW	Nellis AFB
W	-	WB, WC, WD, WF	4536, 4537, 4538, 4539 CCTS	4525 FWW	Nellis AFB
Z	-	ZD, ZE	436, 478 TFS	4531 TFW	Homestead AFB

* *indicates not carried*
\+ *indicates code assigned while with USAFE, anticipating CONUS move*

F-16D Falcon 86-0041 **WA**, 64 AS 57 FWW, Nellis AFB, with black and yellow checkered tail stripe, on aggressor camouflage.
Photo: Patrick Martin, CFB Namao, 18 May 1990.

The **FB** tail codes repeated for 47 TAS 313 TAW, and 43 TFS 15 TFW. Note single codes for all but one CCTW and the FWW. The following CONUS wings adopted a common tail code close to the AFM66-1 date of 1/4/72 (*noted with initial common code assigned components*):

AH	1 SOW	317, 415, 547, 549 SOS, 4407 CCTS	Hurlburt Field
BA	67 TRW	12, 45, 91 TRS	Bergstrom AFB
CC	27 TFW	481, 522, 524 TFS	Cannon AFB
DB	463 TAW	18 TATS, 772, 773 TAS	Dyess AFB
ED	33 TFW	58 TFS	Eglin AFB
EL	23 TFW	74, 75, 76 TFS	England AFB
FB	313 TAW	47, 48 TAS	Forbes AFB
FF	1 TFW	27, 71, 94 TFS, 4501 TFRS	MacDill AFB
GA	35 TFW	434 TFS, 4435 TFRS, 4452, 4535 CCTS, 35 OMS	George AFB
HO	49 TFW	7, 8, 9, 417 TFS	Holloman AFB
JO	363 TRW	16, 18 TRS, 33 TRTS, 62 TRS	Shaw AFB
LK	314 TAW	16 TATS, 61, 62 TAS	Little Rock AFB
LM	316 TAW	36, 37, 38 TAS	Langley AFB
MB	354 TFW	353, 355, 356 TFS, 4554 TFRS	Myrtle Beach AFB
MO	347 TFW	389, 390, 391 TFS	Mountain Home AFB
NA	474 TFW	428, 429, 430 TFS	Nellis AFB
PB	317 TAW	39, 40, 41 TFS	Pope AFB
SJ	4 TFW	334, 335, 336 TFS	Seymour-Johnson AFB
ZF	31 TFW	307, 308, 309 TFS	Homestead AFB

Air Defense-Tactical Air Command

Air Defense Command declined after Air National Guard units gradually assumed more of the air defense mission. Regular Air Force air defense dedicated assets declined until 1/10/79 when interceptor units realigned from Aerospace Defense Command (ADCOM) to Air Defense Tactical Air Command (ADTAC).

Further decline in active Air Force air defense units, saw the withdrawal of the air defense dedicated F-106 and arrival of the F-15. Tail codes were **LY**, **IS** and **TC** assigned to three F-15 fighter interceptor squadrons (*48, 57 and 318 FIS*). In the process the former colourful FIS markings giving way to standard black TAC tail codes.

Alaskan Air Command

Alaskan Air Command redesignated from the major operator of aerial assets in World War II, Eleventh Air Force on 18/12/45. The AAC operated primarily as an Air Defense tasked command until the early 1960s, when the emphasis changed to include support of

HISTORY OF TAIL CODES

SAC operations. Coded tactical operations began with the arrival of **FC** tail coded F-4E in 1970. By the end of 1972 all units adopted the **AK** tail code. On 7/7/89 Alaskan Command activated as a subordinate to US Pacific Command to control AAC. On 9/8/90 the AAC further reassigned to Pacific Air Forces command and redesignated to original World War II title, Eleventh Air Force.

Tactical Air Command - Military Airlift Command (MAC)

Tactical airlift units started applying tail codes on C-7, C-123 and C-130 in the summer of 1968. Numerous temporary deployments in Southeast Asia and other locations occurred with tail codes applied. Most notable, at RAF Mildenhall and Rhein-Main AB, West Germany, which rotated C-130 temporarily attached squadrons. These deployments under 513 and 322 TAW control, continued until a permanent TAS was assigned.

Under AFM66-1 concept wing common tail codes were adopted by the airlift units in June 1972. These short lived tail codes lasted until first of December 1974 when MAC assumed control of all tactical airlift assets. All tail codes were eliminated from C-7, C-123, and C-130 tactical transports (*marked as* 1/12/74+ *in text*) within TAC, ANG, and AFRES.

United States Air Force Reserve (AFRES)

Tail coding of AFRES aircraft generally began in mid 1972. Air Force Reserve tactical units adopted the TAC standard pre AFM66-1 tail code method. Tail codes maintained through a sometimes very complex changing command structure involving Groups and wings. As with Air National Guard units, flying squadrons were stationed separately from like controlled units thus AFM66-1 had no effect. Several units took years before opting to utilize tail codes.

Reserve special operations, tactical fighter, and tactical transport squadrons flew tail coded A-10A, A-37A/B, C-7A, C-123K, C-130A/B, F-4C/D/E, F-16A/B/C/D, F-105B/D/F and CH-3E aircraft. Tail codes were dropped on tactical transport types on 1/12/74 when MAC assumed control of all regular force tactical airlift units.

Air National Guard (ANG)

Air National Guard tactical units first applied tail codes on Federal Activated Duty in response to the seizure of USS Pueblo, on 24 June 1968. This precipitated deployment reaction from TAC and included called-up ANG units under federal active duty. Tail codes were assigned to units for deployments in CONUS and Asian bases. The initial units, coded and deployed in CONUS were:

CS	138 TFS	F-86H	140 TFW	Cannon AFB
CT	104 TFS	F-86H	140 TFW	Cannon AFB
XA	119 TFS	F-100C/F	113 TFW	Myrtle Beach AFB
XB	121 TFS	F-100C/F	113 TFW	Myrtle Beach AFB
RB	154 TRS	RF-101	123 TRW	Little Rock AFB
RG	165 TRS	RF-101	123 TRW	Richards Gebaur AFB
RJ	192 TRS	RF-101	123 TRW	Richards Gebaur AFB

These units are listed among initial tail coded units. The majority of tactical Air National Guard units followed suit by 1972. As tail codes were assigned to individual squadrons, the variation was rather large. The bulk of tail codes abbreviating state name such as; **SD** "South Dakota", **IA** "Iowa" and **OK** "Oklahoma." Others representing close population centres such as **BC** "Battle Creek", **WG** "Greater Wilmington Airport Delaware" and **SG** "Schenectady Airport New York." In addition to personnel, the following five National Guard tactical fighter squadrons deployed to RSVN as complete units, adopting tail codes within regular force wings:

BP	127 TFS	F-100C/F	354 TFW	*25/6/68 - 10/6/69
BO	166 TFS	F-100C/F	354 TFW	*4/7/68 - 10/6/69
SG	136 TFS	F-100C	31 TFW	14/6/68 - 18/5/69
SM	188 TFS	F-100C/F	31 TFW	25/12/66 - 10/9/70
VS	120 TFS	F-100C/F	35 TFW	4/67 - 18/4/69

Deployment dates to Kunsan AB, ROK

Air National Guard flying squadrons number between 101 and 199, thus easily identified. The Air Force concept AFM66-1 did not affect ANG tail codes, as units were individually based, remote from controlling structures.

The sixteen C-7A, C-130A, B and E equipped Tactical Airlift Squadrons started carrying tail codes in April 1970. Air National Guard C-130 airlift squadrons attempted a system of ending tail codes with the letter **G**, eight of the fifteen doing so. Tail codes dropped on Air National Guard, regular and AFRES airlift units when TAC acquiesced to MAC control on 1/12/74. Some tail codes carried as late as October 1975. Many tactical Guard units did not apply tail codes on aircraft until the 1980s, while others, such as the 188 TFS (**NM**), New Mexico Air National Guard did not apply assigned codes.

United States Air Forces Europe (USAFE)

During 1970 the USAFE emulated the PACAF standard tail code system. The first letter of the tail code represented the wing, usually duplicating the parent base name. The second letter designated the squadron. The letters **R, S, T, U** and **V** designated within USAFE to avoid duplication of majority tail codes utilized by TAC and PACAF units. The initial noted units:

TAIL CODE

A - AR, AS, AT	1, 30, 32 TRS	10 TFW	RAF Alconbury
B - BR, BS, BT, BU, BV	39 TEWS, 22, 23, 53, 525 TFS	36 TFW	Bitburg AB, Germany
C - CR	32 TRS	17 AF	Camp New Amsterdam, Netherlands
H - HR, HS	10, 496 TFS	50 TFW	Hahn AB, Germany
U - UR, UT	79, 55, 55 TFS	20 TFW	RAF Upper Heyford
L - LR, LS, LT	492, 493, 494 TFS	48 TFW	RAF Lakenheath
R - RR, RS	38 TRS, 526 TFS	26 TRW	Ramstein AB, Germany
T - TJ, TK, TL	307, 353, 613 TFS	401 TFW	Torrejon AB, Spain
W - WR, WS, WT	78, 91, 92 TFS	81 TFW	RAF Bentwaters
Z - ZR, ZS	17 TRS	86 TFW	Zweibrucken AB, Germany

There were two exceptions to **R, S, T, U** and **V** system. First, the 401 TFW using **J, K** and **L** as second letters. This due to the **TS** and **TT** tail codes in prior usage by the 22 and 602 SOS. These 56 Special Operations Wing units flew the A-1E/G/H/J from Nakhon Phanom RTAFB. The second exception, 20 TFW, started with **U** as the initial letter. This abruptly abandoned due to possible usage of **US** as a tail code (*un-serviceable or United States*) and switched to **J_** range codes.

On the first of April 1972, the tail code system changed with USAFE with the implementation of AFM66-1, wing maintenance concept. As a result, the single two-letter tail code now designated entire wing. This new common wing tail code, usually already used within the wing, applied during the later half of 1972. The initial wing code assignment noted as:

AR	10 TRW	1, 30, 32 TRS	RAF Alconbury
BT	36 TFW	22, 53, 525 TFS	Bitburg AB, Germany
HR	50 TFW	10, 313, 496 TFS	Hahn AB, Germany
LK	48 TFW	492, 493, 493 TFS	RAF Lakenheath
RS	26 TRW	38 TRS, 526 TFS	Ramstein AB, Germany
SP	52 TFW	23, TFS, 39 TEWS	Spangdahlem AB, Germany
TJ	401 TFW	612, 613, 614 TFS	Torrejon AB, Spain
UH	20 TFW	55, 77, 79 TFS	RAF Upper Heyford
WR	81 TFW	78, 91, 92 TFS	RAF Bentwaters
ZR	86 TFW	17 TRS	Zweibrucken AB, Germany

The 48 TFW started with the **LK** tail code, before switching to **LN** during F-4D conversion. In January 1973 several inter wing changes occurred including the 26 TRW and 86 TFW switched bases and tail codes **RS** and **ZR**. The 32 TFS maintained the **CR** tail code after AFM66-1.

F-4D Phantom 66-0227 **LN**, 492 TFS 48 TFW, RAF Lakenheath, without squadron colours. Photo: Bob Archer, 13 August 1976.

Air Force Systems Command (AFSC)

The Air Force Systems Command has two primary locations for aircraft operations utilizing tail codes. The Air Force Flight Test Center at Edwards AFB controls the 6512 Test Squadron through the 6510 Test Wing. The Armament Division based at Eglin AFB controls the 3246 Test Wing, 3247 Test Squadron. Other facilities such as Wright Patterson fly uncoded aircraft. In addition several tactical fighter wings had test designated and tasked squadrons assigned. These units adopted standard TAC tail codes along with regular units. These units provided several examples in variation of the standard tail code practise. This due to paint schemes carried on from previous users, mixed with special test markings. Tail code application also varied due to the combination of special purpose markings. Not all types carried tail codes. The 6520 Test Group, at Hanscom AFB, exhibited HH on aircraft tails in the late fifties. Although similar to current presentation these black superimposed codes were not true codes.

HISTORY OF TAIL CODES

F-102A Delta Dagger 57-0842 "Happy Hanscom" **HH** 6520 Test Group, Hanscom Field. Photo: T. Cuddy 1958-59, Isham collection.

Air Force Logistics Command (AFLC)

The United States Air Force operates five Air Logistics Centers throughout United States. These overhaul and repair facilities usually are without permanently assigned aircraft. The only tail code in standard appearance is at Warner Robbins with a single F-15 switching between **WR** and **RG** tail code. Stored F-105 went through a similar sequence of codes.

Air Training Command (ATC)

Air Training Command applied tail codes to T-37 and T-38 in Flying Training Wings. The aircraft, painted in special blue and white (*FS.595a 15044 and 17925*) horizontally split scheme adopted in the mid 1980s. Tail codes and serials were painted red. These codes are not recognised as true tail codes by Air Training Command except **NT** as carried by the T-43A of the 454 Flying Training Squadron at Mather AFB. In addition, the 71 FTW aircraft carried a very different stylized **OK** code.

F-4D Phantom 65-0748 **XT,** 134 TFS 158 TFG, Vermont ANG, Burlington IAP. Aircraft refinishes followed T.O. 1-1-4 to the letter (see Page 239), painting **XT** rather than the correct **VT** for 134 TFS. Photo: Marty Isham.

F-4D Phantom 66-7725 **SP**, 170 TFS 183 TFG, Illinois ANG, Springfield Airport. The 170 TFS painted an F-4D with **SP** tail code for Springfield before realizing **SP** was assigned within the USAFE. Photo: Charles B Mayer, Volk Field ANGB, 8 August 1984.

F-4D Phantom 66-7582 89 TFS **TanZi** painted to represent commander's name of the 89 TFS, if only for a very short period. Photo: Walter Dramen.

United States Air Forces Pacific

3d Tactical Fighter Wing
8th Tactical Fighter Wing
12th Tactical Fighter Wing
14th Air Commando - Special Operations Wing
18th Tactical Fighter Wing
31st Tactical Fighter Wing
35th Tactical Fighter Wing
37th Tactical Fighter Wing
49th Tactical Fighter Wing
51st Fighter Interceptor - Air Base - Composite (Tactical) -Fighter Wing
54th Tactical Fighter Wing
56th Air Commando Wing
314th Tactical Airlift Wing
315th Air Commando - Special Operations Wing - Tactical Airlift Wing
326th Air Division
347th Tactical Fighter Wing
354th Tactical Fighter Wing
355th Tactical Fighter Wing
366th Tactical Fighter Wing
374th Tactical Airlift Wing
388th Tactical Fighter Wing
405th Fighter Wing
432nd Tactical Reconnaissance - Tactical Fighter Wing
460th Tactical Reconnaissance Wing - Group
463d Tactical Airlift Wing
474th Tactical Fighter Wing
475th Tactical Fighter Wing
483d Tactical Airlift Wing
633d Special Operations Wing

Wing Summary PACAF
3d Tactical Fighter Wing

The 3 Tactical Fighter Wing transferred from England AFB, Louisiana on 8 November 1965, to Bien Hoa AB, RSVN. The initial tail coded units in 1967 noted as F-100D/F equipped 90, 510 and 531 TFS and the A-37B equipped 604 AS. These units applied **CB**, **CE**, **CP** and **CK** tail codes during 1967. The 8 AS **CF** tail coded A-37B also assigned in late 1969. The 90 TFS recoded **CG** while reequipping with A-37B and redesignating 90 AS. The 3 TFW units gradually inactivated by 1970 as Vietnamization occurred. The 310 and 311 SOS also attached for brief periods from the 315 SOW in 1969 before providing their assets to other units. The 3 TFW continued as a paper unit until 31/10/70. The wing moved to Kunsan AB, ROK without personnel or equipment on 15/3/71. The 475 TFW based at Misawa AB, Japan transferred existing resources to the 3 TFW established at Kunsan AB, ROK. The 3 TFW the 35, 36 and 80 TFS with **UP**, **UK** and **UD** tail coded F-4. Both the 44 TFS (3/4 - 2/6/72, 28/7 - 8/9/72) and 67 TFS (2/6/72 - 28/7/72, 8/9/72 - 16/10/72) attached during 1972 from the 18 TFW Kadena AB tail coded **ZL** and **ZG**. The common wing tail code of **UP** was not fully implemented and may not have been officially assigned

The 3 TFW moved to Clark AB, Philippines on 16/9/74 replacing the 405 FW. The three former components remained at Kunsan AB, ROK under the 8 TFW. In addition to the non-operational 68 TFS, the former 405 FW units 1 Test Squadron and 90 TFS with **PN** tail code also assigned to 3 TFW on transfer date. The 25 TFS (*a paper unit*) also assigned for two days in December 1975 before moving on to the 18 TFW based at Kadena AB, Okinawa. The 3 TFS previously assigned to the 388 TFW at Korat RTAFB with **JH** tail code A-7D arrived in December 1975 as a further **PN** tail coded F-4 operator. The non-operational 68 TFS inactivated on 30/9/75. The 1 TS inactivated in October 1978.

8th Tactical Fighter Wing

The 8 Tactical Fighter Wing formerly at George AFB, arrived at Ubon RTAFB in December 1965. The 8 TFW inaugurated tail code application by January 1967. The three initial current F-4C operators started coding with **F** range tail codes in early 1967 were:

FG	433 TFS	F-4C	(*F-4D arrived 7/67; re 4 TFS 33 TFW*)
FP	497 TFS		
FY	555 TFS	F-4C	(*F-4D arrived 5/67; re 40 TFS 33 TFW*)

The former F-104C equipped 435 TFS adopted **FO** tail code after exchanging equipment to the F-4 in July 1967. The reason for picking **G**, **O**, **P** and **Y** letters is unknown. The units noted after initial tail coding 13 BS, 16 SOS and 25 TFS, flying B-57, AC-130 and F-4D coded **FK/FS**, **FT** and **FA**. The 555 TFS reassigned to the 432 TRW with the new tail code **OY** at Udorn RTAFB, in May 1968. Several F-4 units attached from CONUS based wings during 1972-73, maintaining CONUS tail codes. Known deployments include:

SA	334 TFS	4 TFW	F-4E	11/4/72 - 8/7/72
SC-SJ*	336 TFS	4 TFW	F-4E	12/4/72 - 15/9/72
SJ	335 TFS	4 TFW	F-4E	8/7/72 - 12/72
SJ	334 TFS	4 TFW	F-4E	25/9/72 - 12/3/73
ZF	308 TFS	31 TFW	F-4E	11/12/72 - 11/1/73
SJ	336 TFS	4 TFW	F-4E	9/3/73 - 7/9/73
ED	58 TFS	33 TFW	F-4E	8/6/73 - 14/9/73

*(336 TFS recoded from **SC** to **SJ** during deployment)*

Wing common tail code of **WP** affected all components for 16 SOS, 25, 433, 435 and 497 TFS in January 1973. As Ubon RTAFB operations phased down in 1974 the 8 TFW replaced the 3 TFW at Kunsan AB, ROK on 16/9/74. Units adopted were F-4D operators 35 and 80 TFS and for a short time (*between 16/9/74 and 30/9/74*) and the non-operational 36 TFS. The **WP** tail code applied to all three squadrons on 8 TFW control. The F-4D equipped 497 TFS rejoined the 8 TFW in 1978, until reassigned to the 51 CW and coded **OS**. The 35 and 80 TFS started reequipping F-16A/B on 15/5/81 with the arrival of the first example. The 8 TFW upgraded to the F-16C/D in 1988.

12th Tactical Fighter Wing

The 12 Tactical Fighter Wing deployed to Cam Ranh Bay AB, RSVN on 8/11/65. The F-4C equipped 391, 557, 558 and 559 TFS coded mounts late in 1966 **XT**, **XC**, **XD** and **XN**. In response to the seizure of USS Pueblo, the 391 TFS moved to 475 TFW Misawa AB, Japan in July 1968, taking **XD** tail coded F-4C of 558 TFS. The 558 TFS assumed control over the **XT** tail coded former 391 TFS F-4C.

The 12 TFW transferred in name only to Phu Cat AB, RSVN, and assumed 37 TFW assets on 31/3/70. The 37 TFW tail codes of **HB** and **HK** maintained for 389 and 480 TFS. The wing inactivated on 17/11/71. The wing redesignated to 12 Flying Training Wing on 22/3/72 at Randolph AFB, with coded T-37 and T-38 trainers, on 1/5/72.

14th Air Commando Wing
14th Special Operations Wing

The 14 Air Commando Wing activated at Nha Trang AB, RSVN on 8/3/66. The Wing adopted **E_** range tail codes between April and December 1967. Initial units noted as 1, 4, 5, 6 and 9 ACS coded **EC**, **EN**, **EO**, **ET** and **ER**. Redesignated as the 14 Special Operations Wing on 1/8/68 and moved headquarters to Phan Rang AB, RSVN on 15/10/69. The 90 Attack Squadron assigned on 31/10/70 from the 3 TFW with **CG** tail coded A-37B, and further reassigned to the 483 TAW on 1/9/71. The 604 ACS detached and assigned to the 3 TFW, Bien Hoa AB, RSVN (*coded **CK** in late 1968*) on 15/11/67 and 1/3/70. Wing also controlled uncoded AC-119 operations including the AFRes activated 71 SOS between 20/12/68 and 18/6/69. The 1 SOS transferred on 20/12/67 to the 56 SOW and recoded **TC**. The 14 SOW inactivated on 30/9/71. The South Vietnamese Air Force C-47 equipped 415 Transport Squadron, 33 Transport Wing also coding in the **E_** range (**EA** *through* **EZ**). This system, although unrelated to USAF system, other than appearance, are easily confused with 14 SOW C-47.

UNITED STATES AIR FORCES PACIFIC

18th Tactical Fighter Wing

The 18 Tactical Fighter Wing stationed at Kadena AB, Okinawa since 1954 adopted **Z_** range tail codes in 1967. Units noted as 12 (*F-105*), 44 and 67 TFS (*F-4*), 19 TEWS (*EB-66*) and 15 TRS (*RF-4*) tail coded **ZA**, **ZL**, **ZG**, **ZT** and **ZZ**. The 12 TFS sent the **ZB** tail coded Detachment 1 to the 388 TFW in the Wild Weasel role. The 19 TEWS inactivated in October 1970. The 1 SOS assigned during the 1972-73 period and tail coded EB-57E **GT**. Wing recoded **ZZ** post June 1972 and the 25 TFS added in late 1975. Starting in 1979 the 12, 44 and 67 converted to the F-15C/D at Eglin AFB, interrupting the 33 TFW conversion. Squadrons then deployed back to Kadena AB, Okinawa upon conversion. The 25 TFS inactivating on 22/8/80 without converting to the F-15. The 15 TRS transferred to newly established 460 TRG in 1989 and recoded **GU**.

31st Tactical Fighter Wing

Activated at Tuy Hoa AB, RSVN on 16/12/66 the 31 Tactical Fighter Wing adopted tail codes in the **S_** range during 1968. Initial tail coded units 136 (*New York ANG*), 188 (*New Mexico ANG*), 306, 308, 309 TFS flew F-100 with **SG**, **SK**, **SD**, **SM**, and **SS** tail codes. Further F-100 added with the 416, 355 TFS with tail codes **SE** and **SP**. Operations reduced until late 1970 when the 31 TFW returned to Homestead AFB on 15/10/70. All regular force tactical fighter squadrons except the 355 TFS joined the 4403 TFW based England AFB. Squadrons temporarily maintaining Tuy Hoa AB, assigned tail codes until F-100 passed to ANG units.

35th Tactical Fighter Wing

The 35 Tactical Fighter Wing assigned to Phan Rang AB, RSVN replacing the 366 TFW which moved to Da Nang AB, RSVN on 10/10/66. The assigned units 352, 614 and 615 TFS remaining at Phan Rang AB, RSVN. The 120 TFS (*Colorado ANG*) arrived early 1968 and tail codes **VS**, **VM**, **VP**, and **VZ** adopted by the 35 TFW. The 8 and 13 BS spent numerous periods attached from the 405 FW, at Clark AB, Philippines flying B-57 before coding. The 8 BS adopted the 405 FW range tail code of **PQ** on assignment to the 35 TFW.

After redesignating 8 AS and 8 SOS the squadron returned to 35 TFW on 30/9/70 with **CF** tail coded A-37. The 8 SOS later reassigned to the 315 TAW on 31/7/71 when the 35 TFW inactivated. The 612, 614 and 615 TFS reassigned to the 401 TFW at Torrejon AB, Spain the 352 TFS inactivated on 31/7/71. The 120 TFS returned to Buckley Field, Colorado. Wing reactivated at George AFB, on 1/10/71.

37th Tactical Fighter Wing

The 37 Tactical Fighter Wing activated on 1/3/67 at Phu Cat AB, RSVN. Initial tail coded units 355, 416, TFS along with Detachment 1, of 612 TFS, coded F-100 **HP**, **HE** and **HS** in 1968. The F-100 of 174 TFS (*Iowa ANG*) added in May 1968 with **HA** tail code. Two F-4D units, the 389 and 480 TFS added with tail codes **HB**, and **HK** in 1969. The 355 and 416 TFS reassigned to the 31 TFW at Tuy Hoa AB, RSVN with tail codes **SP** and **SE**. The 174 TFS returned to Iowa in May 1969, while 612 TFS Detachment 1 reassigned to the 35 TFW. The wing inactivated on 31/3/70 replaced by the 12 TFW, moving in from Phu Cat AB, RSVN to control remaining 389 and 480 TFS.

49th Tactical Fighter Wing

The 49 Tactical Fighter Wing deployed from Holloman AFB, to Takhli RTAFB on 13/5/72 bolstering air power forces in Southeast Asia. The 49 TFW deployed until 27/10/72.

HB	7 TFS	F-4D	recoded **HO**	mid 1972
HC	8 TFS	F-4D	"	
HD	9 TFS	F-4D	"	
HE	417 TFS	F-4D	"	

All units recoded **HO** Takhli RTAFB under the AFM66-1 concept before returning to Holloman AFB in October 1972. As wing movement not a permanent change of station, code entries are under the TAC CONUS section.

51st Fighter Interceptor Wing
51st Air Base Wing
51st Composite Wing (Tactical)

The 51 Fighter Interceptor Wing was assigned to Naha AB, Okinawa during 1950. The first tail usage within the 51 FIW started with the 82 FIS F-102A adopting the **NV** tail code in 1968. The wing moved to Osan AB, ROK in November 1971 becoming 51 Air Base Wing without 82 FIS. Redesignated 51 Composite Wing (Tactical) on 30/9/74 and 51 Tactical Fighter Wing on 1/1/82. Wing assigned **OS** tail code for components. The wing squadron based and operated from several locations utilizing **GU**, **SU** tail codes as well as **OS**. Components included the 19 TASS with OV-10A, OA-37B and OA-10A (**OS**), 25 TFS A-10A (**OS** *and* **SU**), 36 TFS F-4E, F-16 (**OS**) and 497 TFS F-4D, E (**OS** *and* **GU** *tail codes*).

54th Tactical Fighter Wing

The 54 Tactical Fighter Wing activated on 15/6/70, at Kunsan AB, ROK, taking the place of the 354 TFW. Two F-4E units attached, 16 TFS from Eglin AFB, 33 TFW with **ED** tail codes (15/6/70 *and* 9/70) and the 478 TFS from Homestead AFB, 4531 TFW with **ZE** tail codes (15/6/70 *and* 2/9/70). The 54 TFW inactivated on 31/10/70.

56th Air Commando Wing
56th Special Operations Wing

The 56 Air Commando Wing designated and activated on 8/4/67 at Nakhon Phanom RTAFB. Squadrons initially coded units in late 1967 include the 602, 606 and 609 SOS with tail codes **TT**, **TO** and **TA**. The 1 SOS reassigned from the 14 SOW in December 1967 and recoded **TC**. Wing redesignated to 56 Special Operations Wing on 1/8/68 adding the 22 SOS, coded **TS** on 25/10/68. Many detachments and temporary deployments of 56 SOW assets occurred. Black tail codes augmented the standard white codes on A-1 within Special Operations Squadrons. Perhaps the white painted tail codes were too distinctive to the wrong people. The 609 SOS inactivated in 1969, 22 and 602 SOS in 1970, 606 SOS in 1971 and 1 SOS in 1972. The 361 TEWS added to wing operations in 1972 from the 460 TRW flying **AJ** tail coded C-47. The 361 TEWS inactivated in June 1974. The 56 SOW operated several units flying uncoded U-10, CH-53, QU-22, AC-119, H-34, OV-10 and O-1. Remaining uncoded units inactivated on 30/6/75 and the wing transferred to MacDill AFB, designating as 56 Tactical Fighter Wing flying **MC** tail coded F-4E.

314th Tactical Airlift Wing

The 314 Tactical Airlift Wing operated C-130E with the 50, 345, 346 and 776 TAS tail coded **DE, DH, DY** and **DL**, from Ching Chaun Kang AB, Taiwan. The 314 TAW maintained a large detachment at Tuy Hoa AB, RSVN known as "Task Force" for most of the Southeast Asian conflict. The 346 TAS replaced by the 21 TAS in May 1971. The 314 TAW reassigned to Little Rock AFB on 31/5/71. The 374 Tactical Airlift Wing absorbed the former 314 TAW assets and tail codes.

315th Air Commando Wing
315th Special Operations Wing
315th Tactical Airlift Wing

The 315 Air Commando Wing, Troop Carrier, designated on 21/2/66 and was assigned to Tan Son Nhut AB, RSVN on 8/3/66. The "Troop Carrier" title dropped on 1/8/67. Organized on 8/3/66 at Tan Son Nhut AB, RSVN and equipped with C-123B. Components 19, 309, 310 and 311 ACS, converted from C-123B to the jet assisted C-123K by early 1968. The 315 ACW moved to Phan Rang AB, RSVN on 15/6/67. Tail codes **WE, WH, WM** and **WV** introduced late in 1967 or early in 1968. On 1/8/68 the 315 ACW redesignated to 315 Special Operations Wing. Component units also redesignated to Special Operations Squadrons. Wing controlled the 12 ACS/SOS equipped UC-123 spray aircraft between 15/10/66 and 30/9/70 at Bien Hoa AB, RSVN.

Yet further designation change affected on 1/1/70 to 315 Tactical Airlift Wing, with Special Operations Squadrons redesignating as Tactical Airlift Squadrons. The 19, 309, 310 and 311 TAS maintained tail codes **WE, WH, WM** and **WV**. The 315 TAW assumed control of the 8 SOS with **CF** tail coded A-37 from co-based 35 TFW at Phan Rang AB, RSVN on 31/7/71 until 15/1/72. The 9 SOS flew **ER** tail coded C-47 on reassignment from 14 SOW on 30/9/71. Wing trained crews for South Vietnamese Air Force during 1971. Wing inactivated on 31/3/72, with many assets turned over to SVAF.

326th Air Division

The 326 Air Division replaced the 15 ABW as controlling unit for the 22 TASS on 4/4/80. This only flying and coded component flew **WH** tail coded OV-10A from Wheeler AFB.

347th Tactical Fighter Wing

The 347 Tactical Fighter Wing initially applied tail codes while assigned to Yokota AB, Japan. Application of tail codes in the **G_** range applied to F-105 and F-4. The 35, 36, and 80 TFS coded **GG, GL** and **GR**. The 556 RS assigned mid 1968 and flew B-57 and C-130, with **GT** tail codes. The 34 TFS assigned, but detached to the 388 TFW on 15/1/68. Assigned to the 388 TFW on 15/1/68 and tail coded **JJ**. The 35, 36, 80 TFS reassigned to the 3 TFW with **U_** range tail codes. The wing moved to Mountain Home AFB, on 15/5/71 as F-111F wing.

Wing returned to Southeast Asia on 30/7/73 to control the former 474 TFW F-111A units, 428 and 429 TFS at Takhli RTAFB. Wing used **HG** wing tail codes on F-111A. The 347 TFW moved to Korat RTAFB on 12/7/74 and inactivated on 30/6/75. Reactivated three months later at Moody AFB on 30/9/75 as an F-4E wing, with **MY** tail codes.

F-111A 67-0102 **HG**, 428 TFS 347 TFW, Takhli RTAFB, with red tail stripe. Also visible F-4E 67-368 **ED**, 58 TFS 8 TFW, and a pair from the 336 TFS 8 TFW with **SJ** tail code.

UNITED STATES AIR FORCES PACIFIC

354th Tactical Fighter Wing

The 354 Tactical Fighter Wing units were gradually assigned to the Southeast Asian theatre from Myrtle Beach AFB in the pre-tail code years. Wing title assigned to Kunsan AB, ROK replacing the 4 TFW on 2/7/68. Personnel primarily activated from ANG status. Wing tactical components comprised of units rotated from CONUS. Known deployments include:

BO	127 TFS	Ohio ANG	F-100C/F	5/7/68 - 10/6/69
BP	166 TFS	Kansas ANG	F-100C/F	5/7/68 - 10/6/69
ZG	68 TFS	4531 TFW	F-4D	20/6/69 - 9/12/69
ZF	560 TFS	4531 TFW	F-4D	23/6/69 - 17/12/69
SA	334 TFS	4 TFW	F-4D	*16/12/69 - 31/5/70
SB	335 TFS	4 TFW	F-4D	8/12/69 - 23/5/70
ED	16 TFS	4531 TFW	F-4E	29/5/70 - 14/6/70
ZE	478 TFS	4531 TFW	F-4E	21/5/70 - 14/6/70

The wing assets passed to the 54 TFW on 14/6/70 when the wing transferred to Myrtle Beach AFB, on 15/6/70 equipping with A-7D. A second tour in Southeast Asia began with a wing split on 16/10/72. Units rotated **MB** tail coded A-7D to Korat RTAFB until 23/5/74. During this period the 353, 355 and 356 TFS, plus the 354 and 358 TFS from 355 TFW Davis-Monthan (*formerly coded* **DM**) assigned for combat duty. Many 353 TFS recoded to **JH** for 3 TFS 388 TFW before activation in early 1973. Official noted deployment dates were:

MB/JH	353 TFS	354 TFW	A-7D	10/10/72 - 15/3/73
MB	354 TFS	355 TFW	A-7D	14/1/73 - 5/7/73
MB	355 TFS	354 TFW	A-7D	10/10/72 - 22/4/74
MB	356 TFS	354 TFW	A-7D	10/10/72 - 4/5/74
MB	358 TFS	355 TFW	A-7D	28/12/73 - 15/5/74

*Believe a/c either borrowed from 354 TFW or recoded to 354 TFW standard **MB** for deployment.*

F-4D Phantom 66-7491 **SB**, 335 TFS 354 TFW, Kunsan AB, ROK. Photo: T Matsuzaki, Yokota AB, Japan, 9 January 1970.

F-4E Phantom 67-0231 **ED**, 16 TFS enroute to assignment at 354 TFW, Kunsan AB, Korea. Photo: Martin collection, Yokota AB, Japan, 2 April 1970.

A-7D Corsair 70-0957 **MB**, 356 TFS 354 TFW, Korat RTAFB. Photo: Don Larsen, 26 October 1972.

355th Tactical Fighter Wing

The 355 Tactical Fighter Wing transferred to Takhli RTAFB on 8/11/65 from McConnell AFB, primarily operating F-105. The 41 and 42 TEWS, 333, 354 and 357 TFS carried tail codes **RC**, **RH**, **RK**, **RM** and **RU** in early 1968 (*some units possibly in early 1967*). The 44 TFS attached from the 3288 TFW in late 1969 recoding their F-105 **RE** from **JE**. Units began phasing out for wing inactivation on 10/12/70, with the last aircraft leaving Takhli RTAFB, on 7/10/70. The wing reactivated as 355 TFTW at Davis-Monthan AFB on 1/4/77 primarily with A-7D, attaching units to the 354 TFW at Korat RTAFB.

366th Tactical Fighter Wing

The 366 Tactical Fighter Wing moved to Phan Rang AB, RSVN from Holloman AFB on 20/3/66, then on to Da Nang AB, RSVN on 10/10/66. The wing adopted a separate tail code system, than the later excepted PACAF system. The three F-4C squadrons 389, 390 and 480 TFS started applying tail codes to F-4C in January 1967. The first of two letters represented the squadron, the second the individual aircraft. Thus possible tail codes:

AA to **AZ**	389 TFS	F-4C
BA to **BZ**	390 TFS	F-4C
CA to **CZ**	480 TFS	F-4C

This system continued throughout the F-4D conversion process. Late in 1969 the 390 TFS recoded **LF**, while 480 and 389 TFS transferring to Phu Cat AB, RSVN and adopted the 37 TFW tail codes **HB** and **HK**, thus ending this unique system. The 4 and 421 TFS arrived in April 1969 from CONUS with F-4E coded **LA** and **LC**. Both left in May 1972, joining the 432 TRW although based at Takhli RTAFB until moving to Udorn RTAFB on 31/10/72. The two squadrons had an unconventional tail code history as both maintained the **LA** and **LC** tail codes on subsequent transfers. The 35 TFS attached for the period between 3/4/72 and 12/6/72 flying **UP** tail coded F-4D, from the 3 TFW. The **AN** tail coded EC-47 of the 362 TEWS reassigned on 1/2/72 from the 483 TAW and inactivated on 12/6/72. The wing reassigned to Takhli RTAFB on 27/6/72, then reassigned to Mountain Home AFB, on 31/10/72.

F-4C Phantom 66-8820 **AW**, 389 TFS 366 TFW, Da Nang AB, RSVN. Note the red and white fuselage lines, canopy and rudder markings, in addition to red drop tanks and pylon tips.

UNITED STATES AIR FORCES PACIFIC

374th Tactical Airlift Wing

The 374 Tactical Airlift Wing was assigned to Naha AB, Okinawa in August 1966 replacing 6315 Operations Group as the reporting unit for C-130A units. Operated four squadrons of C-130A, the 21, 35, 41 and 815 TAS applied tail codes **YD**, **YJ**, **YP** and **YU** during 1968. The 347 TAW also controlled the Tachikawa AB, Japan 815 TAS with **MA** tail coded C-130A for under a year. Wing maintained a large detachment at Cam Ranh Bay AB, RSVN until operations ceased by 27/4/71. Wing transferred to the former 314 TAW location at Ching Chaun Kang AB, Taiwan. Assumed three of the four 314 TAW based squadrons; 50, 345 and 776, with tail codes **DE**, **DH** and **DL**. A fourth squadron the 21 TAS arrived with the wing assuming assets and **DY** tail code of 346 TAS. The 21 and 345 TAS transferred with wing to Clark AB, Philippines on 15/11/73. The 374 TAW also controlled Korat RTAFB based 7 ACCS flying **JC** tail coded EC-130E on 22/5/74 from 388 TFW until 31/3/75.

388th Tactical Fighter Wing

The 388 Tactical Fighter Wing moved to Korat RTAFB from McConnell AFB on 8/4/66 with F-105 assets. The 35, 44, and 469 TFS coded early in 1968, with **J_** range tail codes **JJ**, **JE** and **JV**. The 35 TFS attached from the 3 TFW flying **UP** tail coded F-4D between 12/6/72 and 10/10/72. In 1969 the 44 TFS reassigned to the 355 TFW and the 34 and 469 TFS reequipped with the F-4E. The 3 TFS activated between 15/3/73 and 22/12/75 flying **JH** tail coded A-7D. The 16 SOS flew **WP** tail coded AC-130 and attached from 8 TFW between 19/7/74 and 8/12/75 removing codes shortly after arrival. The 42 TEWS with **JW** tail coded EB-66C/E was also assigned between 23/9/70 and 17/1/74. The 469 TFS inactivated in October 1972, the 34 TFS reequipping with F-4D in October 1974 before inactivating in December 1975.

The Wild Weasel role arrived at Korat RTAFB with **ZB** tail coded F-105 of Detachment 1 - 12 TFS in September 1970. This unit evolved two months later into the 6010 WWS. A year later the **JB** tail coded 17 WWS replaced the 6060 WWS. Detachment 1 - 561 TFS attached from the 35 TFW flying **WW** F-105G between 1/2/73 and 5/9/73 operating F-105G. The 388 TFW title reassigned to Hill AFB on 23/12/1975 to operated **HL** tail coded F-4D.

405th Fighter Wing

The 405 Fighter Wing replaced the 6200 Air Base Wing, at Clark AB, Philippines on 9/4/59. The initial coded units during 1968 were; 64, 509 FIS (*F-102*), 523 TFS (*F-100*), 8 and 13 BS (*B-57*) tail coded **PE**, **PK**, **PN**, **PQ** and **PV**. The 405 FW maintained detachments of coded F-102 at Bien Hoa AB, Da Nang AB and Don Muang Airport, Thailand. The 8 and 13 BS assigned to the 35 TFW when initial tail codes applied. The 13 BS, 64 and 509 FIS inactivated 1/1968, 5/1969 and 7/1970. The 1 Test Squadron activated in April 1970 using **DS** and **PA** tail coded F-4. Application of wing common tail code **PN** in 1972 to remaining 1 TS and 523 TFS. The 90 TFS activated within the 405 FW in late 1972, achieved operational status in August 1973. The 523 TFS inactivated in August 1973. The wing also controlled the 774 TAS with **QW** tail codes, (*non-operational after* 2/9/72) and inactivated on 15/9/72. The 3 TFW replaced 405 FW Clark AB, Philippines on 16/9/74 assuming the then current **PN** tail coded 1 TS and 90 TFS F-4 operators.

432d Tactical Reconnaissance Wing
432d Tactical Fighter Wing

Activated at Udorn RTAFB on 18/9/66, the 432 Tactical Reconnaissance Wing previously inactivated at Shaw AFB during 1959. Under initial coding of assigned units; 13 TFS, 11 and 14 TRS, tail coded **OC**, **OO** and **OZ**. The 555 TFS reassigned from 8 TFW adopting the **OY** tail code. The 11 TRS inactivated in November 1970. The 432 TRW hosted a special detachment of two aircraft in the spring of 1971 from 57 FWW tail coded **WZ**. During 1972 the following tactical fighter units attached.

ED	58 TFS	33 TFW	F-4E	29/4/72 - 14/10/72
ZF	307 TFS	31 TFW	F-4E	29/7/72 - 28/10/72
ZF	308 TFS	31 TFW	F-4E	9/5/72 - 29/7/72
WZ	*414 TFS	57 FWW	F-4D	6/72 - fall 72
PN	523 TFS	405 FW	F-4E	9/4/72 - 25/10/72

414 TFS deployment is rather special. Not mentioned in 432 TRW history. Believed to still be a classified event.

The **LA** and **LC** tail coded F-4E of the 4 and 421 TFS assigned in May 1972, although based at Takhli RTAFB until joining other components at Udorn RTAFB on 31/10/72. Components 4, 13, 25, 421, 555 TFS and 14 TRS recoded with **UD** tail code during August 1973. The 4 SOS detachment with **OS** tail coded C-47 assigned between 10/12/69 and 29/5/70. The 555 TFS redesignated 555 TFTS and assigned to 58 TFTW Luke AFB, replaced by 25 TFS on 5/7/74. Wing redesignated 432 Tactical Fighter Wing on 15/11/74. All wing operations ceased on 30/11/75 and wing inactivated on 23/12/75. The wing redesignated as the 432 Tactical Drone Group on 23/12/75, activating on 1/7/76 at Davis-Monthan AFB, controlling uncoded DC-130 and CH-3E equipped units. The 432 TDG inactivated on 1/4/79.

The 432 TFW reactivated, replacing the 6112 ABW at Misawa AB, Japan on 1/7/84. The 432 TFW received the first F-16A on 2/4/85 and activated three maintenance squadrons. The 13 TFS activated on 4/7/85 operating F-16A/B before switching to F-16C/D a year later. The 14 TFS activated on 1/4/87 and also operated the F-16C/D. The choice of wing code was between **MJ** and **MW** with the former requested by 5 Air Force in September 1984.

460th Tactical Reconnaissance Wing
460th Tactical Reconnaissance Group

The 460 Tactical Reconnaissance Wing assigned to Ton Son Nhut AB, RSVN on 18/2/66. Some units previously assigned directly to 2 Air Division. The **A_** range tail codes adopted by 460 TRW on initial coding during 1967 (*possible 1968 for the 45 TRS*). The 12 (*RF-4*), 16 (*RF-4*), 45 TRS (*RF-101*), flew with **AC**, **AE**, **AH** tail codes. In addition the 360, 361 and 362 TEWS (*formerly TRS, assigned during 1966/67*) also tail coded C-47 **AJ**, **AL** and **AN**. Phase-down began in 1970 with completion on 31/8/71. The reconnaissance squadrons reassigned to CONUS and the 483 TAW. The 460 TRW inactivated on 31/8/71.

The 460 TRG consolidated with 460 TFW on 31/1/84. Reactivated as 460 TRG on 19/9/89 and activated on 1/10/89 controlling the 15 TRS, flying **GU** tail coded RF-4C until inactivated in late 1990.

463d Tactical Airlift Wing

The 463 Tactical Airlift Wing initially co-based at Machan and Clark AB, Philippines with C-130B. Airlift squadrons 29, 772, 773 and 774 tail coded **QB**, **QF**, **QG** and **QW** in 1968. A large detachment known as "Det.1" established at Ton Son Nhut AB, RSVN. The 29, 772 and 773 TAS inactivated by October 1971, 774 TAS reassigned to co-based 405 FW when the wing inactivated on 31/12/71.

474th Tactical Fighter Wing

The 474 Tactical Fighter Wing detached personnel and F-111A to Takhli RTAFB on or about 27/9/72 from Nellis AFB. All three squadrons; 428, 429 and 430 TFS tail coded **NA** before arrival at Takhli RTAFB. The 430 TFS returned to rear echelon operations at Nellis AFB on 22/3/73. The 428 and 429 TFS reassigned to the purposefully activated 347 TFW at Takhli RTAFB on 30/7/73. Aircraft recoded **HG** on or about transfer. As wing movement considered a deployment not a permanent change of station, code entries are under TAC CONUS section.

F-111A 67-0066 **NA**, 429 TFS 474 TFW, Takhli RTAFB, with yellow tail stripe. Also unusual combination of grey and white tail code presentation. Photo: Martin collection, Udorn RTAFB, mid-1972.

475th Tactical Fighter Wing

The 475 Tactical Fighter Wing assigned to Misawa AB, Japan on 15/1/68, until 15/3/71. Initially coded units were 67, 356 and 391 TFS with tail codes **UP**, **UK** and **UD**. Non-operational 45 TRS assigned between 15/1/68 and 5/3/71, and the 612 TFS between 15/1/68 and 15/3/71. The **LC** tail coded F-4E of the 421 TFS, delayed on delivery flight to Da Nang AB, (*formerly 16 TFS*) attached between 23/4/69 and 25/6/69 from the 366 TFW. Wing assets used to reform the 3 TFW at Kunsan AB, ROK. Redesignated 475 Air Base Wing on 20/10/71 and activated 1/11/71 at Yokota AB, Japan. The 556 RS assigned as the only flying unit flying **GT** tail coded EB-57E until reassigned to the 18 TFW.

483d Tactical Airlift Wing

The 483 Tactical Airlift Wing activated at Cam Ranh Bay AB, RSVN on 15/10/66 in preparation to receive ex-army transport aircraft. Six US Army Aviation Companies based in Vietnam transferred all C-7 assets to newly created Air Force units 1/1/67. The army units were:

17 AC	Assigned Camp to Holloway (*An Khe*) before moving to Phu Cat AB, RSVN, on 23/12/66 leaving detachment. Assets to 537 TAS (**KN**).
57 AC	Vung Tau AB, RSVN, transferred C-7 assets to 535 TAS (**KH**).
61 AC	Vung Tau AB, RSVN, detachment Can Tho, RSVN, until in late 1967. Assets to 536 TAS (**KL**).
92 AC	Initially assigned Qui Nhon before moving to Phu Cat AB, RSVN. Had detachments Da Nang and Pleiku AB, RSVN (*withdrawn 12/67*). Assets to 459 TAS (**KE**).
134 AC	Based at Can Tho, RSVN, before moving to Cam Ranh Bay AB, RSVN. Detachments noted at Bangkok, Thailand from new base. Assets to 457 TAS (**KA**).
135 AC	Based at Dong Ba Thin, RSVN before moving to Cam Ranh Bay AB, RSVN. Detachment based Nha Trang AB, RSVN, until December 1967. Assets to 458 TAS (**KC**).

Several non-TAS units attached and assigned as other wings inactivated during phase down of operations in Southeast Asia. The 360, 361 and 362 TEWS flying **AJ**, **AL** and **AN** tail coded C-47 subtypes, assigned from the inactivating 460 TRW on 31/8/71. The 360 TEWS reassigned to the 377 ABW on 1/2/72, 361 TEWS changed status to non-operational on 15/10/71, inactivating on 1/12/71. The 363 TEWS assigned to the 366 TFW on 1/2/72 maintaining tail code. The 90 SOS flying **CG** tail coded A-37B, assigned after 14 SOW inactivation on 1/9/71. Wing Headquarters and maintenance squadron based Cam Ranh Bay AB, RSVN until inactivated 31/5/72.

633d Special Operations Wing

The 633 Special Operations Wing activated at Pleiku AB, RSVN on 9/7/68. Wing received only flying component the 6 SOS, on 15/7/68 with **ET** tail codes from the 14 SOW. The wing inactivated on 15/3/70.

UNITED STATES AIR FORCES PACIFIC

Squadron/Code Summary PACAF

A
389 Tactical Fighter Squadron   *366 Tactical Fighter Wing
Da Nang AB, RSVN

F-4C	late 1966/mid 67* - 1/68
F-4D	1/68 - 24/6/69

Squadron deployed with the 366 TFW to Da Nang AB, RSVN on 10/10/66. Followed the 480 TFS in transferring to the 37 TFW at Phu Cat AB, RSVN on 15/6/69. Remained attached to 366 TFW until assigned on 24/6/69 and recoded to **HB**. Two small red and one white stripe on rudder carried as squadron markings. The following individual tail codes noted on F-4C **AA**, **AD**, **AG**, **AH**, **AS**, **AT**, **AW**, **AX** (*2 aircraft*) and **AY**. The F-4D tail codes noted **AD** and **AW** on unidentified aircraft. Following tail codes carried on unidentified F-4 models **AB**, **AK**, **AJ**, **AU** and **AY**.

AC
12 Tactical Reconnaissance Squadron   460 Tactical Reconnaissance Wing
RF-4C   1968* - 31/8/71   Tan Son Nhut AB, RSVN

Assigned to the 460 TRW, on 2/9/66 and tail coded **AC** during 1968. Orange noted as the squadron colour. Reassigned to the 67 TRW at Bergstrom AFB with **BC** tail code on 31/8/71. One source suggests codes applied in early 1967.

AE
16 Tactical Reconnaissance Squadron   460 Tactical Reconnaissance Wing
RF-4C   1967* - 15/3/70   Tan Son Nhut AB, RSVN

The 16 TRS arrived at Tan Son Nhut AB, RSVN on 31/10/65 with RF-4C. Became a component of the 460 TRW on 18/2/66. Squadron colour noted as yellow. Application of **AE** tail code noted in early 1967. The 16 TRS moved to Misawa AB, Japan joining the 475 TFW on 16/3/70, tail coding RF-4C **UE**.

AH
45 Tactical Reconnaissance Squadron   460 Tactical Reconnaissance Wing
RF-101C   1968* - 31/12/70   Tan Son Nhut AB, RSVN

The 45 TRS took the place of the 15 TRS at Tan Son Nhut AB, RSVN in early 1965 flying RF-101. Unit tail code **AH** applied between mid and late 1968. Squadron colours appear to have changed from blue and white, to blue only. The 45 TRS continued as Detachment 1 - 45 TRS after 8/7/66, until 31/12/70 (*controlling unit non-operational within 475 TFW*). Other sources claim unit returned to Davis-Monthan AFB to inactivate. Unit later reactivated on 15/10/71 with **BB** tail coded RF-4C at Bergstrom AFB.

RF-101C Voodoo 56-176 "Kathy's Clown" **AH**, 45 TRS 460 TRW, Tan Son Nhut AB, RSVN, 1969. Photo: unknown

AJ
360 Tactical Electronic Warfare Squadron

1968* - 31/8/71	460 Tactical Reconnaissance Wing
31/8/71 - 1/2/72	483 Tactical Airlift Wing
1/2/72 - 24/11/72	377 Air Base Wing
24/11/72 - 1/7/73	463 Tactical Airlift Wing
1/7/73 - 31/7/73	+1 Special Operations Wing

* non-operational Dyess AFB + status unknown

EC-47N/P/Q   1968* - 24/11/72   Ton Son Nhut AB, RSVN

The C-47 was equipped 360 TEWS assigned to the 460 TRW between 8/4/66 and 31/8/71. Activated from the 360 TRS based at Ton Son Nhut AB, RSVN. Forward operating locations noted at Phu Bhy AB, RSVN, and Nakhon Phanom RTAFB. Blue noted

TAIL CODE

as squadron colour. Assigned to the 483 TAW, on 31/8/71 and 377 ABW on 1/2/72, maintaining **AJ** tail code. Reassigned to the 463 TAW at Dyess AFB, non-operational after 24/11/72 and also assigned to 1 SOW Hurlburt Field between 1/7/73 and 31/7/73 with unknown tail code status.

AL
361 Tactical Electronic Warfare Squadron

1966* - 31/8/71	460 Tactical Reconnaissance Wing
31/8/71 - 1/12/71	483 Tactical Airlift Wing
15/10/71 - 1/12/71	*(Non-operational)*
1/12/71 - 1/9/72	unknown possible inactive
1/9/72 - 30/6/74	56 Special Operations Wing

EC-47N/P/Q   1968* - 30/6/74   Nha Trang AB, RSVN

Activated with some assets of the 361 TRS and assigned to the 460 TRW on 8/4/66. The 361 TRS activated at Nha Trang AB, RSVN on 8/4/66. Detachment 1 activated 8/66 at Pleiku AB, RSVN. Detachment aircraft arriving on 8/9/66. Detachment 1, became 362 TEWS on 1/2/67. Squadron also operated from operating location "A" Vung Tuo AB, RSVN and "B" at Phu Cat AB, RSVN (*time frame unknown*). Unit assigned to 483 TAW on 31/8/71 maintaining **AL** tail code. Status unknown between 1/12/71 and 1/9/72. Squadron assigned to the 56 SOW and possibly based Nakhon Phanom RTAFB, with unknown tail code status until inactivated on 30/6/74.

AN
362 Tactical Electronic Warfare Squadron

1968* - 31/8/71	460 Tactical Reconnaissance Wing
31/8/71 - 1/2/72	483 Tactical Airlift Wing
1/2/72 - 27/6/72	366 Tactical Fighter Wing

EC-47N/P/Q C-47H   1968* - 27/6/72   Pleiku AB, RSVN

Activated from Detachment 1 - 361 TEWS on 1/2/67 and assigned to 460 TRW. Two known detachment locations include Da Nang AB and Detachment 2 at Nakhon Phanom RTAFB (*November 1970*). Squadron reassigned to the 483 TAW between 31/8/71 and 1/2/72, and to the 366 TFW until 27/6/72 maintaining the **AN** tail code. Reassigned to the 56 TFW between 1/9/72 and 30/6/74, with unknown tail code status.

EC-47Q Dakota 45-1102 **AN**, 362 TEWS 366 TFW, Da Nang AB, RSVN. Did not survive rocket attack on 12 April 1972. Photo: John Winston, 13 April 1972.

B
390 Tactical Fighter Squadron   366 Tactical Fighter Wing
                                                          Da Nang AB, RSVN

F-4C   mid-1967* - 1/68
F-4D   1/68 - 1969

The 390 TFS assigned with 366 TFW on 10/10/66 and transferred together in October 1966 to Da Nang AB, RSVN. Blue noted as the squadron colour. Recoded to **LF** when the 366 TFW adopted a squadron common tail code system in 1969. The individual tail codes **BT** and **BY** noted on F-4C, **BN** and **BQ** on F-4D and **BD**, **BF**, **BL** and **BY** on unidentified F-4.

BO   Ohio ANG
166 Tactical Fighter Squadron   354 Tactical Fighter Wing
F-100C/F   5/7/68* - 10/6/69   *Kunsan AB, ROK

The F-100 equipped 166 TFS deployed from Lockbourne AFB to Kunsan AB, between 25/6/68 and 4/7/68 then and assigned to the 354 TFW. The F-100 returned to Ohio on 10/6/69 and control reverted to the 121 TFW. This Ohio ANG unit coded **BO** during deployment, with blue noted as the squadron colour.

UNITED STATES AIR FORCES PACIFIC

BP Kansas ANG
127 Tactical Fighter Squadron   **354 Tactical Fighter Wing**
F-100C/F   5/7/68* - 10/6/69   Kunsan AB, ROK

This Kansas ANG unit coded **BP** during deployment from McConnell AFB to Kunsan AB, ROK on 25/6/68 and assigned to the 354 TFW. The 127 TFS returned to Kansas on 10/6/69. Red noted as squadron colour.

C_
480 Tactical Fighter Squadron   **366 Tactical Fighter Wing**
    Da Nang AB, RSVN

F-4C   mid-1967* - 1/68
F-4D   1/68 - 15/4/69

The 480 TFS moved to Da Nang AB, RSVN with uncoded F-4C within the 366 TFW on 10/10/66. The squadron colour of green noted. The 480 TFS transferred to the 37 TFW on 15/4/69 and recoded **HK**. The **CH**, **CW** and **CY** tail codes noted on F-4C, **CM**, **CO**, **CS**, **CW** and **CY** on F-4D and **CV** noted on unidentified F-4.

CB
90 Tactical Fighter Squadron   **3 Tactical Fighter Wing**
F-100D/F   1967* - 11/69   Bien Hoa AB, RSVN

Squadron assigned to the 3 TFW, moving to Bien Hoa AB, RSVN on 7/2/66 flying F-100D/F. Coded **CB** with blue squadron markings. Redesignated to 90 AS in 11/69 with A-37B coded **CG** within the 3 TFW.

CE
510 Tactical Fighter Squadron   **3 Tactical Fighter Wing**
F-100D/F   1967* - 15/11/69   Bien Hoa AB, RSVN

The 510 TFS moved from England AFB to Bien Hoa AB, RSVN on 7/11/65. Coded **CE** with purple as squadron colour. Inactivated on 15/11/69 until assigned to the 81 TFW flying **WR** coded A-10A.

CF
8 Attack Squadron   15/11/69 - 30/9/70   **3 Tactical Fighter Wing**
8 Special Operations Squadron   30/9/70 - 31/7/71   **35 Tactical Fighter Wing**
    31/7/71 - 15/1/72   **315 Tactical Airlift Wing**
    15/1/72 - 15/12/72   **377 Air Base Wing**
A-37B   15/11/69 - 15/12/72   Bien Hoa AB, RSVN

Squadron formerly designated 8 Bombardment Squadron flying **PQ** tail coded B-57 within the 35 TFW until 15/11/69. The 8 AS transferred on the same day to the 3 TFW with assets of the 604 SOS, (**CK** *coded A-37B*) 3 TFW at Bien Hoa AB, RSVN with the **CF** tail code. Yellow noted as squadron colour. Squadron redesignated as 8 SOS and assigned to the 35 TFW on 30/9/70. Further reassigned to the 315 TAW on 31/7/71, maintaining **CF** tail code and base until inactivated on 15/12/72.

CG
90 Attack Squadron   11/69 - 31/10/70   **3 Tactical Fighter Wing**
90 Special Operations Squadron   31/10/70 - 1/9/71   **14 Special Operations Wing**
    1/9/71 - 15/4/72   **483 Tactical Airlift Wing**
A-37B   11/69 - 15/4/72   Bien Hoa AB, RSVN

Squadron formerly flew **CB** tail coded F-100 when designated 90 TFS within the 3 TFW. Redesignated to 90 Attack Squadron and reequipped with A-37, recoded with **CG** tail code during November 1969. Reassigned to the 14 SOW on 31/10/70, and again to 483 TAW, on 1/9/71 maintaining equipment and **CG** tail code. Further reassigned to the 405 FW on 15/12/72 to fly **PN** coded F-4E.

CK
604 Air Commando Squadron   late 1967* - 15/11/67   unknown
    15/11/67 - 1/8/68   **14 Air Commando Wing**
    (detached to 3 Tactical Fighter Wing)
604 Special Operations Squadron   1/8/68 - 30/9/70   **3 Tactical Fighter Wing**
A-37A/B   late 1967* - 30/9/70   Bien Hoa AB, RSVN

Squadron moved from England AFB to Bien Hoa AB, RSVN on 23/7/67. The controlling unit unknown from arrival until assignment to the 14 SOW on 15/11/67 (*attached 3 TFW, thus* **CK** *tail code*). Flew first mission on 15/8/67 with uncoded A-37. The **CK** tail codes applied late in 1967. Redesignated to 604 SOS on 1/8/68, and assigned to the 3 TFW on 1/3/70. Green squadron markings noted. Squadron inactivated on 30/9/70.

CP
531 Tactical Fighter Squadron   **3 Tactical Fighter Wing**
F-100D/F   1967* - 6/7/70   Bien Hoa AB, RSVN

Squadron activated within the 3 TFW on 7/12/65. The 531 TFS coded F-100D/F **CP** in 1967 with red noted as squadron colour. The 531 TFS inactivated on 6/7/70.

F-100D Super Sabre 55-2881 **CP**, 531 TFS 3 TFW, Bien Hoa AB, RSVN, with red fin cap outlined in white, similar treatment for name block on canopy.

DE
50 Tactical Airlift Squadron

	1968* - 31/5/71	314 Tactical Airlift Wing
	31/5/71 - 15/8/73	374 Tactical Airlift Wing
C-130E	1968* - 8/2/73	Ching Chuan Kang AB, Taiwan

Assigned on 23/2/66 as one of three 314 TAW C-130E squadrons. The DE tail code assigned in July 1968, with red noted as squadron colour. The 374 TAW replaced the 314 TAW, which moved to Little Rock AFB on 31/5/71. The three original squadrons maintained codes and colours until 1973. The 50 TAS ceased operations on 8/2/73 and inactivated on 15/8/73.

DH
345 Tactical Airlift Squadron

	1968* - 31/5/71	314 Tactical Airlift Wing
	31/5/71 - 15/11/73	374 Tactical Airlift Wing
		Ching Chuan Kang AB, Taiwan
	15/11/73 - 31/10/75	374 Tactical Airlift Wing
C-130E	1968* - 1/12/74+	Clark AFB, Philippines

The 345 TAS assigned on 25/3/66 to the 314 TAW. One of three C-130 operators to code during 1968 within the 314 TAW. The 345 TAS coded C-130E **DH** in 1968 with yellow squadron colour unconfirmed. The 374 TAW replaced the 314 TAW on 31/5/71.

C-130E Hercules 63-7825 **DH**, 345 TAS 374 TAW, Clark AB, Philippines. Photo: Don Larsen, Korat RTAFB, May 1974.

DL
776 Tactical Airlift Squadron

	1968* - 31/5/71	314 Tactical Airlift Wing
	31/5/71 - 15/11/73	374 Tactical Airlift Wing
		Ching Chuan Kang AB, Taiwan
	15/11/73 - 31/10/75	374 Tactical Airlift Wing
C-130E	1968* - 1/12/74+	Clark AB, Philippines

Squadron assigned on 25/3/66 to the 314 TAW. Squadron C-130 tail coded **DL** during 1968, white noted as squadron colour. The 374 TAW replaced the 314 TAW on 31/5/71. The three original squadrons maintained tail codes within 374 TAW. The 776 TAS inactivated on 31/10/75.

UNITED STATES AIR FORCES PACIFIC

C-130E Hercules 62-1806 **DL**, 766 TAS 374 TAW, Ching Chuan Kang AB, Taiwan. Photo: Don Larsen, Udorn RTAFB, 16 December 1971.

DS
1 Test Squadron   **405 Fighter Wing**
F-4   between 30/4/70 - 1972   **Clark AB, Philippines**

The 1 TS carried the **DS** tail codes on F-4 seen in Japan. Unit later confirmed with **PA** coded F-4, with few confirmed sightings with **DS** tail code noted.

DY
346 Tactical Airlift Squadron   **314 Tactical Airlift Wing**
C-130E   15/3/69 - 31/5/71   **Ching Chuan Kang AB, Taiwan**

The 346 TAS assigned as fourth squadron within the 314 TAW at Ching Chuan Kang AB, Taiwan after initial coding. The tail code **DY** applied on assignment. The 346 TAS inactivated on 31/5/71 when 314 TAW returned to CONUS. Place taken by 21 TAS (*previously flew C-130A with YD tail code at Naha AB*) arriving with 374 TAW on 31/5/71. Unconfirmed squadron of colour black.

DY
21 Tactical Airlift Squadron

                                        31/5/71 - 15/11/73   **374 Tactical Airlift Wing**
                                                                       Ching Chuan Kang AB, Taiwan
                                        15/11/73 -   **374 Tactical Airlift Wing**
                                                                             Clark AB, Philippines

C-130E   31/5/71 - 1/12/74+

The 21 TAS arrived at Ching Chuan Kang AB, Taiwan with the 374 TAW from Naha AB, Okinawa on 31/5/71. Squadron previously flew **YD** tail coded C-130A. The 346 TAS 314 TAW, providing assets. The wing moved to 31/5/71 and reactivated at Clark AB, Philippines with the 21 TAS. Unconfirmed squadron colours of blue or black.

EA
16 Special Operations Squadron   **8 Tactical Fighter Wing**
AC-130A   1967* - 4/69   **Nha Trang AB, RSVN**

As originally due to activate during August 1968 within the 14 SOW, the 16 SOS, initially assigned the **EA** tail code. Activated within the 8 TFW at Ubon RTAFB on 30/10/68 with the single AC-130A prototype. Additional AC-130 delivered and tail code changed to **FT** during April 1969. Black noted as squadron colour.

EC
1 Air Commando Squadron   1967* - 20/12/67   **14 Air Commando Wing**
A-1E   1967* - 20/12/67   **Pleiku AB, RSVN**

Organized in the summer of 1964 at Bien Hoa AB, RSVN with A-1E, moving to Nha Trang AB, RSVN during 1966. Involved with the training of SVAF crews with Vietnamese marked A-1. Assigned to the 14 SOW on 8/3/66 and tail coded **EC** during mid 1967. Squadron reassigned to the 56 SOW based at Nakhon Phanom, RTAFB on 20/12/67 and recoded **TC**. Possible C-47 and A-1G used, coding details unknown.

A-1E Skyraider 133914 **EC**, 1 SOS 14 SOW, Pleiku AB. Photo: unknown 1969.

EL

3 Air Commando Squadron	1/5/68* - 1/8/68	14 Air Commando Wing
3 Special Operations Squadron	1/8/68 -15/9/69	14 Special Operations Wing
AC-47D	1/5/68* - 15/9/69	Nha Trang AB, RSVN

Squadron replaced the 14 ACS with AC-47 at Nha Trang AB, RSVN during May 1968. Redesignated to 3 SOS on 1/8/68 and inactivated in late 1969.

AC-47D Dakota 45-1057, **EL** 3 SOS 14 SOW, Pleiku AB, RSVN. Photo: Norm Taylor, 11 November 1968.

EN

4 Air Command Squadron	1967* - 1/8/68	14 Air Commando Wing
4 Special Operations Squadron	1/8/68 - 15/12/69	14 Special Operations Wing
	15/12/69 - least 29/5/70	Phan Rang AB, RSVN
		unknown
AC-47D	1967* - 15/12/69	Nha Trang AB, RSVN

Assigned to the 14 SOW on 8/3/66, moving to Ton Son Nhut AB, RSVN in May 1966. Coded aircraft **EN** in late 1967 redesignated 4 SOS on 1/8/68 and inactivated on 15/12/69. Black, or red with black noted as squadron colours. Forward operating locations noted at Phu Cat, Da Nang, Bien Hoa, Pleiku AB, RSVN and Nakhon Phanom RTAFB. Reporting unit and tail code unknown after 15/12/69 with a detachment assigned to the 432 TFW between 10/12/69 and 29/5/70 with **OS** tail coded AC-47D.

AC-47D Dakota 44-76625, **EN** 4 SOS 14 SOW, Nha Trang AB, RSVN, note Spook emblem and black underside. Photo: Norm Taylor, 25 March 1969.

UNITED STATES AIR FORCES PACIFIC

EO
5 Air Commando Squadron	1968* - 1/8/68	14 Air Commando Wing
5 Special Operations Squadron	1/8/68-15/10/69	14 Special Operations Wing
		Nha Trang AB, RSVN

C-47D, SC-47D   1968* - 15/10/69
U-10A/B   1968* - 15/10/69

Activated within the 14 ACW on 8/3/66. Unit moved to several bases including Bien Hoa AB, RSVN. Redesignated 5 SOS and inactivated on 15/10/69. U-10 detachments noted at Da Nang, Pleiku, Bien Hoa and Bien Thuy AB, RSVN.

C-47D Dakota 43-48272, **EO** 5 SOS 14 SOW, Na Trang AB, RSVN. Photo: Bob Burgess, Tan Son Nhut AB, RSVN, 14 January 1968.

ER
9 Air Commando Squadron	1967* - 5/67	14 Air Commando Wing
		Nha Trang AB, RSVN
9 Air Commando Squadron	5/67 - 1/8/68	14 Air Commando Wing
9 Special Operations Squadron	1/8/68 - 30/9/71	14 Special Operations Wing
		Pleiku AB, RSVN
	30/9/71 - 29/2/72	315 Tactical Airlift Wing
		Phan Rang AB, RSVN
	(*possible detached 9/1/72 - 29/2/72*)	Tan Son Nhut AB, RSVN

AC-47D   1967* - 29/2/72

The 9 ACS assigned to the 14 ACW on 25/1/67. Tail code applied while squadron assigned to the 14 ACW, at Nha Trang AB, RSVN, moving to Pleiku AB, RSVN in May 1967. Redesignated to 9 SOS on 1/8/68. Squadron operated numerous forward operating locations and detachments during tenure. Known locations include Bien Tuy, Da Nang, Bien Hoa, Phu Cat, Tuy Hoa AB, RSVN and Ubon RTAFB. Squadron also operated uncoded O-2B. Reassigned to the 315 TAW on 30/9/71 when the 14 SOW inactivated. Squadron reactivated on 1/3/88 within the 1 SOW CONUS replacing the 55 ARRS operating uncoded HC-130.

ET
6 Air Commando Squadron	29/2/68* - 7/68	14 Air Commando Wing
		Nha Trang AB, RSVN
	7/68 - 1/8/68	14 Air Commando Wing
6 Special Operations Squadron	1/8/68 -15/7/68	14 Special Operations Wing
	15/7/68 - 15/3/69	633 Special Operations Wing
		Pleiku AB, RSVN

A-1E/H   29/2/68* - 15/3/69

Squadron deployed on 20/2/68 to Nha Trang AB, RSVN from England AFB (*with 4410 CCTW, flying* **IK** *tail coded A-37*). Squadron moved to Pleiku AB, RSVN, during July 1968 and redesignated 6 SOS on 1/8/68. Further reassigned to co-based 633 SOW and inactivated on 15/3/70. Red noted as squadron colour.

FA
25 Tactical Fighter Squadron
8 Tactical Fighter Wing
F-4D   28/5/68* - 1/73   Ubon RTAFB

Assigned to the 8 TFW on 28/5/68, from the 33 TFW at Eglin AFB. Black and yellow checkered, or solid black fin cap carried as squadron markings. Later a combination of both noted. Recoded to **WP** as wing common code in January 1973.

F-4D Phantom 68-8745 **FA**, 25 TFS 8 TFW, Ubon RTAFB, withcheckered fin cap. Photo: Don Larsen, 24 August 1971.

FG
433 Tactical Fighter Squadron　　　　　　　　　　　　　　　　　　　　　　　　　**8 Tactical Fighter Wing**
　　Ubon RTAFB

F-4C	early 1967* - least 10/67
F-4D	7/67 - 1/73

The 433 TFS assigned to the 8 TFW on 25/7/64. The 433 TFS adopted the **FG** tail code, displaying blue and orange horizontal rudder stripes in early 1968. Later green and black fin cap carried. Reequipped with F-4D on the arrival of the 4 TFS, 33 TFW from Eglin AFB, assuming the 433 TFS title on arrival in July 1967. Recoded to wing common tail code of **WP** in January 1973.

F-4D Phantom 66-7680, 66-8815 **FG**, 433 TFS 8 TFW, Ubon RTAFB. Photo: Martin collection.

FK
13 Bombardment Squadron　　　　　　　　　　　　　　　　　　　　　　　　　　　**8 Tactical Fighter Wing**
B-57G　　　　　late 1970 - 12/4/72　　　　　　　　　　　　　　　　　　　　　　　　　**Ubon RTAFB**

Originally tail coded **FS** with the 15 TFW, deploying with code to 8 TFW at Ubon RTAFB. Attached on 1/10/70 and assigned on 31/10/70. Tail code changed to **FK** shortly after arrival. Although still attached to 8 TFW, status changed to non-operational after 12/4/72 and transferred while non-operational to the 405 FW on 24/12/72. Colours not noted.

FO
435 Tactical Fighter Squadron　　　　　　　　　　　　　　　　　　　　　　　　　**8 Tactical Fighter Wing**
F-4D　　　　　25/7/67* - 1/73　　　　　　　　　　　　　　　　　　　　　　　　　　　**Ubon RTAFB**

The 435 TFS first attached to the 8 TFW in July 1966. Assigned to Udorn RTAFB with F-104C standing down on 19/7/67 and transferring F-104 to Puerto Rico ANG starting on 25/7/67. The F-4D assets came from the 4 TFS 33 TFW. Adopted **FO** tail code with red colour noted for markings on F-4D, changing to black 1968. Recoded **WP** as wing common tail code in January 1973.

FP
497 Tactical Fighter Squadron　　　　　　　　　　　　　　　　　　　　　　　　　**8 Tactical Fighter Wing**
　　Ubon RTAFB

F-4C	early 1967* - 11/67
F-4D	11/67 - 1/73

The 497 TFS was one of three F-4 units coded within the 8 TFW at Ubon RTAFB in 1967. The 497 TFS adopted **FP** as tail code plus a small blue and orange horizontal stripes at the top of rudder, later changing to black fin cap. Squadron F-4D had black painted underside for night role. Recoded to **WP**, in January 1973 and moved with the 8 TFW to Kunsan AB, ROK on 16/9/74.

UNITED STATES AIR FORCES PACIFIC

F-4D Phantom 66-8761 **FP**, 497 TFS 8 TFW, Ubon RTAFB, note black underside. Photo: Don Larsen, 24 August 1971.

FS
13 Bombardment Squadron   **8 Tactical Fighter Wing**
B-57G   **15/9/70 - late 1970**   **Ubon RTAFB**

Squadron attached to the 8 TFW on 31/10/70 with **FK** tail code. Assigned on 31/10/70, changing tail code to **FS** shortly after arrival at Ubon RTAFB.

FT
16 Special Operations Squadron   **8 Tactical Fighter Wing**
                                                                Ubon RTAFB
AC-130A   **4/69 - 5/74**
AC-130E/H   **7/73 - 5/74**

Squadron recoded from **EA** to **FT** with April 1969. Further recoding to **WP** as 8 TFW common code in May 1974.

AC-130A Hercules 55-0029 **FT**, 16 SOS 8 TFW, Ubon RTAFB, black with camouflage topside, plus red serial and tail code. Photo: Don Larsen, Korat RTAFB, 11 May 1974.

FY
555 Tactical Fighter Squadron   **8 Tactical Fighter Wing**
                                                                Ubon RTAFB
F-4C   **1/67* - least 12/6/67**
F-4D   **28/5/67 - 1/6/68**

The 555 TFS attached on 25/1/66 and assigned on 25/3/66 to 8 TFW. The 555 TFS utilized the **FY** tail code. The 40 TFS 33 TFW transferred from Eglin AFB, with F-4D renumbering to 555 TFS on arrival in May 1967. Attached to the 432 TRW at Udorn RTAFB on 28/5/68 and assigned on 1/6/68 with **OY** tail code.

GG
35 Tactical Fighter Squadron
347 Tactical Fighter Wing
F-4C   **1968* - 15/3/71**   **Yokota AB, Japan**

Assigned to 347 TFW on 15/1/68 with F-105D/F, converting to F-4C later in 1968. Unconfirmed **GG** tail code usage on F-105. Detached between 22/3/68 and 10/6/68 to unknown location. Squadron transferred to 3 TFW flying **UP** tail coded F-4C on 15/3/71. Assets used to form the 67 TFS (**ZG** *tail code*) within 18 TFW. Squadron markings noted as blue fin caps.

F-4C Phantom 64-0660 **GG**, 35 TFS 347 TFW Yokota AB, Japan. Photo: T Matsuzaki, 4 May 1968.

GL
36 Tactical Fighter Squadron
347 Tactical Fighter Wing

Yokota AB, Japan

F-4C   1968* - 15/5/71

The 36 TFS assigned to the 374 TFW on 15/1/68 flying the F-105D/F and later converted to the F-4C. Red noted as squadron colour. Squadron transferred to the 3 TFW at Kunsan AB, ROK on 15/5/71, with coded F-4D **UK**. Former F-4C assets assigned to the 44 TFS activated on 14/5/71 with **ZL** tail codes.

GR
80 Tactical Fighter Squadron
347 Tactical Fighter Wing

Yokota AB, Japan

F-105D   1968* - 2/68
F-4C   2/68 - 15/3/71

Squadron assigned to the 347 TFW on 15/1/68 flying the F-105D/F. Squadron F-105 coded G**R** in early 1968 and converted to F-4C in February 1968. Status changed to non-operational on 15/2/71, until transferred to the 3 TFW in March 1971 and recoded **UD**. Blue and yellow noted as squadron colour.

F-105D Thunderchief 61-0093 **GR**, 80 TFS 347 TFW, Yokota AB, Japan. Photo: Martin collection.

UNITED STATES AIR FORCES PACIFIC

F-4C Phantoms 63-7598 and 64-0721 **GR**, 80 TFS 347 TFW, Yokota AB, Japan. Photo: Martin collection.

GT
556 Reconnaissance Squadron	1/7/68 - 15/5/71	347 Tactical Fighter Wing
	15/5/71 - 1/11/71	6100 Air Base Wing
	1/11/71 - 30/6/72	475 Tactical Fighter Wing
		Yokota AB, Japan
EB-57E	1/7/68* - 1972	
RC-130B-ii	1971	

The 556 RS initially tail coded **GT** at Yokota AB, Japan, within the Yokota base **G_** range tail code, in 1968. Controlling units between 15/5/71 and 1/11/71 unconfirmed, but believed to have included the 6100 ABG/ABW. Reassigned to the 475 ABW on 1/11/71 until 30/6/72. There are some odd occurrences connected with this RC-130 operator. (*RC-130B noted in November-December 1971 at Udorn RTAFB, listed at base transit office as from Yokota AB, Japan. Also noted at about the same time are, **GT** tail coded RC-130B on delivery to 7406 CSS, 7404 CSW, October 1971. [Five aircraft and others later] This unit did not use tail codes, but absorbed previously coded aircraft from other units.*)

GT
21 Special Operations Squadron		18 Tactical Fighter Wing
EB-57E	15/12/72 - 1973	Kadena AB, Okinawa

The 1 SOS previously assigned within the 56 SOW flying **TC** tail coded A-1 until 15/12/72. Little known of this unit. Black noted as squadron colour. Believe follow on unit connected to the 556 RS flying with 347 TFW, thus continuation of **G** range tail code assigned in 1968.

EB-57E Canberra 55-4279 **GT**, 1 SOS 18 TFW, Kadena AB, Okinawa. Photo: Hideki Nagakubo, 1971-72.

GU
497 Tactical Fighter Squadron		51 Tactical Fighter Wing
F-4E	7/9/84 - 1/10/89	Taegu AB, ROK

Formerly operated **OS** tail coded F-4E within same wing based at Osan AB, ROK. Squadron applied the **GU** tail code on move to Taegu AB, ROK late 1984. Blue fin caps noted on grey F-4E. The 497 TFS inactivated in late 1989 with code reused by RF-4C of the 15 TRS.

TAIL CODE

F-4E Phantom 67-0351 "Spirit of Freedom" **GU**, 497 TFS 51 CW(T), Taegu AB, ROK, with blue fin cap. Photo: Wallace T. Van Winkle, 3 November 1986.

GU
15 Tactical Reconnaissance Squadron   **460 Tactical Reconnaissance Group**
RF-4C   1/10/89 - late 1990   **Taegu AB, ROK**

Control of 15 TRS assumed from 51 TFW. Reconnaissance RF-4C recoded from **ZZ** to **GU** on assignment to 460 TRG. Unit and group to inactivated in late 1990.

HA   **Iowa ANG**
174 Tactical Fighter Squadron   **37 Tactical Fighter Wing**
F-100C/F   14/5/68* - 11/5/69   **Phu Cat AB, RSVN**

The Iowa National Guard 174 TFS activated on 26/1/68. Assigned from the 185 TFG Sioux City MAP to the 37 TFW on 14/5/68, until 11/5/69. The 37 TFW tail code maintained after return to CONUS (*see ANG section*).

HB
389 Tactical Fighter Squadron   15/6/69 - 31/3/70   **37 Tactical Fighter Wing**
                                                                           31/3/70 - 15/10/71   **12 Tactical Fighter Wing**
F-4D   15/6/69 - 15/10/71   **Phu Cat AB, RSVN**

Attached from the 366 TFW on 15/6/69 and assigned to the 37 TFW on 24/6/69 (*formerly tail coded* **A_** *within the 366 TFW*) recoded to **HB**. Squadron remained at Phu Cat AB, RSVN within the 12 TFW after 37 TFW inactivated, maintaining **HB** tail code along with red squadron colour. Unit transferred without personnel or equipment to Mountain Home AFB with 347 TFW, to fly **MP** tail coded F-111F on 15/10/71. (*The* **HB** *tail code also used by the 7 TFS, 49 TFW from July 1968 and October 1971.*)

F-4D Phantom 66-7531 **HB**, 389 TFS 12 TFW, Phu Cat AB, RSVN, with red and white title block on canopy. Photo: Don Larsen, Udorn RTAFB, 6 November 1971.

UNITED STATES AIR FORCES PACIFIC

HE
416 Tactical Fighter Squadron   **37 Tactical Fighter Wing**
F-100D/F   1968* - 27/5/69   **Phu Cat AB, RSVN**

The 416 TFS assigned to the 37 TFW with F-100 on 15/4/67. Tail coded **HE** with blue squadron markings. Reassigned to the 31 TFW on 27/5/69 moving to Tuy Hoa AB, RSVN and recoding **SE**.

HG
347 Tactical Fighter Wing   30/7/73 - 12/7/74   **Takhli RTAFB**
    12/7/74 - 30/6/75   **Korat RTAFB**

428 Tactical Fighter Squadron
F-111A   30/7/73 - 30/6/75

Unit reassigned from 474 TFW operations at Takhli RTAFB on 30/7/73. Recoded from **NA** tail code to **HG** with red fin stripe. Codes maintained on some F-111A for weeks after return to Nellis AFB on 30/6/75.

429 Tactical Fighter Squadron
F-111A   30/7/73 - 30/6/75

Second former 474 TFW squadron reassigned to the 347 TFW at Takhli RTAFB on 30/7/73. Recoded from **NA** tail code to **HG**, with yellow fin stripe carried. Tail codes maintaining on some F-111 weeks after return to Nellis AFB.

F-111A 67-081 **HG**, ex 429 347 TFW, Takhli RTAFB, with yellow tail stripe. Photo: Don Logan, Nellis AFB, 12 June 1975, on return from South East Asia, before replacement of **HG** tail code with 474 TFW code **NA**.

HK
480 Tactical Fighter Squadron   15/4/69 - 31/3/70   **37 Tactical Fighter Wing**
    31/3/70 - 17/11/71   **12 Tactical Fighter Wing**
F-4D   15/4/69 - 17/11/71   **Phu Cat AB, RSVN**

Squadron attached from the 366 TFW on 15/4/69 (*carried a* **B_** *range tail code*). Recoded **HK** on arrival with the 37 TFW. Remained at Phu Cat AB, RSVN within the 12 TFW after 37 TFW inactivated on 31/3/70. The **HK** tail code maintained with green squadron markings. Unit inactivated on 17/11/71 and reactivated on 15/11/76 with **SP** tail coded F-4D within 52 TFW, USAFE.

HP
355 Tactical Fighter Squadron   **37 Tactical Fighter Wing**
F-100D/F   1968* - 15/5/69   **Phu Cat AB, RSVN**

Squadron attached to the 37 TFW on 3/2/68 and assigned on 5/7/68, at Phu Cat AB, RSVN. Green noted as the squadron colour. Transferred to the 31 TFW at Tuy Hoa AB, RSVN on 15/5/69, with tail code change of **SP**.

HS
612 Tactical Fighter Squadron - Detachment 1   **37 Tactical Fighter Wing**
F-100D/F   1968* - 13/4/69   **Phu Cat AB, RSVN**

The 612 TFS - Detachment 1 attached to the 37 TFW on 8/6/67 and assigned 13/4/69 flying **HS** tail coded F-100D/F. Detachment 1 relocated to 35 TFW on 14/4/69 and coded **VS**. Remainder of unit moved to Phan Rang AB, RSVN on 13/4/69 within the 35 TFW.

JB
17 Wild Weasel Squadron   **388 Tactical Fighter Wing**
F-105G   1/12/71 - 29/10/74   **Korat RTAFB**

The 17 WWS activated from assets of the 6010 WWS, with **ZB** tail coded F-105G. The **ZB** F-105 noted up until a year after recoding date. Operational until 29/10/74, and squadron inactivated on 15/11/74. Black noted as squadron colour. The assets used to form the 562 TFS 35 TFW at George AFB, in October 1974.

F-105G Thunderchief 63-8291 "Muttley the Wonder Dog" **JB**, 17 WWS 388 TFW, Korat RTAFB, displaying shark mouth. Photo: Don Larsen, 29 January 1973.

JC
7 Airborne Command and Control Squadron

30/4/72 - 22/5/74	**388 Tactical Fighter Wing**
22/5/74 - 31/3/75	**374 Tactical Airlift Wing**
EC-130E **30/4/72 - 31/3/75**	**Korat RTAFB**

Squadron assigned to the 388 TFW on 30/4/72 and transferred to the 374 TAW control at Clark AB on 22/5/74. The squadron remained at Korat RTAFB until 31/3/75. Possibly not coded **JC** until mid 1973 with tail codes removed late in 1974.

EC-130E Hercules 62-1857 **JC**, 7 ACCS 388 TFW, Korat RTAFB. Photo: Don Larsen, 10 May 1974.

JE
44 Tactical Fighter Squadron
388 Tactical Fighter Wing
F-105D/F **1968* - 10/10/69** **Korat RTAFB**

Assigned to the 388 TFW, from the 18 TFW on 25/4/67 with F-105D/F. The "Vampires" tail coded F-105 **JE** in 1968 and yellow squadron markings noted. Attached on 10/10/69 and assigned on 15/10/69 to the 355 TFW at Takhli RTAFB and recoded **RE**.

JH
3 Tactical Fighter Squadron **388 Tactical Fighter Wing**
A-7D **15/3/73 - 22/12/75** **Korat RTAFB**

The 3 TFS activated on 15/3/73 with **JH** tail coded A-7D. Most assets came from the withdrawing 353 TFS 354 TFW. The aircraft started coding before squadron start up date in February 1973. Used a combination of **JH** and **MB** tail coded A-7D for some time. Many A-7D assigned from other 354 TFW units. This led to the confusion of squadron colours. Red adopted as standard tail stripe colour. Originally scheduled to form as 6014 TFS, but reversed before effective date. Assigned to the 3 TFW on 15/12/75 with **PN** coded F-4E.

UNITED STATES AIR FORCES PACIFIC

A-7D Corsair 71-0309 **JH**, 3 TFS 388 TFW, Korat RTAFB. Photo: Don Larsen, 28 April 1974.

JJ
34 Tactical Fighter Squadron

388 Tactical Fighter Wing
Korat RTAFB

F-105D/F	1/68* - 7/5/69
F-4E	7/5/69 - 1/10//74
F-4D	1/10/74 - 23/12/75

Attached from the 347 TFW on 15/1/68 and assigned on 15/5/71, flying F-105D/F until 7/5/69 with **JJ** tail coded F-105. The 40 TFS deployed from Eglin AFB to Korat AFB in May 1969 with F-4E and redesignated 34 TFS on arrival. The 40 TFS designation returned to 33 TFW at Eglin AFB. Squadron non-operational between 29/6/74 and 1/7/74 for unknown reason. Black colour noted as fin cap. One source has the 34 TFS initially coding in late 1966.

F-4E Phantom 67-0290 **JJ**, 34 TFS 388 TFW, Korat RTAFB, displaying shark mouth. Photo: Don Larsen, 28 April 1974.

JV
469 Tactical Fighter Squadron

388 Tactical Fighter Wing
Korat RTAFB

F-105D/F	1968* - 11/69
F-4E	11/69 - 31/10/72

Squadron assigned to the 388 TFW on 8/4/66 at Korat RTAFB. The 469 TFS F-105D/F flew with **JV** tail codes. The 40 TFS deployed from Eglin AFB with **JV** tail coded F-4E and redesignated 469 TFS on arrival at Korat RTAFB in November 1969. The 40 TFS designation returned to 33 TFW operations at Eglin AFB. Green noted as squadron colour.

TAIL CODE

JW
42 Tactical Electronic Warfare Squadron   **388 Tactical Fighter Wing**
EB-66C/E   **23/9/70 - 17/1/74**   **Korat RTAFB**

    The 42 TEWS recoded EB-66C/E from **RH** on transfer from the 355 TFW at Takhli RTAFB. Attached on 21/9/70 and assigned on 15/10/70 to the 388 TFW, with **JW** tail codes. Non-operational after 17/1/74 until inactivation on 15/3/74.

EB-66E Destroyer 54-0443 **JW**, 42 TEWS 388 TFW, Korat RTAFB. Photo: Don Larsen, Udorn RTAFB, 30 November 1971.

KA
457 Tactical Airlift Squadron   **483 Tactical Airlift Wing**
C-7A   **1968* - 30/3/72**   **Cam Ranh Bay, RSVN**

    The 457 TAS activated on 1/1/67 with army assets at Cam Rang Bay AB, RSVN. The 457 TAS operated until stand down between 25-30/3/72. Believed involved with training of SVAF crews after February 1972. Squadron inactivated on 30/4/72. Red or blue colours carried on C-7.

KC
458 Tactical Airlift Squadron   **483 Tactical Airlift Wing**
C-7A   **1968* - 1/3/72**   **Cam Ranh Bay, RSVN**

    The 458 TAS adopted former army C-7A on 1/1/67. Squadron active between 1/1/67 and 1/3/72. Colour red carried as full or partial fin cap.

C-7A Caribou 62-4184 **KC**, 458 TAS 483 TAW, Cam Ranh Bay AB, RSVN, with red fin cap, in original US Army camouflage. Photo: McDonald, 1972.

KE
459 Tactical Airlift Squadron   **483 Tactical Airlift Wing**
C-7A   **1968* - 1/6/70**   **Phu Cat, RSVN**

    The third airlift squadron to adopt former army C-7A on 1/1/67. Squadron had detachment at Da Nang AB, RSVN until withdrawn early in 1970. Operational between 1/1/67 and 15/5/70. Inactivated on 1/6/70, squadron colour of white noted.

KH
535 Tactical Airlift Squadron   **483 Tactical Airlift Wing**
C-7A   **1968* - summer 1970**   **Vung Tau, RSVN**
C-7A   **summer 1970 - 24/1/72**   **Cam Ranh Bay, RSVN**

    The fourth C-7A unit activated on 1/1/67 to fly former army C-7. Moved from Vung Tau AB, RSVN to Cam Ranh Bay AB, RSVN in the summer of 1970. The 535 TAS detached between 15/3/69 and 25/6/70 to unknown location. Possible detachments at Phu Cat and Da Nang AB, RSVN. Squadron colours white or green noted. The 535 TAS inactivated on 24/1/72.

UNITED STATES AIR FORCES PACIFIC

C-7A Caribou 63-9725 **KH**, 535 TAS 483 TAW, Cam Ranh Bay AB, RSVN, with partial green fin cap. Photo: Don Larsen, Udorn RTAFB, 20 October 1971.

KL
536 Tactical Airlift Squadron   **483 Tactical Airlift Wing**
C-7A   1968* - summer 1970   Vung Tau, RSVN
C-7A   summer 1970 - 15/10/71   Cam Ranh Bay, RSVN

The fifth C-7A unit to form with former Army C-7 within the 483 TAW. The 536 TAS flew from Vung Tau AB, RSVN until the summer of 1970 when moved to Cam Ranh Bay AB, RSVN. Detached from wing between 15/3/69 and 30/6/70, as did the 535 TAS. Squadron colour of yellow noted.

KN
537 Tactical Airlift Squadron   **483 Tactical Airlift Wing**
C-7A   1968* - 1/6/70   Phu Cat, RSVN

The sixth C-7A unit activated on 1/1/67 with former army C-7. The C-7A flew from Phu Cat AB, RSVN until inactivated on 31/8/71.

LA
4 Tactical Fighter Squadron   **366 Tactical Fighter Wing**
                                          12/4/69 - 27/6/72   Da Nang AB, RSVN
                                          27/6/72 - 29/10/72   Takhli RTAFB
                                                                                                   432 Tactical Reconnaissance Wing
                                          29/10/72 - 8/73   Udorn RTAFB
F-4E   12/4/69 - 8/73

Formerly assigned to the 33 TFW at England AFB with **EB** tail codes. Assigned to the 366 TFW on 12/4/69 flying **LA** tail coding F-4E. Squadron moved with wing to Takhli RTAFB on 27/6/72 maintaining the **LA** tail code. Also maintained the **LA** tail code on attachment, 29/10/72 and assignment on 31/10/72 to the 432 TRW at Udorn RTAFB. Recoded **UD** in August 1973 with other 432 TRW units. Yellow-orange fin caps noted as squadron markings.

LC
421 Tactical Fighter Squadron   23/4/69 - 25/6/69   **475 Tactical Fighter Wing**
                                                                                                 Misawa AB, Japan
                          (attached while enroute to 366 TFW, assumed coded for delivery)
                                          25/6/69 - 31/5/72   **366 Tactical Fighter Wing**
                                                                                                 Da Nang AB, RSVN
                                          31/5/72 - 31/10/72   parent unit unknown at RTAFB Takhli
                                          31/10/72 - 8/73   **432 Tactical Reconnaissance Wing**
                                                                                                     Udorn RTAFB
F-4E   23/4/69 - 8/73

The 16 TFS 33 TFW originally scheduled deployment to reequip the 421 TFS on arrival Da Nang AB, RSVN in April 1969. Aircraft delayed in Japan and South Korea until 27/6/72. Not confirmed if aircraft coded before arrival Da Nang AB, RSVN on 25/

6/69. Officially assigned to the 366 TFW on 16/4/69 and attached to the 475 TFW at Misawa AB, Japan on 23/4/69, until 25/6/69 (*prior to delivery*). Remained with the 366 TFW at Da Nang AB, RSVN until May 1972. Reporting unit unknown between 31/5/72 and assignment to the 432 TRW at Udorn RTAFB on 31/10/72. Recoded to **UD** tail codes within the 432 TRW in August 1973. Red noted as squadron colour.

LF
390 Tactical Fighter Squadron   **366 Tactical Fighter Wing**
F-4D   1969 - 30/6/72   **Da Nang AB, RSVN**

The **B_** range codes of the 390 TFS exchanged for **LF** during 1969 within the 366 TFW. Squadron non-operational after 15/6/72. The squadron colour of blue noted. Squadron reassigned to the 347 TFW Mountain Home AFB on 30/6/72 flying (**MQ**) tail coded F-111F.

MA
815 Tactical Airlift Squadron   **1968* - 1/11/68 315 Air Division**
                                               1/11/68 - 19/10/69   **374 Tactical Airlift Wing**
C-130A   **1968* - 19/10/69**   **Tachikawa AB, Japan**

The C-130A equipped 815 TAS originally assigned to the 315 Air Division during 1968. Squadron reassigned to the 374 TAW at Naha AB, Taiwan on 1/11/68. Non-operational after 19/10/69 and inactivated on 15/12/69. Red noted as squadron colour.

MD
Detachment - 561 Tactical Fighter Squadron   **23 Tactical Fighter Wing**
F-105F/G   7/4/72 - 1/7/72   **Udorn RTAFB**

The 561 TFS sent a detachment to Udorn RTAFB from McConnell AFB with F-105F/G between 7/4/72 and 1/7/72. These aircraft carried **MD** tail codes for deployment. The detachment may have continued at Udorn RTAFB after 23 TFW control ended on 1/7/72. Later returned to Korat RTAFB with **WW** tail coded F-105G.

MJ
432 Tactical Fighter Wing   **1/7/84 - current 31/12/90**   **Misawa AB, Japan**

13 Tactical Fighter Squadron
F-16A/B   4/7/85 - 27/2/87
F-16C/D   31/7/86 - current 31/12/90

The 13 TFS activated within the 432 TFW on 4/7/85. The **MJ** tail coded F-16A/B assigned prior to activation date as the first F-16A arrived from the 363 TFW at Shaw AFB on 2/4/85. Squadron F-16 carried a black and white check tail stripe along with the **MJ** tail code. The 13 TFS converted to F-16C/D close to a year later.

F-16C Falcon 85-1554 **MJ**, 13 TFS 432 TFW, Misawa AB, Japan, with black and white checkered tail stripe. Photo: Masanori Ogawa, Yokota AB, Japan 6 September 1987.

14 Tactical Fighter Squadron
F-16C/D   1/4/87 - current 31/12/90

Redesignated from TRS status on 5/6/84 and activating on 1/4/87. Operations commenced with **MJ** tail coded F-16C/D on 3/4/87. First squadron maintenance F-16C delivered on 31/7/86. Squadron F-16C/D carried a black and yellow check tail stripe.

NV
82 Fighter Interceptor Squadron   **51 Fighter Interceptor Wing**
T/F-102A   1968* - 31/5/71   **Naha AB, Okinawa**

One of only three tail coded F-102 Fighter Interceptor Squadrons. Attached to the 51 FIW on 17/2/66 and assigned 25/6/66 until 31/5/71. Deployed detachment to Bien Hoa AB, RSVN late 1968.

UNITED STATES AIR FORCES PACIFIC

OC
13 Tactical Fighter Squadron   **432 Tactical Reconnaissance Wing**
   Udorn RTAFB

F-4C   9/67* - 10/67
F-4D   21/10/67 - 8/73

   Squadron attached to the 432 TRW on 21/10/67 and assigned on 15/11/67 with F-4C. Tail coded **OC** by mid 1967 and recoded within wing to **UD** standard in August 1973. The F-4D came from the 16 TFS 33 TFW, arriving from Eglin AFB during October 1967. Unit changed designation to 13 TFS on arrival. Blue fin cap carried on F-4.

OO
11 Tactical Reconnaissance Squadron   **432 Tactical Reconnaissance Wing**
RF-4C   1968* - 10/11/70   **Udorn RTAFB**

   The 11 TRS reassigned from the 67 TRW at Mountain Home AFB on 25/10/66. Black noted as squadron colour carried in fin cap form. Inactivated on 10/11/70 with RF-4 assets transferred to Shaw AFB.

OS
4 Special Operations Squadron - detachment   **432 Tactical Reconnaissance Wing**
AC-47D   10/69 - 29/10/70   **Udorn RTAFB**

   The 4 SOS flew **EN** tail coded AC-47D within the 14 SOW until October 1969. Controlling unit unknown after October 1969. A detachment known as the "432 Spooky Operations" performed air base defense missions at Udorn RTAFB with three **OS** tail coded AC-47D until 29/5/70. It is believed the 4 SOS was stationed at Phan Rang AB during this period with either **OS** or maintaining **EN** tail code.

AC-47D Skytrain 43-0010 **OS**, 4 SOS 432 TRW, Udorn RTAFB, displaying spook and mission scores with black underside. Photo: J Ward Boyce, June 1970.

OS
51 Air Base Wing   1/11/71 - 30/9/74
51 Composite Wing (Tactical)   30/9/74 - 1/1/83
51 Tactical Fighter Wing   1/1/82 - current 31/12/90
                     Osan AB, ROK

19 Tactical Air Support Squadron
OV-10A   least 11/75 - 1983*
OA-37B   least 5/83 - late 1985
OV-10A   mid 1985 - 1990
OA-10A   mid 1990 - current 31/12/90
                     Suwon AB, ROK

   The 19 TASS Squadron assigned to the 51 CW on 30/9/74, possibly not coded until November 1975. Blue noted as squadron colour. The 19 TASS assigned to the 5 TACG between January 1980 and June 1986. The 19 TASS switched equipment several times. The squadron moved to Suwon AB from Osan AB, ROK and converted to the OA-10A.

OV-10A Bronco 68-3816 **OS**, 19 TASS 51 TFW, Osan AB, ROK. Photo: Masanori Ogawa, Yokota AB, Japan, 30 August 1986.

25 Tactical Fighter Squadron   **Suwon AB, ROK**
A-10A   1/82 - 1/1/84
A-10A   1990 - current 31/12/90

Previously flew **ZZ** tail coded F-4D within the 18 TFW until 22/8/80. Activated on 1/2/81 but without personnel or equipment until January 1982. Small red lightning flash carried on tail fins. Green unconfirmed as squadron colour. Changed tail code to **SU** on 1/1/84 from **OS** within same wing and maintaining equipment. Squadron later moved to Osan AB and recoded to **OS**.

36 Tactical Fighter Squadron
F-4E   30/9/74 - by 6/1/89
F-16C/D   6/1/89 - current 31/12/90

Formerly flew **UK** tail coded F-4E within the 3 TFW. Assigned to the 51 CW (T) on 30/9/74 flying **OS** tail coded F-4E with a red fine cap.

497 Tactical Fighter Squadron
F-4E   1/1/82 - 7/9/84

Formerly flew **WP** tail coded F-4D within the 8 TFW at Kunsan AB, ROK, before recoding to **OS** and assigned to the 51 TFW. Blue fin caps carried on 497 TFS F-4E. Tail code changed to **GU** and moved to Taegu AB, ROK, on 7/9/84. Possible F-4D carried the **OS** tail code but unconfirmed.

OY
555 Tactical Fighter Squadron   **432 Tactical Reconnaissance Wing**
F-4D   1/6/68* - 8/73   **Udorn RTAFB**

Originally attached to the 432 TRW on 28/5/68 and assigned 1/6/68 from the 8 TFW. Squadron recoding from **FY** to **OY** and carried a green fin cap as squadron markings on F-4D. Under common wing codes the 555 TFS adopted the **UD** tail code.

F-4D Phantom 65-0683 **OY**, 555 TFS 432 TRW, Udorn RTAFB, with green fin cap. Photo: Don Larsen, 20 January 1972.

OZ
14 Tactical Reconnaissance Squadron   **432 Tactical Reconnaissance Wing**
RF-4C   1968* - 8/73   **Udorn RTAFB**

The 14 TRS attached to the 432 TRW on 28/10/67 and assigned on 6/11/67. Tail code **OZ** assigned during 1968. Red fin cap carried on squadron RF-4C. Recoded to **UD** in August 1973.

UNITED STATES AIR FORCES PACIFIC

PA
1 Test Squadron   405 Fighter Wing
F-4C   30/4/70 - 1973   Clark AB, Philippines

Activated on 30/4/70 within the 405 FW until reassignment to the 3 TFW on 16/9/74. The 405 FW history has the 1 TS unit detached for full period to unknown controlling unit (*possibly 6200 TFTG*). Unit coded **DS**, **PA**, and finally, **PN** under AFM66-1 wing common tail code in 1972. Squadron F-4C noted up to January 1973 with **PA** tail codes. Yellow trim noted on F-4.

F-4C Phantom 64-0820 **PA**, 1 TS 405 FW, Clark AB, Philippines. Photo: Grant Matsuoka, Yokota AB, Japan, February 1973.

PE
64 Fighter Interceptor Squadron   405 Fighter Wing
T/F-102A   1968* - 12/5/69   Clark AB, Philippines

Activated within the 405 FW on 10/6/66 and tail coded **PE** during 1968. One of only three coded and camouflaged F-102 users. Both blue and yellow noted as squadron colour. Unit status change to non-operational after 1/12/69 and inactivated on 15/12/69. Reactivated within the 57 FWW on 15/10/72 as 64 FWS flying F-5E in spring 1987.

PK
509 Fighter Interceptor Squadron   405 Fighter Wing
F/TF-102A   1968* - 17/7/70   Clark AB, Philippines

Squadron activate within the 405 FW on 9/4/59 and tail coded F-102 **PK** during 1968. Red noted as squadron colour. Maintained detachments at Don Muang Airport, Thailand, Da Nang and Ton Son Nhut AB, RSVN before inactivating in July 1970. Reactivated within 81 TFW USAFE during 1981, with **WR** tail coded A-10A.

PN
523 Tactical Fighter Squadron   405 Fighter Wing
                                                                                    Clark AB, Philippines
F-100D   1968* - by 1970
F-4C/D   by 1970 - 1972*

Activate within the 405 FW on 20/11/65 and coded **PN** during 1968. The 523 TFS converted from F-100, to F-4 by 1970. Detachment maintained at Tainan, Formosa with F-4 and deployed F-4D to the 432 TRW, at Udorn on 9/4/72 until 25/10/72. Red fin cap carried by F-4D (*unconfirmed F-4E usage*). Maintained **PN** as wing common tail code in 1972.

PN
405 Fighter Wing   1972* - 16/9/74   Clark AB, Philippines
3 Tactical Fighter Wing   16/9/74 - current 31/12/90   Clark AB, Philippines

1 Test Squadron
F-4C/D   1972* - 1/80

Activated within the 405 FW on 30/4/70, coded **DS**, **PA** and finally with **PN** tail coded in 1972. Dates for **DS** - **PA** change not known. Yellow and blue trim noted. Reassigned to the 3 TFW on 16/9/74. F-4E usage unconfirmed. Operated in the test role for PACAF F-4 users.

3 Tactical Fighter Squadron
F-4E   15/12/75 - current 31/12/90

Formerly assigned to the 388 TFW flying the **JH** coded A-7D at Korat RTAFB. Assigned to the 3 TFW on 15/12/75 flying **PN** coded F-4E. Blue fin cap carried.

90 Tactical Fighter Squadron
F-4D   15/12/72 - 1973
F-4E   1973 - current 31/12/90
F-4G   1/7/79 - current 31/12/90

Activated within the 405 FW on 15/12/72 at Clark AB, Philippines. Squadron status non-operational before 31/8/73. Flew **PN** tail coded F-4E and reassigned to the 3 TFW on 16/9/74 maintaining tail code and red squadron markings. The Wild Weasel role added with F-4G in 1979.

F-4G Phantom 69-0275 **PN**, 90 TFS 3 TFW, Clark AB, Philippines. Photo: Henk Scharringa, 3 August 1979.

523 Tactical Fighter Squadron
F-4D   1972* - 31/8/73

Maintained **PN** tail code under AFM66-1 concept before 405 FW adopted **PN** wing common code in 1972. Deployed to the 432 TRW on 9/4/72 until 25/10/72 (*unconfirmed F-4E usage*). The 523 TFS transferred to the 27 TFW, at Cannon AFB on 31/8/73, flying **CC** tail coded F-111.

PQ
8 Bombardment Squadron   **35 Tactical Fighter Wing**
B-57B/C/E   1967* - 15/11/69   **Phan Rang AB, RSVN**

Reasoning for the tail code **PQ**, due to squadron attaching to the 405 FW until early 1968. The 8 BS spent seven periods attached to the 35 TFW before assignment on 15/1/68. The last B-57 left RSVN on 15/10/69. Training detachment maintained at Clark AB, Philippines with four B-57C. Yellow noted as squadron colour. The 8 BS inactivated with the 35 TFW. Squadron and reactivated within 3 TFW as the 8 AS flying **CF** tail coded A-37B. Squadron returned as such to 35 TFW on 30/9/70.

B-57E 55-4282 **PQ**, 8 BS 35 TFW, Phan Rang AB, RSVN. Photo: John Siefert, Bien Hoa AB, RSVN, May 1968.

PV
13 Bombardment Squadron   **405 Fighter Wing**
B-57B/C/E   1967* - 15/1/68   **Clark AB, Philippines**

Assigned to the 405 FW flying B-57 since 1964. Deployed in turn with the 8 BS to the 35 TFW based at Phan Rang AB, RSVN. Coded for short period **PV** and inactivated on 15/1/68. "Grimreapers" colour noted as red. Reactivated on 8/2/69 within the 15 TFW with **FK** tail coded B-57. Returned to the 405 FW as non-operationally on 24/12/72 until inactivated on 30/9/74.

QB
29 Tactical Airlift Squadron   **463 Tactical Airlift Wing**
C-130B   1968* - 1/7/70   **Clark AB, Philippines**

The 29 TAS assigned as one of four 463 TAW C-130B squadrons coded C-130B **QB** in July 1968. Non-operational after 1/7/70 and inactivated on 31/10/70. Reactivated within the 316 TAW at Langley AFB on 1/4/71.

UNITED STATES AIR FORCES PACIFIC

C-130B Hercules 61-0969 **QB**, 29 TAS 463 TAW Det. Ton Son Nhut AB. Photo: Martin collection, Cam Ranh Bay AB, RSVN, 1969.

QF
772 Tactical Airlift Squadron   **463 Tactical Airlift Wing**
C-130B   1968* - 1/6/71   **Clark AB, Philippines**

The 772 TAS coded C-130B **QB** during July 1968. Squadron status non-operational after 1/6/71 and inactivated on 15/6/71. Red noted as squadron colour. Reactivated on 1/6/72 and coded **DB** within the 463 TAW at Dyess AFB.

QG
773 Tactical Airlift Squadron   **463 Tactical Airlift Wing**
C-130B   15/7/68* - 15/10/71   **Clark AB, Philippines**

The 773 TAS coded C-130B **QG** during July 1968, with blue noted as the squadron colour. Non-operational after 15/10/71 inactivating on 31/10/71. Reactivated on 1/6/72 within the 463 TAW at Dyess AFB with **DB** codes.

C-130B Hercules 60-0297 **QG**, 773 TAS 463 TAW, Cam Ranh Bay AB, RSVN. Photo: Martin collection, Cam Ranh Bay AB, RSVN, 1969.

QW
774 Tactical Airlift Squadron   15/7/68 - 31/12/71   **463 Tactical Airlift Wing**
                                          31/12/71 - 2/9/72   **405 Fighter Wing**
C-130B   1968* - 2/9/72   **Clark AB, Philippines**

The 774 TAS tail coded **QW** within the 463 TAW during 1968. When the 463 TAW inactivated on 31/12/71 the 774 TAS transferred to 405 FW. Green noted as squadron colour. Non-operational after 2/9/72 and inactivated on 15/9/72. Reactivated on 1/8/73 with **DB** tail codes within the 463 TAW at Dyess AFB.

RB   **Arkansas ANG**
154 Tactical Reconnaissance Squadron   27/7/68 - 15/11/68   **7th Air Force**

	Kentucky ANG		
165 Tactical Reconnaissance Squadron		2/69 - 20/4/69	7th Air Force
	Nevada ANG		
192 Tactical Reconnaissance Squadron		15/11/68 - 2/69	7th Air Force
RF-101G	summer 1968 - 20/4/69		Itazuke AB, Japan and ROK, locations

Three ANG RF-101 units rotated on detachment to Itazuke AB, Japan starting on 27/7/68. The initial 154 TRS RF-101G coded **RB** in the summer of 1968. Uncoded aircraft noted well into 1969, each unit took turn on deployment, thus all three units flew **RB** tail coded RF-101G within PACAF. Operations based from Itazuke AB, Japan, but most missions flown over Korea. The 154, 165, and 192 TRS reported to the 123 TRW when federally activated in 1968. The **RG** tail code also noted within PACAF operations, probably due to limited aircraft transfers. (*See special note on* **RB**, **RG**, *and* **RJ** *under ANG section*)

RF-101G Voodoo 54-1481 **RB**, 192 TRS, Itazuke AB, Japan. Photo: T Matsuzaki, Yokota AB, Japan, 8 November 1968.

RC
41 Tactical Electronic Warfare Squadron   355 Tactical Fighter Wing
EB-66B/C   1968* - 31/10/69   Takhli RTAFB

Originally activated as the 41 Tactical Reconnaissance Squadron on 29/10/65 the 41 TEWS spent periods (*uncoded*) assigned to 2 AD and 460 TRW. Also assigned to the 432 TRW before assignment on 15/8/67 to the 355 TFW. Inactivated within the 355 TFW on 31/10/69.

RE
44 Tactical Fighter Squadron   355 Tactical Fighter Wing
F-105D/F   15/10/69 - 10/12/70   Takhli RTAFB

Recoded **RE** on detachment from the 388 TFW at Korat RTAFB on 10/10/69 with **JE** tail code. Assigned to the 388 TFW on 15/10/69 until inactivating on 10/12/70. Black noted as squadron colour. Reactivated within the 18 TFW flying **ZL** tail coded F-4C on 14/5/71.

RH
42 Tactical Electronic Warfare Squadron   355 Tactical Fighter Wing
EB-66B/C/E   1968* - 23/9/70   Takhli RTAFB

Replaced the 4660 TEWS on 1/1/68 and tail coded squadron EB-66 **RH** during 1968. Red and white checked fin cap displayed as squadron markings. Squadron detached to the 388 TFW on 23/9/70 and assigned on 15/10/70 at Korat RTAFB while recoding to **JW**.

RK
333 Tactical Fighter Squadron   355 Tactical Fighter Wing
F-105D/F   3/68* - 10/12/70   Takhli RTAFB

Squadron redeployed to Korat RTAFB on 4/12/65 (*personnel only*) from the 4 TFW Seymour-Johnson AFB. Red squadron colour noted. The F-105D/F tail coded **RK** in early 1968 inactivating on 10/12/70. Assigned non-operationally to the 23 TFW and 58 TFTW. Reactivated flying **DM** tail coded A-7D with the 355 TFW at Davis-Monthan AFB on 31/7/71.

RM
354 Tactical Fighter Squadron   355 Tactical Fighter Wing
F-105D/F   2/68* - 10/12/70   Takhli RTAFB

Assigned to the 355 TFW on 27/11/65 and tail coded **RM** until inactivating on 10/12/70. Blue noted as squadron colour. Carried as paper squadron within the 4453 CCTW until 1/4/71. Reactivated within 355 TFW at Davis-Monthan AFB on 1/7/71 flying **DA** tail coded A-7D.

RU
357 Tactical Fighter Squadron   355 Tactical Fighter Wing
F-105D/F   3/68* - 10/12/70   Takhli RTAFB

Assigned to the 355 TFW on 29/1/66 and applied **RU** tail code in early 1968. Yellow noted as squadron colour. Inactivated on 10/12/70 and carried as a paper unit at McConnell AFB. Reactivated on 1/7/71 as 357 TFTS with **DC** tail coded A-7D.

F-105D Thunderchief 61-0176 **RU**, 357 TFS 355 TFW, Takhli RTAFB. Photo: Michael A Noreen, Nakhon Phanom RTAFB, July 1969.

SD
306 Tactical Fighter Squadron   **31 Tactical Fighter Wing**
F-100D/F   **1968* - 28/9/70**   **Tuy Hoa AB, RSVN**
   The 306 TFS moved with the 31 TFW to Tuy Hoa AB, RSVN in December 1966. Tail coded **SD** at Tuy Hoa AB, RSVN during 1968. Red noted as squadron colour. Non-operational after 8/9/70 inactivated on 28/9/70. Reassigned to the 4403 TFW at England AFB with **SD** coded F-100. Returned to the 31 TFW on 30/10/70 at Homestead AFB flying **ZD** coded F-4E.

SE
416 Tactical Fighter Squadron   **31 Tactical Fighter Wing**
F-100D/F   **28/5/69 - 28/9/70**   **Tuy Hoa AB, RSVN**
   The 416 TFS formerly coded **HE** within the 37 TFW based at Phu Cat AB, RSVN, reassigned to the 31 TFW on 28/5/69. Tail coded **SE** on arrival. Status changed to non-operational after 5/9/70 with a blue tail stripe carried. Reassigned on 28/9/70 to the 4403 TFW at England AFB, with **SE** coded F-100.

SG New York ANG
136 Tactical Fighter Squadron   **31 Tactical Fighter Wing**
F-100C   **1968* - 25/5/69**   **Tuy Hoa AB, RSVN**
   New York ANG unit deployed to Tuy Hoa AB, RSVN within the 31 TFW on 14/6/68 until 25/5/69. Squadron coded **SG** during 1968.

SK New Mexico ANG
188 Tactical Fighter Squadron   **31 Tactical Fighter Wing**
F-100C/F   **14/6/68* - 18/5/69**   **Tuy Hoa AB, RSVN**
   New Mexico ANG unit deployed from Kirkland AFB to the 31 TFW at Tuy Hoa AB, RSVN. Squadron tail coded **SK** after arrival on 7/6/68. Tail codes removed upon return to CONUS.

SM
308 Tactical Fighter Squadron   **31 Tactical Fighter Wing**
F-100D/F   **1968* - 5/10/70**   **Tuy Hoa AB, RSVN**
   Squadron assigned to the 31 TFW on 25/12/66 and tail coded F-100 **SM** during 1968. Squadron non-operational after 10/9/70. Reassigned to the 4403 TFW on 15/10/70. Blue and white noted as squadron colour.

SP
355 Tactical Fighter Squadron   **31 Tactical Fighter Wing**
F-100D/F   **15/5/69 - 30/9/70**   **Tuy Hoa AB, RSVN**
   Squadron transferred from the 37 TFW where coded **HP**. Flew operationally until 20/9/70 inactivating on 30/9/70. Blue noted as colour. Reactivated on 1/11/70 with **MB** tail coded A-7D as component of the 354 TFW at Myrtle Beach AFB.

SS
309 Tactical Fighter Squadron   **31 Tactical Fighter Wing**
F-100D/F   **1968* - 5/10/70**   **Tuy Hoa AB, RSVN**
   The 309 TFS moved with the 31 TFW to Tuy Hoa AB, RSVN in December 1966. Blue noted as squadron colour. Tail coded F-100D/F **SS** in 1968 declared non-operational after 10/9/70 until transferring on 5/10/70 to the 4403 TFW at England AFB, before returning to the 31 TFW at Homestead AFB on 30/10/70, flying with **ZE** tail coded F-4E.

SU
25 Tactical Fighter Squadron **51 Tactical Fighter Wing**
A-10A **1/1/84 - 1990** Suwon AB, ROK

The 25 TFS changed tail code from **OS** to **SU** on 1/1/84, maintaining wing and equipment. Possible change from green to red markings with the **SU** tail code. Small red lightning flash carried on tail fins. Squadron later returned to Osan AB, ROK and recoded **OS**.

A-10A Thunderbolt 80-0246 **SU**, 25 TFS 51 TFW, Suwon AB, ROK, with green fin cap and red lightning flash. Photo: Y. Toda, Kadena AB, Okinawa, February 1985.

TA
609 Air Commando Squadron 1967* - 1/8/68 **56 Air Commando Wing**
609 Special Operations Squadron 1/8/68 - 1/12/69 **56 Special Operations Wing**
  Nakhon Phanom RTAFB

A-26A/K 1967* - 1/12/1969
T-28D 1967* - 1969

Squadron equipped with A-26 on 15/5/67 (*The A-26 designation used because basing of bomber designated aircraft not permitted by treaty in Thailand during period assigned*). Known as "Nightflyers" or "Nimrods" with yellow and black markings. Redesignated to 609 SOS, on 1/8/68, and inactivating on 1/12/69.

A-26 Invader 64-17660 **TA**, 609 SOS 56 SOW, Nakhon Phanom RTAFB, Brig Edwin White, Wing commander's aircraft. Photo: Michael A Noreen, June 1969.

UNITED STATES AIR FORCES PACIFIC

A-26A Invader 64-17651 **TA**, 609 SOS 56 SOW, Nakhon Phanom RTAFB, with black tail code and underside. Photo: Bob Garrard, Davis-Monthan MASDC Arizona 6 August 1970.

TC
1 Air Commando Squadron	20/12/67 - 1/8/68	56 Air Commando Wing
1 Special Operations Squadron	1/8/68 -15/12/72	56 Special Operations Wing
A-1E/G/H/J	20/12/67* - 15/12/72	Nakhon Phanom RTAFB

Organized in 1964 at Bien Hoa AB, RSVN and reassigned to the 56 SOW from 14 SOW (*between 8/3/66 and 20/12/67 tail coded* **EC**). The 1 ACS, "Hobo's" carried markings of green and yellow. Temporary detachment may have been established at Da Nang AB, RSVN with A-1 during 1969-70. Presentation of tail code unusual as dark codes with light outline applied. Reassigned to the 18 TFW Kadena AB, Okinawa flying **GT** tail coded EB-57 on 15/12/72.

TO
606 Air Commando Squadron	1968* - 1/8/68	56 Air Commando Wing
606 Special Operations Squadron	1/8/68 - 15/6/71	56 Special Operations Wing
		Nakhon Phanom RTAFB
C-123B	1968* - 15/6/71	
T-28D	late 1967* - 15/6/71	

The 606 ACS activated flying the T-28D, while C-123B added later in 1968. Redesignated to 606 SOS, on 1/8/68. One source states the 606 SOS inactivated on 30/1/71 while others on 15/6/71. Red noted as squadron colour.

C-123B Provider 54-0577 **TO**, 606 ACS 56 ACW, Nakhon Phanom RTAFB, with red and white serial card in nose window with black tail code. Photo: Cope, July 1968.

TAIL CODE

T-28D Trojan 49-1583 **TO**, 606 SOS 56 SOW, Nakhon Phanom RTAFB. Photo: Norm Crocker, October 1968.

TS
22 Special Operations Squadron		**56 Special Operations Wing**
A-1E/G/H/J	25/10/68 - 18/7/70	**Nakhon Phanom RTAFB**

The 22 SOS activated within the 56 SOW on 25/10/68. Squadron known as "Zorro's." Operated **TS** tail coded A-1E/G/H/J. Status changed to non-operational on 18/7/70 and squadron inactivated on 30/9/70.

TT
602 Air Commando Squadron	1968* - 1/8/6856	**Air Commando Wing**
602 Special Operations Squadron	1/8/68 - 31/12/70	**56 Special Operations Wing**
A-1E/H/J	1968* - 20/12/70	**Nakhon Phanom RTAFB**

Squadron transferred from the 14 SOW before code usage. Reassigned to the 56 ACW on 8/4/67 and redesignated 602 SOS on 1/8/68. Status changed to non-operational on 20/12/70 and inactivated 31/12/70. Black and gold noted as colour noted.

A-1J Skyraider 142063 **TT**, 602 SOS 56 SOW, Nakhon Phanom RTAFB. Photo: Captain Michael A Noreen, May 1969.

UD
391 Tactical Fighter Squadron		**475 Tactical Fighter Wing**
F-4C/D	22/7/68* - 28/2/71	**Misawa AB, Japan**

Formerly flew **XT** tail F-4C within the 12 TFW at Cam Ranh Bay AB, RSVN. Brought **XD** tail coded F-4C of the 558 TFS 12 TFW to the 475 TFW assignment. Yellow noted as squadron colour. Reactivated within the 366 TFW on 30/6/71 with F-111A at Mountain Home AFB.

UD
432 Tactical Reconnaissance Wing	early 1973* -15/11/74	**Udorn RTAFB**
432 Tactical Fighter Wing	15/11/74 - 23/12/75*	

UNITED STATES AIR FORCES PACIFIC

4 Tactical Fighter Squadron
F-4E   8/73 - 23/12/75
The 4 TFS assigned to the 432 TRW and coded F-4E **LA** on 31/10/72, transferring from the 366 TFW at Takhli RTAFB. Squadron maintained the **LA** tail code until changed to **UD** in August in 1973 under AFM66-1 concept. Yellow noted as squadron colour. Non-operational after 7/12/75 and transferred to the 388 TFW at Hill AFB, on 23/12/75 with **HL** tail coded F-4D.

13 Tactical Fighter Squadron
F-4D   8/73 - 30/6/75
Squadron recoded from **OC** tail code in August 1973. Blue continued as the squadron colour on F-4D until inactivated on 30/6/75. Squadron later reactivated within 56 TFW flying on 13/1/76 with **MC** coded F-4E.

14 Tactical Reconnaissance Squadron
RF-4C   8/73 - 30/6/75
Squadron recoded RF-4C from **OZ** to **UD** in August 1973. Red maintained as squadron colour until inactivation on 30/6/75.

25 Tactical Fighter Squadron
F-4D   5/7/74 - 18/12/75
Squadron formerly tail coded **WP** within the 8 TFW. Transferred from 8 TFW on 5/7/74 replacing the 555 TFS. The 25 TFS remained with the 432 TRW until 18/12/75. Reassigned to 3 TFW for two days as paper unit, then on to 51 Control Wing at Osan AB, ROK, in 1980.

421 Tactical Fighter Squadron
F-4E   8/73 - 23/12/75
Squadron assigned to the 432 TRW with **LC** F-4E on 31/10/72, from the 366 TFW at Takhli RTAFB. Tail code **LC** continued until assigned **UD** tail code August in 1973 under AFM66-1 concept. Red noted as squadron colour. The 421 TFS assigned to 388 TFW at Hill AFB on 23/12/75 with **HL** tail coded F-4D.

555 Tactical Fighter Squadron
F-4D   8/73 - 5/7/74
Squadron recoded from **OY** to **UD** in late 1973 under wing common code concept of AFM66-1. Unit also hosting several uncoded specially equipped F-4E marked "RRRRibt." The 555 TFS transferred in number only to the 58 TFTW on 5/7/74 and replaced by the 25 TFS on 5/7/74.

UD
80 Tactical Fighter Squadron   **3 Tactical Fighter Wing**
                                                                                Kunsan AB, ROK
F-4D   15/3/71 - by 16/9/74
F-4E   8/7/74 - 16/9/74
Squadron formerly flew **GR** tail coded F-105 and F-4C within the 347 TFW. Reassigned to the 3 TFW on 15/3/71 flying **UD** tail coded F-4D. Yellow noted as squadron colour. Reassigned to the 8 TFW on 16/9/74, flying **WP** tail coded F-4D while remaining at Kunsan AB, ROK.

UE
16 Tactical Reconnaissance Squadron   **475 Tactical Fighter Wing**
RF-4C   16/3/70 - 15/2/71   **Misawa AB, Japan**
Squadron transferred from the 460 TRW at Ton Son Nhut AB, RSVN formerly flying **AE** tail coded RF-4C. Operated **UE** tail coded RF-4C under one year before reassignment to Shaw AFB on 15/2/71 with **JM** tail code. Blue noted as squadron colour.

RF-4C Phantom 64-1041 **UE**, 16 TRS 475 TRW, Misawa AB, Japan. Photo: Grant Matsuoka, Yokota AB, Japan, March 1970.

TAIL CODE

UK
356 Tactical Fighter Squadron
F-4C/D   1968* - 15/3/71

475 Tactical Fighter Wing
Misawa AB, Japan

The 356 TFS assigned to the 475 TFW on 15/1/68 and tail coded **UK** during 1968. Green noted as squadron colour. Squadron inactivated at Misawa AB, Japan on 15/3/71 and reactivated on 15/5/71 within the 354 TFW at Myrtle Beach AFB flying **MN** tail coded A-7D.

F-4C Phantom 63-7433 **UK**, 356 TFS 475 TFW, Misawa AB, Japan. Photo: Martin collection.

UK
36 Tactical Fighter Squadron

3 Tactical Fighter Wing
Kunsan AB, ROK

F-4D   15/5/71 - 28/1/73
F-4E***   12/71 - 16/9/74

Squadron previously flew **GL** tail coded F-4C within the 347 TFW, at Yokota AB, Japan. Assigned to the 3 TFW on 15/5/71 with **UK** tail coded F-4D. The 36 TFS converted to F-4E during December 1971. Red noted as squadron colour carried as both trim and fin cap. Transferred non-operationally to the 8 TFW until further reassigned to the 51 CW, on 30/9/74 flying **OS** tail coded F-4E.

UP
67 Tactical Fighter Squadron
F-4D   1968* - 15/3/71

475 Tactical Fighter Wing
Misawa AB, Japan

The 67 TFS assigned to the 475 TFW on 15/1/68, and tail coded F-4D **UP** during 1968. Red noted as squadron colour. Reassigned on 15/3/71 to 18 TFW with tail coded **ZG**.

UP
35 Tactical Fighter Squadron

3 Tactical Fighter Wing
Kunsan AB, ROK

F-4D   15/3/71 - by 1974
F-4E   8/7/74 - 16/9/74

Previously flew **GG** tail coded F-4C while assigned to the 347 TFW at Yokota AB, Japan. Assigned on 15/3/71 to the 3 TFW flying **UP** tail coded F-4D until F-4E conversion in July 1974. Squadron attached to the 366 TFW between 3/4/72 and 12/6/72 and the 388 TFW between 12/6/72 and 10/10/72. Light blue noted as squadron colour. Reassigned to the 8 TFW flying **WP** tail coded F-4D, on 16/9/74. Several **UP** tail coded F-4 were noted after the 35 TFS was reassigned to the 8 TFW. This may have been the start of wing common usage that was not completed.

F-4D Phantom 66-7648 **UP**, 35 TFS 8 TFW, Kunsan AB, ROK, with light blue fin cap, late in recoding to **WP**. Photo: Bruce Trombecky, Yokota AB, Japan, December 1974.

UNITED STATES AIR FORCES PACIFIC

VM
352 Tactical Fighter Squadron
F-100D/F   1968* - 31/7/71   **35 Tactical Fighter Wing**
Phan Rang AB, RSVN

Reassigned while flying uncoded F-100 from the 366 TFW to the 35 TFW on 10/10/66. Adopted the **VM** tail code on F-100 during 1968. Squadron inactivated on 31/7/71.

F-100F Super Sabre 58-1232 in markings of **VM**, 120 TFS Colorado ANG 35 TFW Phan Rang AB, RSVN, after units return to Buckley Field, Colorado. Photo: Doug Remington, Langley AFB, 5 October 1970.

VP
614 Tactical Fighter Squadron
F-100D/F   1968* - 18/7/71   **35 Tactical Fighter Wing**
Phan Rang AB, RSVN

The 614 TFS moved to Phan Rang AB, RSVN from England AFB on 13/9/66. Squadron reassigned from 366 TFW to 35 TFW on 10/10/66 while uncoded. May not have been active after 18/7/71. Some 614 TFS F-100 noted with a red fin cap outlined in white. Squadron transferred to the 401 TFW at Torrejon AB, Spain on 31/7/71 to fly **TK** coded F-4E. Sources disagree on date as USAFE records show the 614 TFS, assigned 15/7/71 but assigned to the 401 TFW on 15/7/71.

F-100F Super Sabre 58-1222 **VP**, 614 TFS 35 TFW, Phan Rang AB, RSVN. Photo: Don Larsen, Udorn RTAFB, 26 February 1971.

VS Colorado ANG
120 Tactical Aircraft Squadron
F-100C/F   4/67* - 18/4/69   **35 Tactical Fighter Wing**
Phan Rang AB, RSVN

Colorado ANG 120 TFS from Buckley ANGB, assigned to the 35 TFW between 30/4/68 and 18/4/69. The 120 TFS returned to CONUS with **VS** tail codes still applied at the end of active tour. Blue fin caps noted on F-100C/F.

VS
612 Tactical Fighter Squadron   **35 Tactical Fighter Wing**

| F-100D/F | 14/4/69 - 31/7/71 | Phan Rang AB, RSVN |

The 612 TFS **VS** tail coded F-100 distinguishable from 120 TFS by virtue of F-100D usage rather the F-100C (*although both units flew the F-100F*). Blue noted as squadron colour. The 612 TFS (*non-operational with 475 TFW*) attached Detachment 1 to the 35 TFW between 14/4/69 and 15/3/71. The 612 TFS reassigned to the 401 TFW, at Torrejon AB, Spain in July 1971 to fly **TJ** tail coded F-4E.

VZ

| 615 Tactical Fighter Squadron | | 35 Tactical Fighter Wing |
| F-100D/F | 14/4/69 - 31/7/71 | Phan Rang AB, RSVN |

Squadron transferred from England AFB on 18/7/66 to Phan Rang AB, RSVN. Unit assumed from 366 TFW on 10/10/66 while uncoded. Green noted as squadron colour. Detachment 1, moved from 37 TFW on 14/4/69. Full 615 TFS transferred by 15/3/71 and inactivated on 31/7/71. The USAFE records have the 615 TFS reassigned to the 401 TFW on 15/7/71 flying **TK** tail coded F-4E.

WE

19 Air Commando Squadron	1967* - 1/6/68	315 Air Commando Wing
19 Special Operations Squadron	1/6/68 - 1/1/70	315 Special Operations Wing
19 Tactical Airlift Squadron	1/1/70 - 1/5/71	315 Tactical Airlift Wing
		Phan Rang AB, RSVN

| C-123B | 1967* - 1968 |
| C-123K | 1967* - 1/5/71 |

Squadron flew **WE** tail coded C-123B from 8/3/66 until conversion to C-123K during 1968. Designation changed to 19 SOS on 1/6/68 and 19 TAS on 1/1/70. Squadron not operational after 1/5/71 and inactivated on 10/6/71. Yellow noted as squadron colour.

C-123K Provider 54-0696 **WE**, 19 ACS 315 ACW, Phan Rang AB, RSVN. Photo: Bob Burgess, Ton Son Nhut AB, RSVN, 30 April 1968.

WH

309 Air Commando Squadron	1967* - 1/6/68	315 Air Commando Wing
309 Special Operations Squadron	1/6/68 - 1/1/70	315 Special Operations Wing
309 Tactical Airlift Squadron	1/1/70 - 31/7/70	315 Tactical Airlift Wing
		Phan Rang AB, RSVN

| C-123B | 1967* - 1968 |
| C-123K | 1968* - 31/7/70 |

Squadron flew **WH** tail coded C-123B from 8/3/66 and converted to C-123K by 1968. Designation changed to 309 SOS on 1/6/68 and 309 TAS on 1/1/70, non-operational on 1/7/70 and inactivating on 31/7/70. Red noted as squadron colour.

C-123B Provider 54-0598 **WH**, 309 TAS 315 ACW, Phan Rang AB, RSVN. Taken Ton Son Nhut AB, RSVN, 24 March 1968. Photo: Bob Burgess.

UNITED STATES AIR FORCES PACIFIC

WH
22 Tactical Air Support Squadron   **326 Air Division**
OV-10A   **early 1984 - 11/9/88**   **Wheeler Field, Hawaii**

Squadron previously flew blue fin capped O-2. Equipment changed in 1984 to OV-10A maintaining markings. The **WH** tail code applied in early 1984. Fin tip colour from blue to black during September and October 1986. Squadron inactivated on 22/9/88, reactivating on 14/10/88 with **NF** tail coded OV-10A.

OV-10A Bronco 67-14699 **WH**, 22 TASS 326 AD, Wheeler AFB. Photo: Grant Matsuoka, March 1984.

WM
310 Air Commando Squadron	1967* - 1/6/68	315 Air Commando Wing
310 Special Operations Squadron	1/6/68 - 1/1/70	315 Special Operations Wing
310 Tactical Airlift Squadron	1/1/70 - 26/1/72	315 Tactical Airlift Wing
		Phan Rang AB, RSVN

C-123B   1967* - 1968
C-123K   1968* - 26/1/72

Squadron flew **WM** tail coded C-123B from 8/3/66 converted to C-123K by 1968. Designation changed to 310 SOS on 1/6/68 and 310 TAS on 1/1/70. Attached to the 315 TAW between 16/1/72 and 26/1/72, then inactivated. Blue noted as squadron colour.

WP
8 Tactical Fighter Wing   1/73 - 16/9/74   **Ubon RTAFB**
                                          16/9/74 - current 31/12/90   **Kunsan AB, ROK**

16 Special Operations Squadron
AC-130A   5/74 - 8/12/74
AC-130H   5/74 - 8/12/74

Squadron recoded from **FT** tail code at Ubon RTAFB. Attached to the 388 TFW based at Korat RTAFB between 19/4/74 and 8/12/75. The **WP** tail code removed shortly after arrival at Korat RTAFB. The 16 SOS reassigned to 1 SOW Hurlburt Field on 12/12/75.

25 Tactical Fighter Squadron
F-4D   1/73 - 5/7/74

The 25 TFS recoded from **FA** to **WP** tail code, under AFM66-1 wing common code concept in April 1974. Squadron F-4 carried yellow a fin cap. Transferred on 5/7/74 to the 432 TRW replacing the 555 TFS and tail coded **UD**.

F-4D Phantom 66-8709 **WP**, 25 TFS 8 TFW, Udorn RTAFB, with yellow fin cap. Photo: Don Larsen, Korat RTAFB, early 1974.

35 Tactical Fighter Squadron
F-4D	16/9/74 - 11/81
F-16A/B	14/9/81 - 1988
F-16C/D	5/88 - current 31/12/90

Reassigned from the 3 TFW flying **UP** tail coded F-4E on 16/9/74, recoding **WP** on arrival. Squadron colour noted as light blue and carried as a fin cap. Equipped with F-4D before upgrading to F-16A/B in 1981 and F-16C/D in 1988.

80 Tactical Fighter Squadron
F-4D	16/9/74 - 11/81
F-16A/B	14/9/81 - 1988
F-16C/D	5/88 - current 31/12/90

Squadron reassigned from the 3 TFW on 16/9/74. Squadron colour yellow carried as fin cap. Squadron equipment changed from F-4D to F-16A/B in 1981, and F-16C/D in 1988.

F-16A Falcon 80-580 **WP**, 80 TFS 8 TFW, Kunsan AB, ROK, with yellow fin cap. Photo: Kadena September 1983.

433 Tactical Fighter Squadron
F-4D	1/73 - 23/7/74

Squadron recoded from **FG** tail code to wing standard **UD** with green squadron colour noted. Inactivated on 23/7/74 at Ubon RTAFB. Reactivated within the 57 FWW on 1/11/76 flying **WA** tail coded F-15A/B.

435 Tactical Fighter Squadron
F-4D	1/73 - 8/8/74

Squadron recoded from **FO**, and inactivated on 8/8/74. Red noted as squadron colour. Reactivated on 1/1/77 with **HM** tail coded AT-38B with the 479 TTW.

497 Tactical Fighter Squadron   Taegu AB, ROK
F-4D	1/73 - 16/9/74
F-4D	11/78 - 1/1/82

The 497 TFS recoded from **FP** tail code early in 1974. Squadron colours noted as blue and black. Inactivated on 16/9/74 and reactivated with ex 474 TFW F-4D in November 1978. Squadron F-4D noted with a red fin cap and **WP** tail code at Taegu AB, ROK. Squadron F-4D were the last in Korea. Reassigned to the 51 CW in 1982 flying **OS** coded F-4E.

WV
311 Air Commando Squadron	1967* - 1/6/68	315 Air Commando Wing
311 Special Operations Squadron	1/6/68 - 1/1/70	315 Special Operations Wing
	(*attached*) 15/11/69 - 15/12/69	3 Tactical Fighter Wing
311 Tactical Airlift Squadron	1/1/70 - 5/10/71	315 Tactical Airlift Wing

UNITED STATES AIR FORCES PACIFIC

Phan Rang AB, RSVN

C-123B 1967* - 1968
C-123K 1968 - 5/10/71

Squadron flew **WV** tail coded C-123B from 8/3/66 converting to the C-123K by 1968. Status changed to 311 SOS on 1/6/68 and 311 TAS on 1/1/70. Status changed to non-operational on 15/9/71 before inactivating on 5/10/71. Forward operating locations noted at Da Nang and Tan Son Nhut AB, RSVN with the latter lasting until squadron inactivated on 5/10/71. Detached briefly between 15/11/69 and 15/12/69 to the 3 TFW.

WW
Detachment 1, 561 Tactical Fighter Squadron **388 Tactical Fighter Wing**
F-105G 1/2/73 - 5/9/73 **Korat RTAFB**

Attached from the 35 TFW although not assigned, flew **WW** tail coded F-105G during 1973. Detachment F-105G carried yellow tail stripe.

F-105G Thunderchief 63-8319 **WW**, Detachment 1, 561 TFS 388 TFW, Korat RTAFB, with yellow tail stripe and canopy sides. Photo: Don Larsen 29 January 1973.

XC
557 Tactical Fighter Squadron **12 Tactical Fighter Wing**
F-4C 1966* - 31/3/70 **Cam Ranh Bay AB, RSVN**

The 557 TFS assigned to the 12 TFW on 1/12/65, coding assigned F-4C in June 1968. Squadron status changed to non-operational on 10/3/70 until inactivated on 31/3/70 with a red fin cap carried.

F-4C Phantom 63-7534 "Mystic Skater" **XC**, 557 TFS 12 TFW, Cam Ranh Bay AB, RSVN. Photo: T Matsuzaki, Yokota AB, Japan, December 1969.

XD
558 Tactical Fighter Squadron **12 Tactical Fighter Wing**
F-4C 1966* - 22/7/68 **Cam Ranh Bay AB, RSVN**

Squadron assigned to the 12 TFW on 25/4/62 transferring with wing to Cam Ranh Bay AB, RSVN during 1965. The **XD** tail coded F-4C utilized green or blue as the squadron colour. The 391 TFS took **XD** tail coded F-4C of the 558 TFS to assignment at Misawa AB, Japan on 22/7/68. The 558 TFS assumed the former 391 TFS **XT** tail coded F-4C at Cam Ranh Bay AB, RSVN. Thus a tail code change for the 558 TFS on 22/7/68.

XD
391 Tactical Fighter Squadron **12 Tactical Fighter Wing**
F-4C 22/7/68 - 22/7/68 **Cam Ranh Bay AB, RSVN**

The normally **XT** tail coded 391 TFS transferred to 475 TFW Misawa AB, Japan on 22/7/68. Squadron took the **XD** coded mounts of 558 on assignment. Aircraft recoded to **UD** at destination.

XN
559 Tactical Fighter Squadron 12 Tactical Fighter Wing
F-4C   1966* - 31/3/70   Cam Ranh Bay AB, RSVN

The 559 TFS assigned to the 12 TFW on 27/12/65. Moved to Cam Ranh Bay AB, RSVN with the wing in January 1966. Tail coded F-4C **XN** during June 1968 and applied blue fin caps. Squadron status changed to non-operational after 23/3/70 until inactivated on 31/3/70. Squadron redesignated and activated in 1972 as 559 FTS 12 FTW flying T-37.

XT
391 Tactical Fighter Squadron 12 Tactical Fighter Wing
F-4C   1966* - 22/7/68   Cam Ranh Bay AB, RSVN

The 391 TFS attached to the 12 TFW on 26/1/66 and assigned on 23/6/66. Squadron transferred to the 475 TFW at Misawa AB, Japan on 22/7/68 with the **XD** tail coded F-4C of the 558 TFS. Yellow trim noted. Squadron recoded to **UD** within the 475 TFW.

XT
558 Tactical Fighter Squadron 12 Tactical Fighter Wing
F-4C   22/7/68 - 31/3/71   Cam Ranh Bay AB, RSVN

Squadron originally flew **XD** tail coded F-4C until 391 TFS moved to Misawa AB, Japan taking the 558 TFS **XD** tail coded aircraft. Squadron assumed the former 391 TFS, **XT** tail coded F-4C on 22/7/68. Status changed on 10/3/70 to non-operational until inactivated on 31/3/71.

F-4C Phantom 64-0659 **XT**, 558 TFS 12 TFW Cam Ranh Bay AB, RSVN. Photo: Martin collection.

YD
21 Tactical Airlift Squadron 374 Tactical Airlift Wing
                                                                      Naha AB, Okinawa
C-130A   1968* - 27/4/71
AC-130A   1970 - 1971

One of four squadrons formerly assigned to the 6315 Operations Group at Naha AB, Okinawa, reassigned to the 374 TAW on 8/8/66 and tail coded C-130A **YD** in 1968. Limited use of AC-130A also noted. The 374 TAW reduced operations and by 27/4/71 all C-130 reassigned from wing. The 374 TAW transferred on 31/5/71 to the former 314 TAW operations base at Ching Chuan Kang AB, Taiwan. The 21 TAS reassigned to replace the 346 TAS at new 347 TAW location. Codes changing from **YD** to **DY** on reassignment.

YJ
35 Tactical Airlift Squadron 374 Tactical Airlift Wing
C-130A   1968* - 24/3/71   Naha AB, Okinawa

Assigned to the 374 TFW on 8/8/66 from the 6315 Operation Group. The **YJ** tail code carried on C-130A by the end of 1968. Operations ceased on 24/3/71 and squadron inactivated on 31/3/71.

C-130A Hercules 55-0047 **YJ**, 35 TAS 374 TAW, Naha AB, Okinawa. Photo: Roy Lock, 2 June 1970.

UNITED STATES AIR FORCES PACIFIC

YP
41 Tactical Airlift Squadron   **374 Tactical Airlift Wing**
C-130A   **1968* - 21/2/71**   **Naha AB, Okinawa**

Squadron assigned to the 374 TAW on 8/8/66. The **YP** tail codes applied to C-130A during 1968. Operations ceased and squadron inactivated on 21/2/71.

YU
817 Tactical Airlift Squadron   **374 Tactical Airlift Wing**
C-130A   **1968* - 27/4/70**   **Naha AB, Okinawa**

The last of four squadrons within the 374 TAW originally assigned to the 6315 Operations Group at Naha AB, Okinawa to reassign on 8/8/66. Tail codes carried on squadron C-130A by the end of 1968. Flying operations ceased on 10/4/70 and unit inactivated on 15/6/70. The 374 TAW ran down operations and by 27/4/71 all C-130A reassigned from wing. The 374 TAW transferred to the former 314 TAW operations base at Ching Chuan Kang AB, Taiwan.

ZA
12 Tactical Fighter Squadron   **18 Tactical Fighter Wing**
F-105D/F   **9/67* - 15/6/72**   **Kadena AB, Okinawa**

Squadron activated within the 18 TFW at Kadena AB, Okinawa during 1952. A yellow tail stripe carried on F-105D/F and coded **ZA** by September 1968. The Detachment 1 assigned to Korat RTAFB in the "Wild Weasel" role with **ZB** codes in September 1970.

F-105D Thunderchief 62-4375 **ZA**, 12 TFS 18 TFW, Kadena AB, Okinawa, with yellow fin cap. Photo: Hideki Nagakubo, Yokota AB, Japan, 18 May 1971.

ZB
Detachment 1 - 12 Tactical Fighter Squadron   **18 Tactical Fighter Wing**
F-105F/G   **24/9/70 - 1/11/70**   **Korat RTAFB**

Air Force Times quote "24/9/70 the first flight of F-105 arrived at Korat RTAFB, from inactivating (*units at*) Takhli RTAFB, and formed Det 1 - 12 TFS... grew in size and in November 1970 the 6010 WWS unique in the USAF was formed at Korat." Squadron maintaining the **ZB** tail code and reassigned to the 388 TFW on 1/11/70.

ZB
6010 Wild Weasel Squadron
388 Tactical Fighter Wing
F-105F/G   **1/11/70 - 1/12/71**   **Korat RTAFB**

Activated from the assets of Detachment 1, 12 TFS. By 1/11/70 the 6010 WWS activated, replacing Detachment 1, 12 TFS. The F-105F/G tail coded **ZB** with 6010 WWS in turn replaced by the 17 WWS on 1/12/71 with **JB** tail codes. Squadron F-105G noted with **ZB** tail coded F-105G as late as January 1972.

F-105G Thunderchief 63-8302 **ZB**, 6010 WWS 18 TFW, Korat RTAFB. Photo: Martin collection, 18 January 1972.

TAIL CODE

ZG
67 Tactical Fighter Squadron

18 Tactical Fighter Wing
Kadena AB, Okinawa

F-4C   15/3/71 - 10/73*
F-4C (ww)   15/3/71 - 10/73

Squadron transferred from the 475 TFW at Misawa AB, Japan and assigned to 18 TFW on 15/3/71. Formation assets came from the 35 TFS 347 TFW at Yokota AB, Japan. Between 23/9/72 and 18/2/73, 6 Wild Weasel F-4C deployed to Korat RTAFB for Linebacker operations. This was the combat debut of the Wild Weasel modified F-4C. The 67 TFS attached to the 3 TFW, between 2/6/72 and 28/7/72. Carried white outlined red fin cap. Squadron maintained a detachment at Ching Chuan Kang, Taiwan from 15/11/72 until 1979. Recoded in June 1972 to common wing code **ZZ**, although **ZG** lasted until at least 10/73.

F-4C Phantom 63-7474 **ZG**, 67 TFS 18 TFW, Korat RTAFB, with white outline, red fin cap. Photo: Don Larsen, 1 November 1972.

ZL
44 Tactical Fighter Squadron
F-4C   15/3/71 - 12/72

18 Tactical Fighter Wing
Kadena AB, Okinawa

The 44 TFS formerly assigned to 355 TFW flying **RE** tail coded F-105D/F, activated within the 18 TFW on 15/3/71. Operational after 14/5/71 with **ZL** tail coded F-4C reassigned from the 36 TFS 347 TFW (*ex-tail code* **GL**). Detached to the 3 TFW at Kunsan AB, ROK between 3/4/72 and 2/6/72 and also 28/7/72 and 8/9/72, replacing units deployed to RSVN. Conversion to F-4D provided from the 388 TFW and 432 TRW in June 1975. Squadron carried diagonal dark orange and black fin cap. Tail code changed to **ZZ** post December 1972.

F-4C Phantom 64-0750 **ZL**, 44 TFS 18 TFW, Kadena AB, Okinawa, with diagonal orange and black fin cap. Photo: David Davenport, Detachment 1, Ching Chuan Kang AB, Taiwan, 2 October 1973.

ZT
19 Tactical Electronic Warfare Squadron
EB-66E   31/12/68 - 30/10/70

18 Tactical Fighter Wing
Kadena AB, Okinawa

The 19 TEWS reassigned from the 363 TRW at Shaw AFB on 31/12/68. The 19 TEWS applied **ZT** as tail code on EB-66E. Squadron established a detachment at Osan AB, ROK during December 1968 in response to the USS Pueblo seizure. Squadron also initiated a detachment at Itazuke AB, Japan on 10/5/69 until squadron inactivated on 30/10/70.

UNITED STATES AIR FORCES PACIFIC

EB-66E Destroyer 54-0542 **ZT**, 19 TEWS 18 TFW, Kadena AB, Okinawa. Photo: Bob Burgess, Davis Monthan AFB, 23 August 1974.

ZZ
15 Tactical Reconnaissance Squadron		18 Tactical Fighter Wing
RF-4C	1967* - 6/72	Kadena AB, Okinawa

Squadron attached to the 18 TFW on 15/3/60 and assigned on 20/4/70. Detachment maintained for unknown period at Osan AB, ROK. Squadron RF-4C carried black and yellow checked tail stripe as markings. The **ZZ** tail code adopted during 1967 and maintained as wing code post 1972.

ZZ
18 Tactical Fighter Wing	10/73 - current 31/12/90	Kadena AB, Okinawa

12 Tactical Fighter Squadron
F-4D 29/11/75 - least 5/79
F-15C/D 1/80 - current 31/12/90

Squadron previously active with **ZA** tail coded F-105D/F until March 1972. Reactivated with F-4D in 1975 until conversion to the F-15C/D at Eglin AFB starting in January 1980. Officially operational with F-15C/D on 1/4/80. Squadron carried yellow tail stripes until 1982. Markings of red, yellow and blue in triangular pattern, with yellow dominant, adopted 1982.

25 Tactical Fighter Squadron
F-4D 19/12/75 - 22/8/80

Squadron previously flew **UD** tail coded F-4 within the 432 TRW. Activated as a paper unit within the 3 TFW between 18/12/75 and 19/12/75. Assigned **UD** tail coded F-4D on activation on 19/12/75, with green squadron markings. The 25 TFS left out of wing's conversion process to F-15C/D conversion inactivating on 22/8/80. Squadron reactivated in November 1981, with **SU** tail coded A-10A within the 51 CW.

44 Tactical Fighter Squadron
F-4C post 10/73 - 6/75
F-4D 6/75 - 1979
F-15C/D 29/9/79 - current 31/12/90

Squadron carried blue trim on assigned F-4. Converted to F-15C/D at Eglin AFB in late 1979. Deployed F-15C/D to Kadena AB, Okinawa during January 1980. Squadron F-15 carried black tail stripes switching post 1982, to triangle markings of red, yellow and prominent black.

67 Tactical Fighter Squadron
F-4C (ww) post 10/73 - 1/9/80
F-15C/D 7/79 - current 31/12/90

The 67 TFS recoded from **ZG** while flying Wild Weasel F-4C. Squadron returned to Korat RTAFB on 20/4/75 with F-4C Weasel for air coverage of Saigon embassy evacuation, returning on 2/5/75. Squadron attached to 3 TFW, between 8/9/75 and 16/10/75. Changed role with conversion to F-15C/D at Eglin AFB starting on 14/7/79. Redeployed back Kadena AB, Okinawa in September 1979. Carried red stripes until 1982, changing to yellow, blue and dominant red stylized tail markings.

F-15C Eagle 78-0497 **ZZ**, 67 TFS 18 TFW, Kadena AB, Okinawa, with yellow, blue and dominant red stylized tail markings. Photo: Don Abrahamson, Tyndall AFB, 13 October 1984.

TAIL CODE

15 Tactical Reconnaissance Squadron
RF-4C 1972* - 1/10/89
 Squadron maintained **ZZ** as wing common tail code post AFM66-1 concept. The 15 TRS transferred to Taegu AB, ROK during 1989 and recoded **GU** with assignment to 460 TRG Taegu AB, ROK maintaining yellow tail stripe.

RF-4C Phantom 68-0581 **ZZ**, 15 TRS 18 TFW, Kadena AB, Okinawa. Photo: Masanori Ogawa, Yokota AB, Japan, 6 September 1987.

6T
6 Special Operations Squadron   **14/633 Special Operations Wing**
A-1E/H 1968* - 1969   **Phu Cat AB, RSVN**
 Squadron previously assigned to the 14 SOW at Pleiku AB, RSVN with A-1 tail coded **ET**, then assigned 633 SOW. Several A-1 carried **6T** tail code, possibly a detachment, established at Phu Cat AB, RSVN with 14 or 633 SOW. A second theory concerns experimentation with an undocumented different code system.

A-1H Skyraider 52-609 (134609) **6T**, Det. 6 SOS 14 SOW, Phu Cat AB, RSVN. Photo: S Pargeter, Isham collection, November 1969.

Alaskan Air Command

21st Composite - Tactical Fighter Wing
343d Tactical Fighter Group - Composite Wing - Tactical Fighter Wing

Wing Summary AAC

21st Composite Wing
21st Tactical Fighter Wing

The 21 Composite Wing activated at Elmendorf AFB on 8/6/66 controlling several uncoded units. The 43 TFS arrived from the 15 TFW, Langley AFB on 23/6/70 with **FC** tail coded F-4E. The 343 TFG activated within the 21 CW on 15/11/70 with the 18 TFS flying F-4E. Reports have the 18 TFS flying **FS** tail coded F-4E for a short period between October 1977 and the end of 1978. On 1/1/80 the 343 TFG inactivated and the 18 TFS reassigned directly to the 21 CW.

The 21 CW redesignated to 21 Tactical Fighter Wing on 1/10/79. The 43 TFS started conversion to the F-15A/B in March 1982 with completion in October 1982. With further conversion to F-15C/D and assignment of additional aircraft the 43 TFS divided assets to form an additional squadron, the 54 TFS on 8/5/87. Completion of wing transformation to the F-15C/D occurred on 12/8/88.

343d Tactical Fighter Group
343d Composite Wing
343d Tactical Fighter Wing

Initially redesignated as 343 Tactical Fighter Group on 9/11/77 and assigned to the 21 Composite Wing on 15/11/77. Group operated **FC** tail coded F-4E of the 18 TFS until the group inactivated on 1/1/80 and the 18 TFS reassigned directly to the 21 TFW. Reactivated on 1/10/81 as the 343 Composite Wing at Eielson AFB replacing the 5010 Combat Support Group. The 18 TFS reassigned from the 21 TFW on 1/1/82 and completed conversion to the **AK** tail coded A-10A by the end of 1982. The group redesignated to 343 Tactical Fighter Wing status on 8/6/84. An uncoded component, the 25 TASS converted to **AK** tail coded OV-10A in 1986. In 1989 the OV-10A retired and the 25 TASS inactivated. The squadron replaced by a TASS dedicated flight within the A-10A equipped 18 TFS.

ALASKAN AIR COMMAND

Squadron/code Summary AAC

AK
343 Composite Wing   1/10/81 - 8/6/84
343 Tactical Fighter Wing 8/6/84 - current 31/12/90

Eielson AFB, Alaska

18 Tactical Fighter Squadron
A-10A   1/10/81 - current 31/12/90
   Squadron assigned from the 21 TFW on 1/1/82 with **FC** tail coded F-4E. The 18 TFS completed conversion to A-10 by the end of 1982. Squadron colours not normally carried until July 1983. Squadron A-10A carried blue fin caps with a black fox superimposed. One of the few squadrons to apply a shadow to tail codes on all assigned aircraft.

A-10A Thunderbolt 80-0240 **AK**, 18 TFS 343 TFW, Eielson AFB, with twin double sided light blue fin caps containing black fox on outer surfaces, tail code and serial in shadow. Photo: Patrick Martin, CFB Comox, 4 August 1990.

25 TASS
OV-10A   1986 - 1989
The 25 TASS reequipped from the uncoded O-2 in 1986, to the OV-10A. The **AK** tail coded OV-10A continued until 1989. The squadron inactivated and the TASS role assigned to a TASS dedicated flight within the 18 TFS, with further A-10.

AK
21 Composite Wing   3/82 - 8/6/84
21 Tactical Fighter Wing   8/6/84 - current 31/12/90

Elmendorf AFB, Alaska

43 Tactical Fighter Squadron
F-15A/B   1/3/82 - 12/8/88
F-15C/D   1987 - current 31/12/90
The 43 TFS converted from **FC** tail coded F-4E operations to **AK** coded F-15A/B by March 1983. A gold squadron colour initially carried until changed to blue bands with grey dipper effective in February 1985. Later, the addition of a North Star to Dipper motif applied.

54 Tactical Fighter Squadron
F-15C/D   8/5/87 - current 31/12/90
The 54 TFS activated 8/5/87 with the division of 43 TFS F-15C/D. The F-15 carried a yellow tail stripes.

F-15C Eagle 81-0020 **AK**, 54 TFS 21 TFW, Elmendorf AFB, with single sided yellow tail stripes. Photo: Patrick Martin, CFB Comox, 4 August 1990.

FC
43 Tactical Fighter Squadron   **21 Composite Wing**
F-4E   **23/6/70 - 1972**   **Elmendorf AFB, Alaska**
The 43 TFS tail coded F-4E FB in July 1968 within the 15 TFW and reassigned to the 21 CW, at Elmendorf AFB, arriving on 23/6/70 with former 45 TFS 15 TFW FC tail coded F-4E. Blue fin cap outlined in white carried as squadron markings.

FC
21 Composite Wing   **1977 - 1/1/80**
21 Tactical Fighter Wing   **1/1/80 - late 1982**
                                                                                                 Elmendorf AFB, Alaska

18 Tactical Fighter Squadron
F-4E   **15/11/77 - late 1982**
The 18 TFS activated within the 21 CW but assigned to the 343 TFG on 15/11/77. On inactivation of the 343 TFG, on 1/1/80 the 18 TFS directly assigned to the 21 TFW. The squadron F-4E carried a white fin cap. The 18 TFS reassigned to the reactivated 343 CW on 1/1/82. Squadron completed A-10 conversion by year end. Aircraft carried FC tail code until the A-10 conversion thus, the FC code carried while assigned to the 343 CW.

43 Tactical Fighter Squadron
F-4E   **1972* - 1/3/82**
The 43 TFS maintained FC as wing common tail code post 1972, with a blue fin cap. On 1/3/82 the squadron converted to AK coded F-15A/B. The last F-4E left Alaska on 16/11/82.

F-4E Phantom 68-0483 **FC**, 43 TFS 21 CW, Elmendorf AFB, with blue fin cap outlined in white. Photo: Robert Redden, July 1971.

Tactical Air Command - Continental United States

1st Air Commando - Special Operations - 834th Tactical Composite - 1st Special Operation Wing
1st Tactical Fighter Wing
4th Tactical Fighter Wing
15th Tactical Fighter Wing
23d Tactical Fighter Wing
24th Composite Wing
27th Tactical Fighter Wing
28th Air Division
31st Tactical Fighter Wing
33d Tactical Fighter Wing
35th Tactical Fighter - Tactical Training - Tactical Fighter Wing
37th Tactical Fighter Wing
49th Tactical Fighter Wing
56th Tactical Fighter - Tactical Training Wing
57th Fighter Weapons - Tactical Training - Fighter Weapons Wing
58th Tactical Fighter Training - Tactical Training Wing
64th Tactical Airlift Wing
67th Tactical Reconnaissance Wing
68th Tactical Air Support Group
75th Tactical Reconnaissance Wing
313th Tactical Airlift Wing
314th Tactical Airlift Wing
316th Tactical Airlift Wing
317th Tactical Airlift Wing
325th Tactical Training Wing
347th Tactical Fighter Wing
354th Tactical Fighter Wing
355th Tactical Fighter Wing
363d Tactical Reconnaissance - Tactical Fighter Wing
366th Tactical Fighter Wing
388th Tactical Fighter Wing
405th Tactical Training Wing
463d Tactical Airlift Wing
464th Tactical Airlift Wing
474th Tactical Fighter Wing
479th Tactical Fighter Wing
507th Tactical Air Control Wing
516th Tactical Airlift Wing
602d Tactical Air Control Wing

4403d Tactical Fighter Wing
4410th Combat Crew Training Wing
4442d Combat Crew Training Wing
4450th Tactical Group
4453d Combat Crew Training Wing
4510th Combat Crew Training Wing
4525th Fighter Weapons Wing
4531st Tactical Fighter Wing

TACTICAL AIR COMMAND - CONTINENTAL U.S.

Wing Summary TAC - CONUS

1st Tactical Fighter Wing

The 1 Tactical Fighter Wing moved from Hamilton AFB to MacDill AFB on 1/10/70. Units and tail codes assumed from the inactivating 15 TFW. Wing operated with **F_** tail code range on F-4E assigned to the 45, 46, 47 TFS, 4530 TFTS and B-57 equipped 4452 CCTS with tail codes **FB, FD, FE, FF** and **FS**. The 4501 TFRS activated, replacing the 4530 TFTS flying **FF** tail coded F-4E. All F-4 Tactical Fighter Squadrons inactivated on 1/7/71 and replaced by the 27, 71 and 94 TFS, utilizing existing tail codes **FD, FB,** and **FE**. The B-57 equipped 4424 CCTS inactivated on 30/6/72. Under wing common tail code, all F-4E adopted the **FF** tail code as the wing tail code in mid 1972.

On 30/6/75, the 1 Tactical Fighter Wing reassigned with 27, 71 and 94 TFS to Langley AFB, converting to F-15. The wing maintained the **FF** tail code, with the first F-15 received on 9/1/76. The 56 TFW at MacDill AFB assumed all F-4 assets, including the 4501 TFRS, recoding to **MC**.

1st Air Commando Wing
1st Special Operations Wing
834th Tactical Composite Wing
1st Special Operations Wing

The 1 Special Operations Wing originally established in August 1944, as 1 Air Commando Group. The group reactivated and organized in April 1962, and redesignated as 1 Air Commando Wing on 1/6/63. The 1 ACW assigned **I** range tail codes during July 1968. Tail codes actually assigned to the 1 ACW, but the wing redesignated to 1 Special Operations Wing on 8/7/68. Aircraft types operated include A-37, C-47, C-119, C-123, T-28, UH-1 and U-10. The 1 SOW Headquartered at England AFB from 15/1/66 until 15/7/69. Units initially coded in July 1968 included; Detachment 1, Detachment 2, 71, 317, 319, 603 ACS, 4412, 4413, and 4532 CCTS, with tail codes **IA, IB, IC, ID, IE, IF, IG, IH** and **II**. The 4406 CCTS with **IJ** tail codes, assigned during October 1968. When the wing designation changed to SOW, Air Commando Squadrons renamed to Special Operations Squadrons (*coded aircraft types operated included A-37, C-47, C-119, C-123 and C-130*). On 15/7/69, the 1 SOW and the Eglin Air Force Auxiliary Field No.9 (*hereafter called Hurlburt Field*) based 4410 CCTW, exchanged bases and components. The 1 SOW adopting the former 4410 CCTW, **A** range tail codes. All **I** range tail coded components lost in the switch, these units included the 71, 317, 319 ACS, 4406, 4412, 4413, 4532 and 4406 CCTS tail coded; **IC, ID, IE, IJ, IG, IH, II** and **IJ**.

Units gained on 15/7/69 included 4407, 4408, 4409 and 4410 CCTS with tail codes **AD, AO, AP** and **AQ**. These units flew the A-1, C-123, UH-1 and T-28 aircraft. The 4408 CCTS moved to Lockbourne AFB and reassigned to the 317 TAW, changing assigned tail code to **OD**. The 317 SOS, returned to the 1 SOW from the 4410 CCTW, (**IE** *tail code*) adopting new equipment and the now unused **AO** tail code. On 15/10/69 the 4409 and 4410 CCTS redesignated to 549 TASTS and 547 SOS (*later TASTS*) with tail codes **AP** and **AQ**. Possibly Detachment 1 and 2 evolved into the 7 SOF and coded **AA**, while Detachment 2 recoded to **AB**.

Under wing common tail codes adopted in 1972 the 1 SOW recoded all remaining component assigned aircraft to **AH**. Units noted recoding to **AH** included 549 TASTS, 547 TASTS, 317 SOS, 603 SOTS and 4407 CCTS with codes; **AP, AQ, AO, AF** and **AD**. Later, the OV-10A equipped 549 TASTS recoded **FL** and moved to Patrick AFB. In addition, the 8, 16 and 20 SOS, flying C-130, UH-1 and CH-3 added after AFM66-1 wing common code **AH** adopted. The 360 TEWS assigned between 1/7/73 and 31/7/73, to the 1 SOW, with an unknown tail code status. The 4410 SOTG inactivated on 31/7/73, resulting in assignment of the 6 SOTS, flying **IJ** tail coded A-37, until reassigned to the 23 TFW on 1/1/74, without wing common code. Wing redesignated to the 834 Tactical Composite Wing, on merger with USAF Special Operations Force on 1/7/74, and redesignated back to the 1 SOW on 1/7/75.

4th Tactical Fighter Wing

The 4 Tactical Fighter Wing stationed at Seymour Johnson AFB, since 1957 flew F-86, F-100, F-105, F-4D/E and F-15E. Three current squadrons, 334, 335 and 336 TFS, applied the **SA, SB,** and **SC** tail codes, to F-4D during July 1968. The 4 TFW deployed to Kunsan AB, ROK, during 1-2/68 following the seizure of USS Pueblo. The 334 TFS moved on to Kwang-ju AB, ROK in March 1968 until returning to Seymour Johnson AFB, at the end of July 1968. The 335 TFS and 336 TFS returned in June and July 1968. The wing reequipped with F-4E during 1970-71.

The 4 TFW maintained F-4E deployments with the 8 TFW in South East Asia between, April 72 and September 1973, under "Constant Guard" deployments. The 334 and 336 TFS went to Ubon RTAFB, in April 1972 beginning a complex rotation of 4 TFW fighter assets. Known deployments include:

SA	334 TFS	4 TFW	F-4E	11/4/72 - 8/7/72
SC-SJ	336 TFS	4 TFW	F-4E	12/4/72 - 15/9/72
SJ	335 TFS	4 TFW	F-4E	8/7/72 - 12/72
SJ	334 TFS	4 TFW	F-4E	25/9/72 - 12/3/73
SJ	336 TFS	4 TFW	F-4E	9/3/73 - 7/9/73

(*336 TFS recoded during deployment*)

The 4 TFW adopted the **SJ** wing common tail code under AFM66-1 concept in 1972. The 337 TFS activated in 1982, also flying **SJ** tail coded F-4E, until inactivating three years later. The first F-15E arrived on 29/12/88, and the 4 TFW reequipped by the end of 1990.

15th Tactical Fighter Wing

The 15 Tactical Fighter Wing activated at MacDill AFB, Florida in 1962. In 1968 initial tail coded F-4E squadrons include the 43, 45, 46 and 47 TFS with tail codes, **FB, FC, FD** and **FE**. The B-57 operated with the 13 BS and the 4424 CCTS, both tail coded **FK**. The 13 BS reassigned to the 8 TFW at Ubon RTAFB, recoding to **FS** after arrival. The 43 TFS reassigned to Elmendorf AFB on 1/4/70, taking the former 45 TFS, **FC** tail codes F-4E. The remaining 45 TFS switched codes from **FC** to **FB** (*formerly used by the*

43 TFS). The 15 TFW inactivated on 1/10/70, with the remaining 45, 46, 47 TFS and 4424 CCTS, reassigned to the 1 TFW, maintaining **FB, FD, FE** and **FS** tail codes.

23d Tactical Fighter Wing

The 23 Tactical Fighter Wing flew F-105 as main equipment when tail codes applied while assigned to McConnell AFB, during July 1968. The 560, 561, 562, 563 TFS and 4519 CCTS assigned tail codes **MC, MD, ME, MF** and **MG** in July 1968. The 560 TFS transferred to the 4531 TFW, possibly before tail codes applied. The remaining squadrons transferred to the 35 TFW in the "Wild Weasel" role on 1/7/72. Detachments with **WW** and **MD** tail codes sent to South East Asia. The 419 TFTS replaced the 4519 CCTS, during 1969, then inactivated in 1971.

The 23 TFW reassigned to England AFB, to fly A-7D on 1/7/72 with the 74 and 75 TFS as components. The 76 TFS added during October 1972. Under common wing concept all 23 TFW squadrons flew **EL** tail coded A-7D. The 6 SOTS assigned between 1/1/74 and 15/9/74 flying **IJ** tail coded A-37, not adopting the 23 TFW **EL** tail code. The first A-10A arrived on 23/9/80, which entirely replaced the A-7D operations by July 1981. The last A-7D ferried out to ANG units on 14/8/81.

24th Composite Wing

The 24 Composite Wing controlled various attached units as part of Southern Command. The command inactivated in 1976 and control passed to Tactical Air Command. The only tail coded component, the 24 SOS adopted the **HW** tail code. As the USAF downgraded force levels in Panama the **HW** A-37 withdrew, along with Pan American Air Academy, to Homestead AFB, where the tail codes were removed.

27th Tactical Fighter Wing

The 27 Tactical Fighter Wing, tail coded F-100 **CA, CC, CD** and **CE** within the 481, 522, 524 and 4427 TFS, in July 1968. Conversion started during October 1969 to the F-111E. The F-100 phased out during mid 1972, with the **C** range tail codes passing to F-111. In a complex transfer of assets the F-111E lasted a short time before reassignment to the 20 TFW at RAF Upper Heyford. Swing wing F-111 operations commenced again on 28/10/70 as the 27 TFW selected to operate the F-111D model. The 474 TFW at Nellis AFB, loaned F-111A in 1971, until significant numbers of F-111D were available. Very few **C** range, tail coded F-111E noted. Under AFM66-1 concept, wing common tail code **CC** adopted during 1972 for all F-111D squadrons. The 523 TFS replaced the 481 TFS on 31/8/73. The 481 TFS, activating for a second period on 15/1/76 replacing the inactivating 4427 TFTS, until again inactivating on 8/7/80. Former SAC FB-111A redesignated to F-111G and began operations at Cannon AFB within the activated 428 TFTS in April 1990.

28th Air Division

The 28 Air Division controlled two tail coded units, the 41 ECS and 7 ACCS, flying EC-130 with **DM** and **KS** coded EC-130. The 7 ACCS further controlled by the 52 AW & CW within the 28 Air Division. Tail codes dropped on change of camouflage schemes by EC-130.

31st Tactical Fighter Wing

The 31 Tactical Fighter Wing activated at Homestead AFB in May 1962. Wing assigned to Tuy Hoa AB, RSVN, during December 1966. The 31 TFW returned to Homestead AFB on 15/10/70 and assumed assets from the tenant 4531 TFW. Initial F-4E units noted as; 436, 478, 560 and 68 TFS, coded **ZD, ZE, ZF** and **ZG**. The 478 and 560 TFS inactivated on 31/10/70, while the 68 TFS reassigned to the 4403 TFW at England AFB and 436 TFS to 479 TFW, at George AFB. The 306, 309 and 308 TFS, reassigned from the 4403 TFW, to the 31 TFW, assuming **ZD, ZE,** and **ZF** tail coded F-4E. All three formerly assigned to the 31 TFW at Tuy Hoa, RSVN. The 307 TFS transferred from 401 TFW on 14/7/71 replacing the 306 TFS, and assuming the **ZD** tail coded F-4E. Under common wing tail code concept 1972, **ZF** was adopted for squadrons. The inactive 306 TFS redesignated to 306 TFTS on 5/6/78, and reactivated on 1/7/78. Wing designation changed to 31 TTW on 30/3/81, while the 306, 307 and 309 TFS redesignated as TFTS on 1/7/83, 9/10/80 and 1/7/82. All units began conversion to the F-4D during 1981-82. The wing redesignated to 31 TFW on 1/10/85. During wing conversion to F-16A/B, the 306 TFS inactivated on 1/10/86. The 307, 308 and 309 TFS redesignated to TFS on 9/5/88, 1/10/86 and 15/4/86. Wing changed tail code from **ZF** to **HS** starting on 1/12/86, with both tail codes carried well into 1987. Wing conversion to F-16C/D started in late 1990.

33d Tactical Fighter Wing

The 33 Tactical Fighter Wing activated at Eglin AFB on 1/4/65. Initial tail coded units comprised of 4, 16, 40 TFS and 4533 TTS(T), later coded; **EB, ED, EE** and **EG**. The 33 TFW provided F-4 formation assets for six squadrons in South East Asia.

4 TFS	F-4D assets 7/67	to 433 TFS	8 TFW	**FG**
40 TFS	F-4D assets 5/67	to 555 TFS	8 TFW	**FY**
16 TFS	F-4D assets 10/67	to 13 TFS	366 TFW	**OC**
25 TFS	F-4D self 5/68	to 8 TFW	8 TFW	**FA**
40 TFS	F-4E assets 11/68	to 469 TFS	388 TFW	**JV**
16 TFS	F-4E assets 4/69	to 421 TFS	366 TFW	**LC**
4 TFS	F-4E self 4/69	to 366 TFW		**LA**
40 TFS	F-4E assets 5/69	to 34 TFS	388 TFW	**JJ**

The 4 TFS left for South East Asia and the 40 TFS inactivated in mid 1969. In 1970 the 58 TFS replaced the 16 TFS. The 4533 TTS(T) inactivated on 12/4/71, replaced by TAWC assigned 4485 TS. The F-4 usage continued after common wing tail code **ED** assigned on remaining 16 TFS. The 59 TFS became operational in July 1973. The wing tail code of **ED** changed to **EG** during October 1978. The F-15A/B replaced the F-4E during 1979. The 60 TFS joined operations early in 1979 with conversion to the F-15C/D starting in October 1984. The process halted to allow priority conversion of the 18 TFW, to proceed at Eglin AFB. The first F-15C and F-15D received within the 33 TFW, on 2/5/84 and 23/2/84.

TACTICAL AIR COMMAND - CONTINENTAL U.S.

35th Tactical Fighter Wing
35th Tactical Training Wing
35th Tactical Fighter Wing

The 35 Tactical Fighter Wing replaced the 479 TFW at George AFB, on 1/10/71. The 35 TFW has gone through three distinctive phases.

35 Tactical *Fighter* Wing	1/10/71 - 1/7/84
35 Tactical *Training* Wing	1/7/84 - 5/10/89
35 Tactical *Fighter* Wing	5/10/89 - current 31/12/90

Wing initially activated at George AFB, with all F-4 units reassigned from the inactivating 479 TFW, on 1/10/71. The units noted 4535, 4452 CCTS, 434 TFS, and 35 OMS with UH-1, coded **GA**, **GC**, **GD** and **GE**. The activated 4435 TFRS, replaced the 4546 TTS, on 35 TFW assignment date, with the **GB** tail code. Under AFM66-1 common wing tail code concept, the wing recoded **GA**. The 4535 and 4452 CCTS inactivated on 1/12/1972, with the replacement 20 and 21 TFTS activated on the same day.

The date of Base Flight folding is unknown. The 561 and 562 TFS assigned in the "Wild Weasel" role with F-105F and G on 15/7/73 and 31/10/74. The 563 TFTS assigned to the 35 TFW on 31/10/74. The 563 TFS status changed to non-operational during July 1977. The 39 TFTS also assigned in July 1977 with F-4C, F-4C (ww) then later redesignating 563 TFS. The 434 TFS redesignated to 434 TFTS, and remained non-operational until reassigned as an AT-38B unit within the 479 TTW in July 1977.

Detachment 1, 561 TFS deployed to Korat, RTAFB, with **WW** tail coded F-105G between 1/2/73 and 5/9/73. By June 1979, the wing started recoding the F-105 with **WW** tail code, thus becoming a two tail code wing. The first F-105G replacements, the F-4G, arrived on 28/4/78. The last F-105 left for Air Guard duty on 12/7/80. The F-4G equipped 39 TFS, 561, 562 TFS and 563 TFTS, all carried the **WW** tail code, with two exceptions, of **GA** tail code. The Weasel squadrons also operated **GA** tail coded F-4E, switching to **WW** codes.

The "Wild Weasel" operations passed to the co-based 37 TFW on 30/3/81. The 561, 563 TFS and 562 TFTS, reassigned to the 37 TFW. Wing redesignated on 1/7/84, to 35 Tactical Training Wing. The wing status returned to 35 Tactical Fighter Wing designation on 5/10/89, when F-4E/G "Wild Weasel" operations returned to the 35 TFW. The co-based 37 TFW designation reassigned to F-117 operations at Tonopah. Only the 561 TFS and 562 TFTS returned to the 35 TFW control with **WW** codes from the 37 TFW.

F-4F Phantom 72-1118 (*37+08*) Luftwaffe **GA**, 35 TFW George AFB, in standard German camouflage colours and pattern. Photo: Martin collection, 10 October 1973.

37th Tactical Fighter Wing

The 37 Tactical Fighter Wing previously inactivated on 31/3/70 at Phu Cat AB, RSVN. The wing reactivated on 30/3/81, with F-4E/G "Wild Weasel" assets from the co-based 35 TFW at George AFB. The 561, 563 TFS, and 562 TFTS, coded **WW** and equipped with F-4E/G. The 563 TFS inactivated, and control of the remaining assets returned to 35 TFW on 5/10/89.

Wing moved to F-117 operations at Tonopah on the same day, replacing the 4450 Tactical Group controlling F-117 operations with activated 415, 416 TFS and 417 TFTS.

F-4E Phantom 74-1048 **WW**, 37 TFW, George AFB, displaying colours of all three squadrons, red, yellow and blue, plus shadow codes and "**37 TFW**." Photo: Marty Isham, Nellis AFB, 6 May 1987.

49th Tactical Fighter Wing

The 49 Tactical Fighter Wing, based at Holloman AFB, New Mexico, tail coded F-4D of 7, 8 and 9 TFS **HB**, **HC**, and **HD** in July 1968 on return from USAFE. The 417 TFS added on 15/11/70 with **HA** tail codes, switched to the **HE** code very shortly thereafter. The 49 TFW had dual based roles to reinforce USAFE in time of conflict. Occasional deployments made to European shores to prove the "dual basing" concept.

The 49 TFW deployed to Takhli RTAFB during May 1972 with individual squadron tail codes (*see PACAF section*). Wing returned to Holloman AFB in October 1972, after AFM66-1 concept and all units recoded to **HO**. The 417 TFS inactivated in early 1973. The 49 TFW converted to the F-15A/B started with maintenance examples in June 1977.

F-4D Phantom; 66-0472 **HC**, 8 TFS; 65-603 non-standard application of **HB** tail code, 7 TFS; 66-7678 **HE**, 417 TFS all 49 TFW, with yellow, blue and red fin caps. Replacement F-4D enroute to Southeast Asia. Photo: Doug Remington, McChord AFB, 11 February 1971.

56th Tactical Fighter Wing
56th Tactical Training Wing

Prior to activation on 30/6/75 as the 56 Tactical Fighter Wing the 56 SOW flew uncoded OV-10A and CH-53, and **T_** range, tail coded A-1 up until 30/6/75, from Nakhon Phanom RTAFB. Wing redesignated and transferred to MacDill AFB, on 30/6/75 with F-4 assets reassigned from the 1 TFW. The 1 TFW along with 27, 71 and 94 TFS moved to Langley AFB, to convert to F-15A/B.

The 56 TFW assumed the 61, 62, 63 TFS and 4501 TFRS. The **MC** tail code adopted by wing F-4. The 4501 TFRS inactivated during early 1976 and replaced by the 13 TFTS. The 56 TFW converted from the F-4E to F-4D between 5/10/77 and 29/9/78. Further re-equipment in the form of F-16A/B, occurred between 22/10/79 and 1/7/82. Along with the F-16A/B the wing changed role, reflected by redesignating 56 Tactical Training Wing, on 1/7/82. The 72 TFTS replaced the 13 TFTS in mid 1981. The wing redesignated to 56 Tactical Training Wing on 1/10/81, components had redesignated TFTS. Wing further converted to F-16C/D in 1989.

57th Fighter Weapons Wing
57th Tactical Training Wing
57th Fighter Weapons Wing

The 57 Fighter Weapons Wing activated on 15/10/69, assuming control of the former 4525 FWW units at Nellis AFB. Flying units 4536, 4537, 4538 and 4539 CCTS, flew F-100, F-105, F-4 and F-111, with tail codes **WB**, **WC**, **WD** and **WF**. All four unit replaced by 65, 66, 414 and 422 FWS on 15/10/69 while maintaining assets and tail codes. The 4525 FWW originally assigned **WA** as wing tail code in addition to individual squadron codes (*detachments used* **WA** *tail code*). The **WA** tail code appeared in wing use during October 1971, rather than the normal TAC standard of June 1972.

Wing redesignated to 57 Tactical Training Wing, on 1/4/77, and further redesignating back to 57 Fighter Weapons Wing on 1/3/80. Throughout the wing name change many redesignation and a variety of equipment changes occurred at the squadron levels. On 30/12/81 the 66, 414, 433 FWS inactivated with assigned equipment of A-10, F-4, F-15 to the like named divisions of USAF Fighter Weapons School.

Detachments of 57 FWW (*TTW/FWW*) activated on need, at sites away from home base. There have been numerous detachment numbers repeated for different operations at different times. Often, tail codes of the site adopted. The larger confirmed, documented and unclassified detachments are listed in text. Detachment 1, progressed through **LA** and **DM** tail coded A-7D and **LF** tail coded F-16. Detachment 2, started at Cannon AFB with **CC** tail coded F-111 and continued with **MO** at Mountain Home AFB (also used **NA** coded F-111A with standard black and yellow fin caps). A term also served at Edward AFB, with unknown types. Detachment 3, started at Mountain Home AFB, between 15/8/71 and 1/5/72, moving to Nellis AFB, between 1/8/77 and 15/8/77, then on to McClellan AFB on 15/8/77. Replaced by the F-111 equipped 431 FWS, on 1/10/80 and redesignated 431 TES on 1/6/81. A Detachment 16 operated from Hill AFB including foreign **HL** tail coded F-16. The F-15 operated with Det 1/HQ USAF Tactical Fighter Weapons Center, Operating Location AA at Luke AFB.

TACTICAL AIR COMMAND - CONTINENTAL U.S.

F-5E Tiger 72-1386 **WA**, 65 AS 57 FWW, Nellis AFB, with black and yellow checkered tail stripe. Photo: Patrick Martin, 9 January 1989.

A-7D Corsair 71-0295 **WA**, 57 FWW, Nellis AFB, with black and yellow checkered tail stripe. Photo: Don Larsen, 17 May 1973.

58th Tactical Fighter Training Wing
58th Tactical Training Wing

The 58 Tactical Fighter Training Wing initially activated on 15/10/69 with 4510 CCTW F-100 assets of 4511, 4514, 4515, and 4517 CCTS, coding **LA** and the F-5 of 4441 CCTS coded **LZ**. All F-100 carried the wing assigned tail code of **LA**. The 4514 CCTS inactivated on 15/12/69, replaced by the 310 TFTS forming on the same day. The 4511, 4515, and 4517 CCTS followed on 18/1/70, replaced by 311, 426 and 550 TFTS. The 310 TFTS flew A-7D before joining the 426 and 550 TFTS flying the F-4C. The F-5 operations at Williams AFB, carried the **LZ** tail code until late 1974, when switched to **LA** wing standard.

Units not intending F-16 conversion including 425, 461 and 550 TFTS transferred to newly activated, co-based 405 TFTW, and maintained the **LA** tail code. The 58 TFTW recoded **LF**, on 1/1/83 operating F-16, although some aircraft received and tail coded before the official date. The 310 and 311 TFTS converted to F-16A/B with **LF** tail code. The 312 and 314 TFTS added with **LF** tail coded F-16C/D.

TAIL CODE

64th Tactical Airlift Wing

The 64 Tactical Airlift Wing tail coded C-130E operations during 1968 at Sewart AFB in the **S** range. The two assigned units 61 and 62 TAS, tail coded **ST** and **SR**. The 64 TAW moved to Little Rock AFB, on 9/3/70. The 64 TAW inactivated on 31/5/71, with the 314 TAW assuming assets and maintaining tail codes.

67th Tactical Reconnaissance Wing

The 67 Tactical Reconnaissance Wing flew three RF-4C squadrons and one F-4D squadron, when the **K** range codes applied in July 1968. The 7, 10, 22 TRS applied tail codes **KT**, **KR**, **KS** and the F-4D of the 417 TFS coded **KB** at Mountain Home AFB. The 417 TFS reassigned to Holloman AFB, late in 1970 and the 10 TRS inactivated during June 1971.

On 15/7/71, the 67 TRW, reassigned to Bergstrom AFB, and replaced the inactivating 75 TFW. The former 75 TRW units 4, 9, and 91 TRS maintained the tail codes **BB**, **BC** and **BA** within the 67 TRW. The 22 TRS did not follow 67 TRW to Bergstrom AFB inactivating on 15/7/71. The 7 TRS moved with the wing maintaining the **KT** tail code until inactivated during October 1971 with the 4 TRS. After the 67 TRW move the 12 and 45 TRS replaced the 9 and 4 TRS, during August and October 1971, maintaining **BC** and **BB** tail code. All remaining squadrons (12, 45 *and* 91 TRS) recoded to **BA** under the AFM66-1 common wing tail code concept. The 62 TRTS assigned from 363 TRW, at Shaw AFB, in July 1982.

68th Tactical Air Support Group

The 68 TASG controlled the **VA** tail coded 703 SOS CH-3 operations, between initial coding and reassignment to 507 TAIRCW. The 68 TASG inactivating on 15/1/70.

75th Tactical Reconnaissance Wing

The 75 Tactical Reconnaissance Wing controlled three RF-4C squadrons on initial coding of components during July 1968. The 4, 9, and 91 TRS tail coded RF-4C **BB**, **BC** and **BA** at Bergstrom AFB. The 75 TRW inactivated on 15/7/71, with the 67 TRW assuming control, and maintaining tail codes.

313th Tactical Airlift Wing

The 313 Tactical Airlift Wing activated at Forbes AFB, on 1/10/64. The C-130 operator, 47 TAS tail coded **FB** in July 1968. The 38 TAS assigned from the 316 TAW, and coded **FH** on 1/10/69. The 48 TAS replaced the 38 TAS on 15/11/71, and assumed the **FB** tail code. Under the AFM66-1 concept the 48 TAS also adopted the **FB** tail code as a wing standard. The 47 TAS reassigned to the 463 TAW in July 1973, while the 48 TAS inactivated on 6/8/73, followed by the wing on 30/9/73.

314th Tactical Airlift Wing

The 314 Tactical Airlift Wing ceased operations at Ching Chuan Kang AB, Taiwan on 31/5/71. On that date, the 314 TAW reassigned to Little Rock AFB, replacing the 64 TAW controlling the 61 and 62 TAS with **ST** and **SR** tail codes. The 16 TATS, with **TE** tail codes added in June 1971, from the inactivating 4442 CCTW. Under the AFM66-1 common wing tail code concept, the 61 and 62 TAS recoded C-130 aircraft to **LK** during 1972. The 32, 48 and 50 TAS added further **LK** tail coded C-130 to the wing during August and September 1973.

316th Tactical Airlift Wing

The 316 Tactical Airlift Wing activated at Langley AFB on 25/11/65, with C-130E operations beginning in April 1966. The 36, 37 and 38 TAS assigned between 1966 and 1967. Tail codes **LM**, **LN** and **LO** assigned on 10/7/68. The 38 TAS reassigned to the 313 TAW and recoded **FH** between 1/7/69 and 15/11/71. All units recoding to **LM** under common wing tail codes in 1972.

317th Tactical Airlift Wing

The 317 Tactical Airlift Wing assigned to Lockbourne AFB from USAFE on 20/6/64. In July 1968 the 39 and 40 TAS tail coded C-130 **OA** and **OB**. The C-123 equipped the 4408 CCTS with **OD** tail codes reassigned from 1 SOW on 22/9/71, inactivating during 1971. The 317 TAW moved to Pope AFB, on 31/8/71 taking the place of the 464 TAW. Assets and tail codes **PB** and **PG** absorbed from the 777 and 778 TAS. In addition, the 41 TAS activated and adopted the **PR** tail code with assets from the 779 TFS. The AFM66-1 common wing tail code concept assigned the **PB** tail code to 39, 40 and 41 TAS during 1972.

325th Tactical Training Wing

Formerly titled, 325 Fighter Wing (*Air Defense*) and 325 Fighter Weapons Wing, the wing redesignated to 325 Tactical Training Wing on 1/10/83. Controls the F-15A/B training mission at Tyndall AFB. The former 2 FWS, also redesignated on the same date to 2 TFTS. Two further units, the 1 TFTS activated and assigned on 1/1/84, while the 95 FITS redesignated 95 TFTS on 1/4/84. All three squadrons operate **TY** tail coded F-15A/B.

347th Tactical Fighter Wing

The 347 Tactical Fighter Wing moved from Yokota AB, Japan, (**G_** range F-4C) to Mountain Home AFB, on 15/5/71. Flight operations commenced with factory fresh F-111F. The 391 TFS transferred to the 347 TFW to fly **MO** coded F-111F in June 1971. This was followed by the 4589 TFS on 1/9/71 and the 4590 TFS on 1/1/72 with **MP** and **MQ** tail coded F-111F. The latter two squadrons assigned as provisional units, pending transfer of 389 and 390 TFS under the 12 and 366 TFW, in South East Asia with F-4, on 15/10/71 and 30/6/72. All three units adopted the **MO** tail code under the common wing tail code concept in mid 1972. The 366 TFW replaced the 347 TFW at Mountain Home AFB on 30/10/72.

The 347 TFW reactivated at Takhli RTAFB on 30/7/73, assuming control of the former 474 TFW deployed F-111A units from Nellis AFB. The 347 Tactical Fighter Wing previously based at Korat RTAFB until 30/9/75 when reassigned to Moody AFB. Initial assigned F-4E equipped units 68 and 70 TFS, adopted the common wing tail code **MY**. The 339 TFS joined flying operations by 4/5/76, inactivating on 1/9/83 and replaced by the 69 TFS. The 347 TFW converting to F-16A/B and completed F-16C/D conversion in December 1990.

354th Tactical Fighter Wing

The 354 Tactical Fighter Wing moved, without personnel or equipment, from Kunsan AB, ROK, and replaced the 4554 TFW at Myrtle Beach on 15/6/70. Initial tail coded units included the 511 TFS, tail coded **MR**. The 4430 CCTS also assigned but tail code

TACTICAL AIR COMMAND - CONTINENTAL U.S.

details unknown. The 356 and 355 TFS coded **MN**, and **MB**, assigned during 1970 and 1971. The 511 TFS replaced by the 353 TFS on 15/7/71 maintaining the **MR** tail code. Under the AFM66-1 common wing tail code concept the 353, 355 and 356 TFS recoded to **MB**. The 4554 TFRS assigned between 1972 and 1975, also with A-7D.

After wing common tail code the 354 TFW divided into two elements in October 1972. The first went to Korat RTAFB, and the second remained at Myrtle Beach AFB. Other units attached to the 354 TFW during the South East Asia deployment. The A-7D gave way to the much larger A-10A starting on 9/3/77 with the first example for maintenance training. The three remaining squadrons 353, 355 and 356 TFS re-equipped and declared operational by August 1978.

355th Tactical Fighter Wing

The 355 Tactical Fighter Wing reactivated at Davis-Monthan AFB, on 1/7/71. The 355 TFW previously inactivated at Takhli RTAFB on 10/12/70. The original A-7D operations transferred from Luke AFB under the 58 TFTW. A switch of units took place in which the 355 TFW, at Davis-Monthan AFB operated the A-7D, replacing the 4453 CCTW. The wing operated the F-4C in the training role and inactivated on 30/9/71. After a period of dual control, the F-4C training role transferred to the 58 TFTW at Luke AFB. Units assumed by 355 TFW on 1/7/71 including the 11 Tactical Drone Squadron, 354 and 357 TFS with **DF**, **DA** and **DC** tail codes. The 40 and 333 TFS assigned in October and July 1971 with tail codes **DD** and **DM** with A-7D. The last F-4C operated between 1/10/71 and 8/10/71 (*attached*). The 358 TFS replaced the 40 TFS in June 1972. All units adopted the **DM** tail code under common wing tail code during 1972. During 1973-74, the 354 and 358 TFS deployed to Korat RTAFB, under the 354 TFW control, utilizing the **MB** tail code for deployment. The A-7D gave way to the large A-10A, starting with the first A-10A on 14/2/76. The wing redesignated to the 355 Tactical Fighter Training Wing in September 1979.

363d Tactical Reconnaissance Wing
363d Tactical Fighter Wing

Shaw AFB has been the hub of reconnaissance activity within Tactical Air Command for many years. The 363 Tactical Reconnaissance Wing comprised of 4414, 4415, 4417 CCTS and 29 TRS flying RF-101, RF-4C, RB-66 and RF-101 with **JK**, **JL**, **JN** and **JO** tail codes during 1968. The inactivated 4416 TES, also assigned the **JM** tail code. The CCTS units redesignated to 31, 33, and 39 TRTS in October 1969. The 39 TRTS further redesignated to 39 TEWTS in 1970. The 18 TRS with **JP** tail coded RF-101 assigned in 1970. In 1971 the 16 TRS and 22 TRS, flying **JM** and **JO** tail coded RF-101 also assigned. The 62 TRS replaced the 22 TRS maintained **JO** tail code, until inactivating itself on 1/7/71. The 31 TRTS inactivated on 18/2/71. Under the AFM66-1 wing common tail code concept, the remaining assigned units; 16, 18, 62 TRS and 33 TRTS recoded to **JO**, named after the Chief of Maintenance's wife! The 18 TRS and 33 TRTS inactivated on 30/9/79 and 1/10/82. The wing redesignated to 363 Tactical Fighter Wing on 1/10/81, with wing tail code changed, officially to **SW** on 1/10/82, although aircraft noted with **JO** tails codes as late as 3/2/83. The only RF-4C equipped, 16 TRS recoded to **SW**. The first four **SW** coded F-16A arrived for wing maintenance training on 26/3/82, in company of a **SW** coded RF-4C, with bulk deliveries in June 1982. New units 17 and 19 TFS activated in July and April 1982 with F-16A/B. The wing further converted to F-16C/D during 1985 and 1986, with a third squadron, the 33 TFS, added in early 1985, with F-16C/D.

366th Tactical Fighter Wing

The 366 Tactical Fighter Wing moved from Takhli RTAFB, to Mountain Home AFB, on 31/10/72, assuming control of the former 347 TFW F-111 assets. The assumed squadrons 389, 390 and 391 TFS, maintained the **MO** tail code. Under "Ready Switch" all converted from F-111F to F-111A. The F-111F reassigned to the 48 TFW at RAF Lakenheath, while the former 48 TFW F-4D moved to the 474 TFW operations at Nellis AFB. The Nellis AFB F-111A transferred to 366 TFW at Mountain Home to complete the triangle movement. The 388 TFS added during 1977, converting to EF-111A and redesignated to 388 ECS, in 1981. The role then passed to redesignated 390 ECS in 1984. The 389 TFS redesignated TFTS in 1979.

F-111F 70-2366 **MO**, 366 TFW, Mountain Home AFB, with bi-centennial markings. Photo: Jim Meehan, unknown location, March 1979.

388th Tactical Fighter Wing

The 388 Tactical Fighter Wing title reassigned from Korat RTAFB to Hill AFB on 23//12/75 to control F-4D assets. The three assigned squadrons 4, 34 and 421 TFS, F-4D and adopted the tail code **HL**. F-16A/B conversion started on 6/1/79. The 16 TFTS, added during 1980, redesignating 16 TFS 1983, and inactivated during 1986. Further conversion to F-16C/D models completed in mid 1990.

405th Tactical Training Wing

The 405 Tactical Training Wing activated at Luke AFB, during August 1979, assuming the 58 TFTW assets not slated for F-16 conversion. Initial noted coded units 425, 461, 550 and 555 TFTS. The 426 TFTS assigned in 1981. All components maintained **LA** tail code while, the 58 TTW adopted the **LF** tail code on 1/1/83. The first F-15E model received during April 1988.

463d Tactical Airlift Wing

The 463 Tactical Airlift Wing activated at Dyess AFB, on 1/6/72, replacing the 516 TAW. Previously the 463 TAW, inactivated at Clark AB, Philippines on 31/12/71. All squadrons carried the **DB** tail code as activation occurred after the common wing tail code concept in mid 1972. Three units initially activated 772, 773 TAS and 18 TATS. A fourth unit, the 47 TAS assigned in July 1973, and replaced by the 774 TAS, in August 1973. The 463 TAW maintained the **DB** tail code until the MAC transfer of TAC airlift assets on 1/12/74. The wing aircraft carried four colours, as flight colours, thereby making squadron identification impossible.

464th Tactical Airlift Wing

The 464 Tactical Airlift Wing based at Pope AFB, started flying the C-130 during 1963. Assigned airlift squadron 777, 778 and 779 TAS, tail coded **PB**, **PG** and **PR** in July 1968. The 464 TAW was replaced by 317 TAW on 31/8/71, from Lockbourne with 39 and 40 TAS, plus 41 TAS from 374 TAW maintaining 464 TAW codes.

474th Tactical Fighter Wing

The 474 Tactical Fighter Wing activated from the assets of the 4525 CCTW at Nellis AFB on 20/1/68, before code application. The 4527 CCTS activated during January 1968. The 428 and 429 TFS designations arrived in July 1968 and the 430 TFS in October 1968, all with F-111A. Units coded **ND**, **NA**, **NB**, and **NC** starting in July 1968. Under common wing tail code concept, all components recoded with the **NA** tail code in mid 1972.

The 474 TFW deployed to Takhli RTAFB, leaving a rear echelon at Nellis AFB. The 430 TFS returned to Nellis AFB, on 22/3/73. The 428 and 429 detached on 23/3/73 and assigned on 30/7/73 to the newly activated 347 TFW, at Takhli RTAFB. Both units returned to 474 TFW control on 15/6/75, from Korat RTAFB (*347 TFW moved 12/7/74*). The 474 TFW converted to F-4D under "Ready Switch." The wing further converted to F-16A/B in early 1982. The 474 TFW inactivated in 1988.

479th Tactical Fighter Wing

The 479 Tactical Fighter Wing started flying the F-4 in 1965, at George AFB. The initial assignment of codes and actual application, provided a very complex set of circumstances. Tail codes initially assigned in 1968 within the 479 TFW include 68, 431, 434, 476 TFS and 4452 CCTS, coded **GA**, **GB**, **GC**, **GD** and **GE**.

The **GA** tail code not taken up by the 68 TFS, as unit reassigned before initial tail code application date. The **GA** tail code, taken up by 4535 CCTS as initial usage in October 1968. The 476 TFS did not carry the assigned **GD** tail code, as the squadron inactivated during September 1968. The now vacated **GD** tail code assumed by the 434 TFS after the **GC** tail code used for a short period. The **GC** code applied to the 4452 CCTS rather than the initial assigned **GE**. The **GE** tail code taken up by Base Flight. The inactive 436 TFS assigned between 30/10 and 8/3/71.

The 4546 TTS, assigned to the 479 TFW, flew F-4 with a red and white checked fin cap, along with **GB** tail code, vacated by the 431 TFS, inactivation in May 1970. The 4546 TTS, not listed by official sources, assigned between 1970 and 1971. On 1/10/71, the 35 TFW replaced the 479 TFW, at George AFB. All remaining coded units reassigned to the 35 TFW, while the 479 TFW inactivated.

The 479 TFW redesignated to 479 Tactical Training Wing, on 22/10/76, while inactive. The 479 TFTW reactivated on 1/1/77, at Holloman AFB, replacing the 4479 TFTW (*Provisional*) operating **HM** tail coded AT-38B in the advance tactical training role. Three squadrons initially activated 434, 435 and 436 TFTS and tail coded **HM**. The 465 TFTS assigned post 1977, and replaced by the 416 TFTS on 14/3/79, which in turn replaced by the 433 TFTS, on 1/9/83, all maintaining the **HM** tail code.

507th Tactical Air Control Wing

The 507 TAIRCW controlled the 703 TASS flying **VA** tail coded CH-3 on 15/1/70, replacing the 68 TASG. The 703 SOS redesignated to 703 TASS on the same day. Squadron recoded to **SR** before inactivating on 26/5/85. The 21 TASS tail coded assigned OT-37B **SR** in 1986. Equipment changed to OV-10A in October 1988. The 20 TASS added in 1990 with further **SR** tail coded OV-10A.

516th Tactical Airlift Wing

The 516 Tactical Airlift Wing operated the C-130 from Dyess AFB, starting in July 1963. Three squadrons 346, 347 and 348 TAS, tail coded **DB**, **DY** and **DZ**, formed the initial complement. The 4449 CCTS, flying C-7 assigned on 27/8/69, with **TD** tail codes, replaced on 15/10/69, by the 18 TATS. The 346 TAS reassigned to 374 TAW, at Ching Chuan Kang AB, Taiwan, in March 1969. The 516 TAW inactivated on 1/6/72, replaced by the 463 TAW, which previously inactivated at Clark AB, Philippines, on 31/12/71. The 347 and 348 TAS inactivated with the 516 TAW, on 1/6/72.

602d Tactical Air Control Wing

The 602 Tactical Air Control Wing (*TAIRCW*) initially activated as 602 Tactical Control Group on 1/3/66 and redesignated 602 Tactical Air Control Wing on 1/10/76. The wing had numerous ground based sub elements, as well as flying units with uncoded O-1E and OV-10 assets from various bases. The 602 TAIRCW assigned to Davis-Monthan AFB on 1/9/82, controlled the 27 TASS flying **VV** tail coded OV-10A from George AFB between 1984 and 1990. The 23 TASS assigned in 1981, flying **NF** coded OA-37 until March 1988, adding OA-10A in 1987. The 22 TASTS activated within the 602 TAIRCW flying **NF** coded OV-10A and OA-10A in the training role.

834th Tactical Composite Wing

The USAF Special Operations Force merged with the 1 SOW, resulting in the 834 Tactical Composite Wing title on 1 July 1974. One year later, on 1 July 1975, the wing redesignated back to the 1 Special Operations Wing. All details noted in the 1 SOW entry of **AH** tail code.

TACTICAL AIR COMMAND - CONTINENTAL U.S.

4403d Tactical Fighter Wing
The 4403 TFW assigned as the tenant wing at England AFB, between 15/9/70 and 1/7/72. The wing absorbed the returning Tactical Fighter Squadrons from the 31 TFW at Tuy Hoa AB, RSVN. Units assigned for a short period before reassignment to the 31 TFW, on wing return to Homestead AFB, replacing existing F-4E squadrons. The F-100 assets transferred to ANG units. It is unknown if tail codes officially assigned or perhaps carried on from 31 TFW application at Tuy Hoa AB, RSVN. Units noted:

SD	306 TFS	28/9/70 - 30/10/70	to 31 TFW replacing 436 TFS with ZD F-4E
SE	416 TFS	28/9/70 - 1/4/72	
SM	308 TFS	5/10/70 - 30/10/70	to 31 TFW replacing 560 TFS with ZF F-4E
SS	309 TFS	5/10/70 - 30/10/70	to 31 TFW replacing 478 TFS with ZE F-4E

The 416 TFS maintained as a paper unit until 1/7/72, as holding unit for a 23 TFW, activated A-7D squadron. The 68 TFS assigned with unknown status on 30/10/70, formerly flying **ZG** tail coded F-4E within the 4531 TFW. The 23 TFW arrived from McConnell AFB, replaced the 4403 TFW on 1/7/72. The 4403 TFW inactivating on 1/7/72.

4410th Combat Crew Training Wing
4410th Special Operations Training Group
The 4410 Combat Crew Training Wing coded four components on 10/7/68. Tail codes **AD, AO, AP** and **AQ** assigned to 4407, 4408, 4409 and 4410 CCTS, flying A-1, C-123, UH-1 and T-28. On 15/7/69, the 4410 CCTW and England AFB based 1 SOW, switched bases and components. The 4410 CCTW, adopted the former 1 SOW, **I** range tail codes. All four initially **A** coded, units passed to the 1 SOW on 15/7/69. The **I** ranged tail coded components gained in the switch noted 71, 317, 319 ACS, 4406, 4412, 4413, and 4532 CCTS, with tail codes **IC, ID, IE, IJ, IG, IH,** and **II**. These units flew A-37, C-47, C-119, C-123 and C-130. The Air Commando Squadron redesignated to Special Operations Squadron shortly after the initial tail code assignment on 10/7/68. The 514 AS, flying A-37, added later with **IK** tail codes, replaced by 6 SOTS, with **IJ** tail codes. The 6 SOTS inactivating during January 1974. The 317 SOS inactivated in April 1970, and the 319 SOS recoded to **AG** tail codes and returned to the 1 SOW 16 days later. The 427 SOTS replaced the 4406 CCTS on 1/7/70, inactivated itself on 15/7/72. The 415 SOTS replaced the 4413 CCTS, and later reassigned to 1 SOW and tail coded **AH**. Inactivation dates of the 71 SOS and 4412 CCTS are unknown. The 4410 CCTW redesignated to 4410 Special Operations Training Group on 15/9/70 and inactivated on 31/7/73. The remaining tail coded unit, 6 SOTS reassigned to 1 SOW on wing inactivation.

4442d Combat Crew Training Wing
The 4442 Combat Crew Training Wing at Sewart AFB, operated C-130E in the training role. The **TS** tail code assigned on 10/7/68 to formations 4446, 4447 and 4449 CCTS (*the formation dates are unknown, 4448 CCTS existence is also unconfirmed, possible ground training unit*). The 4447 CCTS inactivating on 1/3/69, while the 4446 and 4449 CCTS inactivated on 9/3/70 when the wing moved to Little Rock AFB. Assets used to form the 16 TATS with **TE** tail code. The 4442 CCTW inactivated on 1/8/71, with the 16 TATS reassigned to the co-based 314 TAW, retaining the **TE** tail code.

4450th Tactical Group
The 4450 Tactical Group was activated on 15/10/79 to control F-117 operations and associate function units. The 4451 Test Squadron equipped with A-7 from the 23 TFW staring in May 1981. Further examples of A-7D and A-7K added by December 1981. The 4451 Test Squadron tail coded assigned A-7 **LV** by late 1984 until 1988, when A-7 reassigned to ANG units. Group inactivated and replaced by the 37 TFW on 5/10/89.

4453d Combat Crew Training Wing
The 4453 Combat Crew Training Wing operated as an F-4 training wing at Davis-Monthan AFB when tail coding TAC assets began. Wing common tail code **DM** assigned on 10/7/68. The 4453 CCTW units 4454, 4455 and 4456 CCTS flew F-4 while the 4472 SS(SPA) operated the DC-130A drone carrier.

The F-4 operations reassigned to the 58 TFTW at Luke AFB. The switch brought A-7D to Davis-Monthan AFB. The 4453 CCTW F-4C assets used to form the 310, 426 and 550 TFTS at Luke AFB. Wing operated alongside the 355 TFW (*actually the same personnel*) between 355 TFW activation on 1/7/71 and 4453 CCTW inactivation on 30/9/71.

4510th Combat Crew Training Wing
The 4510 Combat Crew Training Wing assigned the **LA** tail code at Luke AFB on 10/7/68. All based components tail coded **LA**. The F-100 equipped 4511, 4514, 4515 and 4517 CCTS reassigned to the 58 TTW, on 15/10/69. The Williams AFB assigned 4441 CCTS redesignated to 425 TFTS on transfer to 58 TFW, maintaining the separately assigned **LZ** tail code.

F-100F Super Sabre 56-3776 **LA**, 4510 CCTW, Luke AFB. Photo: Tom Waller, Reese AFB, summer 1968.

4525th Fighter Weapons Wing

The 4525 Fighter Weapons Wing activated on 1/9/66 to control four Nellis AFB assigned Combat Crew Training Squadrons. During initial coding of units on 10/7/68 the 4536, 4537, 4538 and 4539 CCTS flying F-100, F-105, F-4 and F-111, tail coded **WB**, **WC**, **WD** and **WF**. In addition the 4525 FWW was assigned the **WA** tail code for use on detachments. The 57 FWW replaced the 4525 FWW on 15/10/69 with all units carrying a black yellow checkered tail stripe.

4531st Tactical Fighter Wing

During the 31 TFW tenure in South East Asia, starting in 1966, the 4531 Tactical Fighter Wing was assigned as the tenant unit at Homestead AFB, flying F-4C with conversion to F-4D starting on 8/2/67 and F-4E on 13/11/68. Components 68, 436, 478 and 560 TFS, tail coded **ZG**, **ZD**, **ZE** and **ZF**. Noted F-4 deployments from the 4531 TFW to locations in South East Asia include:

ZG	68 TFS	354 TFW	F-4E	20/6/69 - 9/12/69
ZF	560 TFS	354 TFW	F-4D	23/6/69 - 17/12/69
ZE	478 TFS	354 TFW	F-4E	21/5/70 - 15/6/70
ZE	478 TFS	54 TFW	F-4E	15/6/70 - 2/9/70

Four component squadrons assigned to the 31 TFW on return from Tuy Hoa AB, RSVN on 15/10/70.

*Special Note: The 516 TAW **DY**, **DZ**: The TET offensive in 1968 necessitated CONUS C-130 assets moving to South East Asia and the Far East for deployments. Initial contributions; Dyess AFB - 347 TAS tail code **DY**, Langley AFB - 38 TAS tail code **LO**, and Pope AFB - 779 TAS, tail code **PR**, sent in February 1968. Units from the Dyess AFB, 516 TAW commitment did not rotate squadron-for-squadron with aircraft as other wings did. The initial 347 TAS personnel replaced by 348 TAS in September/October 1968 (*aircraft not involved in transfer*). The 347 TAS crews went back to Dyess AFB and operated the former 348 TAS aircraft. Thus the **DY** tail coded C-130E were flown by 348 crews in CONUS while 348 TAS personnel flew **DZ** tail coded C-130E in Southeast Asia. To further complicate matters, in December 1968 the 346 TAS personnel rotated to Southeast Asia to operate the **DY** tail coded C-130E. In the same period the 348 TAS crews operated the 346 TAS **DB** tail coded aircraft from Dyess AFB. The last step was the 346 personnel taking the **DY** tail coded aircraft PCS (*permanent change of station*) to Ching Chuan Kang AB, Taiwan on 15/3/69 as part of the 314 TAW.

TACTICAL AIR COMMAND - CONTINENTAL U.S.

Squadron/Code Summary TAC - CONUS

AA
7 Special Operations Flight - (Detachment 1)　　　　　　　　　　　　　　　**1 Special Operations Wing**
　　Otis AFB, Massachusetts

C-47	1/7/69 - 1/4/70
UC-123K	1/7/69 - 31/5/72
U-10B	1/7/69 - 1971

　　Activated from Detachment 1, 1 SOW. Blue maintained as flight colour on some **AA** tail coded C-47, C-123 and U-10. Maintained by 1 SOW on component switch with 4410 CCTW on 15/7/69. Inactivated on 31/5/72. Possible tail code not allocated until 15/7/69, as **A** range codes assigned to 4410 CCTW, before 15/7/69.

U-10B Super Courier 63-8091 **AA**, Detachment 1 - 1 SOW, with blue fin cap. Photo: Tom Brewer, Eglin AFB, 23 August 1971, unknown location.

AB
Detachment 2　　　　　　　　　　　　　　　　　　　　　　　　　　　　　　**1 Special Operations Wing**
C-130E　　　　　　　　　　15/7/69 - 15/11/71　　　　　　　　　　　　　　　　**Pope AFB, North Carolina**

　　Tail code assigned to Detachment 2, 1 SOW, maintained until redesignated to 318 SOS on 15/11/71.

AB
318 Special Operations Squadron　　　　　　　　　　　　　　　　　　　　　　**1 Special Operations Wing**
C-130E　　　　　　　　　　15/11/71 - 1/6/74　　　　　　　　　　　　　　　　　**Pope AFB, North Carolina**

　　Activated to replace Detachment 2, 1 SOW on 15/11/71, formerly carried the **IB** tail code. Assumed C-130E assets and brown squadron colour, inactivating on 1/6/74.

AD
4407 Combat Crew Training Squadron　　　　　10/7/68* - 15/7/69　　　　　**4410 Combat Crew Training Wing**
　　　　　　　　　　　　　　　　　　　　　　　　15/7/69 - 30/4/73　　　　　　**1 Special Operations Wing**
　　　　　　　　　　　　　　　　　　　　　　　　　　　　　　　　　　　　　　　Hurlburt Field, Florida

A-1E/G/H	10/7/68* - 1972*
T-28D	1969 - 1972*

　　Activated within the 441606 CCTW on 1/12/67 and tail coded **AD** in July 1968. Reassigned from the 4410 CCTW on 15/7/69, when the 1 SOW moved to Hurlburt Field. Equipped with A-1G when assigned to 4410 CCTW. Recoded to **AH** common wing tail code in 1972. Green noted as squadron colour.

AF
603 Special Operations Squadron　　　　　　　　　　　　　　　　　　　　　　**1 Special Operations Wing**
　　　　　　　　　　　　　　　　　　　　　　　　　　　　　　　　　　　　　　　Hurlburt Field, Florida

A-26	15/7/69 - 15/5/71
A-37B	15/7/69 - 15/5/71*

　　Recoded **AF** as 1 SOW switched to **A** range, tail codes from **I** range during wing switch on 15/7/69. Squadron inactivated on 15/5/71, with assets transferring to AFRES units.

A-37B Dragonfly 68-10824 **AF**, 603 SOS 1 SOW, Hurlburt Field. Photo: Doug Remington, Langley AFB, 7 May 1970.

AG
319 Special Operations Squadron   **1 Special Operations Wing**
C-123K   **30/7/69 - 15/1/72**   **Hurlburt Field, Florida**

Operated up until 15/7/69 within the 1 SOW flying C-123, with **IE** tail code when reassigned with tail code to the 4410 CCTW. The squadron returned 16 days later as 319 SOS, operating **AG** tail coded C-123, U-10A and uncoded O-1 and A-262 until inactivated on 15/1/72. Orange noted as squadron colour.

C-123K Provider 54-0635 **AG**, 319 SOS 1 SOW, Hurlburt Field, with partial very faded orange fin cap. Photo: Doug Remington, Langley AFB, 7 May 1970.

AH
415 Special Operations Training Squadron   **1 Special Operations Wing**
                                                                   Hurlburt Field, Florida

AC-119G	**15/7/71 - pre 1972***
AC-119K	**15/7/71 - 1972***
AC-130A	**15/7/71 - 1972***

The 415 SOTS previously carried the **IH** tail code within the 4410 SOTG at Lockbourne AFB. Recoded to **AH** and moved to Hurlburt Field on 15/7/71. Under AFM66-1, **AH** maintained as wing common tail code.

TACTICAL AIR COMMAND - CONTINENTAL U.S.

AC-119K Flying Boxcar 53-7839 **AH**, 415 SOTS 1 SOW, Hurlburt Field. Photo: Tom Brewer, 6 February 1972.

AH
1 Special Operations Wing	1972* - 1/7/74
834 Tactical Composite Wing	1/7/74 - 1/7/75
1 Special Operations Wing	1/7/75 - by 1980

Hurlburt Field, Florida

16 Special Operations Squadron
AC-130H	12/12/75 - by 1980

Squadron reassigned from the 8 TFW, at Kunsan AB, ROK, to Hurlburt Field. Activate with AC-130H on 12/12/75. Tail code usage is unconfirmed as codes were generally removed from AC-130 before formation date.

20 Special Operations Squadron
UH-1N	1/1/76 - by 1980
CH-3E	1/1/76 - by 1980

Activated within the 1 SOW on 1/1/76 flying UH-1N and CH-3E. Codes dropped by helicopters by 1980.

317 Special Operations Squadron
C-123K	1972* - 1973
UH-1N/P	1972* - 24/6/71
A-1E/G/H	1972* - 26/10/72
T-28D	1972* - 30/4/74
CH-3E	1972* - 4/74

Recoded from **AO** under common wing tail code. Inactivated on 30/4/74, with red noted as squadron colour.

415 Special Operations Training Squadron
AC-119K	1972* - 26/10/72
AC-130A	1972* - 30/6/75

Under AFM66-1, **AH** maintained as wing common tail code. Red noted as squadron colour. Squadron inactivated on 30/6/75.

AC-130A Hercules 54-1630 **AH**, 415 SOTS 1 SOW, Hurlburt Field. Photo: Ken Buchanan, Eglin AFB, September 1972.

547 Tactical Air Support Training Squadron
U-10   1972* - 30/4/75
   Squadron previously tail coded **AQ** within the 1 SOW. Also flew uncoded types O-1E, U-10A and UH-1F/P. Unconfirmed code usage on UH-1F/P. Red noted as the squadron colour.

549 Tactical Air Support Training Squadron
UH-1F/P   1972* - 15/12/75
   The 549 TASTS previously tail coded **AP** within the 1 SOW. Red used as squadron colour on UH-1 and uncoded OV-10A. Squadron recoded to **FL** tail code on transfer to Patrick AFB and redesignated to 549 TASTG on 15/12/75. Possibly the OV-10A tail coded before unit moved.

603 Special Operations Training Squadron
C-47   1/7/73 - 1/7/74
   Squadron inactivated on 1/7/74 as the 603 SOTS flying **IF** tail coded A-37B until 15/5/71. Reactivated as the 603 SOTS on 1/7/73 to train C-47 MAP crews, flying **AH** coded C-47 from 1/7/73 until 1/7/74. Red noted as squadron colour.

4407 Combat Crew Training Squadron
A-1E/G/H   1972* - 30/4/73
AT/T-28D   1972* - 30/4/73
   Recoded from **AD** to **AH** under common wing tail code during 1972 and inactivated on 30/4/73. Possible the T-28 and A-1 left the 4407 CCTS during 1972. Red tail stripe carried as squadron markings.

AT-28D Trojan "54-711" **AH**, 4407 CCTS 1 SOW, Hurlburt Field, with red tail stripe. Photo: Tom Brewer, 16 June 1972.

A-1E Skyraider 52-133919 **AH**, 4407 CCTS 1 SOW, Hurlburt Field, with red tail stripe. Photo: Tom Brewer, 15 June 1972.

7 Special Operation Flight
UH-1N   1972* - 31/5/72
   Flight previously flew **AA** tail coded C-47, UC-123K and U-10B starting at Otis AFB. Possible unit moved to Hurlburt before **AH** tail coded UH-1N flown. It is not known if the UC-123K recoded to **AH**.

TACTICAL AIR COMMAND - CONTINENTAL U.S.

UH-1N Twin Huey 69-6619 **AH**, 7 SOF 1 SOW, Hurlburt Field. Photo: Jack Morris, Eglin AFB, 15 June 1973.

AO
4408 Combat Crew Training Squadron	10/7/68* - 15/7/69	4410 Combat Crew Training Wing Hurlburt Field
	15/7/69 - 31/7/691	Special Operations Wing Hurlburt Field
	31/7/69 - 22/9/69	1 Special Operations Wing
C-123K	10/7/68* - 22/9/69	Lockbourne AFB, Ohio

Operated C-123 between 15/7/69 and 22/9/69, and tail coded **AO**, with green noted as squadron colour. The 4408 CCTS reassigned to 317 TAW at Lockbourne AFB between 22/9/69 and 15/8/71 with **OD** tail codes. Tail code **AO** reused by unrelated 317 SOS on 15/4/70.

AO
317 Special Operations Squadron	15/4/70 - 30/4/74	1 Special Operations Wing Hurlburt Field, Florida
C-123K	15/4/70 - 1972*	
UH-1N/P	15/4/70 - 1972*	
A-1E	15/4/70 - 1972*	
U-10D	15/4/70 - 1972*	

Assigned to the 1 SOW for two separate periods in time, the first period between 1/7/64 and 15/7/69. The squadron flew AC-47 with **ID** tail codes from England AFB. Reassigned to the 4410 CCTW, between 15/7/69 and 15/4/70, continuing with the **ID** tail code at England AFB (*C-47 usage unconfirmed with* **AO** *tail code*). The 317 SOS returned to the 1 SOW control for second tour between 15/4/70 and 30/4/74, using **AO** tail codes. Tail code vacated by unrelated 4408 CCTS. The C-47 operations dropped for a variety of other types. Squadron also operated C-123, UH-1, A-1, and U-10. Recoded in 1972 with **AH** as wing common tail code. Green noted as squadron colour.

U-10D Super Courier 63-13100 **AO**, 317 SOS 1 SOW, Ramsey AFB, with green fin cap. Photo: Denis Hughes, 23 June 1972.

UH-1N Twin Huey 69-6603 **AO**, 317 SOS 1 SOW, Hurlburt Field. Photo: Doug Remington, Langley AFB, 21 September 1970.

AP
4409 Combat Crew Training Squadron	10/7/68* - 15/7/69	4410 Combat Crew Training Wing
	15/7/69 - 15/10/69	1 Special Operations Wing
UH-1F/P	10/7/68* - 15/10/69	Hurlburt Field, Florida

Reassigned from the 4410 CCTW on 15/7/69, within the 1 SOW move to Hurlburt Field. Also flew uncoded OV-10A, U-10D and O-1E. Replaced by the 549 TASTS on 15/10/69.

AP
| 549 Tactical Air Support Training Squadron | | 1 Special Operations Wing |
| UH-1F/P | 15/10/69 - 1972 | Hurlburt Field, Florida |

The 549 TASTS activated when the 4409 CCTS inactivated on 15/10/69 and assumed the **AP** tail code. Squadron continued to operated uncoded OV-10A, U-10D and O-1E in addition to **AP** tail coded UH-1. Recoded with **AH** wing common tail code in 1972.

AQ
4410 Combat Crew Training Squadron	10/7/68* - 15/7/69	4410 Combat Crew Training Wing
	15/7/69 - 15/10/69	1 Special Operations Wing
UH-1F/P	10/7/68* - 1/10/69	Hurlburt Field, Florida

Unit transferred from the 4410 CCTW when the 1 SOW moved to Hurlburt Field on 15/7/69. Operated uncoded O-1E, O-2A and U-10A along side of **AQ** tail coded UH-1.

AQ
547 Special Operations Training Squadron	15/10/69 -	1 Special Operations Wing
547 Tactical Air Support Training Squadron	- 30/4/75	1 Special Operations Wing
U-10	15/10/69 - 1972	Hurlburt Field, Florida

The 547 SOTS activated on 15/10/69 replacing the inactivating 4410 CCTS at Hurlburt Field. Recoded to **AH** as wing common tail code during 1972. Squadron also operated uncoded O-1E and possibly O-2. UH-1F/P coded operations are unconfirmed. Recoded to **AH** under AFM66-1 common tail code in 1972.

BA
91 Tactical Reconnaissance Squadron	10/7/68* - 15/7/71	75 Tactical Reconnaissance Wing
	15/7/71 - 1972	67 Tactical Reconnaissance Wing
RF-4C	10/7/68* - 15/7/71	Bergstrom AFB, Texas

The 91 TRS activated on 1/7/67 with RF-4C. Squadron reassigned to the 67 TRW on 15/7/71. Red fin cap carried on RF-4C. The **BA** tail code maintained under AFM66-1 wing common concept post 1972.

BA
| 67 Tactical Reconnaissance Wing | 1972* - current 31/12/90 | Bergstrom AFB, Texas |

12 Tactical Fighter Squadron
RF-4C 1972* - current 31/12/90

Recoded from **BC** under common wing tail code during 1972. Red fin cap carried with several RF-4C noted with white fin cap.

45 Tactical Reconnaissance Squadron
RF-4C 1972* - 31/10/75

The 45 TRS recoded from **BB** under common wing tail code during 1972. Blue fin cap noted on RF-4C.

62 Tactical Reconnaissance Training Squadron
RF-4C 1/7/82 - 31/12/89

TACTICAL AIR COMMAND - CONTINENTAL U.S.

Squadron reassigned from the 363 TRW at Shaw AFB and redesignating from 62 TRS flying **JO** coded RF-4C. Inactivated with **BA** coded RF-4C on 31/12/89.

91 Tactical Reconnaissance Squadron
RF-4C   **1972* - current 31/12/90**
   The 91 TRS maintained **BA** tail code under wing common code during 1972. Red fin cap with two rows of white stars carried on RF-4C.

BB
4 Tactical Reconnaissance Squadron   18/11/66 - 15/7/71   **75 Tactical Reconnaissance Wing**
                                              15/7/71 - 15/10/71   **67 Tactical Reconnaissance Wing**
RF-4C   **10/7/68* - 15/10/71**   **Bergstrom AFB, Texas**
   The 4 TRS activated on 18/11/66 within the 75 TRW flying RF-4C with the **BB** tail code. Later reassigned to the 67 TRW when the 75 TRW inactivated on 15/7/71. The 4 TRS inactivated three months later while RF-4C carried a light blue fin cap.

RF-4C Phantom 66-0400, **BB** 4 TRS 75 TRW, Bergstrom AFB, with light blue fin cap. Photo: Doug Remington, Langley AFB, 7 October 1970.

BB
45 Tactical Reconnaissance Squadron   **67 Tactical Reconnaissance Wing**
RF-4C   **15/10/71 - 1972**   **Bergstrom AFB, Texas**
   The 45 TRS activated within the 67 TRW, assuming assets of the inactivating 4 TRS on 15/10/71. Blue fin cap carried on RF-4C. Formerly assigned to the 460 TRW, flying **AH** tail coded RF-101.

RF-4C Phantom 67-0430, **BB** 45 TRS 67 TRW, Bergstrom AFB, with blue fin cap. Photo: Doug Remington, McChord AFB, 2 February 1972.

BC
9 Tactical Reconnaissance Squadron   10/7/68* - 15/7/71   **75 Tactical Reconnaissance Wing**
                                              15/7/71 - 31/8/71   **67 Tactical Reconnaissance Wing**
RF-4C   **10/7/68* - 31/8/71**   **Bergstrom AFB, Texas**
   Squadron activated on 1/9/69 with RF-4C. The 9 TRS reassigned to the 67 TRW on 15/7/71 on inactivation of the 75 TRW. Yellow fin cap carried on RF-4C. Inactivated on 31/8/71 and place taken by the 12 TRS on the same day.

RF-4C Phantom 67-0455, **BC** 9 TRS 67 TRW, Bergstrom AFB, with yellow fin cap. Photo: Doug Remington, McChord AFB, 17 July 1971.

BC
12 Tactical Reconnaissance Squadron   **67 Tactical Reconnaissance Wing**
RF-4C   31/8/71 - 1972   **Bergstrom AFB, Texas**

  The 12 TRS activated with former assets and tail code of the 9 TRS on 31/8/71. Squadron reassigned from the 460 TRW at Tan Son Nhut AB, RSVN flying **AC** tail coded RF-4C. Red fin cap carried on RF-4C. Recoded **BA** under common wing tail code during 1972.

CA
481 Tactical Fighter Squadron   **27 Tactical Fighter Wing**
                                                                                            Cannon AFB, New Mexico
F-111D/F   10/7/68* - 27/10/71
F-111E   30/9/69 - by 7/71
F-111A   10/69 - 11/71

  Squadron F-100 initially coded during July 1968. Conversion began to F-111 in late 1969 with a green tail stripe carried. Status changed to non-operational between 5/9/68 and 30/6/69 as well as 31/7/71 and 12/11/72, due to conversion process. Recoded under the AFM66-1 concept to **CC** during 1972.

CC
522 Tactical Fighter Squadron   **27 Tactical Fighter Wing**
                                                                                            Cannon AFB, New Mexico
F-100D/F   10/7/68* - 19/7/72
F-111E   10/71 - 11/71
F-111A   1971
F-111D   5/72 - 1972*

  Initially coded F-100 during July 1968, switching to F-111 in 1972. Status changed to non-operational between periods 19/6/69 and 9/69, as well as 31/3/71 and 15/9/71 due to conversions. Under wing common tail code, **CC** maintained after 1972 with a red tail stripe.

CC
27 Tactical Fighter Wing   1972* - current 31/12/90   **Cannon AFB, New Mexico**

481 Tactical Fighter Squadron
F-111D   12/72 - 31/8/73
F-111D   15/1/76 - 8/7/80

  The 481 TFS recoded from **CA** to **CC** under common wing tail code. Squadron inactivated on 31/8/73 and replaced by the 523 TFS, also coded **CA** on 8/7/80. Reactivated on 15/1/76 to replaced the inactivating 4427 TFRS. The 481 TFS flew until further inactivating on 8/7/80. Green tail stripe carried on F-111D.

522 Tactical Fighter Squadron
F-100D/F   1972* - 19/7/72
F-111D   5/72 - current 31/12/90

  Under 1972 wing common tail codes, the 522 TFS maintained the **CC** tail code. Red tail stripe carried, changing to fin cap during 1982 on F-111D.

523 Tactical Fighter Squadron
F-111D   31/8/73 - current 31/12/90

  Formerly flew **PN** tail coded F-4E within the 405 FW at Clark AB until 31/8/73. Assets assumed from the 481 TFS with a blue tail stripe changing to fin cap in the early eighties.

524 Tactical Fighter Squadron
F-100D/F   1972* - 19/7/72
F-111D   1972* - current 31/12/90

  Flew F-100 until converting to F-111D in 1972. Status changed to non-operational between 7/3/69 and July 1969. The 524 TFS recoded to **CC** common wing tail code. Yellow tail stripe carried on F-100 and F-111D until change to fin cap in 1981.

TACTICAL AIR COMMAND - CONTINENTAL U.S.

4427 Tactical Fighter Replacement Squadron
F-111D   8/72 - 15/1/76

Recoded **CC** under AFM66-1 common wing code concept. Blue tail stripe carried until squadron replaced by the reactivated 481 TFS.

428 Tactical Fighter Training Squadron
F-111G   1/6/90 - current 31/12/90

The 428 TFS activated as the first squadron with F-111G, *(former FB-111A from SAC)*. Assigned to the 27 TFW, until the planned reactivation of 474 TFW.

CC
Detachment 2   **57 Fighter Weapons Wing**
F-111   1/10/70 - 1/5/72   **Cannon AFB, New Mexico**

Activated at Cannon AFB on 1/10/70 inactivating on 1/5/72.

CD
524 Tactical Fighter Squadron   **27 Tactical Fighter Wing**
                                                           Cannon AFB, New Mexico

F-100D/F	10/7/68* - 19/7/72*
F-111A	- 1972
F-111E	- 1972
F-111D	27/10/71 - 1972*

The 524 TFS flew F-100 until converting to the F-111 in 1972. Changed status to non-operational between 7/3/69 and 7/69. Yellow tail stripe carried, recoded **CC** under AFM66-1 common wing tail code concept. The **CD** tail application on F-111A and F-111E is unconfirmed.

F-100F Super Sabre 56-3867, **CD** 524 TFS 27 TFW, Cannon AFB, with yellow tail stripe. Photo: Doug Remington, Langley AFB, 20 May 1970.

CE
4427 Tactical Fighter Replacement Squadron   **27 Tactical Fighter Wing**
F-111D   1/11/71 - 1972   **Cannon AFB, New Mexico**

Squadron activated after F-111E and F-111A left the wing. Purple tail stripe carried with **CE** tail code. Recoded **CC** under AFM66-1 concept in 1972.

F-111D 68-0087, **CE** 4427 TFRS 27 TFW, Cannon AFB, with purple tail stripe. Photo: USAF via Marty Isham.

DA
354 Tactical Fighter Squadron
A-7D   1/7/71 - 1972

355 Tactical Fighter Wing
Davis-Monthan AFB, Arizona

Previously inactivated, with **RM** tail coded F-105D in 1970 within the 355 TFW at Takhli RTAFB. Carried as paper unit within the 4453 CCTW between 1/4/71 and activation on 1/7/71 within the 355 TFW flying **DA** tail coded A-7D. Recoded under common wing tail code **DM** in 1972. Blue tail stripe carried by A-7D.

DB
346 Tactical Airlift Training Squadron
C-130E   10/7/68* - 15/3/69

516 Tactical Airlift Wing
Dyess AFB, Texas

Activated on 1/4/63 to operate the C-130E. Aircraft coded **DB** during July 1968. Crews used the 347 TAS, **DY** tail coded aircraft on detachment to Southeast Asia. On 15/3/69 changed permanent station and assignment to the 374 TAW at Ching Chuan Kang AB, Taiwan taking the **DY** tail coded C-130E. Black noted as squadron colour. *See Special **DY** and **DZ** note at the end of wing summary.

DB
463 Tactical Airlift Wing   1972* - 1/12/74   Dyess AFB, Texas
Wing aircraft carried red, blue and white tail stripes as flight colours.

18 Tactical Airlift Training Squadron
C-7A   1/6/72* - 25/8/72

The 18 TATS assigned to the 463 TAW between 1/6/72 and 31/8/72. Squadron non-operational after 25/8/72. Squadron was the only flying component of 516 TAW when absorbed by the 463 TAW at Dyess AFB where tail coded **TD** within the 516 TAW. Assigned **DB** tail code within the 463 TAW and a carried white tail band.

47 Tactical Airlift Squadron
C-130E   6/7/73 - 1/8/73

The 47 TAS assigned from 313 TAW were previously coded **FB**. After less than one month operations place taken by the 774 TAS within the 463 TAW.

772 Tactical Airlift Squadron
C-130E   1/6/72* - 1/12/74+

Activated flying **DB** tail coded C-130E on 1/6/72. Tail code maintained until MAC control on 1/12/74. Previously inactivated flying **QF** tail coded C-130B on 1/6/71 at Clark AB under the 463 TAW.

773 Tactical Airlift Squadron
C-130E   1/6/72* - 1/12/74+

Activated flying **DB** tail coded C-130E on 1/6/72. Tail codes maintained until MAC control on 1/12/74. Previous flew **QG** coded C-130B until 15/10/71 at Clark AB within the 463 TAW.

C-130E Hercules 63-7829 **DB**, 773 TAS 463 TAW, Dyess AFB, with blue flight tail stripe. Photo: Doug Remington, McChord AFB, 5 June 1972.

774 Tactical Airlift Squadron
C-130E   1/8/73 - 1/12/74+

The 774 TAS assigned on 1/8/73 to the 463 TAW replacing inactivating 47 TAS as the third 463 TAW C-130E squadron. Unit dropped tail codes on MAC control 1/12/74. Previously active with **QW** tail coded C-130B until 15/9/72 at Clark AB, Philippines within the 405 FW.

DC
357 Tactical Fighter Squadron
A-7D   1/7/71 - 1972

355 Tactical Fighter Wing
Davis-Monthan AFB, Arizona

Squadron formerly flew **RU** tail coded F-105 within the 355 TFW at Takhli RTAFB in 1970. Reactivated as a "paper unit" within the 4453 CCTW on 22/3/71 until reactivated within the 355 TFW on 1/7/71. Flew **DC** tail coded A-7D, with yellow tail stripe. Recoded **DM** under common wing tail code.

TACTICAL AIR COMMAND - CONTINENTAL U.S.

DD
40 Tactical Fighter Squadron
A-7D   1/10/71 - 1/6/72

355 Tactical Fighter Wing
Davis-Monthan AFB, Arizona

The 40 TFS previously flew F-4E with **EE** tail codes within the 33 TFW, at Eglin AFB. Reactivated on 1/10/71 flying **DD** tail coded A-7D. Inactivated on 1/6/72 and replaced by the 358 TFS on the same day with **DM** tail codes and green tail stripe. It is likely that some cross coding (**DD** *and* **DM**) occurred in mid 1972, close to date of change as the AFM66-1 concept of wing common tail codes took effect in the same period.

A-7D Corsair 70-1051, **DD** 40 TFS 355 TFW, Davis-Monthan AFB, with green tail stripe. Photo: Don Larsen, 18 March 1972.

DF
11 Tactical Drone Squadron
DC-130A   1/7/71 - 1972

355 Tactical Fighter Wing
Davis-Monthan AFB, Arizona

Squadron replaced the 4472 SS(SPA) 4453 CCTW on 1/7/71. Recoded to **DM** under AFM66-1 concept. Black noted as squadron colour, but green tail stripe also carried on DC-130A.

DM
4453 Combat Crew Training Wing   10/7/68* - 30/9/71   Davis-Monthan AFB, Arizona

4454 Combat Crew Training Squadron
F-4C/D   10/7/68* - 16/8/71

Squadron code assigned in July 1968 as F-4C training unit within the 4453 CCTW. Unit inactivated with assets reassigned to 58 TFTW at Luke AFB in August 1971. Red fin cap carried by F-4C.

F-4C Phantom 63-7418, **DM** 4454 CCTS 4453 CCTW, Davis-Monthan AFB. Photo: Doug Remington, McChord AFB, 12 March 1971.

4455 Combat Crew Training Squadron
F-4C   10/7/68* - 8/10/71

The 4455 CCTS F-4C coded **DM** during July 1968. Only the 4455 CCTS reassigned from 4453 CCTW control to 355 TFW, although lasting only eight days before inactivation. White outlined blue fin cap carried.

F-4C Phantom 63-7602, **DM** 4455 CCTS 4453 CCTW, Davis-Monthan AFB, with white outlined blue fin cap. Photo: Doug Remington, Langley AFB, 16 July 1970.

4456 Combat Crew Training Squadron
F-4C/D   10/7/68* - 30/7/71

Code assigned to squadron on 10/7/68 while flying F-4 in the training role until inactivated on 15/1/71. White outlined green fin cap carried by F-4.

4472 Combat Crew Training Squadron   10/7/68* - 1/7/69
4472 Support Squadron (Special Projects Activity) 1/7/69 - 1/7/71
DC-130A   10/7/68* - 1/7/71

Squadron coded within the 4453 CCTW during July 1969. Redesignated SS(SPA) in July 1969. Recoded **DF** and replaced by the 11 TDS on 1/7/71.

DM
333 Tactical Fighter Training Squadron   **355 Tactical Fighter Wing**
A-7D   16/7/71 - 1972   **Davis-Monthan AFB, Arizona**

The 333 TFS formerly flew **RK** tail coded F-105 within the 355 TFW at Takhli RTAFB. Assigned to the 355 TFW in May 1971 with the assets from the 58 TFTW at Luke AFB. Maintained the **DM** as common wing tail code with a red tail stripe.

DM
355 Tactical Fighter Wing   1972* - 1/9/79
355 Tactical Training Wing   1/9/79 - current 31/12/90

Davis-Monthan AFB, Arizona

11 Tactical Drone Squadron
DC-130A   1972* - 1/7/76

Recoded **DM** common wing tail code from **DF**. Tail codes removed in late 1975. Reassigned to 432 Tactical Drone Group on 1/7/76, before inactivated in March 1979 (*The co-based 22 TDS flew uncoded EC-130E*).

DC-130A Hercules 57-0497, **DM** 11 TDS 355 TFW, Davis-Monthan AFB, with like coded drone. Photo: David Davenport, Pope AFB, 13 October 1972.

333 Tactical Fighter Training Squadron
A-7D   1972* - 1976
A-10A   3/1976 - 15/2/90

Maintained the **DM** tail code under common wing code, with red tail stripe maintained on the A-7D. Redesignated to 333 TFTS and was the first tactical unit to fly the A-10A. Red fin tail stripe initiated on the A-10A and later replaced by red and white checkered fin caps.

TACTICAL AIR COMMAND - CONTINENTAL U.S.

A-10A Thunderbolt 75-0260, **DM** 333 TFTS 355 TTW, Davis-Monthan AFB, 1990 A-10 demonstration team aircraft displaying all three squadrons colours, and numbers on outer surfaces, with tail code and "**355 TTW**" in shadow. Photo: Patrick Martin, Hillsboro, 15 June 1990.

354 Tactical Fighter Squadron
A-7D   1972* - 1/4/79

Recoded from **DA** under AFM66-1 common wing tail code concept to **DM**. Detached between 12/1/73 and 5/7/73 to the 454 TFW operations at Korat RTAFB with **MB** tail codes, carrying a blue tail stripe. Inactivated on 1/4/79.

357 Tactical Fighter Squadron   1972* - 1/7/76
357 Tactical Fighter Training Squadron   1/7/76 - current 31/12/90
A-7D   1972* - 1/7/76
A-10A   1976 - current 31/12/90

Recoded **DM** from **DC** tail code under AFM66-1 concept. Yellow tail stripe maintained on A-7D, while yellow fin caps with black lightning bolt carried by the A-10A.

A-7D Corsair 72-0233, **DM** 357 TFS 355 TFW, Davis-Monthan AFB, with yellow tail stripe. Photo: Don Larsen, Kaneohe Bay MCAS, 1 November 1973.

A-10A Thunderbolt 76-0532, **DM** 357 TFS 355 TTW, Davis-Monthan AFB, with twin yellow fin caps and black lightning bolt on outer surfaces. Photo: Patrick Martin, Abbotsford IAP, 8 August 1985.

358 Tactical Fighter Training Squadron
A-7D   1/6/72* - mid 1978
A-10A   1978 - current 31/12/90

Designated 358 TFTS on 18/5/72 and activated on 1/6/72 with assets from **DD** tail coded 40 TFS. Green tail stripe carried. Detached to Korat RTAFB between 12/1/73 and 5/7/73. Flew **MB** tail coded A-7D while on detachment (*possibly borrowed from the 354 TFW*). Conversion to A-10A completed by mid 1978. Green fin caps carried by A-10A and amended in early eighties with white stylized Canine figure head. Fins caps further changing to black by October 1990.

4455 Combat Crew Training Squadron
F-4C   1/10/71 - 8/10/71

When the 355 TFW replaced the 4453 CCTW, the 4455 CCTS reassigned maintaining **DM** tail code for eight days before inactivated.

DM
Detachment 1   **57 Fighter Weapons Wing**
A-7D   15/7/71 - 1/7/72   **Davis-Monthan AFB, Arizona**

When the 58 TFTW at Luke AFB switched from A-7 to F-4C operations with 355 TFW at Davis-Monthan AFB the 57 FWW detachment moved as well. Unit inactivated on 1/7/72. The 65 FWS activated flying A-7D with **WA** tail code at Nellis AFB on 23/6/72 before flying F-5E. Black and yellow checkered tail stripe carried as squadron markings.

DM
41 Electronic Combat Squadron   **28 Air Division**
EC-130H   19/3/82 - 4/87   **Davis-Monthan AFB, Arizona**

The 41 ECS activated on 1/7/808 with **DM** tail coded EC-130H in the electronic warfare role. Codes dropped on camouflage change from European One to light grey camouflage by 1987. Unconfirmed reports of regular C-130E/H also tail coded.

TACTICAL AIR COMMAND - CONTINENTAL U.S.

EC-130H Hercules 73-1581 **DM**, 41 ECS 522 AW & WC, Davis-Monthan AFB. Photo: GB a/c Slides, July 1982.

DY
347 Tactical Airlift Squadron   **516 Tactical Airlift Wing**
C-130E   10/7/68* - 1/6/72   Dyess AFB, Texas

The 347 TAS activated within the 516 TAW on 1/7/63 and tail coded C-130 **DY** by 10/7/68 with blue tail stripe. The 347 TAS inactivated along with wing on 1/6/72. *See Special **DY** and **DZ** note.

DZ
348 Tactical Airlift Squadron   **516 Tactical Airlift Wing**
C-130E   10/7/68* - 1/6/72   Dyess AFB, Texas

The 348 TAS activated within the 516 TAW on 5/7/68 and coded C-130E **DZ** by 10/7/68, with a blue tail stripe carried. The 348 TAS inactivated along with wing on 1/6/72. *See Special **DY** and **DZ** note.

EB
4 Tactical Fighter Squadron   **33 Tactical Fighter Wing**
F-4E   10/7/68* - 12/4/69   Eglin AFB, Florida

The 4 TFS activated within the 33 TFW flying F-4D on 20/6/65. The F-4D assets provided to form the 435 TFS with **FG** tail codes at Ubon AB, RTAFB in July 1967. The 435 TFS was formerly based Udorn RTAFB with F-104C. Squadron tail code of **EB** assigned in July 1968 on F-4E with stylized red and white fin cap. Continued until 12/4/69 when reassigned to the 366 TFW at Da Nang, RSVN with **LA** tail coded F-4E.

ED
16 Tactical Fighter Squadron   **33 Tactical Fighter Wing**
F-4E   10/7/68* - 9/70   Eglin AFB, Florida

Assets used to reform squadrons in Southeast Asia, each time the 16 TFS designation continuing at Eglin AFB. The first time on 17/10/67 F-4D assets absorbed by the 13 TFS and tail coded **OC** at Udorn RTAFB. The 16 TFS reequipped with F-4E and tail coded **ED** in July 1968 with stylized blue and white fin cap. The second asset transferred affected in April 1969 and providing the 421 TFS with **LC** tail coded F-4E. The aircraft did not reach the 421 TFS at Da Nang until June 1969, but stopped with the 475 TFW enroute. Each time the 16 TFS reformed at Eglin AFB. Attached on 29/5/70 to the 354 TFW at Kunsan AB, ROK and continuing with the replacement of 354 TFW by the 54 TFW on 14/6/70. The 16 TFS position taken by the 58 TFS on 1/9/70 within the 33 TFW.

ED
58 Tactical Fighter Squadron   **33 Tactical Fighter Wing**
F-4E   1/9/70 - 1972   Eglin AFB, Florida

Activated on 1/9/70 and assuming assets and **ED** tail code of the 16 TFS. Operational status reached on 1/11/70 and detached to the 432 TRW at Udorn RTAFB between 29/4/72 and 14/10/72. Under common wing tail code concept the squadron maintained **ED** code post 1972. Squadron colour blue displayed as fin cap.

ED
33 Tactical Fighter Wing   1972* - 10/78   Eglin AFB, Florida

58 Tactical Fighter Squadron
F-4E   1972* - 10/78

The **ED** wing tail code maintained under AFM66-1 concept. Squadron returned to Southeast Asia for a second tour to at Udorn RTAFB between 8/6/73 and 14/9/73 and attached to 8 TFW. Continued to fly **ED** coded F-4E until the wing recoded **EG** by October 1978. Blue fin cap carried by F-4E.

TAIL CODE

59 Tactical Fighter Squadron
F-4E   1973 - 10/78

The 59 TFS activated within the 33 TFW on 1/9/70, non-operational until 1/7/73 when flying F-4E with **ED** tail code. Tail code carried until Oct 1978 when the wing recoded to **EG**. Yellow fin caps carried.

EE
40 Tactical Fighter Squadron   **33 Tactical Fighter Wing**
F-4E   10/7/68* - 7/5/69   **Eglin AFB, Florida**

First activated within the 33 TFW flying F-4 on 20/6/65. Squadron assets used to form squadrons in Southeast Asia. Twice reformed, the first time on 25/5/67 with F-4D passed 555 TFS at Ubon RTAFB and tail coded **FY**. The second time in November 1968 with F-4E passed to the 469 TFS and tail coded **JV** prior to delivery. The last time, on 10/5/69 when F-4E passed to the 34 TFS tail coded **JJ**. The squadron status changed to non-operational until inactivating on 15/10/70. Blue fin cap with diagonal centred white checkered pattern, carried on F-4E.

EG
4533 Tactical Training Squadron (Test)   **33 Tactical Fighter Wing**
                                                                                       Eglin AFB Florida

F-4D	10/7/68* - 12/4/71
F-4E	10/7/68* - 12/4/71
RF-4C	- 12/4/71

Designated and organized at Eglin AFB on 7/12/67 as a component of the 33 TFW. All black fin cap carried on some F-4D with a white checkered pattern through centred third of cap. Replaced by the TAWC assigned 4485 TS on 12/4/71.

RF-4C Phantom 67-0435, **EG** 4533 TTS(T) 33 TFW, Eglin AFB. Photo: Tom Brewer, 1 April 1971.

EG
33 Tactical Fighter Wing   10/78 - current 31/12/90   **Eglin AFB, Florida**

58 Tactical Fighter Squadron
F-4E   10/78 - 3/79
F-15A/B   1/79 - 1984
F-15C/D   10/84 - current 31/12/90

Squadron previously flew **ED** tail coded F-4E, until conversion to F-15A/B in January 1979. Squadron F-15 conversion achieved at Luke AFB and operational in March 1979. Blue tail stripes carried by F-15. Converted to F-15C/D in late 1974.

F-15D Eagle 83-0046, **EG** 58 TFS 33 TFW, Eglin AFB, displaying inner black bands with eagle motif and single sided blue tail stripes. Photo: Norm Taylor, Shaw AFB, 15 October 1985.

TACTICAL AIR COMMAND - CONTINENTAL U.S.

59 Tactical Fighter Squadron
F-4E   10/78 - 3/79
F-15A/B   3/79 - 1984
F-15C/D   1984 - current 31/12/90

Activated within the 33 TFW on 1/9/70, non-operational until 1/7/73. Converted to F-15A/B in 1979, and F-15C/D in October 1984. Initial conversion to F-15 achieved at Luke AFB, operational by March 1979. F-15 carried yellow tail stripes.

F-15A Eagle 76-0015, **EG** 59 TFS 33 TFW, Eglin AFB, displaying inner black bands with eagle motif and single sided red tail stripes. Photo: Doug Remington, McChord AFB, 15 January 1984.

60 Tactical Fighter Squadron
F-15A/B   early 79 - 10/84
F-15C/D   10/84 - current 31/12/90

Squadron activated within the 33 TFW on 1/9/71 and activated late in 1978 to complete three squadron wing. Conversion training at Luke AFB, completed by end 1979. Conversion to the F-15C/D started in October 1984, maintaining red tail stripe.

EL
23 Tactical Fighter Wing   1/7/72 - current 31/12/90   **England AFB, Louisiana**

74 Tactical Fighter Squadron
A-7D   1/7/72 - 1980-81
A-10A   1980 - current 31/12/90

Activated within the 23 TFW, flying **EL** coded A-7D. A blue tail stripe adorned squadron A-7D, adding white stars and "74" by 1979. Deployed to Korat RTAFB between 2/7/73 and 15/8/73. Converted to A-10A and declared operational on 6/3/81. The 74 TFS A-10A carried the same markings as the A-7D, later changing to blue fin caps with a lighting bolt.

A-7D Corsair 71-0338, **EL** 74 TFS 23 TFW, England AFB, with blue tail stripe. Photo: Don Larsen, Nellis AFB, 20 May 1973.

75 Tactical Fighter Squadron
A-7D   1/7/72 - 1980-81
A-10A   1980 - current 31/12/90

The 75 TFS activated within the 23 TFW, at England AFB on 1/7/72. Squadron A-7D carried a white outlined black tail stripe, changing to black and white checkered later. Converted to A-10A and maintained the same markings. Later changing to checkered fin caps by mid 1987, later with white "75" centred.

76 Tactical Fighter Squadron
A-7D   1/10/72 - 11/6/81
A-10A   1981 - current 31/12/90

Following the 75 TFS, the 76 TFS activated within the 23 TFW, on 1/10/72, at England AFB, flying the A-7D. A red tail stripe carried, adding white stars and "76" by 1978. The 76 TFS converted to A-10A, and carried the latter A-7D style markings as a fin cap.

A-10A Thunderbolt 79-0179, **EL** 76 TFS 23 TFW, England AFB, displaying shark mouth and single sided red fin caps with white stars. Photo: Patrick Martin, Nellis AFB, 9 January 1989.

FB
43 Tactical Fighter Squadron		**15 Tactical Fighter Wing**
F-4E	10/7/68* - 23/6/70	MacDill AFB, Florida

The 43 TFS assigned the **FB** tail code on 10/7/68, and reassigned to the 21 Control Wing, based at Elmendorf AFB on 15/7/70, taking 45 TFS **FC** tail coded F-4E. Aircraft arrived at destination on 23/6/70. A blue fin cap, outlined in white carried by F-4E. The **FB** tail code assigned to both 43 TFS and 47 TAS (*C-130*) and was the only conflict within original assigned tail codes on 10/7/68.

FB
45 Tactical Fighter Squadron	6/70 - 1/10/70	**15 Tactical Fighter Wing**
	1/10/70 - 1/7/71	**1 Tactical Fighter Wing**
F-4E	6/70 - 1/7/71	MacDill AFB, Florida

The 45 TFS absorbed former 43 TFS **FB** tail coded F-4E in June 1970. The 43 TFS took the former 45 TFS **FC** tail coded F-4E to Alaska. The 15 TFW inactivated and was replaced by the 1 TFW on 1/10/70 at MacDill AFB. A red fin cap, with white outline carried by F-4E. On 1/7/71, the 45 TFS assets transferred to 71 TFS, **FB** tail code maintained.

F-4E Phantom 67-0305 **FB**, 45 TFS 15 TFW, MacDill AFB, with white outlined red fin cap. Photo: Doug Remington, Langley AFB, 18 July 1970.

FB
71 Tactical Fighter Squadron		**1 Tactical Fighter Wing**
F-4E	1/7/71 - 1972	MacDill AFB, Florida

On 1/7/71 the 71 TFS replaced the 45 TFS, maintaining the **FB** tail code and red fin cap. Recoded **FF** under AFM66-1 wing common code concept.

FB
47 Tactical Airlift Squadron		**313 Tactical Airlift Wing**
C-130E	10/7/68* - 1972	Forbes AFB, Kansas

The 47 TAS operated C-130 from 1/10/64. The 47 TAS assigned **FB** on 10/7/68, maintaining the **FB** as common wing tail code, post 1972. The **FB** tail code assigned to both 47 TAS and 43 TFS (*F-4E*) and was the only conflict within original assigned tail codes on 10/7/68.

FB
313 Tactical Airlift Wing	1972* - 1/12/74+	Forbes AFB, Kansas

47 Tactical Airlift Wing	
C-130E	1972* - 6/7/73

TACTICAL AIR COMMAND - CONTINENTAL U.S.

The **FB** tail code maintained after AFM66-1 common wing tail code concept. The squadron transferred to 463 TAW and recoded to **DB** on 6/7/73, as prelude to the wing closure on 30/9/73. A black coloured stripe carried on C-130E.

48 Tactical Airlift Squadron
C-130E   1972* - 6/8/73

The 48 TAS recoded from **FH** to **FB** under the AFM66-1 common wing tail code concept in 1972. The Squadron inactivated on 6/8/73 and the wing on 30/9/73. Squadron reassigned to Little Rock AFB, within the 314 TAW on 6/8/73, with **LK** tail coded C-130E, with a yellow tail stripe.

FC
45 Tactical Fighter Squadron   **15 Tactical Fighter Wing**
F-4E   10/7/68* - 6/70   **MacDill AFB, Florida**

Squadron assigned **FC** tail code on 10/7/68. The **FC** tail coded F-4E taken by 43 TFS to Alaska in June 1970. The 45 TFS absorbed the former 43 TFS **FB** coded F-4E, in effect, changing squadron tail code to **FB**.

FD
46 Tactical Fighter Squadron   1/7/62 - 1/10/70   **15 Tactical Fighter Wing**
                                          1/10/70 - 1/7/71   **1 Tactical Fighter Wing**
F-4E   10/7/68* - 1/1/71   **MacDill AFB, Florida**

Initially **FD** tail code assigned in July 1968 to 46 TFS. Tail code maintained through the 15 TFW inactivation and replacement by 1 TFW. Yellow fin cap carried by assigned F-4E. On 1/7/71 the 27 TFS replaced the 46 TFS, maintaining **FD** tail code.

FD
27 Tactical Fighter Squadron   **1 Tactical Fighter Wing**
F-4E   1/7/71 - 1972   **MacDill AFB, Florida**

On 1/7/71 the 27 TFS replaced the 46 TFS within the 1 TFW. The assets, **FD** tail code and yellow fin cap maintained. Squadron recoded to **FF** in 1972 under common wing tail code.

FE
47 Tactical Fighter Squadron   1/7/62 - 1/10/71   **15 Tactical Fighter Wing**
                                          1/10/71 - 1/7/71   **1 Tactical Fighter Wing**
F-4E   10/7/68* - 1/7/71   **MacDill AFB, Florida**

Initially assigned the **FE** tail code in July 1968. Tail code maintained throughout the 15 TFW replacement by the 1 TFW at MacDill AFB on 1/10/70. Squadron F-4E carried green fin cap. On 1/7/71 the 94 TFS replaced by the 47 TFS, maintaining the **FE** tail code.

FE
94 Tactical Fighter Squadron   **1 Tactical Fighter Wing**
F-4E   1/7/71 - 1972   **MacDill AFB, Florida**

On 1/7/71, the 94 TFS activated and replaced the 47 TFS. The 47 TFS assets, **FE** tail code and green fin cap maintained. Squadron recoded to **FF** under wing common tail code in 1972.

(FF)
4530 Tactical Fighter Training Squadron   **15 Tactical Fighter Wing**
F-4E   10/7/68* - 1/10/71   **MacDill AFB, Florida**

Assumed the role from 4530 TTS which did not have permanently assigned aircraft on 1/10/70, although crest seen on F-4. Inactivated on 1/10/71, and replaced by the 4501 TFRS, assuming assets and codes.

FF
4501 Tactical Fighter Replacement Squadron   **1 Tactical Fighter Wing**
F-4E   1/10/71 - 1972   **MacDill AFB, Florida**

Squadron activated within the 1 TFW on 1/10/71 with **FF** tail coded F-4E, with white fin caps (*unconfirmed F-4D usage*). Maintained **FF** as wing common tail code under AFM66-1.

FF
1 Tactical Fighter Wing   1972* - 30/6/75   **MacDill AFB, Florida**
                                          30/6/75 - current 31/12/90   **Langley AFB, Virginia**

27 Tactical Fighter Squadron
F-4E   1972* - 30/6/75
F-15A/B   30/6/76 - 4/11/82
F-15C/D   11/81 - current 31/12/90

Recoded from **FD** to **FF** tail code in 1972. Assets assigned to the 56 TFW on 30/6/75. The 27 TFS moved to Langley AFB, to fly F-15A/B. Yellow fin cap carried on F-4E and yellow tail stripes on F-15.

F-15C Eagle 81-0052 **FF**, 27 TFS 1 TFW, Langley AFB, with single sided yellow tail stripes. Photo: Doug Remington, 4 September 1983.

71 Tactical Fighter Squadron
F-4E	1972* - 30/6/75
F-15A/B	1/76 - 11/81
F-15C/D	11/81 - current 31/12/90

Recoded from **FB** tail code under common wing tail code in 1972. Assets reassigned to the 56 TFW on 30/6/75. The 71 TFS moved to Langley AFB to fly F-15A/B. The F-4E carried red fin caps and red tail stripes on F-15.

94 Tactical Fighter Squadron
F-4E	1972* - 30/6/75
F-15A/B	30/6/75 - 4/11/81
F-15C/D	4/11/81 - current 31/12/90

Recoded from **FE** code under common wing tail code concept in 1972. Assets reassigned to the 56 TFW on 30/6/75 with 94 TFS moving to Langley AFB to fly F-15A/B. Green fin cap carried by F-4E and blue tail stripes on F-15.

F-4E Phantom 66-0295 **FF**, 94 TFS 1 TFW, MacDill AFB, with blue fin cap. Photo: Ken Buchanan, 1 August 1972.

4501 Tactical Fighter Replacement Squadron
F-4E	1972* - 30/6/75

Squadron maintained the **FF** tail code and white fin cap, post AFM66-1 common wing tail code concept. Recoded to **MC** when reassigned to the 56 TFW, on 30/6/75.

F-4E Phantom 67-0213 **FF**, 4501 TFRS 1 TFW, MacDill AFB, with white fin cap. Photo: Ken Buchanan, McCoy AFB, 3 March 1973.

TACTICAL AIR COMMAND - CONTINENTAL U.S.

FH
38 Tactical Airlift Squadron   **313 Tactical Airlift Wing**
C-130E   1/7/69 - 15/11/71   **Forbes AFB, Kansas**

  The 38 TAS reassigned from 316 TAW, where coded **LO** between July 1968 and 1/7/69. Flew C-130E with **FH** tail code as a component of the 313 TAW. Replaced by the 48 TAS on 15/11/71, assuming assets and tail code. Yellow tail stripe carried by C-130E. Unit returned to **LO** tail coded operations within the 316 TAW.

FH
48 Tactical Airlift Squadron   **313 Tactical Airlift Wing**
C-130E   15/11/71 - 1972   **Forbes AFB, Kansas**

  The 48 TAS replaced the 38 TAS on 15/11/71, maintaining the **FH** tail code and yellow tail stripe. Under the AFM66-1 concept, the squadron recoded to **FB**, as common wing tail code standard, again maintaining the yellow stripe.

FL
549 Tactical Air Support Training Squadron
                                                 549 Tactical Air Support Training Group/1 Special Operations Wing
                                                                                                 Patrick AFB, Florida

OV-10A   15/12/75 - 11/3/87*
OT-37B   unknown - 11/3/87

  Squadron previously flew **AH** tail coded UH-1 and possible OV-10 from Hurlburt Field until reassigned to 549 TASTG on 15/12/75 at Patrick AFB. The group itself assigned to the 1 SOW on the same date. Initially assignment date of OT-37B is unknown. Red markings noted when unit recoded to **PF** on 11/3/87.

OV-10A Bronco 67-14608 FL, 549 TASTS 549 TASTG, Patrick AFB. Photo: Norm Taylor, Shaw AFB, 12 October 1984.

FS
4424 Combat Crew Training Squadron   15/10/68 - 1/10/70   **15 Tactical Fighter Wing**
                                             1/10/70 - 30/6/72   **1 Tactical Fighter Wing**
                                                                       MacDill AFB, Florida

B-57C   15/10/68 - 30/6/72
B-57E   1971 - 1972
B-57G   late 1971 - 30/6/72

  Unit activated on 15/10/68 with **FS** tail code. Control passed to the 1 TFW when the 15 TFW inactivated at MacDill AFB (*Unconfirmed if B-57E tail coded*). The 4424 CCTS inactivated on 30/6/72. Black noted as squadron colour. Assets transferred to ANG unit before tail code removal.

B-57G Canberra 53-3877 FS, 4424 CCTS 1 TFW, MacDill AFB. Photo: W H Strandberg, 28 August 1971.

FS
13 Bombardment Squadron   **15 Tactical Fighter Wing**
B-57G   8/2/69 - 15/9/70   **MacDill AFB, Florida**

The 13 BS formerly assigned within the 405 FW and tail coded **PV**. Activated within the 15 TFW to operate B-57G on 8/2/69. 15 TFW records show squadron attached to the 8 TFW, Ubon RTAFB on 15/9/70 and assigned on 1/10/70. The 8 TFW records show squadron attached on 1/10/70 and assigned on 31/10/70. Deployed with **FS** tail code, switching to **FK** shortly after arrival at Ubon RTAFB. Shared the **FS** tail code with 4424 CCTS for short period.

B-57E Canberra 55-4248 **FS**, 13 BS 15 TFW, MacDill AFB. Photo: Doug Remington, Langley AFB, 8 June 1970.

(GA)
68 Tactical Fighter Squadron   **479 Tactical Fighter Wing**
                                                                              George AFB, California

Tail code assigned to 68 TFS with F-4D, but not carried. In theory the 68 TFS should have coded **GA**, but squadron departed prior to application to the 4531 TFW at Homestead AFB during August 1968, then the 4535 CCTS assumed the **GA** tail code.

GA
4535 Combat Crew Training Squadron   25/9/68 - 1/10/71   **479 Tactical Fighter Wing**
                                            1/10/71 - 1972   **35 Tactical Fighter Wing**
                                                                        George AFB, California

F-4D	25/9/68 - 8/69
F-4E	5/69 - 1972*
F-4C	2/70 - 1972*

Squadron reassigned from the 4531 TFW on 25/9/68, with the assets of the inactivating (*and uncoded*) 476 TFS. The F-4D tail coded **GA** code within the 479 TFW. The F-4E added in May 1969 until squadron F-4C operations added in 1970. Assigned to the 35 TFW on 1/10/71 and maintained the **GA** tail code. Further maintained **GA** as tail code after AFM66-1 concept 1972. Both red and white fin caps noted.

F-4E Phantom 66-0382 **GA**, 4535 TFTS 35 TFW, George AFB, with red fin cap. Photo: Don Larsen, Davis-Monthan AFB, 28 April 1972.

GA
35 Tactical Fighter Wing   1972* - 1/7/84*
35 Tactical Training Wing   1/7/84 - 5/10/89
35 Tactical Fighter Wing   5/10/89 - current 31/12/90
                                                                              George AFB, California

20 Tactical Fighter Training Squadron
F-4C	1/12/72 - by 1981
F-4E	by 1981 - current 31/12/90
F-4F	1972 - 1975

TACTICAL AIR COMMAND - CONTINENTAL U.S.

The 20 TFTS activated within the 35 TFW on 1/12/72 replacing the 4452 CCTS as an F-4 training unit. By 1981 only F-4E operated within the wing. Initially carried blue fin cap, changing to silver wedge outlined in black. German Air Force F-4F operated within 20 TFTS before replacement with German owned F-4E in 1975.

F-4E Phantom 75-635 Luftwaffe **GA**, 20 TFTS 35 TFW, George AFB, displaying German flag colours of black, red and yellow at tail band and "1st GAFTS" on tail. Photo: Mick Roth, October 1989.

21 Tactical Fighter Training Squadron   1/12/72 - 9/10/80
21 Tactical Fighter Squadron   9/10/80 - 5/10/89
21 Tactical Fighter Training Squadron   5/10/89 - current 31/12/90
F-4C   1/12/72 - 1980
F-4E   1980 - current 31/12/90

Activated on 1/12/72, replacing the 4535 CCTS as a F-4C training unit. Squadron redesignated to 21 TFS on 9/10/80. Initial markings of white stripe and small red fin cap changing to all white fin cap by 1974. Further changed to all red fin cap during 1975 until colour change to black by 1978. Several variations noted including black wedge outlined in silver. Also carried black cat in circle badge on tail. Further redesignated to 21 TFS on 9/10/80, squadron known as "Cheetah." Further redesignated to 21 TFTS, possibly on 5/10/89.

F-4E Phantom 67-0311 **GA**, 21 TFTS 35 TFW, George AFB, with silver outlined black wedge. Photo: Patrick Martin, Fairchild AFB, 15 May 1987.

39 Tactical Fighter Training Squadron   1/7/77 - 9/10/80
39 Tactical Fighter Squadron   9/10/80 - 11/5/84
F-4C   1/7/77 - by 6/6/79
F-4C (ww)   1/7/77 - by 6/6/79
F-4E   by 22/11/80 - 11/5/84

The 39 TFTS assigned to the 35 TFW on 1/7/77. Designated to TFS status on 9/10/80 and inactivated on 11/5/84. Squadron F-4C carried white fin cap with red "ww" centred, F-4E carried white tail stripe (*also operated* **WW** *F-4G*).

431 Tactical Fighter Training Squadron
F-4D   1972* - 1972
F-4E   15/1/76 - 1/1/78

Squadron flew the F-4E within the 479 TFW and tail coded **GB** until 1/6/70. The 431 TFTS moved to England AFB on 30/10/70. Reactivated at George AFB, as 431 TFTS, with **GA** tail code, replacing the 4435 TFRS, on 15/1/76. The 431 TFTS further inactivated on 1/10/78, F-4E carried red fin caps and canopy rails.

434 Tactical Fighter Squadron   1972* - 10/10/75
434 Tactical Fighter Training Squadron   10/10/75 - 1/1/77
F-4D   1972*
F-4E   1972* - 11/1/77

Recoded under common wing tail code concept the 434 TFS changed **GD** tail codes for **GA** 1972. Continued until 10/10/75, when redesignation to 434 TFTS. F-4D carried white fin cap. Flew until 11/1/76 when entering period of non-operation. Transferred on 1/1/77 and reestablished at Holloman AFB within the 479 TTW flying **HM** coded AT-38B.

561 Tactical Fighter Squadron
F-105F/G   15/7/73 - 12/7/80
F-4E   - 30/3/81

Activated on 15/7/73 and started recoding **WW** by June 1979. Previously assignment included **MD** tail code within the 23 TFW. Possibly operated both **GA** and **WW** tail codes until the last F-105 left on 12/7/80. Equipment changed to F-4G (*all coded* **WW**) and squadron transferred to 37 TFW, also at George AFB, on 30/3/81. Yellow tail stripe carried.

562 Tactical Fighter Squadron
F-105F/G   31/10/74 - 12/7/80
F-4E   - 30/3/81

Squadron activated on 3/10/74 from assets of 17 WWS 388 TFW at Korat RTAFB (*tail coded* **JB**). Green tail stripe carried. Recode to **WW** in 1978.

563 Tactical Fighter Training Squadron   31/7/75 - 1/7/77
563 Tactical Fighter Squadron   1/7/77 - 30/3/81
F-105F/G   31/7/75 - 1/7/77
F-4E   - 30/3/81

Squadron activated on 31/7/75 flying in the training role until transferred to the 37 TFW, also at George AFB. Previously coded **MF** until July 1972, within the 23 TFW. Designation changed to 563 TFS on 1/7/77 and status changed to non-operational, until reassigned to the 37 TFW, on 30/3/81. The F-4 carried a red fin cap. (*Possibly a paper unit between 1/7/77 until 12/2/82, see* **WW**)

4435 Tactical Fighter Replacement Squadron
F-4C   1972* - 15/1/76
F-4E   1972* - 1/12/72

Squadron recoded from **GB** under AFM66-1 concept in 1972. Squadron reequipped with F-4E before replaced by the 431 TFTS on 15/1/76.

4452 Combat Crew Training Squadron
F-4D   1972* - 1/12/72
F-4E   1972* - 10/72

Previously tail coded **GC** within the 35 TFW. Tail code changed to wing standard of **GA** by 7/72. A blue fin cap carried by F-4D. Replaced by the 20 TFTS on 1/12/72.

F-4D Phantom 65-0672 **GA**, 4452 CCTS 35 TFW, George AFB, with blue fin cap. Photo: Doug Remington, McChord AFB, 10 June 1972. Deployed to McChord for AWACS program.

4535 Combat Crew Training Squadron
F-4C   1972* - 1/12/72

Maintained **GA** as common wing tail code post 1972. Replaced by the 21 TFTS on 1/12/72. Variations of red and white markings carried as fin cap changing to all red during 1972.

F-4E Phantom 67-0376 **GA**, 4435 TFRS 35 TFW, George AFB, with white fin cap. Photo: Doug Remington, McChord AFB, 29 September 1972.

TACTICAL AIR COMMAND - CONTINENTAL U.S.

35 OMS
UH-1P   late 1972* - pre 1988
Operated as base flight with **GE** tail coded UH-1 until recoded **GA** late in 1972. Date of operations termination unknown.

UH-1P Huey 63-13163 **GA**, 35 OMS 35 TFW, George AFB. Photo: Tom Brewer, 18 September 1974.

GB
431 Tactical Fighter Squadron   **479 Tactical Fighter Wing**
                                                                      George AFB, California

F-4D	10/7/68* - 1/1/69
F-4D	1/3/69 - 6/69
F-4E	by June 1969 - 31/5/70*

Squadron assigned to the 479 TFW on 15/6/68 and tail coded F-4D **GB** under initial coding in July 1968. Converted to F-4E by June 1969, non-operational between January and March 1969. Operations terminated on 31/5/70 and replaced by the 4546 TTS assuming **GB** coded assets. Reactivated as the 431 TFTS 35 TFW, with **GA** tail coded F-4E in 1976.

GB
4546 Tactical T Squadron   **479 Tactical Fighter Wing**
                                                                      George AFB, California

F-4E	31/5/70 - 2/71
F-4C	1971 - 1/10/71

Unit existence unconfirmed as not carried in either 35 or 479 TFW official histories. Believed activated on 1/7/68 operating F-4E between 1/1/69 and 1/3/69, pooled with 431 TFS. Operations resumed on 1/6/70 replacing the 431 TFS and assuming red and white large checkered fin capped F-4E by 31/5/70. The F-4C added in 1971, adopting all white squadron markings. Squadron replaced by 4435 TFRS within the 35 TFW on 1/10/71.

F-4E Phantom 68-0340 **GB**, 4546 TTS 479 TFW, George AFB, with large red and white checkered fin cap. Photo: Doug Remington, Langley AFB, 23 September 1970.

GB
4435 Tactical Fighter Replacement Squadron   **35 Tactical Fighter Wing**
F-4C   1/10/71 - 1972   **George AFB, California**

The 4435 TFRS activated on 1/10/71 replacing the 4546 TTS. The 35 TFW also replaced 479 TFW on the same day. Recoded to **GA** under AFM66-1 influence.

GC
434 Tactical Fighter Squadron   **479 Tactical Fighter Wing**
F-4D   10/7/68* - 9/68   **George AFB, California**

Squadron assigned to the 479 TFW in 1957 and flew the F-4D since October 1966. The 434 TFS, tail coded F-4D **GC** in July 1968. Recoded in September 1968 to **GD**.

TAIL CODE

GC
4452 Combat Crew Training Squadron   5/69 - 1/10/71   **479 Tactical Fighter Wing**
1/10/71 - 1972   **35 Tactical Fighter Wing**
George AFB, California

F-4E	5/69 - 8/70
F-4C	2/70 - 10/70
F-4D	3/72 - 1972*

Activated on 16/1/67 with F-4 aircraft and assigned tail coded **GC** on 10/7/68. Originally assigned the **GE** tail code on 10/7/68. Code not taken up as **GC** tail code vacated by the 434 TFS. Unit assigned to 35 TFW on 1/10/71. Blue tail stripe, outlined in white, carried on F-4E, F-4C, with blue fin cap on F-4D. Model of F-4 flown between October 1970 and early 1972 is unknown. Adopted common wing tail code of **GA** in 1972.

F-4E Phantom 68-0345 **GC**, 4452 CCTS 479 TFW, George AFB, with blue fin cap outline in white. Photo: Doug Remington, Langley AFB, 7 May 1970.

(GD)
476 Tactical Fighter Squadron   **479 Tactical Fighter Wing**
George AFB, California

The 476 TFS tail code assigned but not carried by squadron F-4 as inactivated on 25/9/68. Assets assigned to the 4535 CCTS with **GA** tail codes. The **GD** code taken up by the 434 TFS September 1970.

GD
434 Tactical Fighter Squadron   9/68 - 1/10/71   **479 Tactical Fighter Wing**
1/10/71 - 1972   **35 Tactical Fighter Wing**
George AFB, California

F-4D	9/68 - 5/69
F-4E	5/69 - 1972*

Squadron recoded from **GC** in September 1968. Reassigned to the 35 TFW along with other components within the 479 TFW on 1/10/71. The 434 TFS changed tail code to **GA** under common wing code standard in 1972. The F-4E carried light blue fin cap.

(GE)
4452 Combat Crew Training Squadron   **479 Tactical Fighter Wing**
George AFB, California

Tail code **GE** assigned to the 4452 CCTS while flying F-4C and possibly F-4D, but never carried. In theory tail coded **GE** before **GC**, application in May 1969.

GE
35 OMS   25/9/68 - 1/10/71   **479 Tactical Fighter Wing**
1/10/71 - 1972   **35 Tactical Fighter Wing**
UH-1P   unknown - late 1972   **George AFB, California**

Operated as base flight with **GE** coded UH-1 until recoded **GA** late in 1972.

TACTICAL AIR COMMAND - CONTINENTAL U.S.

UH-1H Huey 64-13161 **GE**, 35 OMS 35 TFW, George AFB. Photo: Jerry Liang, 28 October 1972.

HA
417 Tactical Fighter Squadron   **49 Tactical Fighter Wing**
F-4D   **15/11/70 - 1970**   **Holloman AFB, New Mexico**

Reassigned from the 67 TRW at Mountain Home AFB on 15/11/70 as fourth F-4D unit added to the 49 TFW. A red fin cap with white outline carried as with squadron markings. Tail coded **HA** for a very short period before adopting **HE**.

HB
7 Tactical Fighter Squadron   **49 Tactical Fighter Wing**
F-4D   **10/7/68* - 1972**   **Holloman AFB, New Mexico**

Squadron tail coded F-4D **HB** in July 1968. Deployed to Takhli AB, RTAFB in May 1972 and recoded to **HO** during deployment. A blue fin capped carried by F-4 (*Unusual tail code assignment as* **HB** *tail code also used by 389 TFS 37 TFW, between June 1969 and October 1971*).

HC
8 Tactical Fighter Squadron   **49 Tactical Fighter Wing**
F-4D   **10/7/68* - 1972**   **Holloman AFB, New Mexico**

Squadron tail coded F-4D **HC** in July 1968. Deployed to Takhli AB, RTAFB in May 1972 and recoded to **HO** during deployment. Yellow fin cap carried by squadron F-4.

HD
9 Tactical Fighter Squadron   **49 Tactical Fighter Wing**
F-4D   **10/7/68* - 1972**   **Holloman AFB, New Mexico**

Squadron tail coded F-4D **HD** in July 1968. Deployed to Takhli AB, RTAFB in May 1972 and recoded to **HO** during combat tour. Red fin cap carried by F-4.

HE
417 Tactical Fighter Squadron   **49 Tactical Fighter Wing**
F-4D   **late 1970 - 1972**   **Holloman AFB, New Mexico**

Squadron recoded from short lived **HA** tail code to **HE** within the 49 TFW. Recoded to **HO** tail code during Southeast Asian deployment. Red colour carried as fin cap.

F-4D Phantom 66-0254 **HE**, 417 TFS 49 TFW, Holloman AFB, with red fin cap. Photo: Bob LaBouy, Hamilton AFB, 8 May 1971.

TAIL CODE

HL
388 Tactical Fighter Wing 23/12/75 - current 31/12/90 Hill AFB, Utah

4 Tactical Fighter Squadron
F-4D 23/12/75 - by 9/79
F-16A/B 1/79 - 5/89
F-16C/D 5/89 - current 31/12/90

Squadron reassigned from F-4E operations within the 432 TFW at Udorn RTAFB and tail coded **UD**. The 4 TFS reached operational status at Hill AFB on 9/3/76 with yellow fin capped F-4D. Converted to F-16A/B in 1979 and F-16C/D by June 1979. Squadron F-16 carried black lightning bolt on yellow tail stripe with "4" centred.

F-4D Phantom 65-0676 **HL**, 4 TFS 388 TFW, Hill AFB, with yellow fin cap. Photo: Brian Rogers, 10 September 1979.

16 Tactical Fighter Training Squadron 1/79 - 1/4/83
16 Tactical Fighter Squadron 1/4/83 - 30/6/86
F-16A/B 1/79 - 30/6/86

Previously flew **ED** tail coded F-4E within the 33 TFW. Activated in 1980 as 16 TFTS, redesignating 16 TFS on 1/4/83. Black and white checkered tail stripe carried by F-16. Squadron inactivated on 30/6/86.

F-16A Falcon 82-0929 **HL**, 16 TFS 388 TFW, Hill AFB, with black and white checkered tail stripe. Photo: Doug Remington, McChord AFB, 13 February 1985.

34 Tactical Fighter Squadron
F-4D 23/12/75 - 1/79
F-16A/B 1/79 - 5/89
F-16C/D 5/89 - current 31/12/90

Previously tail coded **JJ** flying F-4D within the 388 TFW at Korat RTAFB. Assigned with wing to Hill AFB and declared operational on 31/3/76, equipped F-4D carrying a red fin capped F-4D with white trim. Squadron converted to F-16A/B during 1979, as the first operational F-16 squadron and F-16C/D by July 1990. The F-16A/B carried red tail stripe. By 1986, white "Rams" and outline added to tail stripe.

TACTICAL AIR COMMAND - CONTINENTAL U.S.

F-16B Falcon 78-0096 **HL**, 34 TFS 388 TFW, Hill AFB, with trial lizard camouflage and red tail stripe. Photo: Martin collection.

421 Tactical Fighter Squadron
F-4D	23/12/75 - 1979
F-16A/B	1979 - 5/90
F-16C/D	5/90 - current 31/12/90

Reassigned from Udorn RTAFB, the 421 TFS formerly flew **UD** tail coded F-4E. Reassigned to fly the **HL** coded F-4D, within the 388 TFW at Hill AFB on 23/12/75. Converted to F-16A/B in the second half of 1979. A black tail stripe carried, containing white "Black Widows", plus red centred hourglass. Further conversion to F-16C/D in 1990.

F-4D Phantom 65-0612 **HL**, 421 TFS 388 TFW, Hill AFB, with a combination of all three squadron markings. Photo: Brian C Rogers, 29 March 1978.

HL
Detachment 16   **57 Fighter Weapons Wing**
F-16A/B   late 7/79 - unknown   **Hill AFB, Utah**

Also known as F-16 Multinational Operational Test and Evaluation programme. Squadron flew F-16 of the Belgische Luchtmacht and Koninklijke Luchtnacht F-16 in addition to USAF. First Belgian aircraft ferried to United States in July 1979. Aircraft flew in national markings in addition to USAF serials and **HL** tail code. Not known if Kongelige Danske Flyvevabnet and Kongelige Norske Luftforsvaret participated with aircraft or personnel only.

F-16A Falcon 78-0118 (*Belgische Luchtmacht FA-03*) **HL**, 57 FWW Det 16 MOT & E, Hill AFB, in Belgian marking. Photo: Iain MacPhearson, 19 October 1979.

HM
479 Tactical Training Wing   1/1/77 - current 31/12/90   **Holloman AFB, New Mexico**

416 Tactical Fighter Training Squadron

AT-38B 14/3/79 - 1/9/83

Squadron last active as a paper holding unit within the 4403 TFW at England AFB on 1/7/72. Redesignated to 416 TFTS on 8/3/79 and activated on 14/3/79. The squadron flew in the advanced training role, carried a grey tail stripe on AT-38B. Inactivated on 1/9/83 and replaced by the 433 TFTS, to bring the original 479 TFW assigned units together.

AT-38B Talon 62-3752 **HM**, 416 TFTS 479 TTW, Holloman AFB, with grey tail stripe. Photo: Doug Remington, McChord AFB, 3 June 1983.

433 Tactical Fighter Training Squadron
AT-38B 1/9/83 - current 31/12/90

Squadron activated with the former assets of the 416 TFTS on 1/9/83. Green tail stripe carried on AT-38B.

434 Tactical Fighter Training Squadron
AT-38B 1/1/77 - current 31/12/90

Previously flew **GA** and **GD** tail coded F-4 within the 35 TFW, and 479 TFW. Assigned to 479 TTW on 1/1/77. AT-38B carried a red tail stripe.

AT-38B Talon 64-13172 **HM**, 434 TFTS 479 TTW, Holloman AFB, displaying "**434 TFTS**" with unusual shadow serial presentation. Photo: Patrick Martin, McChord AFB, 13 July 1990.

435 Tactical Fighter Training Squadron
AT-38B 1/1/77 - current 31/12/90

Activated on 1/1/77 within the 479 TTW. Squadron AT-38B carried a blue tail stripe on AT-38B.

436 Tactical Fighter Training Squadron
AT-38B 1/1/77 - current 31/12/90

Activated on 1/1/77 within the 479 TTW but not operational until 24/4/77, yellow tail stripe carried on AT-38B.

HO
49 Tactical Fighter Wing 1972* - current 31/12/90 Holloman AFB, New Mexico

7 Tactical Fighter Squadron
F-4D 1972* - early 1978
F-15A/B 10/77 - current 31/12/90

Squadron recoded from **HB** to **HO** (*post May 1972*) during Southeast Asian deployment. Converted to the F-15A/B at Luke AFB starting in October 1977, declared operational by December 1978. Squadron F-15A/B carried blue and white checkered tail stripes, changing to all blue by 1983.

TACTICAL AIR COMMAND - CONTINENTAL U.S.

8 Tactical Fighter Squadron
F-4D   1972* - late 1978
F-15A/B   late 1978 - current 31/12/90

Squadron F-4D recoded from **HC** tail code to **HO** during Southeast Asian deployment post May 1972. Converted to F-15A/B in 1978, with yellow tail stripes carried.

F-15A Eagle 77-0115 **HO**, 8 TFS 49 TFW, Holloman AFB, with twin double sided yellow tail stripes. Note wing commander's aircraft behind, three coloured tail stripes. Photo: Patrick Martin, CFB Namao, 17 May 1986.

9 Tactical Fighter Squadron
F-4D   1972* - late 1978
F-15A/B   late 1978 - current 31/12/90

The 9 TFS F-4D recoded from **HD** to **HO** during Southeast Asian deployment. Converted to F-15A/B in during 1978. Red tail stripes carried with white knights helmet and stars, the white portion dropped by mid eighties.

417 Tactical Fighter Squadron
F-4D   1972* - 31/3/77

Squadron recoded from **HE** to **HO** during deployment in Southeast Asia, between 10/5/72 - 30/9/72. Inactivated on 30/3/77, but ceased operations on 31/3/77. Squadron F-4D carried a red tail stripe. Reactivated briefly within the 26 TRW at Zweibrucken AB, Germany.

HS
31 Tactical Fighter Wing   1/12/86 - current 31/12/90   Homestead AFB, Florida

307 Tactical Fighter Training Squadron   1/12/86 - 9/5/88
307 Tactical Fighter Squadron   9/5/88 - 28/4/89
F-4D   1/12/86 - least 5/88
F-16A/B   1988 - by 11/89

Wing recoded from **ZF** to **HS** on 1/12/86 while flying F-4D. Squadron F-4 carried a red fin cap outlined in white, with white scripted "stingers." Converted to F-16A/B in 1988 and inactivated on 28/4/89.

F-4D Phantom 65-0796 **HS**, 307 TFS 31 TTW, Homestead AFB, displaying red and white canopy trim and fin cap containing "STINGERS." Tail code, serial and "**307 TFS**" displayed in shadow. Photo: Keith Snyder, Dyess AFB, 1 May 1988.

F-16A Falcon 81-0806 **HS**, 307 TFS 31 TTW, Homestead AFB, with red and white tail stripe containing "STINGERS." Photo: Patrick Martin, Nellis AFB, 9 January 1989.

308 Tactical Fighter Squadron
F-4D	**1/12/86 - least 10/87**
F-16A/B	**least 10/87 - current 31/12/90**
F-16C/D	**by 10/90 - current 31/12/90**

Wing recoded from **ZF** to **HS** tail code on 1/12/86 while flying F-4D. Conversion to F-16A/B started during period of tail code change from **ZF** to **HS**. The 308 TFS F-16A/B carried a green tail stripe, with white "Knights" and outline. Converted to the F-16A/B in late 1989 and further reequipped with F-16C/D starting on 18/12/90.

309 Tactical Fighter Squadron
F-4D	**1/12/86 - 1987**
F-16A/B	**1/12/86 - current 31/12/90**
F-16C/D	**18/12/90 - current 31/12/90**

Wing recoded from **ZF** to **HS** on 1/12/86. Initially carried a white outlined green band, later adding "Wild Ducks."

HW
24 Special Operations Squadron   **24 Composite Wing**
                                                                       Howard AFB, Panama

UH-1N	**- 1/2/87**
OA-37	**- 1990**

Operated UH-1N and later OA-37 from Howard AFB (*Albrook AFB, also noted as base*). The 24 Composite Wing also controlled attached C-130 units. The 24 CW inactivated on 1/2/87, replaced by direct division control. The 24 SOS operated OA-37 aircraft from Panama, until aircraft moved to Homestead AFB, with the Pan American training facility and **HW** tail codes removed from A-37 on arrival. Tails codes reapplied prior to aircraft transfer to storage in 1990.

UH-1N Twin Huey 69-6636 **HW**, 24 SOS 24 CW, Howard AFB. Photo: Martin collection unknown location.

IA
Detachment 1   **1 Special Operations Wing**
                                                                       Otis AFB, Massachusetts

C-123K	10/7/68* - 1/7/69
C-47	10/7/68* - 1/7/69

TACTICAL AIR COMMAND - CONTINENTAL U.S.

Tail code **IA** assigned to Detachment 1, 1 ACW on 10/7/68. Recoded **AA** as wing switched tail code range within the 4410 CCTW on 15/7/69. Replaced by the 7 SOF on 1/7/1969, thus in theory, 7 SOF could have used the **IA** tail code between 1/7/69 and 15/7/69. Blue noted as squadron colour.

IB
Detachment 2   1 Special Operations Wing
C-130E   10/7/68* - 15/7/69   Pope AFB, North Carolina

Tail code assigned to Detachment 2, on 10/7/68, maintained until replaced by the **AB** tail codes Detachment 2, 1 SOW on 15/7/69.

IC*
71 Special Operations Squadron   1 Special Operations Wing
                                                                       Lockbourne AFB, Ohio and Pease AFB, New Hampshire

AC-119G   10/7/68* - 16/12/68
AC-130A   10/7/68* - 16/12/68

Tail code assigned while unit still designated 71 ACS, applied after redesignated 71 SOS. Activated with uncoded C-119 while based at Bakalar AFB within AFRES. Transferred to TAC on 13/5/68. Based at both Lockbourne and Pease AFB, applying **IC** tail code. Unit transferred (*uncoded*) to Southeast Asia within the 14 SOW. Released from active duty on 18/6/69, reverted to uncoded cargo C-119 within AFRES. Squadron later recoded **HO** with AFRES, flying the A-37A.

ID
317 Air Commando Squadron   10/7/68* - 15/7/69   1 Special Operations Wing
                                       15/7/69 - 15/4/70   4410 Combat Crew Training Wing
EC-47P/Q   10/7/68* - 15/4/70   England AFB, Louisiana

Activated within the 1 SOW on 1/7/64, until reassigned to the 4410 CCTW under wing switch on 15/7/69. Squadron inactivated on 15/4/70. In 1974 squadron returned as the 317 SOS 1 SOW, using **AO** tail coded C-123.

IE
319 Air Commando Squadron   10/7/68* -
319 Tactical Airlift Squadron   - 15/7/69   1 Special Operations Wing
                                       15/7/69 - 30/7/69   4410 Combat Crew Training Wing
                                                                                                 England AFB, Louisiana
UC-123B   10/7/68* - 30/7/69
C-123K   10/7/68* - 30/7/69

Activated within the 1 SOW on 27/4/62 and tail coded **IE** in July 1968. The C-123 operated from England, Cannon and Pope AFB, along with St. Croix. Possible tail code only used by a Eglin AFB detachment. Orange noted as squadron colour. Reassigned to the 4410 CCTW, on 15/7/69, under wing switch with 1 SOW. Squadron returned to the 1 SOW with **AG** tail codes, on 30/7/69 at Hurlburt Field.

IF
603 Air Command Squadron, Strike/Reconnaissance Squadron   1 Special Operations Wing
                                                                                                 Hurlburt Field, Florida
A-26   unknown - 15/7/769
A-37   10/7/68* - 15/7/69*

Activated within the 1 SOW on 1/7/63 and coded A-37 **IF** in July 1968. Flew from England AFB, Cannon AFB and Hurlburt Field. Reactivated as 603 SOTS on 1/7/73 to train C-47 MAP crews flying **AH** tail coded C-47. Recoded **AF** as control maintained by the 1 SOW wing switch on 15/7/69.

IG
4412 Combat Crew Training Squadron   10/7/68* - 15/7/69   1 Special Operations Wing
                                       15/7/69 - 15/9/70   4410 Combat Crew Training Wing
                                       15/9/70 - by 1973   4410 Special Operations Group
AC-47D, C-47D   10/7/68* - by 6/72   England AFB, Louisiana

Squadron activated to the 1 SOW with C-47 on 25/10/67. The 4412 CCTS C-47 tail coded within the 1 SOW, **IG** before reassignment to 4410 CCTW during wing switch on 15/7/69. Red noted as squadron colour.

IH
4413 Combat Crew Training Squadron   10/7/68* - 15/7/69   1 Special Operations Wing
                                       15/7/69 - 1/7/70   4410 Combat Crew Training Wing
                                                                                                 Lockbourne AFB, Ohio
AC-119G   10/7/68* - 1/7/70
AC-119K   8/11/68 - 1/7/70
AC-130A   6/8/68 - 1/7/70

Assigned to the 1 SOW on 1/3/68 and tail coded AC-119 **IH**, in July 1968 adding AC-130 in August 1968. Reassigned to the 4410 CCTW on wing switch with 1 SOW on 15/7/69. Replaced by the 415 SOTS at Lockbourne AFB on 1/7/70.

AC-119G Flying Boxcar 53-8089 **IH**, 4413 CCTS, 4410 CCTW, Lockbourne AFB.
Photo: Doug Remington, Langley AFB, 23 June 1970.

IH
415 Special Operations Training Squadron

	1/7/70 - 15/9/70	4410 Combat Crew Training Wing
	15/9/70 - 19/7/71	4410 Special Operations Training Group
		Lockbourne AFB, Ohio

AC-119G	1/7/70 - 15/7/71
AC-119K	1/7/70 - 28/6/71
AC-130A	1/7/70 - 9/3/71

Squadron replaced the 4413 CCTS at Lockbourne AFB on 1/7/70, assuming equipment and the **IH** tail code. Recoded to **AH** and moved to Hurlburt Field on 15/7/71 and became a component of 1 SOW on 19/7/71.

II
4532 Combat Crew Training Squadron

	10/7/68* - 15/7/69	1 Special Operations Wing
	15/7/69 - 28/7/70	4410 Combat Crew Training Wing
		England AFB, Louisiana

A-37A/B	10/7/68* - 28/7/70

Assigned to the 1 SOW on 25/10/67 and tail coded **II** in July 1968. Transferred to the 4410 CCTW at England AFB on 15/7/69, maintaining the **II** tail code and equipment. A blue and white markings noted on some A-37. Established as the first A-37 training squadron, with the first aircraft received on 1/8/67. Inactivated on 28/7/70 transferring assets to the AFRES units.

IJ
4406 Combat Crew Training Squadron

	1/10/68 - 15/7/69	1 Special Operations Wing
	15/7/69 - 1/7/70	4410 Combat Crew Training Wing
		England AFB, Louisiana

A-37B	1/10/68 - 1/7/70

The 4406 CCTS activated within the 1 SOW with **IJ** tail coded A-37B. The 4406 CCTS reassigned to 4410 CCTW under wing switch on 5/7/69. Replaced within the 4410 CCTW by the 427 SOTS on 1/7/70.

IJ
427 Special Operations Training Squadron

	1/7/70 - 15/9/70	4410 Combat Crew Training Wing
	15/9/70 - 15/7/72	4410 Special Operations Training Group
		England AFB, Louisiana

A-37B	1/7/70 - 15/7/72

The 427 SOTS activated on 1/7/70 replacing the 4406 CCTS, flying **II** tail coded A-37B. Inactivated on 15/7/72 with **IJ** tail code reused by the unrelated 6 SOTS.

IJ
6 Special Operations Training Squadron

	31/7/73 - 1/1/74	1 Special Operations Wing
	1/1/74 - 15/9/74	23 Tactical Fighter Wing
		England AFB, Louisiana

A-37B	31/3/73 - 15/9/74

The 6 SOS 1 SOW activated on 27/4/62. Tail coded **ET** while assigned to the 14 ACW at Nha Trang AB, RSVN, and inactivated on 15/3/70. Title used to replace the 514 AS 4410 CCTW at England AFB with **IK** A-37. The **IK** tail code remained after redesignating to the 6 SOTS 4410 SOTG, then reassigned to the 1 SOW recoded **IJ** on 31/7/73. Further reassigned to the 23 TFW on 1/1/74 and inactivated on 15/9/74. Red noted as squadron colour.

IK
514 Attack Squadron   4410 Combat Crew Training Wing

TACTICAL AIR COMMAND - CONTINENTAL U.S.

A-37B 15/7/69 - 8/1/70 England AFB, Louisiana
Activated within the 4410 CCTW on 15/7/69 with **IK** tail code. Replaced by the 6 SOS on 8/1/70 maintaining the **IK** tail code.

IK
6 Special Operations Squadron 15/4/70 - 31/8/72
6 Special Operations Training Squadron 31/8/72 - 31/7/73
  15/4/70 - 15/9/70 **4410 Combat Crew Training Wing**
  15/9/70 - 31/7/73 **4410 Special Operations Training Group**
A-37B 15/4/70 - 31/7/73 **England AFB, Louisiana**
Squadron replaced the 514 AS with **IK** tail code on 15/4/70. Redesignated to 6 SOTS on 15/9/70 and reassigned to the 1 SOW. Tail coded **IJ** when the 4410 SOTG inactivated on 31/7/73.

IS
57 Fighter Interceptor Squadron **1st Air Force**
F-15C/D 2/7/85 - current 31/12/90 **NAS Keflavik, Iceland**
The 57 FIS "Black Knights" reequipped from uncoded F-4E to **IS** tail coded F-15C/D during July 1985. The F-4 era finished with the last E model departing in February 1986. The **IS** tail code assigned in deference to local linguistic requirements as proper abbreviation would contain an accent over the **I**. Black and white checkered tail bands carried by F-15C/D.

F-15C Eagle 80-0035 **IS**, 57 FIS 1 AF, Keflavik NAS, with black and white checkered tail bands. Photo: Frank MacSorley, May 1986.

JK
4414 Combat Crew Training Squadron **363 Tactical Reconnaissance Wing**
RF-101A/C 10/7/68* - 15/10/69 **Shaw AFB, South Carolina**
Squadron activated at Shaw AFB on 20/1/68, flying RF-101. The 4414 CCTS tail coded **JK** in July 1968. Inactivated on 15/10/69 and replaced by the 31 TRTS maintaining assets and the **JK** tail code. Squadron RF-101 carried black and red trim.

JK
31 Tactical Reconnaissance Training Squadron **363 Tactical Reconnaissance Wing**
RF-101A/C 15/10/69 - 18/2/71 **Shaw AFB, South Carolina**
The 31 TRTS activated on 15/10/69 with assets from the inactivating 4414 CCTS. Uncoded TF-101F dual trainers also flown. Black and red trim also carried until inactivation on 18/2/71.

JL
4415 Combat Crew Training Squadron **363 Tactical Reconnaissance Wing**
RF-4C 10/7/68* - 15/10/69 **Shaw AFB, South Carolina**
Activated on 1/2/67 and tail coded RF-4C **JL** in July 1968, with a white fin cap. Inactivated with assets and tail code, transferring to the activating 33 TRTS on 15/10/69.

JL
33 Tactical Reconnaissance Training Squadron **363 Tactical Reconnaissance Wing**
RF-4C 15/10/69 - 1972 **Shaw AFB, South Carolina**
The 33 TRTS activated and replaced the 4415 CCTS on 15/10/69. Assets and tail codes assumed from the inactivating 4415 CCTS. Squadron colour of white carried as a fin cap. The 33 TRTS recoded under common wing tail code concept to **JO**.

(JM)
4416 Test and Evaluation Squadron **363 Tactical Reconnaissance Squadron**
  Shaw AFB, South Carolina
Squadron activated with the 363 TRW on 1/7/66 until 1/7/67. Assigned **JM** tail code on 10/7/68 even though inactivated a year prior to initial tail code application date.

JM
16 Tactical Reconnaissance Squadron **363 Tactical Reconnaissance Wing**
RF-4C 15/2/71 - 1972 **Shaw AFB, South Carolina**
Reassigned from the 475 TFW at Misawa AB, Japan where squadron RF-101 coded **UE**, until 15/2/71. The RF-4C coded **JM** within the 363 TRW. The tail code changed to **JO** under the common wing tail code concept during 1972.

TAIL CODE

RF-4C Phantom 65-0864 **JM**, 16 TRS 363 TRW, Shaw AFB, with yellow fin cap. Photo: Tom Brewer, Eglin AFB, 11 March 1972.

JN
4417 Combat Crew Training Squadron 363 Tactical Reconnaissance Wing
EB-66B/E   10/7/68* - 15/10/69   Shaw AFB, South Carolina

Squadron assigned **JN** tail code within the 363 TRW on 10/7/68. Squadron replaced by the 39 TRTS maintaining the same assets and tail code on 15/10/69. Red and white trim carried by EB-66.

JN
39 Tactical Reconnaissance Training Squadron   15/10/69 -15/2/70
39 Tactical Electronic Warfare Training Squadron 15/2/70 -15/3/74
                                              363 Tactical Reconnaissance Wing
EB-66B/C/E   15/10/69 - 15/3/74   Shaw AFB, South Carolina

Activated from the assets of the 4417 CCTS in October 1969 and maintained the **JN** tail code. Operated as the 39 TRTS until 15/2/70 when redesignated to 39 TEWTS. Deployments made to Southeast Asia. Squadron, as an exception, did not recode to **JO** with wing under AFM66-1 concept in 1972. Blue tail stripe carried until inactivation on 15/3/74.

EB-66E Destroyer 54-0469 **JN**, 39 TEWTS 363 TRW, Shaw AFB, with blue tail stripe. Photo: Tom Waller, McChord AFB, 17 March 1972.

JO
29 Tactical Reconnaissance Squadron   363 Tactical Reconnaissance Wing
RF-101A/C   10/7/68* - 24/1/71   Shaw AFB, South Carolina

Activated on 20/1/68 and coded RF-101 aircraft **JO** in July 1968. Squadron inactivated on 24/1/71 with assets going to the Michigan ANG. Squadron colour of yellow carried by RF-101.

RF-101C Voodoo 56-0185 **JO**, 29 TRS 363 TRW, Shaw AFB, with unusual white fin cap, as yellow noted as squadron colour. Photo: Ken Buchanan, MacDill AFB, May 1969.

TACTICAL AIR COMMAND - CONTINENTAL U.S.

JO
22 Tactical Reconnaissance Squadron   **363 Tactical Reconnaissance Wing**
                                                                                                        Shaw AFB, South Carolina

RF-4C   15/7/71 - 15/10/71
B-57E   1971 - 15/10/71

    Reassigned from the 67 TRW at Bergstrom AFB on 15/7/71, having flown **KS** tail coded RF-4C. Two B-57E also assigned to the squadron in 1971. The 22 TRS inactivating on 15/10/71, providing assets and code to activating 62 TRS on the same day.

JO
62 Tactical Reconnaissance Squadron   **363 Tactical Reconnaissance Wing**
RF-4C   15/10/71 - 1/7/82   **Shaw AFB, South Carolina**

    Squadron assets assigned from the 22 TRS on 15/7/71 (*Not known if B-57E maintained*). A red fin cap carried, and **JO** tail code maintained as wing common code. Reassigned to the 67 TRW, at Bergstrom AFB, on 1/7/82.

JO
363 Tactical Reconnaissance Wing   1972* - 1/10/81
363 Tactical Fighter Wing   1/10/81 - 1/10/82
                                                                                                        Shaw AFB, South Carolina

16 Tactical Reconnaissance Squadron
RF-4C   1972* - 3/2/83
B-57E   1972* - 9/74

    Recoded from **JM** to **JO** under the AFM66-1 common wing code concept. Squadron was the only RF-4C unit to remain active and recode to **SW** within the 363 TRW/TFW after October 1982. Some **JO** coded aircraft noted until 3/2/83. Operated last the TAC assigned B-57. Black and white tail stripe noted.

18 Tactical Reconnaissance Squadron
RF-4C   1972* - 30/9/79

    Recoded under the AFM66-1 concept from **JP** to **JO** during 1972. Light blue fin cap carried. Squadron inactivated on 30/3/79.

RF-4C Phantom 66-0427 JO, 18 TRS 363 TRW, Shaw AFB, with light blue fin cap. Photo: Doug Remington, McChord AFB, November 1977.

33 Tactical Reconnaissance Training Squadron
RF-4C   1972* - 1/10/82

    Recoded from **JL**, under common wing concept in 1972, with RF-4C carrying white trim. Inactivated on 1/10/82, redesignated 33 TFS on 7/9/84 and reactivated 1/1/85 receiving first **SW** tail coded F-16C on 27/1/85.

62 Tactical Reconnaissance Squadron
RF-4C   1972* - 1/7/82

    Maintained **JO** tail code and red tail stripe, after wing common tail code concept in 1972. Squadron reassigned to the 67 TRW, at Bergstrom AFB, as 62 TRTS, on 1/7/82.

JP
18 Tactical Reconnaissance Squadron   **363 Tactical Reconnaissance Wing**
                                                                                                        Shaw AFB, South Carolina

RF-101A/C   30/1/70 - late 1970
RF-4C   30/11/70 - 1972*

    Assigned to the 363 TRW on 30/1/70 with **JP** tail code. Squadron RF-101 carried light blue fin cap. The RF-101 began leaving 18 TRS on 26/10/70 with the first RF-4C arriving on 13/11/70. Recoded to **JO** as common wing tail code in 1972.

TAIL CODE

RF-101C Voodoo 56-0202 **JP**, 18 TRS 363 TRW, Shaw AFB, with light blue fin cap. Photo: Doug Remington, Langley AFB, 24 September 1970.

RF-4C Phantom 65-0876 **JP**, 18 TRS 363 TRW, Shaw AFB, with light blue fin cap. Photo: Ken Buchanan, MacDill AFB, 4 March 1972.

KB
417 Tactical Fighter Squadron   **67 Tactical Reconnaissance Wing**
F-4D   **10/7/68* - 15/11/70**   **Mountain Home AFB, Idaho**

Squadron assigned **KB** tail code on 10/7/68, in anticipation of move from 50 TFW, USAFE to Mountain Home AFB. The 417 TFS with F-4D was the exception to an all RF-4C wing. Squadron left for Holloman AFB and 49 TFW, to recode **HA**, on 15/11/70, although still assigned to 67 TRW until 10/10/70. A red fin cap with seven white stars carried.

F-4D Phantom 66-0278 **KB**, 417 TFS 67 TRW, Mountain Home AFB, with red fin cap containing seven white stars. Photo: Doug Remington, Langley AFB, 7 July 1970.

KR
10 Tactical Reconnaissance Squadron   **67 Tactical Reconnaissance Wing**
RF-4C   **10/7/68* - 30/6/71**   **Mountain Home AFB, Idaho**

Squadron initial coded **KR** within the 67 TRW. The 10 TRS RF-4C carried a yellow fin cap. Inactivated before the 67 TRW moved to Bergstrom AFB.

KS
22 Tactical Reconnaissance Squadron   **67 Tactical Reconnaissance Wing**
RF-4C   **10/7/68* - 15/7/71**   **Mountain Home AFB, Idaho**

TACTICAL AIR COMMAND - CONTINENTAL U.S.

Squadron flew **KS** RF-4C on initial coding in July 1968. Blue squadron markings noted. Inactivated on 15/7/71, with the squadron transferred to Shaw AFB utilizing the **JO** tail code within the 363 TRW. A light blue fin cap with white falling star centred applied to RF-4C.

KS
7 ACCS   **28 Air Division**
                                                                         522 AW & CW
EC-130E/H   **20/7/83 - least 9/87**   **Keesler AFB, Mississippi**

The 7 ACCS formerly flew **JC** tail coded C-130 within the 388 TFW, then uncoded C-130 at Clark late 1974 within the 374 TAW. Reactivated Keesler AFB in September 1983 with **KS** coded EC-130. Control passed to 522 AW & CW by 11/83.

EC-130E Hercules 62-1857 **KS**, 7 ACCS Keesler Field. Photo: Jerry Geer, Volk Field, September 1987.

KT
7 Tactical Reconnaissance Squadron   **67 Tactical Reconnaissance Wing**
RF-4C   **10/7/68* - 15/7/71**   **Mountain Home AFB, Idaho**
RF-4C   **15/7/71 - 15/10/71**   **Bergstrom AFB, Texas**

Squadron activated on 15/12/67 with RF-4C and initially coded **KT** within the 67 TRW in July 1968. A green fin cap carried with a white lightning bolt on RF-4C. The 7 TRS inactivated on 15/10/71.

RF-4C Phantom 65-0922 **KT**, 7 TRS 67 TRW, Mountain Home AFB, with green fin cap and white lightning flash. Photo: Doug Remington, Langley AFB, 18 August 1970.

LA
4510 Combat Crew Training Wing	10/7/68* - 15/10/69
58 Tactical Fighter Training Wing	15/10/69 - 1/4/77
58 Tactical Training Wing	1/4/77 - 1/1/83
405 Tactical Training Wing	29/8/79 - current 31/12/90

                                                                                            Luke AFB, Arizona

*The 58 TTW recoded to **LF** on 1/1/83, the remaining **LA** tail coded units were reassigned to the 405 TFTW on 29/8/79.*

310 Tactical Fighter Training Squadron
A-7D   15/12/69 - 31/7/71
F-4C   7/5/71 - 4/11/82

Activated with personnel of the 4514 CCTS, the 310 TFTS equipped with A-7D. Three A-7D carried yellow stripe, while normally A-7D carried a green tail stripe. The A-7D reassigned to the 333 TFS on 31/7/71, activating at Davis-Monthan AFB. The squadron reequipped with F-4C starting on 7/5/71 and assumed F-4 training role from Davis-Monthan AFB units. The F-4 carried a green fin cap. The 311 TFTS reassigned to 58 TFTW with **LF** tail coded F-16 on 1/1/83.

A-7D Corsair 68-8226 **LA**, 310 TFTS 58 TFTW, Luke AFB, with green tail stripe. Photo: Tom Brewer, Eglin AFB, 30 May 1971.

311 Tactical Fighter Training Squadron
F-100D	**18/1/70 - 21/8/71**
F-4C	**21/8/71 - 4/11/82**

Squadron activated with assets from the 4515 CCTS on 18/1/70. The 311 TFTS reequipped with F-4C, and assuming the F-4 training role from Davis-Monthan AFB units. The F-4C carried a yellow fin cap. On 1/1/83 the squadron recoded **LF** and reequipped with the F-16A/B, within the 58 TFTW.

F-4C Phantom 63-7426 **LA**, 311 TFTS 58 TFTW, Luke AFB, displaying yellow fin cap plus large yellow and black visibility markings for air combat training. Photo: Ben Knowles, 17 March 1977.

425 Tactical Fighter Training Squadron **Williams AFB, Arizona**
F-5B	**1974 - 8/79 or 5/85**
F-5E	**6/4/73 - 1/9/89**
F-5F	**1985 - 1/9/89**

The 425 TFTS assigned to the 58 TFW on 15/10/69 flying **LZ** tail coded F-5. Recoded to **LA** during 1974. Squadron F-5B noted with a green tail stripe, F-5E with blue or yellow tail stripe. Most F-5 did not carry tail codes during this period. Reassigned to the 405 TTW during August 1979 and inactivated on 1/9/89.

F-5E Tiger 72-1400 **LA**, 425 TFTS 405 TFTW, Williams AFB, with unusual "425 TFTS" and tiger emblem on tail. Photo: Douglas Slowiak, 15 February 1989.

TACTICAL AIR COMMAND - CONTINENTAL U.S.

F-5E Tiger 72-1403 **LA**, 425 TFTS 58 TFTW, Williams AFB, with blue tail stripe and canopy title block. Photo: Martin Collection, Malmstrom AFB, September 1977.

426 Tactical Fighter Training Squadron
F-100D	**18/1/70 - 21/8/71**
F-4C	**21/8/71 - 12/80**
F-15A/B	**1/1/81 - 29/11/90**
F-15D	**by 1989 - 29/11/90**

The 426 TFTS activated with assets of the former 4515 CCTS, on 18/1/70. Status changed to non-operational between 13/9/71 and 2/10/71. Squadron F-4C carried a blue fin cap. Reassigned to the 405 TTW with the F-15 on 1/1/81. Squadron F-15 carried red tail stripes and by 1983 added a yellow centred delta shape. The 426 TFTS inactivated on 29/11/90.

F-15A Eagle 73-0094 **LA**, 426 TFTS 405 TFTW, Luke AFB, with twin double sided red tail stripes and yellow centred delta on each surface. Photo: Patrick Martin, Nellis AFB, 29 June 1984.

461 Tactical Fighter Training Squadron
F-15A/B	**1/7/77 - 3/3/88**
F-15D	**1/83 - 3/3/88**
F-15E	**18/7/88 - current 31/12/90**

The activated on 1/7/77 with assets of the 4461 CCTS. Control passed to the 05 TTW, during August 1979 while maintaining the **LA** tail code. Flew F-15A with yellow tail stripes, later adding yellow stylized marks.

F-15E Strike Eagle 87-0169 **LA**, 461 TFTS, 405 TFTW, Luke AFB, with twin double sided yellow and black tail stripes. Photo: Douglas Slowiak, 30 March 1989.

550 Tactical Fighter Training Squadron.
F-4C   18/1/70 - 8/77
F-15A/B   8/77 - 2/89
F-15E   2-3/89 - current 31/12/90

Activated with assets of the 4517 CCTS on 18/1/70. Control passed to the 405 TTW during August 1979 while maintaining the **LA** tail code. The F-4 carried a red fin cap while F-15 stylized silver wings over black tail stripes.

F-4C Phantom 63-7675 **LA**, 550 TFTS 58 TFTW, Luke AFB, with red fin cap. Photo: Don Larsen, Davis-Monthan AFB, 18 March 1972.

555 Tactical Fighter Training Squadron
F-15A/B   14/11/74 - current 31/12/90
F-15D   by 10/82 - current 31/12/90

Reassigned from the 432 TFW at Udorn, RTAFB operating **UD** tail coded F-4D on 5/7/74. Redesignated 555 TFTS within the 58 TFTW, as initial F-15 training unit. Control passed to the 405 TTW on 29/8/79 while maintaining the **LA** tail code. The F-15 maintained green tail stripes with five white stars, some F-15A noted in 1984 with white outlines added to stripes.

F-15A Eagle 73-0092 **LA**, 555 TFTS 58 TFTW, Luke AFB, with twin double sided green tail stripes containing five white stars on each surface. Photo: Ben Knowles, July 1975.

4461 Tactical Fighter Training Squadron
F-15A/B   23/6/76 - 1/7/77

Activated within the 58 TFTW on 23/6/76 as second F-15 training squadron. Inactivated on 1/7/77 with the 461 TFTS activating on the same day.

4511 Combat Crew Training Squadron
F-100D/F   10/7/68* - 18/1/70

The 4511 CCTS, tail coded F-100 assets in July 1968, while assigned to the 4510 CCTW. Squadron reassigned on 15/10/69 to the 58 TFTW, maintaining the **LA** tail code. Inactivated on 18/1/70 with 311 TFTS activating same day.

4514 Combat Crew Training Squadron
F-100D/F   10/7/68* - 15/12/69

Activated within the 4510 CCTW, on 1/9/66, and tail coded **LA** in July 1968. Reassigned to the 58 TFTW on 15/10/69, maintaining **LA** tail code. Green noted as the squadron colour. Inactivated on 15/12/69 and replaced by the 310 TFTS.

4515 Combat Crew Training Squadron
F-100D/F   10/7/68* - 18/1/70

Activated within the 4510 CCTW, on 1/9/66, and tail coded **LA** during July 1968. Reassigned from the inactivating 4510 CCTW on 15/10/69 to the 58 TFTW maintaining the **LA** tail code. Inactivated on 18/1/70, with the 426 TFTS activated on the same day.

4517 Combat Crew Training Squadron
F-100D/F   10/7/68* - 18/1/70

TACTICAL AIR COMMAND - CONTINENTAL U.S.

Assigned to 4510 CCTW on 1/9/66, tail coded **LA** during July 1968, and reassigned to 58 TFTW on 15/10/69 maintained the **LA** tail code. Inactivated on 18/1/70 with assets reassigned to the activating 550 TFTS.

58 OMS/Base Flight
UH-1F/P
Luke AFB operated both UH-1F and UH-1P. Not a recognized unit, but a staff section. Dates of usage are unknown, operated at least between 1983 and 1987. Reassigned from the 58 TFTW to 405 TTW on activation in August 1979.

UH-1F Huey 65-7925 **LA**, Base flight 405 TFTW, Luke AFB. Photo: Douglas Slowiak, 21 March 1987.

LA
Detachment 1   **57 Fighter Weapons Wing**
A-7D   15/10/69 - 15/7/71   **Luke AFB, Arizona**

Activated at Luke AFB in September 1969 with **WA** tail code. Detachment 1 recoded to **LA** in the same interval as the 4525 FWW was replaced by the 57 FWW. As the exact dates are unknown, it is possible that the **LA** code may have adorned 4525 FWW A-7D, and the **WA** tail code on 57 FWW, assigned A-7D. Both noted with black and yellow checkered tail stripe. Also in this time frame, the 58 TFTW and 355 TFW exchanged roles and equipment. The 57 FWW detachment moved from Luke AFB to Davis-Monthan AFB and recoded **DM**. Also reported as originally Detachment 1 4510 CCTW at Luke AFB except 4410 CCTW became 58 TFTW on 15/10/69 before possible delivery of A-7D.

LA
USAF Tactical Fighter Weapons Centre - Detachment   **1 1/7/74 - 15/5/75**
HQ USAF TFWC Operating Location AA   **15/5/75 - unknown**
    Luke AFB, Arizona

F-15   **1/7/74 - unknown**
Activated on 1/7/74 at Luke AFB as the F-15 Flight Operations Test and Evaluation Detachment. Replaced by the HQ USAF TFWC Operating Location AA on 15/5/75.

LF
58 Tactical Training Wing   **1/1/83* - current 31/12/90**   **Luke AFB, Arizona**
*official date, F-16 noted with **LF** tail code prior.*

310 Tactical Fighter Training Squadron
F-16A/B   6/12/82 - 6/89
F-16C/D   5/89 - current 31/12/90
Converted from **LA** tail coded F-4C operations within the 58 TFW to **LF** tail coded F-16 on 6/12/82. Squadron F-16A/B carried a green tail stripe outlined in yellow with a white star added mid 1980's. Converted to F-16C/D during May 1989.

311 Tactical Fighter Training Squadron
F-16A/B   4/83 - current 31/12/90
Converted from F-4C operations with **LA** tail code. Recoded with F-16 training role to **LF**. A blue tail stripe carried with yellow outline carried on F-16A/B. Noted as the second F-16 unit within wing.

F-16A Falcon 79-0324 **LF**, 311 TFS 58 TFTW, Luke AFB, with blue tail stripe outline in white. Photo: Mike MacGowan, Abbotsford IAP, 9 August 1986.

312 Tactical Fighter Training Squadron
F-16C/D   5/11/84 - current 31/12/90

Activated on 1/10/84, with the first F-16C/D aircraft delivered on 5/11/84. A black tail stripe outlined with red carried by F-16C/D. Centred white star noted in 1990.

F-16D Falcon 83-1175 **LF**, 312 TFTS 58 TFTW, Luke AFB, with red outlined black tail stripe. Displaying "F-16D No 1" on fuselage side, although 83-1174 is actual first F-16D. Photo: Douglas Slowiak, 17 November 1984.

314 Tactical Fighter Training Squadron
F-16C/D   1/10/86 - current 31/12/90

The 314 TFTS activated in 1984, with F-16C/D. The squadron F-16 carried a yellow tail stripe outlined in red.

LF
Detachment 1*57 Fighter Weapons Wing
F-16C   1/4/85 - 1990   Luke AFB, Arizona

Detachment 1 reactivated on 1/4/85, at Luke AFB to conduct F-16C testing.

LK
314 Tactical Airlift Wing   1972* - 1/12/74+   Little Rock AFB Arkansas

16 Tactical Airlift Training Squadron
C-130E   1972* - 1/12/74+

The Little Rock based 64 TATS flew **TE** tail coded C-130E. On commencement of AFM66-1, common wing tail code, recoded to **LK** in 1972 with a white tail stripe. Tail code dropped with MAC control.

32 Tactical Airlift Squadron
C-130E   1/9/73 - 1/12/74+

The 32 TAS previously flew **DE** tail coded C-130 within the 374 TAW at Ching Chuan Kang AB, Taiwan until 8/2/73. The 32 TAS activated within the 314 TAW on 1/9/73 with **LK** tail coded C-130E replacing the 48 TAS. Tail codes carried until MAC control on 1/12/74.

48 Tactical Airlift Squadron
C-130E   6/8/73 - 1/9/73

The 48 TAS assigned from the 313 TAW on 6/8/73 to the 314 TAW with C-130E. Inactivated within the 314 TAW shortly after on 1/9/73 until replaced by the 32 TAS.

50 Tactical Airlift Squadron
C-130E   15/9/73 - 1/12/74+

TACTICAL AIR COMMAND - CONTINENTAL U.S.

The squadron activated within the 314 TAW on 15/8/73, declared operational on 15/9/73. Carried **LK** tail codes until MAC control on 1/12/74.

61 Tactical Airlift Squadron
C-130E 1972* - 1/12/74+

Previously tail coded **ST** before common wing tail code. Tail coded C-130E flown with a green tail stripe. Codes removed on 1/12/74 under MAC control.

62 Tactical Airlift Squadron
C-130E 1972* - 1/12/74+

Previously flew **SR** tail coded C-130 before common wing tail codes. The **LK** coded C-130 flew with a yellow tail stripe. Codes removed 1/12/74 under MAC control.

C-130E Hercules 68-10941 **LK**, 62 TAS 314 TAW, Little Rock AFB, with yellow tail stripe. Photo: David Davenport, at unknown location, 22 April 1974.

LM
36 Tactical Airlift Squadron   316 Tactical Airlift Wing
C-130E 10/7/68* - 1972   Langley AFB, Virginia

The 36 TAS assigned **LM** tail code on 10/7/68. Squadron flew C-130E with the 316 TAW since 1/4/66. Under common tail code concept the squadron maintained **LM** tail code and a red tail stripe after 1972.

LM
316 Tactical Airlift Wing   1972* - 1/12/74+   Langley AFB, Virginia

36 Tactical Airlift Squadron
C-130E 1972* - 1/12/74+

Under AFM66-1 concept, squadron maintained the **LM** tail code. Red tail stripe carried. Tail codes dropped on 1/12/74 when MAC took control of airlift assets.

37 Tactical Airlift Squadron
C-130E 1972* - 1/12/74+

Recoded from **LN** tail code to **LM** under common wing tail code concept during 1972. Tail code and blue tail stripe maintained until MAC control on 1/12/74.

38 Tactical Airlift Squadron
C-130E 1972* - 1/12/74+

Recoded from **LO** to **LM** under common wing tail code concept during 1972. Tail codes maintained until MAC took control of airlift assets on 1/12/74.

LN
37 Tactical Airlift Squadron   316 Tactical Airlift Wing
C-130E 10/7/68* - 1972   Langley AFB, Virginia

Flew C-130E starting on 1/10/66, within the 316 TAW and tail coded **LN** in July 1968. Under common wing code concept AFM66-1, the squadron recoded to **LM**. Squadron colour noted as Blue.

LO
38 Tactical Airlift Squadron   316 Tactical Airlift Wing
                                                    Langley AFB, Virginia

C-130E 10/7/68* - 1/7/69
C-130E 15/11/71 - 1972*

The 38 TAS starting flying C-130E on 1/1/67 within the 316 TAW and tail coded **LO** during July 1968. Reassigned to the 313 TAW on 1/7/69 and recoded to **FH**, between 1/7/69 and 15/11/71. Squadron returned to the 316 TAW resuming the **LO** tail code and further recoded **LM** under common wing tail code concept.

TAIL CODE

LV
4451 Test Squadron   **4450 Tactical Group**
A-7D/K   **by 11/84 - 1988**   **Nellis AFB, Nevada**

    The 4451 Test Squadron flew uncoded A-7 since June 1981. Aircraft tail coded **LV** by late 1984. Markings of either a black or red band with two falcons carried on A-7. Aircraft reported as systems check and as day time mounts for stealth program. Replaced by uncoded AT-38B during 1988.

A-7D Corsair 69-0241 **LV**, 4451 TS 4450 TG, Nellis AFB. Photo: Doug Remington, McChord AFB, 1 September 1986.

LY
48 Fighter Interceptor Squadron

	1/3/83 - 1/7/87	23 Air Division - Air Defense TAC
	1/7/87 - 1/12/87	23 Air Division - 1st Air Force
	1/12/87 - current 31/12/90	24 Air Division - 1st Air Force
F-15A/B	1987 - current 31/12/90	**Langley AFB, Virginia**

    The 48 FIS reequipped from F-106A/B to F-15A/B, starting on 14/8/81. The F-15 applied the **LY** tail code by 1987, with blue tail stripes with four white stars added shortly after.

F-15A Eagle 76-0119 **LY**, 48 FIS 24 AD, Langley AFB, with single sided blue tail stripes with four white stars. Photo: Marty Isham, Nellis AFB, 24 March 1989.

LZ
4441 Combat Crew Training Squadron   **4510 Combat Crew Training Wing**
     Williams AFB, Arizona

F-5A   10/7/68* - 15/10/69
F-5B   10/7/68* - 15/10/69

    Squadron assigned F-5A/B in 1964, with tail code **LZ** applied in July 1968. Unusual original tail code assignment as of four CCTW each adopted a single tail code for all components. The 4441 CCTS providing the sole exception as based at Williams AFB separately from controlling wing at Luke AFB. Blue note as squadron colour and carried as tail stripe. Squadron replaced by the 425 TFTS 58 TTW on 15/10/69 while maintaining base.

LZ
425 Tactical Fighter Training Squadron   **58 Tactical Fighter Training Wing**
     Williams AFB, Arizona

F-5A   15/10/69 - 1973
F-5B   15/10/69 - 1974

    The 425 TFTS replaced the 4441 CCTS on 15/10/69. Squadron F-5B carried a blue tail stripe, while F-5A green. Aircraft recoded to common wing tail code **LA** in 1974.

TACTICAL AIR COMMAND - CONTINENTAL U.S.

127

F-5B Freedom Fighter 72-0439 **LZ**, 425 TFTS 58 TFTW, Williams AFB, with blue tail stripe. Photo: Tom Brewer, Wright-Patterson AFB, 14 July 1973.

MB
355 Tactical Fighter Squadron   **354 Tactical Fighter Wing**
A-7D   **1/11/70 - 1972**   **Myrtle Beach AFB, South Carolina**

The 355 TFS previously operated **SP** tail coded F-100 at Tuy Hoa AB, RSVN until 20/9/70. Squadron reactivated on 1/11/70 with **MB** tail coded A-7D and maintained the **MB** tail code as wing standard.

MB
354 Tactical Fighter Wing   post 5/72* - current 31/12/90   Myrtle Beach AFB, South Carolina

353 Tactical Fighter Squadron
A-7D   1972* - 1976
A-10A   1976 - current 31/12/90

The 353 TFS recoded to **MB** under the AFM66-1 concept, from **MR**. Squadron A-7D carried a red tail stripe. The 353 TFS deployed to Korat RTAFB between 10/10/72 and 15/3/73. Squadron converted to A-10A during 1976 and carried red tail stripes with black panther. The A-10A switched to red fin caps by 1983.

A-10A Thunderbolt 78-0687 **MB**, 353 TFS 354 TFW, Myrtle Beach AFB, with twin red fin caps. Photo: Patrick Martin, CFB Cold Lake, 3 May 1985.

355 Tactical Fighter Squadron
A-7D   1972* - 1977
A-10A   1977 - current 31/12/90

Squadron maintained the **MB** tail code and blue tail stripe under common wing tail code. The 355 TFS deployed to Korat RTAFB between 10/10/72 and 22/4/74 with the advance echelon of the 354 TFW. Squadron re-equipped with A-10A during 1977, reaching operational status on 15/2/78. Squadron A-10 carried white tail bands with six black stars, changing to seven blue stars during 1982-83. By 1984 A-10A carried an all blue fin caps.

A-10A Thunderbolt 77-0199 **MB**, 355 TFS 354 TFW, Myrtle Beach AFB, with single sided white tail stripe containing six black stars. Photo: Ben Knowles, Davis-Monthan AFB, 2 February 1980.

356 Tactical Fighter Squadron
A-7D   1972* - 1977
A-10A   1977 - current 31/12/90

Recoded **MB** from **MN** under the common wing tail code during 1972. Squadron A-7D carried a green tail stripe. Squadron deployed to Korat RTAFB, between 10/10/72 and 4/5/74, with advance echelon of the 354 TFW. Re-equipped with A-10A during 1977 and reached operational status on 15/10/77. Squadron A-10A carried green tail bands outlined in white with four forward facing arrows before switching to green fin caps. One example noted with green and white checkered tail stripe with a white square containing centred green arrows.

A-7D Corsair 69-6244 **MB**, 356 TFS 354 TFW, Myrtle Beach AFB. Photo: David Davenport, Pope AFB, 17 October 1973.

4554 Tactical Fighter Replacement Squadron
A-7D   15/5/72 - 15/10/75

The 4554 TFRS activated within the 354 TFW as a training unit. A yellow tail stripe carried on A-7D. The squadron status non-operational after 13/9/75, and inactivating on 15/10/75.

MC
560 Tactical Fighter Squadron   **23 Tactical Fighter Wing**
F-105D/F   10/7/68* - 25/9/68

Tail code assigned along with the 561, 562, 563 TFS and 4519 CCTS in July 1968. Status changed to non-operational after 19/6/68. Possibly the codes not applied as reassigned to the 4531 TFW Homestead with **ZF** tail coded F-4 on 15/9/68.

MC
56 Tactical Fighter Wing   30/6/75 - 1/10/81
56 Tactical Training Wing   1/10/81 - current 31/12/90

MacDill AFB, Florida

13 Tactical Fighter Training Squadron
F-4E   13/1/76 - 25/8/78
F-4D   25/8/78 - 30/6/82

Previously inactivated with **UD** tail coded F-4D within the 432 TRW at Udorn RTAFB, on 30/6/75. Activated within the 56 TFW on 15/1/76, assuming assets from the inactivating 4501 TFRS. Squadron inactivated on 30/6/82. Squadron replaced by the 72 TFTS on 1/7/81. Later assigned to the 432 TFW, Misawa AB, Japan flying **MJ** tail coded F-16.

TACTICAL AIR COMMAND - CONTINENTAL U.S.

61 Tactical Fighter Squadron   30/6/75 - 1/7/82
61 Tactical Fighter Training Squadron   1/7/82 - current 31/12/90
F-4E   30/6/75 - 30/4/78
F-4D   30/4/78 - 19/11/79
F-16A/B   4/80 - 4-6/89
F-16C/D   4-6/89 - current 31/12/90

The 61 TFS activated with assets of the 27 TFS when the 56 TFW replaced the 1 TFW on 30/6/75. Squadron converted to yellow fin capped F-4D. The last F-4D mission flown on 19/11/79 and was the first squadron within the 56 TFW to complete F-16A/B conversion on 18/4/80. The F-16 carried a yellow tail stripe outlined in white. The squadron redesignated to 61 TFTS on 1/7/82 and completed further conversion to F-16C/D on 28/6/89, adding black "Top Dawg" within the stripe.

F-16 Falcon 79-0397 **MC**, 61 TFTS 56 TTW, MacDill AFB. Photo: Daniel Soulaine, Burlington IAP, May 1987.

F-4D Phantom 66-0244 **MC**, 61 TFS 56 TFW, MacDill AFB, with yellow fin cap. Photo: unknown

62 Tactical Fighter Squadron   30/6/75 - 1/7/82
62 Tactical Fighter Training Squadron   1/7/82 - current 31/12/90
F-4E   30/6/75 - 4/2/78
F-4D   4/2/78 - 14/11/80
F-16A/B   15/10/80 - 6/89
F-16C/D   6/89 - current 31/12/90

The 62 TFS activated within the 56 TFW on 30/6/75. The last F-4D flight occurred on 14/11/80. Conversion to F-16A/B began on 15/10/80 with completion on 1/12/80. Further converted to the F-16C/D completed on 27/6/89. Squadron colour of blue carried as fin cap of varying thickness, with white outline added later.

63 Tactical Fighter Squadron   30/6/75 - 1/7/82
63 Tactical Fighter Training Squadron   1/7/82 - current 31/12/90
F-4E   30/6/75 - 26/5/78
F-4D   26/5/78 - 1/10/81
F-16A/B   1/10/81 - 6/89
F-16C/D   6/89 - current 31/12/90

The squadron converted to F-4D from F-4E by 26/5/78 the F-16A/B by 1/10/81 and the F-16C/D by 31/7/89. A red tail stripe outlined in white carried, with F-16C/D added white "Panthers" within the stripe.

TAIL CODE

F-4D Phantom 66-0277 **MC**, 63 TFTS 56 TTW, MacDill AFB, with red fin cap. Photo: Martin collection.

72 Tactical Fighter Training Squadron

F-16A/B	1/7/82 - 3/90
F-16C/D	11/3/90 - current 31/12/90

The 72 TFTS replaced the 13 TFTS which inactivated on 30/6/82. A black tail stripe outlined in white carried by F-16. The 72 TFTS reequipped with the F-16C/D in March 1990.

4501 Tactical Fighter Replacement Squadron

F-4E	30/6/75 - 15/1/76

The 1 TFW left the 4501 TFRS at MacDill AFB on wing reassignment to Langley AFB, on 30/6/75. The 56 TFW controlled squadron until inactivated on 15/1/76. The 13 TFTS assumed squadron assets when activated on the same day. White noted as squadron colour.

MD

561 Tactical Fighter Squadron   **23 Tactical Fighter Wing**
                                             McConnell AFB, Kansas

F-105D/F	10/7/68* - 1/7/72
F-105G	9/6/70 - 1/7/72

The 561 TFS activated with F-105 on 8/2/64 within the 23 TFW. The **MD** tail code assigned on 10/7/68. A detachment deployed to Udorn RTAFB with **MD** tail coded F-105F/G between 7/4/72 and 1/7/72, leaving only the F-105F at McConnell AFB. A yellow tail stripe carried on F-105. Possible squadron directly assigned on 1/7/72 to the 832 AD before activating within the 35 TFW on 1/7/73 and recoded **GA**.

F-105G Thunderchief 63-8360 **MD**, 561 TFS 23 TFW, McConnell AFB, with yellow tail stripe. Photo: Doug Remington, Langley AFB, 7 October 1970.

ME

562 Tactical Fighter Squadron   **23 Tactical Fighter Wing**
                                             McConnell AFB, Kansas

F-105D	10/7/68* - 1/7/72
F-105F	1/7/72 - 31/7/72

Squadron activated as an F-105 unit on 8/2/64 within the 23 TFW. Tail code **ME** assigned on 10/7/68. Squadron inactivated on 31/7/72 and later reactivated within the 35 TFW, at George AFB, with **GA** tail code.

MF

563 Tactical Fighter Squadron   **23 Tactical Fighter Wing**
                                             McConnell AFB, Kansas

F-105B	1970

TACTICAL AIR COMMAND - CONTINENTAL U.S.

F-105D	10/7/68* - 1/7/72
F-105D T-Stick	unknown
F-105F	- 1/7/72

The third F-105 squadron activated on 8/2/64 within the 23 TFW, at McConnell AFB. Tail code **MF** assigned on 10/7/68. T-Stick II version of F-105D also used for an unknown period. Inactivated on 1/7/72 and reactivated within the 35 TFW, during July 1975.

F-105D Thunderchief T-Stick 60-0465 **MF**, 563 TFS 23 TFW, McConnell AFB, with red tail stripe. Photo: Doug Remington, MacDill AFB, 25 March 1972.

MG
4519 Combat Crew Training Squadron **23 Tactical Fighter Wing**
  McConnell AFB, Kansas

F-105B	10/7/68* - 16/10/69
F-105D	10/7/68* - 16/10/69
F-105F	1968 - 16/10/69
F-105G	1969 - 16/10/69

Activated at McConnell AFB on 1/8/67 and declared operational on 21/1/68, with F-105B/D. Assigned **MG** tail code on 10/7/68. Squadron added F-105G in 1969. The 4519 CCTS inactivated on 16/10/69 and replaced by the 419 TFTS, assuming assets and **MG** tail code.

MG
419 Tactical Fighter Training Squadron **23 Tactical Fighter Wing**
  McConnell AFB, Kansas

F-105B	15/10/69 - 8/5/71
F-105D	15/10/69 - 8/5/71
F-105F	15/10/69 - 8/5/71

Squadron activated at McConnell AFB, on 15/10/69, replacing the 4419 CCTS, assuming assets and **MG** tail code. Operations ceased on 8/5/71 and the squadron inactivated on 1/10/71.

MN
356 Tactical Fighter Squadron **354 Tactical Fighter Wing**
A-7D   15/5/71 - 1972 **Myrtle Beach AFB, South Carolina**

Squadron previously inactivated while flying **UK** tail coded F-4 within the 475 TFW at Misawa AB, Japan, on 15/3/71. Reactivated on 15/5/71 to operate **MN** tail coded A-7D until wing recoded to **MB** under common wing code in mid 1972. A green tail stripe carried by squadron A-7D.

A-7D Corsair 70-0975 **MN**, 356 TFS 354 TFW, Myrtle Beach AFB. Photo: Tom Brewer, Eglin AFB, 18 September 1971.

132 TAIL CODE

MO
391 Tactical Fighter Squadron   **347 Tactical Fighter Wing**
F-111F   **30/6/71 - 1972**   **Mountain Home AFB, Idaho**

The 391 TFS activated with **MO** tail coded F-111F displayed a blue tail stripe, at Mountain Home AFB, on 30/6/71. Squadron maintained the **MO** tail code under the AFM66-1 common wing tail code concept.

MO
347 Tactical Fighter Wing   **1972* - 30/10/72**
366 Tactical Fighter Wing   **31/10/72 - current 31/12/90**

Mountain Home AFB, Idaho

388 Tactical Fighter Training Squadron   **1/7/77 - 28/3/81**
388 Electronic Combat Squadron   **28/3/81 - 28/3/84**
F-111A   **1/7/77 - 1981**
EF-111A   **5/11/81 - 28/3/84**

The 388 TFTS, added as the fourth squadron to the 366 TFW on 1/7/77. Initially activated with F-111A, converted to the electronic role 1981 with EF-111A. The electronic role reassigned to 390 ECS on 28/3/84, with the 388 TFS inactivating. Squadron EF-111A did not carry identification markings.

389 Tactical Fighter Squadron   **15/10/71 - 30/9/79**
389 Tactical Fighter Training Squadron   **30/9/79 - current 31/12/90**
F-111F   **1972* - 1977**
F-111A   **1977 - current 31/12/90**

Squadron recoded from **MP** under common wing code concept during 1972. Reequipped under operation "Ready Switch" to F-111A. The 389 TFS redesignated to 389 TFTS on 30/9/79. A yellow tail stripe carried by F-111, later changing to fin cap.

F-111F 70-2364 **MO**, 389 TFS 366 TFW, Mountain Home AFB, with red tail stripe. Photo: Ben Knowles, McClellan AFB, 18 October 1974.

390 Tactical Fighter Squadron   **30/6/72 - 28/3/84**
390 Electronic Combat Squadron   **28/3/84 - current 31/12/90**
F-111F   **1972* - 1977**
F-111A   **1977 - 28/3/84**
EF-111A   **28/3/84 - current 31/12/90**

Recoded from **MQ** under the common wing tail code concept. Squadron reassigned to the 366 TFW on 31/10/72. The 390 TFS reequipped under "Ready Switch" to F-111A. The green tail stripe changed to fin cap. Assumed electronic countermeasures role from inactivating 388 ECS on 28/3/84 the standard F-111A exchanged for EF-111A "Ravens."

EF-111A Raven 67-0052 **MO**, 390 ECS 366 TFW, Mountain Home AFB, displaying black raven motif. Photo: Patrick Martin, CFB Namao, 18 May 1990.

TACTICAL AIR COMMAND - CONTINENTAL U.S.

F-111F 70-2394 **MO**, 391 TFS 347 TFW, Mountain Home AFB, displaying blue tail stripe of 391 TFS. Photo: Lindsay Peacock, Andrews AFB, 16 September 1972.

391 Tactical Fighter Squadron
F-111F   1972* - 1977
F-111A   1977- current 31/12/90
   The **MO** tail code and blue tail stripe maintained under the AFM66-1 common wing tail code concept.

MO
Detachment 2   **57 Fighter Weapons Wing**
F-111A   1/7/77 - 30/12/81   **Mountain Home AFB, Idaho**
   F-111A FWS activated at Mountain Home AFB with title changed to USAF FWS Detachment 1 (*F-111 Division - Fighter Weapons School*) on 30/12/81.

MO
Detachment 3   **57 Fighter Weapons Wing**
F-111F   15/8/71 - 1/5/72   **Mountain Home AFB, Idaho**
   Activated at Mountain Home AFB. The F-111F model assumed as before operation "ready switch." Detachment 3 also title of testing unit at McClellan AFB. Inactivated and replaced by the 431 TES, on 1/10/80.

MO
USAF FWS Detachment 1   **Mountain Home AFB, Idaho**
F-111   30/12/81 - unknown
   Detachment activated at Mountain Home AFB, on 30/12/81, replacing Detachment 2, 57 FWW also based at Mountain Home AFB. The F-111A carried black and yellow checkered tail stripe when assigned to the FWS.

(MP)
4589 Tactical Fighter Squadron   **347 Tactical Fighter Wing**
F-111F   1/9/71 - 15/10/71   **Mountain Home AFB, Idaho**
   Squadron activated within the 347 TFW and tail coded **MP**. The 4589 TFS inactivated on 15/10/71 and replaced by the 389 TFS on the same day.

(MP)
389 Tactical Fighter Squadron   **347 Tactical Fighter Wing**
F-111F   15/10/71 - 1972   **Mountain Home AFB, Idaho**
   Reassigned from the 12 TFW, flying **HB** coded F-4D at Phu Cat AB, RSVN. Assets and tail code assumed from the inactivated provisional 4589 TFS. Squadron recoded under common wing tail code concept to **MO**.

(MQ)
4590 Tactical Fighter Squadron   **347 Tactical Fighter Wing**
F-111F   1/1/72 - 30/6/72   **Mountain Home AFB, Idaho**
   Squadron activated within the 347 TFW and coded **MQ**. Inactivated on 30/6/72, and replaced by the 390 TFS on the same day.

(MQ)
390 Tactical Fighter Squadron   **347 Tactical Fighter Wing**
F-111F   30/6/72 - 1972   **Mountain Home AFB, Idaho**
   Reassigned from flying the **LF** tail coded F-4D within the 366 TFW, at Da Nang AB, RSVN on 30/6/72. Assets and tail code assumed from the inactivated provisional 4590 TFS. Recoded under common wing tail code concept to **MO** at Mountain Home AFB during 1972. It is possible the 390 TFS never carried the **MQ** tail code as transition occurred in the same period as common wing tail code concept of **MO** introduced.

MR
511 Tactical Fighter Squadron   **354 Tactical Fighter Wing**
A-7D   15/6/70 - 15/7/71   **Myrtle Beach AFB, South Carolina**

Activated within the 354 TFW, on 15/6/70, and becoming operational on 8/9/70. Squadron operated **MR** tail coded A-7D until replaced by the 353 TFS, on 15/7/71. Red tail stripe carried by A-7D. Reactivated in 1988 with the 81 TFW USAFE. Reactivated within USAFE flying the A-10A with **WR** and later **AR** tail code.

MR
353 Tactical Fighter Squadron   **354 Tactical Fighter Wing**
A-7D   15/7/71 - 1972   Myrtle Beach AFB, South Carolina

Squadron reassigned from F-4E operations within the 401 TFW at Torrejon AB, Spain. Squadron replaced the 511 TFS on 15/7/71 and flew **MR** tail coded A-7D, with red tail stripes. Recoded **MB** under the AFM66-1 concept.

MY
347 Tactical Fighter Wing   30/9/75 - current 31/12/90   Moody AFB, Georgia

68 Tactical Fighter Squadron
F-4E	30/9/75 - 1/1/88
F-16A/B	1/1/88 - by 31/12/90
F-16C/D	1990 - current 31/12/90

Squadron reassigned from 3 TFW (*non-operational*) to the 347 TFW, on 30/9/75. Squadron F-4E carried a red tail stripe. The 68 TFS converted to the F-16A/B in 1988 and F-16C in 1990.

69 Tactical Fighter Squadron
F-4E	1/9/83 - 1/1/88
F-16A/B	1/1/88 - by 10/90
F-16C/D	by 7/90 - current 31/12/90

Squadron activated on 1/9/83, from the assets of the 339 TFS, which inactivated on the same day. Silver tail stripe carried as squadron markings.

70 Tactical Fighter Squadron
F-4E	30/9/75 - 1/4/88
F-16A/B	1/4/88 - by 10/90
F-16C/D	by 10/90 - current 31/12/90

Squadron activated within the 347 TFW on 30/9/75. Squadron F-4E carried black and white checkered tail stripe. Converted to F-16A/B 1988 and F-16C/D in 1990.

F-4E Phantom 67-0392 **MY**, 70 TFS 347 TFW, Moody AFB, with black and white checkered tail stripe, with "70 AMU" on tail.
Photo: Doug Remington, McChord AFB, 15 August 1987.

339 Tactical Fighter Squadron
F-4E	30/9/75 - 1/9/83

The 339 TFS activated within the 347 TFW on 30/9/75, non-operational until 4/5/76. Squadron F-4E carried a red tail stripe. Inactivated and replaced by the 69 TFS, on 1/9/83.

NA
428 Tactical Fighter Squadron   **474 Tactical Fighter Wing**
F-111A   11/68* - 1972   Nellis AFB, Nevada

Squadron assigned **NA** tail code on 10/7/68, but not receiving F-111A until return of "Combat Lancer" aircraft. The **NA** tail code maintained as common wing code under AFM66-1. Large blue and white stylized tail band, outlined in black carried.

NA
474 Tactical Fighter Wing   1972* - 1/8/89   Nellis AFB, Nevada
                                                                  27/9/72 - 30/7/73   Takhli RTAFB

428 Tactical Fighter Squadron
F-111A	1972* - 30/7/73
F-111A	15/6/75 - by 8/77
F-4D	by 8/77 - 1982
F-16A/B	1982 - 1//8/89

TACTICAL AIR COMMAND - CONTINENTAL U.S.

Squadron maintained the **NA** tail code as wing standard under AFM66-1 common wing code concept. The 428 TFS F-111A carried a light blue tail stripe. The 428 TFS deployed to Takhli RTAFB in September 1972. Assigned to 347 TFW RTAFB Takhli, on 30/7/73, and tail coded **HG** on assignment.

The 428 TFS returned from Southeast Asia to 474 TFW at Nellis AFB on 15/6/75. The **HG** tail code carried for a short period after squadron returned to Nellis AFB, then returning to the **NA** tail code. Squadron converted to F-4D during operation "Ready Switch." Further conversion to F-16A/B in occurred in 1977. Squadron F-16 carried a blue tail stripe with white skull and cross bones. Reactivated to fly **CC** tail coded F-111G within 27 TFW in April 1990. Squadron inactivated in 1989.

429 Tactical Fighter Squadron
F-111A	1972* - 30/7/73
F-111A	21/6/75 - by 8/77
F-4D	by 8/77 - 1982
F-16A/B	1982 - 1/8/89

Recoded from **NB** to common wing tail code standard of **NA** in 1972. The 429 TFS deployed to Takhli RTAFB, during September and October 1972. Reassigned to 347 TFW at Takhli RTAFB on 30/7/73 and recoded **HG**.

Squadron returned to 474 TFW from Southeast Asia on 21/6/75. A yellow tail stripe carried on **NA** tail coded F-111A. Converted to F-4D during operation "Ready Switch" and further converted to F-16A/B in 1977. The squadron F-16 carried yellow tail stripe with centred black raven. In late 1980's markings changed to dark green band with like coloured raven in a yellow centred disk. The 429 TFS inactivated 1989.

F-16A Falcon 79-0389 **NA**, 429 TFS 474 TFW, Nellis AFB, with yellow tail stripe. Photo: Doug Remington, McChord AFB, 15 April 1983.

F-16A Falcon 79-0380 **NA**, 429 TFS 474 TFW, Nellis AFB, with red outlined black tail stripe containing yellow disk with black raven. Photo: Patrick Martin, Paine Field, 18 August 1987.

430 Tactical Fighter Squadron
F-111A	1972* - by 8/77
F-4D	by 8/77 - 1982
F-16A/B	1982 - 1/8/89

Squadron formerly tail coded **NC**, with F-111A. The 430 TFS recoded **NA** under AFM66-1 common wing code concept. Squadron deployed to Takhli RTAFB, during September and October 1972 and returned to Nellis AFB on 22/3/73. Equipment changed under operation "Ready Switch" to F-4D. Squadron further converted to F-16A/B carrying with a red tail stripe. Markings changed to a red and white striped band before inactivating in 1989.

136   TAIL CODE

NB
429 Tactical Fighter Squadron   **474 Tactical Fighter Wing**
F-111A   10/7/68* - 1972   **Nellis AFB, Nevada**

The 429 received F-111A in early 1968 and by mid year tail coded **NA**. Large yellow and white stylized tail band outlined in black changing to yellow tail stripe by 1971. Possible F-111A not received until August 1968. Recoded to the wing standard **NA** in 1972.

F-111A 67-0074 **NB**, 429 TFS 474 TFW, Nellis AFB, with yellow tail stripe. Photo: Pete Bergagnin, George AFB, 3 April 1971.

NC
430 Tactical Fighter Squadron   **474 Tactical Fighter Wing**
F-111A   3/69* - 1972   **Nellis AFB, Nevada**

Tail code **NC** assigned on 10/7/68 even though not activated within the 474 TFW until 15/9/68, receiving F-111A in March 1969 and coding **NC**. Large red and white stylized tail band, outlined in black carried. Recoded to the wing standard of **NA** in 1972.

F-111A 67-0113 **NC**, 430 TFS 474 TFW, Nellis AFB, large red and white stylized tail band outlined in black. Photo: Martin collection.

ND
4527 Combat Crew Training Squadron   **474 Tactical Fighter Wing**
F-111A   10/7/68* - 15/10/69   **Nellis AFB, Nevada**

Activated on 20/1/68 assigned **ND** tail code on 10/7/68 for application on F-111A. Large green and white stylized tail band, outlined in black carried on F-111A. Squadron inactivated on 15/10/69, at Nellis AFB. Also, but unconfirmed, is the use of F-111E.

NF
602 Tactical Air Control Wing   1/9/82 - current 31/12/90   **Davis-Monthan AFB, Arizona**

22 Tactical Air Support Training Squadron
OV-10A   14/10/88 - current 31/12/90
OA-10A   15/6/88 - current 31/12/90

Previously flew **WH** coded OV-10A from Wheeler Field until reactivated at Davis-Monthan AFB on 14/10/88. Established as FAC training unit for forward air control flying OV-10A and OA-10A.

23 Tactical Air Support Squadron
OA-37B   2/5/81 - 4/3/88
OA-10A   1/10/87 - current 31/12/90

Squadron originally located Bergstrom AFB provided FAC capability flying uncoded O-2. The 23 TASS moved to Davis-Monthan AFB assuming O-2 assets of the 27 TASS on 1/7/80. Unit flew last O-2 mission on 30/10/81 and converted to **NF** tail coded OA-37B on 1/11/81 (*note code prior to 602 TACW activation date*). OA-37B noted with blue and red trim. Became FAC school during October 1987. The 23 TASS started OA-10A conversion in October 1987, absorbed the training role for OA-10A 8/89 and declared operational by January 1989. Squadron OA-10A noted with blue fin caps with three yellow stars on outer surfaces.

TACTICAL AIR COMMAND - CONTINENTAL U.S.

OA-10A Thunderbolt 77-0218 **NF**, 23 TASS 602 TAIRCW, Davis-Monthan AFB, with blue fin caps containing three yellow stars on outer surfaces. Photo: Patrick Martin, Nellis AFB, 9 January 1989.

OA
39 Tactical Airlift Squadron   **317 Tactical Airlift Wing**
C-130A   10/7/68* - 30/6/71   **Lockbourne AFB, Ohio**

The 39 TAS flew C-130A from Lockbourne AFB between 15/4/63 and 30/5/71. Assigned the **OA** tail code for C-130A on 10/7/68. Unit status changed to non-operational on 1/6/71 and inactivated on 30/6/71.

OB
40 Tactical Airlift Squadron   **317 Tactical Airlift Wing**
                                                                                                    Lockbourne AFB, Ohio
C-130A   10/7/68* - 31/8/71
AC-130   14/7/70 - 31/8/71

Flew C-130A from Lockbourne AFB, since 15/4/63 with **OA** tail code assigned on 10/7/68. Also flew the AC-130A between 14/7/70 and 31/8/71. Squadron reassigned with wing to Pope AFB, on 31/8/71. Squadron colours not noted, recoded to **PG** on 31/8/71.

OD
4408 Combat Crew Training Squadron   **317 Tactical Airlift Wing**
C-123K   22/9/69 - 15/8/71   **Lockbourne AFB, Ohio**

The C-123K equipped 4408 CCTS reassigned from 1 SOW, at Lockbourne AFB, with **AO** tail codes. Green noted as the squadron colour. Inactivated within the 317 TAW on 15/8/71.

C-123K Provider 54-0669 **OD**, 4408 CCTS 4410 CCTW, Lockbourne AFB. Photo: Doug Remington, Langley AFB, 1 August 1970.

TAIL CODE

PB
777 Tactical Airlift Squadron
C-130E   10/7/68* - 31/8/71   **464 Tactical Airlift Wing**
                                                                       Pope AFB, North Carolina
  The 777 TAS tail coded C-130E **PB** while assigned to the 464 TAW at Pope AFB. Assets and tail code absorbed by 39 TAS 317 TAW, on 31/8/71. Blue noted as squadron colour with black also noted.

PB
39 Tactical Airlift Squadron
C-130E   31/8/71 - 1972   **317 Tactical Airlift Wing**
                                                                       Pope AFB, North Carolina
  The 39 TAS formerly flew **OA** tail coded C-130A within the 317 TAW based at Lockbourne AFB. Reassigned to Pope AFB within the 317 TAW, on 31/8/71. Assets assumed from the 777 TAS. Under AFM66-1, the common wing code concept, **PB** maintained as the wing code.

PB
317 Tactical Airlift Wing   1972* - 1/12/74+   **Pope AFB, North Carolina**

39 Tactical Airlift Squadron
C-130E   1972* - 1/12/74+
  Under the AFM66-1, common wing code concept the 39 TAS maintained the **PB** tail code post 1972. Blue noted as squadron colour. Codes carried until MAC control 1/12/74.

40 Tactical Airlift Squadron
C-130E   1972* - 1/12/74+
  Under AFM66-1 concept the 40 TAS changed tail codes from **PB** from **PG**. Green noted as squadron colour. Codes carried until MAC control 1/12/74.

41 Tactical Airlift Squadron
C-130E   1972* - 1/12/74+
  Under AFM66-1 concept tail codes change from **PB** from **PR**. A red tail stripe carried. Codes carried until MAC control 1/12/74.

C-130E Hercules 63-7876 **PB**, 41 TAS 317 TAW, Pope AFB, with red tail stripe. Photo: David Davenport, unknown location, 11 June 1974.

PG
778 Tactical Airlift Squadron
C-130E   10/7/68* - 31/8/71   **464 Tactical Airlift Wing**
                                                                       Pope AFB, North Carolina
  The 778 TAS tail coded C-130E in July 1968 as component of 464 TAW. Assets and tail code absorbed by 40 TAS 317 TAW on 31/8/71. Green stripe carried as squadron colour.

PF
549 Tactical Air Support Training Squadron   **549 Tactical Air Support Training Group/**
                                                                       1 Special Operations Wing
                                                                       Patrick AFB, Florida
OV-10A   11/3/87 - 1988
OT-37B   11/3/87 - 1988
  Squadron recoded from **FL** to **PF** on 11/3/87 maintaining red markings. Status unknown after 1988.

PG
40 Tactical Airlift Squadron
C-130E   31/8/71 - 1972   **317 Tactical Airlift Wing**
                                                                       Pope AFB, North Carolina
  The 40 TAS formerly flew **OB** coded C-130A within the 317 TAW at Lockbourne AFB. Squadron transferred to Pope AFB within the 317 TAW on 31/8/71, flying C-130E and tail coded **PG**. Assets assumed from 778 TAS. Under AFM66-1 common wing concept adopted the **PB** tail code during 1972.

TACTICAL AIR COMMAND - CONTINENTAL U.S.

PR
779 Tactical Airlift Squadron　　　　　　　　　　　　　　　　　　　　　　**464 Tactical Airlift Wing**
C-130E　　　　　　　　10/7/68* - 31/8/71　　　　　　　　　　　　　　　　　　**Pope AFB, North Carolina**

　　　　Flew C-130E within the 464 TAW, coding aircraft during July 1968. Assets and **PR** tail code absorbed by 41 TAS 317 TAW on 31/8/71. A red colour stripe carried by squadron C-130E.

PR
41 Tactical Airlift Squadron　　　　　　　　　　　　　　　　　　　　　　　**317 Tactical Airlift Wing**
C-130E　　　　　　　　31/8/71 - 1972　　　　　　　　　　　　　　　　　　　　**Pope AFB, North Carolina**

　　　　The 41 TAS previously flew C-130A with **YP** tail code within the 374 TAW, at Naha AB, Taiwan. Activated within the 317 TAW, at Pope AFB on 31/8/71. Assets absorbed from inactivating 779 TAS 464 TAW. Under common wing tail code, **PB** adopted as wing standard.

SA
334 Tactical Fighter Squadron　　　　　　　　　　　　　　　　　　　　　　**4 Tactical Fighter Wing**
　　　　　　　　　　　　　　　　　　　　　　　　　　　　　　　　　　　　　　Seymour Johnson AFB, North Carolina

F-4D　　　　　　　　　10/7/68* - by mid 1970
F-4E　　　　　　　　　7/70 - 1972*

　　　　Initially tail coded F-4D **SA** during 1968 (*squadron deployed to Kunsan AB, ROK, on 2/68 changing location to Kwang-ju AB, ROK, until 30/7/68 in reaction of to USS Pueblo seizure*). Second deployment to Kunsan AB, between 13/12/69 and 30/5/70, attached to the 354 TFW. Squadron F-4D carried a blue fin cap, with white outline. Conversion to F-4E started in July 1970 and completed on 31/10/70. The first of two deployments to 8 TFW at Ubon AB, RTAFB with F-4E occurred between 11/4/72 and 8/7/72. Wing common tail code **SJ** applied during second deployment between 25/9/72 and 3/73. Squadron F-4E carried blue fin cap and drop tank caps.

F-4D Phantom 67-7618 **SA**, 334 TFS 4 TFW, Seymour-Johnson AFB, displaying squadron commanders blue fin cap with three rows of white dots. Photo: Stephen H Miller, Andrews AFB, May 1969.

SB
335 Tactical Fighter Squadron　　　　　　　　　　　　　　　　　　　　　　**4 Tactical Fighter Wing**
　　　　　　　　　　　　　　　　　　　　　　　　　　　　　　　　　　　　　　Seymour Johnson AFB, North Carolina

F-4D　　　　　　　　　10/7/68* - late 1970
F-4E　　　　　　　　　10/70 - 1972*

　　　　Squadron F-4E assets coded in July 1968. The 335 TFS deployed within the 4 TFW to Kunsan AB, ROK in February 1968 and returning on 1/7/68. Squadron detached to the 354 TFW at Kunsan AB, ROK between 8/12/69 and 23/5/70. Conversion to F-4E started mid October 1970 and completed 16/2/71. A green fin cap carried as squadron markings. Squadron recoded to **SJ** under AFM66-1 wing common tail code in 1972.

SC
336 Tactical Fighter Squadron　　　　　　　　　　　　　　　　　　　　　　**4 Tactical Fighter Wing**
　　　　　　　　　　　　　　　　　　　　　　　　　　　　　　　　　　　　　　Seymour Johnson AFB, North Carolina

F-4D　　　　　　　　　10/7/68* - 7/70
F-4E　　　　　　　　　16/4/70 - 1972*

　　　　Squadron F-4D coded in July 1968. The F-4D carried a yellow fin cap with 12 small dark stars. The 336 TFS deployed to Kunsan AB, ROK in February 1968. Returned on 11/7/68 and converted to F-4E between 16/4/70 and 17/7/70. Detached to the 8 TFW for combat operations between 12/4/72 and 15/9/72. The 336 TFS recoded to 4 TFW common code of **SJ** while at Ubon RTAFB. Yellow fin cap carried by 336 TFS F-4.

SD
306 Tactical Fighter Squadron　　　　　　　　　　　　　　　　　　　　　　**4403 Tactical Fighter Wing**

TAIL CODE

F-100D/F   28/9/70 - 30/10/70   England AFB, Louisiana

Squadron formerly flew **SD** tail coded F-100 within the 31 TFW at Tuy Hoa AB, RSVN. The 306 TFS moved to England AFB and assigned to the 4403 TFW. It is unknown if the **SD** tail code is official, or carried on from the 31 TFW assignment at Tuy Hoa AB. Squadron assigned to replace the 436 TFS assuming the F-4E assets and **ZD** tail code within the 31 TFW on 30/10/70.

SE

416 Tactical Fighter Squadron   **4403 Tactical Fighter Wing**
F-100D/F   28/9/70 - 1/4/72   England AFB, Louisiana

Squadron moved from the 31 TFW base at Tuy Hoa AB, RSVN to England AFB on 28/9/70. It is unknown if the **SE** tail code is official or carried on from the 31 TFW at Tuy Hoa AB. The tail code and assets remained until the F-100 passed to ANG units. Blue noted as the squadron colour. The 416 TFS remained active without flying assets between April and May 1972, acted as holding unit before 23 TFW assigned squadrons arrived at England AFB.

F-100D Super Sabre 55-3710 **SE**. 416 TFS 4403 TFW, England AFB, with blue tail stripe. Photo: Tom Brewer, Eglin AFB, 5 September 1971.

SJ

4 Tactical Fighter Wing   1972* - current 31/12/90   Seymour Johnson AFB, North Carolina

334 Tactical Fighter Squadron
F-4E   1972* - current 31/12/90
F-15E   1990 - current 31/12/90

The 334 TFS recoded to 4 TFW common wing tail code of **SJ** before second combat tour in Southeast Asia, between 25/9/72 and 12/3/73 with the 8 TFW at Ubon RTAFB. A variety of blue markings carried. Squadron F-4E noted with blue fin caps until 1986, when a blue tail stripe outlined with white script "Eagles" was introduced. The 334 TFS was the last 4 TFW squadron converting to F-15E with completion by the end of 1990.

335 Tactical Fighter Squadron
F-4E   1972* - early 1990
F-15E   1/3/90 - current 31/12/90

Squadron attached to Ubon RTAFB between 8/7/72 and December 1972 for combat operations with the 8 TFW. Several F-4E noted in 1972 with black fin cap and green tail stripe. By 1979 a light green fin cap carried by F-4E. A green band outlined in white, with white centred "Chiefs" appeared by May 1985. Converted to F-15E early 1990.

336 Tactical Fighter Squadron
F-4E   1972* - least 1/10/89
F-15E   12/88 - current 31/12/90

The 336 TFS arrived at Ubon RTAFB with **SC** tail codes on 12/4/72, then recoded to **SJ** during the combat tour until 15/9/72. Returned to Ubon RTAFB, between March 1973 and 7/9/73 for second tour. A yellow fin cap carried until changed to a tail stripe before 1983. In the late eighties "Rocket" script added to the tail stripe. The 336 TFS was the first operational F-15E squadron as of 1/10/89. The F-15E carried twin yellow tail stripes outlined in white.

F-4E Phantom 74-1629 **SJ**, 336 TFS 4 TFW, Seymour-Johnson AFB, with yellow tail stripe. Photo: Patrick Martin, Nellis AFB, 29 June 1984.

TACTICAL AIR COMMAND - CONTINENTAL U.S.

F-15E Strike Eagle 88-1690 **SJ**, 336 TFS 4 TFW, Seymour-Johnson AFB, with single sided, white outline yellow tail stripes. Photo: CFB Cold Lake, May 1990.

337 Tactical Fighter Squadron
F-4E   1/4/82 - 1/7/85

The 337 TFS added as the fourth F-4E unit within the 4 TFW on 1/4/82. Squadron aircraft carried a red tail stripe, later with a white outline. On 30/9/85 the 337 TFS inactivated after adding "Falcons" in white script.

SM
308 Tactical Fighter Squadron   **4403 Tactical Fighter Wing**
F-100D/F   5/10/70 - 30/10/70   **England AFB, Louisiana**

The 308 TFS moved from the 31 TFW base at Tuy Hoa AB, RSVN on 5/10/70 with **SM** tail coded F-100 to England AFB. A green squadron colour noted on F-100D/F. It is unknown if the **SM** tail code is official or carried on from 31 TFW, at Tuy Hoa AB. The tail code and assets maintained until the F-100 passed to established ANG units The 308 TFS reassigned to newly based 31 TFW, at Homestead AFB on 30/10/71, flying **ZF** coded F-4E.

SR
62 Tactical Airlift Squadron   10/7/68* - 9/3/70   **64 Tactical Airlift Wing**
                                                                                                Sewart AFB, Tennessee
                                               9/3/70 - 31/5/71   **64 Tactical Airlift Wing**
                                               31/5/71 - 1972   **314 Tactical Airlift Wing**
                                                                                                Little Rock AFB Arkansas
C-130E   10/7/68* - 1972*

The 62 TAS tail coded C-130E **SR** in July 1968. The **SR** tail code maintained after wing assignment to Little Rock AFB in March 1970. Yellow noted as the squadron colour. The 62 TAS reassigned to the 314 TAW on 31/5/71 and recoded **LK** during 1972 under common wing code concept.

SR
703 Tactical Air Support Squadron   **507 Tactical Air Control Wing**
CH-3E   9/4/85 - 28/4/85   **Shaw AFB, South Carolina**

Squadron recoded from **VA** to **SR** on 9/4/85. Squadron inactivated on 26/5/85, thus the **SR** tail code carried for a very short period. Recoded to allow the 149 TFS (*Virginia ANG*) to reuse the **VA** tail code.

SR
507 Tactical Air Control Wing   17/3/86 - current 31/12/90   **Shaw AFB, South Carolina**

20 Tactical Air Support Squadron
OV-10A   1/4/90 -

Squadron activated to fly **SR** tail coded OV-10A on 1/4/90. Squadron colour of red displayed with two white stars and "Misty" on tail.

21 Tactical Air Support Squadron
OT-37B   17/3/86 - 1988
OV-10A   10/88 -

Squadron converted from uncoded O-2 to T-37B starting on 17/3/86. The last O-2 mission flown on 31/7/86. Squadron flew camouflage T-37B and retitled OT-37B. Flew OT-37B until converting to the OV-10A during April 1988. Blue noted as squadron colour.

SS
309 Tactical Fighter Squadron   **4403 Tactical Fighter Wing**
F-100D/F   5/10/70 - 30/10/70   **England AFB, Louisiana**

The 309 TFS reassigned from the 31 TFW at Tuy Hoa AB, RSVN on 5/10/70 with **SS** tail coded F-100. It is unknown if the **SS** tail code is official or carried on from the 31 TFW assignment at Tuy Hoa AB. The tail codes and assets maintained until F-100 passed on to ANG units. Blue noted as the squadron colour. The 309 TFS reassigned to 31 TFW, established at Homestead AFB,

T-37B 68-8064 **SR**, 21 TASS 507 TAIRCW, Shaw AFB. Photo: Norm Taylor, 15 September 1986.

ST

61 Tactical Airlift Squadron	10/7/68* - 20/2/70	64 Tactical Airlift Wing Sewart AFB, Tennessee
	20/2/70 - 31/5/71	64 Tactical Airlift Wing
	31/5/71 - 1972	314 Tactical Airlift Wing Little Rock AFB, Arkansas

C-130E   10/7/68* - 1972*

The 61 TFS tail coded assigned C-130E **ST** tail code at Sewart AFB in July 1968. Squadron maintained the **ST** tail code after the 64 TAW moved to Little Rock AFB in February 1970. The 61 TAS reassigned to the 314 TAW on 31/5/71. Green noted as the squadron colour. Recoded to **LK**, as common wing tail code concept in 1972.

C-130E Hercules 69-6569 **ST**, 61 TAS 64 TAW, Little Rock AFB. Photo: Doug Remington, Langley AFB, 20 May 1970.

SW

363 Tactical Fighter Wing	1/10/82 - current 31/12/90	Shaw AFB, South Carolina

16 Tactical Reconnaissance Squadron
RF-4C   1/10/82 - 15/9/85

The only RF-4C unit to recode within the 363 TFW from **JO** to **SW** due to inactivations and role change to tactical fighter operations. Inactivated on 30/9/89, with the last RF-4C leaving Shaw AFB, on 16/12/89. Squadron RF-4C carried a fin cap (*front half red, second half black and white checkered separated by gold lighting bolt*).

17 Tactical Fighter Squadron
F-16A/B   1/7/82 - late 1985
F-16C/D   12/9/85 - current 31/12/90

The 17 TFS activated with F-16A/B on 1/7/82 becoming operational on 1/10/82. Squadron started converting to F-16C/D on 12/9/85. Black "Owls" in white tail band carried, later changing to "Hooters."

TACTICAL AIR COMMAND - CONTINENTAL U.S.

F-16A Falcon 8-0537 **SW**, 17 TFS 363 TFW, Shaw AFB, with white tail stripe containing black "OWLS." Photo: Patrick Martin, CFB Cold Lake, 23 May 1983.

19 Tactical Fighter Squadron
F-16A/B   1/4/82 - mid 1985
F-16C/D   27/6/85 - current 31/12/90

Activated in April 1982, with F-16A/B displaying black "Gamecocks" in yellow tail stripe. Squadron declared operational on 1/7/82. The 19 TFS further converted to F-16C/D starting on 27/6/85.

33 Tactical Fighter Squadron
F-16C/D   8/3/85 - current 31/12/90

Squadron activated with F-16C/D on 1/10/82 after previously flying RF-4C (*TRS*), with **JO** tail codes until 1/10/82. Squadron F-16C/D carried a light blue tail stripe with yellow "Falcons." A few examples noted with black stripes.

TC
318 Fighter Interceptor Squadron   25 Air Division
F-15A/B   2/88 - 7/12/89   McChord AFB, Washington

The 318 FIS converted from the F-106A/B, to the F-15A/B with the first arrival of a single F-15B on 9/7/83. The **TC** tail code carried for short period starting in February 1988. The 318 FIS inactivated on 7/12/89. Not all F-15A/B carried tail codes due to the inactivation and assets transfer to the 123 FIS Oregon ANG before tail coding completed. Tail coded F-15A/B carried two tone blue tail stripes with a blue stylized star centred.

F-15A Eagle 76-0098 **TC**, 318 FIS 24 AD, McChord AFB, with single sided, two tone blue tail stripes and star, and stylized crew name block. Photo: Patrick Martin, 28 July 1989.

TD
4449 Combat Crew Training Squadron   516 Tactical Airlift Wing
C-7A   27/8/69 - 15/10/69   Dyess AFB, Texas

The 4449 CCTS operated **TD** tail coded C-7A in the training role. On 15/10/69 the 18 TATS activated and replaced the 4449 CCTS.

TD
18 Tactical Airlift Training Squadron   516 Tactical Airlift Wing
C-7A   15/10/69 - 1/6/72   Dyess AFB, Texas

The 18 TATS replaced the 4449 CCTS on 15/10/69 in the C-7 training role. The 463 TAW replaced the 516 TAW on 1/6/72, retaining the 18 TATS while recoding from **TD** to **DB**.

TAIL CODE

C-7A Caribou 60-3766 **TD**, 18 TATS 516 TAW, Dyess AFB. Photo: Doug Remington, Langley AFB, 18 August 1970.

TE
16 Tactical Airlift Training Squadron

9/3/70 - 1/8/71	4442 Combat Crew Training Wing
1/8/71 - 1972	314 Tactical Airlift Wing

C-130E 9/3/70 - 1972 **Little Rock AFB, Arkansas**

Squadron replaced the 4446 CCTS (**TS** *tail code*) on move of the 4442 CCTW from Sewart AFB to Little Rock AFB. The 16 TATS reassigned to the 314 TAW on 1/8/71. The C-130E maintained the **TE** tail code until the inception of AFM66-1 common code concept. All 314 TAW squadron adopting **LK** as tail code, the 16 TATS adding blue tail stripe.

TR
37 Tactical Fighter Wing 5/10/89 - current 31/12/90 **Tonopah Test Range, Nevada**

F-117A Stealth fighter 85-0818 **TR**, 37 TFW, Tonopah Test Range. Photo: Patrick Martin, Abbotsford, 9 August 1991.

F-117A Stealth fighter 85-0813 **TR**, 37 TFW, Tonopah Test Range. Photo: Marty J Isham, Nellis AFB, 17 August 1990.

415 Tactical Fighter Squadron
F-117A 5/10/89 - current 31/12/90

Squadron redesignated from 415 SOS to 415 TFS on 15/9/70. Activated on 5/10/89 within the 37 TFW at Tonopah. Known as the "NightStalkers" with squadron colour of red not carried externally.

TACTICAL AIR COMMAND - CONTINENTAL U.S.

416 Tactical Fighter Squadron
F-117A   5/10/89 - current 31/12/90
   The 416 TFTS redesignated to 416 TFS on 15/9/89 and activated on 5/10/89, within the 37 TFW at Tonopah. The 416 TFS replaced the uncoded 4453 Test and Evaluation Squadron. Known as the "Ghost Riders", with squadron colour of blue not carried externally. Squadron previously active with 479 TFTW.

417 Tactical Fighter Training Squadron
F-117A   5/10/89 - current 31/12/90
A/T-38B   5/10/89 - current 31/12/90
   Last active as a paper squadron until 15/9/87 within the 86 TFW at Ramstein AB, Germany. Redesignated 417 TFTS and activated on 5/10/89 within the 37 TFW at Tonopah. Known as the "Bandits" with squadron colour of yellow not carried externally. Squadron also assigned T-38 noted with different colours, possibly from prior users.

TS
4442 Combat Crew Training Wing   10/7/68* - 9/3/70   Sewart AFB, Tennessee
                                        9/3/70 - 1/8/71   Little Rock AFB, Arkansas

4446 Combat Crew Training Squadron
C-130E   10/7/68* - 9/3/70
   Squadron flew **TS** tail coded C-130E in the training role, until inactivating when the 4442 CCTW moved to Little Rock AFB on 9/3/70. Assets used to form 16 TATS, 4442 CCTW with the **TE** tail code.

4447 Combat Crew Training Squadron
C-130E   10/7/68* - 1/3/69
   Squadron flew **TS** tail coded C-130E in the training role until inactivation on 1/3/69.

4448 Combat Crew Training Squadron
C-130E   10/7/68* - 1/8/71
   The 4448 CCTS (*unconfirmed existence*) believe to have coded **TS** with the other 4442 CCTW components on 10/7/68. May have recoded to **TE** with wing move to Little Rock AFB, on 9/3/70.

4449 Combat Crew Training Squadron   4442 Combat Crew Training Wing
C-130E   10/7/68* - 27/8/69   Sewart AFB, Tennessee
   The formation date of the 4449 CCTS is unknown. Squadron flew the **TE** tail coded C-130E in the training role, until reassigned to Little Rock AFB and replaced by the 16 TATS 4442 CCTW on 9/3/70.

TY
325 Tactical Training Wing   1/10/83 - current 31/12/90   Tyndall AFB, Florida
1 Tactical Fighter Training Squadron
F-15A/B   27/4/84 - current 31/12/90
   Squadron activated on 1/1/84 within the 325 TTW and received first F-15 on 27/4/84. Red tail stripes with **TY** tail code carried by F-15A/B.

2 Tactical Fighter Training Squadron
F-15A/B   1/10/83 - current 31/12/90
   The 2 TFTS redesignated from 2 FWS on 1/10/83, formerly flying F-106. Yellow tail stripes carried with **TY** tail code on F-15A/B.

F-15B 75-0086 **TY**, 2 TFTS 325 TTW, Tyndall AFB, with single sided yellow tail stripes. Photo: Martin collection.

95 Tactical Fighter Training Squadron
F-15A/B   1/4/84 - current 31/12/90
   The 95 FITS redesignated 95 TFTS as the third component equipped with F-15A/B within the 325 TTW on 1/4/83. The **TY** tail code and blue tail stripes carried. Some F-15B noted with additional three white stars.

TAIL CODE

703 Tactical Air Support Squadron 15/1/70 - **507 Tactical Air Control Wing**
 Shaw AFB, South Carolina
CH-3E 1973 - 9/4/85
CH-53C 6/3/70 - 15/11/71

The 703 SOS/TASS operated CH-3E, applying tail codes late in 1969. The CH-53C added in late 1969 and also applied tail codes. Squadron recoded to **SR** on 9/4/85 for a very short period. Yellow noted as squadron colour but not applied. Uncoded O-2A operations also conducted.

CH-3E 67-14707 **VA**, 703 TASS 507 TAIRCW, Shaw AFB. Photo: Thomas S Waller, Barksdale AFB, 17 March 1973.

VV
27 Tactical Air Support Squadron **602 Tactical Air Control Wing**
OV-10A 15/5/84 - 8/6/90 George AFB, California

The 27 TASS activated on 1/7/77 flying uncoded O-2 from Davis-Monthan AFB until July 1980. The 27 TASS reactivated at George AFB under 602 TAIRCW on 15/5/84. The **VV** tail code applied with flight colours of blue and yellow, carried in fin cap form. The 27 TASS inactivated on 8/6/90 at George AFB.

OV-10A Bronco 67-14675 **VV**, 27 TASS 602 TAIRCW, George AFB, with flight markings of twin single sided yellow fin caps. Photo: Doug Remington, 18 May 1985.

WA
4525 Fighter Weapons Wing, Detachment 1 *Luke AFB, Arizona
A-7D 16/9/69 - 15/10/69

Detachment 1 activated under 4225 FWW with **WA** tail coded A-7D. Replaced by Detachment 1 - 57 FWW on 15/10/69 and recoded **LA**. Possible reactivated in 1973 for unknown period with further **WA** tail coded A-7D in addition to 65 FWS aircraft. Detachment A-7D carried 57 FWW standard markings of black and yellow tail stripe.

WA
57 Fighter Weapons Wing 10/71 - 1/4/77*
57 Tactical Training Wing 1/4/77 - 1/3/80
57 Fighter Weapons Wing 1/3/80 - current 31/12/90

Nellis AFB, Nevada

64 Fighter Weapons Squadron 15/10/72 - 30/12/81
64 Tactical Fighter Aggressor Squadron 1/6/81 - 1/4/83
64 Aggressor Squadron 1/4/83 - 5/9/90
F-5E spring 87 - early 1989
F-16C/D by 7/4/89 - 5/10/90

TACTICAL AIR COMMAND - CONTINENTAL U.S.

The 64 FWS activated within the 57 FWW on 15/10/72 flying T-38A. Initially equipped with uncoded T-38A on 23/10/72, with the higher performing F-5E added by 4/5/76. Redesignated to the 64 TFAS on 30/12/81. Last two digits of the F-5E serial repeated in red, outlined in yellow in large format on the nose. The 64 TFAS further redesignated to the 65 Aggressor Squadron on 1/4/83. The application of **WA** tail code started in the spring of 1987. The 65 AS F-16 conversion started with some **NA** tail coded F-16A/B borrowed from the 474 TFW before declared operational on 7/4/89 with F-16C/D. The **WA** tail coded F-16C/D distinguishable from other Nellis **WA** users 422 TES and TFWC by virtue of aggressor camouflage colours while maintaining the black and yellow checkered tail stripe. Squadron replaced by the 4440 TFTG (*Adversary Tactics Division*) maintaining code and most F-16C/D assets on 5/10/90.

F-5E Tiger 74-1572 **WA**, 64 AS 57 FWW, Nellis AFB, with black and yellow checkered tail stripe. Photo: Patrick Martin, 9 January 1989.

F-16C Falcon 86-0251 **WA**, 64 AS 57 FWW, Nellis AFB, with black and yellow tail stripe over aggressor camouflage paint scheme. Photo: Marty Isham, 3 October 1989.

65 Fighter Weapons Squadron	23/6/72 - 30/12/81
65 Tactical Fighter Aggressor Squadron	30/12/81 - 1/4/83
65 Aggressor Squadron	1/4/83 - 7/4/89
A-7D	23/6/72 - 8/75
F-5E	spring 1987 - 7/4/89

Squadron flew **WB** tail coded F-100D/F and inactivated on 31/12/69 until 23/6/72. On reactivation the 65 FWS flew the A-7D between 23/6/72 and August 1975. The 57 FWW flew A-7D with Detachment 1 from Luke (**LA**) and Davis-Monthan AFB (**DM**) before 65 FWS A-7D usage. Work up started on 29/10/75 with the F-5E and squadron declared operational with on 5/11/75. Last two digits of serial aircraft serial number repeated on the nose in blue outlined in white. Squadron redesignated to 64 TFAS on 30/12/81. The **WA** tail code applied to the F-5E started in the spring on 1987. Further redesignated to 65 Aggressor Squadron on 1/4/83 and inactivated on 7/4/89.

66 Fighter Weapons Squadron	1/10/71 - 30/12/81
F-105D/F/G	1/10/71 - 7/1975
F-4C (ww)	9/71 - 7/75
A-10A	1/10/77 - 1/6//81

Squadron formerly flew **WC** tail coded F-105 until September 1971 when role changed to the development of "Wild Weasel" aircraft. "Wild Weasel" development taken over from 414 FWS. The 66 FWS F-105 carried black and yellow checkered tail stripe. Squadron status changed to non-operational between 26/7/75 and 30/9/77. The operational role resumed with **WA** tail coded A-10A on 1/10/77. The 66 FWS replaced by the A-10 division of the FWS on 1/6/81. Squadron carried black and yellow checkered tail stripes.

414 Fighter Weapons Squadron	1/10/71 - 30/12/81
F-4C	1/10/71 - 1972
F-4D	1/10/71 - least 1972

148   TAIL CODE

F-4E   **1/10/71 - 1/6/81**

The 414 FWS recoded from **WD** as an F-4 unit. Assets assumed by the FWS F-4 Division on 30/12/81. The F-4E carried a black and yellow checkered fin cap. (*See WZ for deployment note to Southeast Asia.*)

F-4D Phantom 66-8700 **WA**, 414 FWS 57 FWW, Nellis AFB, with black and yellow checkered fin cap. Photo: Tom Brewer, Eglin AFB, 11 November 1972.

422 Fighter Weapon Squadron	**1/10/71 - 30/12/81**
422 Test and Evaluation Squadron	**1/6/81 - current 31/12/90**
F-111A	**1/10/71 - least 1/73**
F-111E	**1973 - 1987**
F-111D	**- by 1988**
F-111F	**- 1988**
F-16A/B	**- 1989**
F-16/ADV	**1989 - current 31/12/90**
F-16C	**22/7/87 - current 31/12/90**
F-16D	**20/6/87 - current 31/12/90**
F-4E	**least 1980 - 1985**
F-15A/B	**post 30/12/81 - by 1990**
F-15C/D	**by 1989 - current 31/12/90**
F-15E	**1990 - current 31/12/90**
A-10A	**post 30/12/81 - current 31/12/90**

The 422 FWS recoded from **WF** to **WA** in October 1971 primarily equipped with the F-111. Squadron aircraft carried a black and yellow checkered tail stripe until 30/12/81. Squadron redesignated as the 422 TES with F-111 role departing. Squadron redesignated 422 TES on 1/6/81. Several tactical types of aircraft and subtypes utilized. The 422 TES F-16C/D identified by lack of falcon emblem on the tail. Black and yellow checkered tail stripes maintained as standard wing markings.

F-111D 68-0118 **WA**, 422 TES 57 FWW, Nellis AFB, with black and yellow checkered tail stripe. Photo: Marty Isham, 29 April 1989.

F-15C Eagle 82-0028 **WA**, 422 TES 57 FWW, Nellis AFB, with twin double sided black and yellow checkered tail stripes. Aircraft test painted for F-15E Strike Eagle program. Photo: Kansau, 5 December 1986.

TACTICAL AIR COMMAND - CONTINENTAL U.S.

A-10A Thunderbolt 79-0172 **WA**, 422 TES 57 FWW, Nellis AFB, with twin double sided black and yellow checkered tail stripes. Photo: Patrick Martin, 9 January 1989.

431 Fighter Weapons Squadron   1/10/80 -10/12/81
431 Test and Evaluation Squadron   1/6/81 - current 31/12/90

McClellan AFB, California

F-111A	1/10/80 - current 31/12/90
F-111D	- least 4/89
F-111E	by 1981 - current 31/12/90
F-111F	by 1981 - current 31/12/90

The 431 FWS activated to replace Detachment 3 - 57 FWW on 1/10/80. Various versions of the F-111 used in test role. Squadron aircraft carried a black and yellow tail stripe. Squadron redesignated to 431 TES on 30/12/81.

433 Fighter Weapons Squadron
F-15A/B   1/11/76 - 1/6/81

The 433 FWS formerly assigned to the 8 TFW with **WP** tail coded F-4D, as 433 TFS until 23/7/74. Activated within the 57 FWW on 1/11/76 as the F-15 operator until FWS F-15 Division assumed squadron assets in June 1981. Squadron carried 57 FWW standard markings of black and yellow tail stripes.

Adversary Threat Division (ATD)   **4440 Tactical Fighter Training Group/Fighter Weapons School**
F-16C/D   5/10/90 - current 31/12/90

Flying component of 4440 TFTG (*Red Flag*) activated to replaced the inactivating 64 AS on 5/10/90, with F-16C/D maintaining markings. Unit activated to operate a down sized aggressor force.

A-10 Division		**Fighter Weapons School**
A-10A	1/6/81 - current 31/12/90*	
F-4 Division		**Fighter Weapons School**
F-4E	1/6/81 - 8/85	
F-15 Division		**Fighter Weapons School**
F-15A/B	1/6/81 - 1983	
F-15C/D	1/7/83 - current 31/12/90	
F-16 Division		**Fighter Weapons School**
F-16A/B	1/10/81 - by 87	
F-16C/D	by 1987 - current 31/12/90	

The Fighter Weapons School operated four Divisions each with a distinctive type. Divisions activated from the 66, 414 and 433 FWS with assets of A-10, F-4 and F-15 tail coded **WA** on 1/6/81. In addition the F-16 division flew F-16A from 1/10/81 before upgrading to the F-16C/D. The Fighter Weapons School assigned F-16 differ from the 422 TES by Falcon motif on the tail base. The F-15A/B giving way to C/D starting 1/7/83. The last F-4 leaving during August 1985. Components carried 57 FWW standard markings of black and yellow tail stripes.

F-15C Eagle 82-0027 **WA**, F-15 FWS 57 FWW, Nellis AFB, displaying shadow tail code and "**FWS**", eagle motif on inner tail fin and twin double black and yellow checkered tail stripes. Photo: Patrick Martin, 9 January 1989.

Detachment 3 57 Fighter Weapons Wing
F-111 1/8/77 - 15/8/77 Nellis AFB, Nevada
F-111 15/8/77 - 1/10/80 McClellan AFB, California

Detachment 3 reactivated at Nellis AFB on 1/8/77 moving to McClellan AFB on 15/8/77. The **WA** tail code and markings of controlling wing at Nellis AFB maintained. Replaced by the 431 FWS on 1/10/80 maintaining the **WA** tail code.

WB
4536 Combat Crew Training Squadron 4525 Fighter Weapons Wing
F-100D/F 10/7/68* - 15/10/69 Nellis AFB, Nevada

The 4536 CCTS tail coded F-100D/F **WB** within the 4525 FWW, at Nellis AFB during July 1968. The squadron inactivated on 15/10/69 along with the 4525 FWW. Assets and tail code maintained by replacing 65 FWS.

WB
65 Fighter Weapons Squadron 57 Fighter Weapons Wing
F-100D/F 15/10/69 - 31/12/69 Nellis AFB, Nevada

The 65 FWS activated to replace the 4536 CCTS at Nellis on 15/10/69 when the 4525 FWW inactivated. Assets and **WB** tail code maintained. The F-100D/F carried black and yellow checkered tail band. The 65 FWS inactivated on 31/12/69. Squadron reactivated on 23/6/72 with **WA** tail coded A-7D.

WC
4537 Combat Crew Training Squadron 4525 Fighter Weapons Wing
F-105D/F/G 10/7/68* - 15/10/69 Nellis AFB, Nevada

The 4537 CCTS coded **WC** within the 4525 FWW at Nellis AFB during July 1968. In addition to F-105 the 4537 CCTS also flew three uncoded T-39F. Squadron replaced by the 66 FWS on 15/10/69.

WC
66 Fighter Weapons Squadron 57 Fighter Weapons Wing
F-105D/F/G 15/10/69 - 1/10/71 Nellis AFB, Nevada

The 66 FWS assumed assets of the former 4537 CCTS within the 4525 FWW on 15/10/69. The 66 FWS F-105 carried black and yellow checkered tail stripe or band with tail codes until October 1971. Squadron recoded to **WA** in October 1971.

F-105D Thunderchief 61-0069 **WC**, 66 FWS 57 FWW, Nellis AFB, with black and yellow checkered tail stripe. Photo: Doug Remington, Langley AFB, 31 August 1970.

WD
4538 Combat Crew Training Squadron 4525 Fighter Weapons Wing
F-4C/D/E 10/7/68* - 15/10/69 Nellis AFB, Nevada

The 4538 CCTS tail coded F-4 **WD** within the 4525 FWW at Nellis AFB during July 1968. Wing and squadron inactivated on 15/10/69 and replaced by 414 FWS 57 FWW maintaining assets and **WD** tail code.

WD
414 Fighter Weapons Squadron 57 Fighter Weapons Wing
 Nellis AFB, Nevada

F-4C/D 15/10/69 - 1/10/71
F-4E 10/6/72 - unknown
F-4C (ww) - 9/71

The 414 FWS operated as an F-4 unit at Nellis AFB with squadron F-4 tail coding during October 1969. Added "Wild Weasel" role until transferred to the 66 FWS in September 1971. Wing tail code **WA** adopted in October 1971. Standard 57 FWW black and yellow tail stripe carried by F-4.

WD
66 Fighter Weapons Squadron 57 Fighter Weapons Wing
F-4C (ww) 9/71 - 1/10/71 Nellis AFB, Nevada

Squadron assigned to 57 FWW between 15/10/69 and 30/12/81. The 66 FWS formerly flew **WC** tail coded F-105 until September 1971 when "Wild Weasel" development role assumed from the 414 FWS. The squadron F-4 continued to carry the 414 FWS tail code of **WD** until 1/10/71. Tail code changed to **WA** in October 1971.

TACTICAL AIR COMMAND - CONTINENTAL U.S.

WF
4539 Combat Crew Training Squadron   **4525 Fighter Weapons Wing**
F-111A   10/7/68* - 15/10/69   **Nellis AFB, Nevada**

   The 4539 CCTS tail coded F-111A **WF** within the 4525 FWW at Nellis during July 1968. The squadron inactivated and replaced by 422 FWS 57 FWW on 15/10/69. Standard 57 FWW black and yellow tail stripe carried by F-111A.

WF
422 Fighter Weapon Squadron   15/10/69 - 1/10/71   **57 Fighter Weapons Wing**
                                                                                                                                          Nellis AFB, Nevada
F-111A   15/10/69 - by 1972
F-111E   1969 - by 1972
F-111D   - by 1972
F-111F   - 1/10/71

   Squadron activated to replace the 4539 CCTS 4525 FWW assuming assets, **WF** tail code and markings on 15/10/69. Recoded to wing common tail code of **WA** on 1/10/71. Yellow and black checkered tail band carried as squadron markings.

F-111E 68-0011 **WF**, 422 FWS 57 FWW, Nellis AFB, with black and yellow checkered tail stripe. Photo: Doug Remington, Langley AFB, 5 October 1970.

WW
35 Tactical Fighter Wing   4/78 - 1/7/84
37 Tactical Fighter Wing   30/3/81 - 5/10/89
35 Tactical Fighter Wing   5/10/89 - current 31/12/90
                                                                                                                                       George AFB, California

   *The 35 TFW starting using the **WW** tail code after June 1979, changing from **GA**. The **WW** tail code usage continued through assignment of "Wild Weasel" assets to the 37 TFW on 1/7/84 and return to 35 TFW on 5/10/89.

39 Tactical Fighter Training Squadron   1979 - 9/10/80
39 Tactical Fighter Squadron   9/10/80 - 11/5/84
F-4E   9/10/90 - 11/5/84
F-4G   1979 - by 1981

   The 39 TFTS activated in 1979 and redesignated to 39 TFS on 9/10/80 before inactivating on 11/5/84. Squadron also operated **GA** tail coded F-4C (ww) with white fin cap.

561 Tactical Fighter Squadron
F-105G   1978 - 12/7/80
F-4E   1981 - current 31/12/90
F-4G   1978 - current 31/12/90

   The 35 TFW started recoding F-105G from **GA** to **WW** by June 1979. It is possible the squadron operated with both tail codes on F-105 until July 1980. The newly introduced F-4G carried a half yellow fin cap. A few F-4G noted with full fin caps before returning to the half cap with white outline. Detachment assigned to Korat RTAFB during 1973. Assigned to the 37 TFW maintaining equipment, base, tail code and markings, returned from 37 TFW control on 5/10/89.

F-4E Phantom 74-1650 **WW**, 561 TFS 37 TFW, George AFB, with yellow fin cap. Photo: Patrick Martin, Nellis AFB, 9 January 1989.

562 Tactical Fighter Training Squadron
F-105G	**1978 - 12/7/80**
F-4E	**1981 - current 31/12/90**
F-4G	**1978 - current 31/12/90**

The 562 TFS aircraft carried the same variety of blue markings as the 561 TFS. Squadron assigned to 37 TFW between 30/3/81 and 5/10/89 maintaining assets, tail code, base and markings. Squadron F-4 carried half blue fin cap trimmed in white.

F-4E Phantom 74-1044 **WW**, 562 TFTS 35 TFW, George AFB, with grey-blue fin cap. Photo: Patrick Martin, McChord AFB, 13 July 1990.

563 Tactical Fighter Squadron
F-4E	**1981 - 30/3/81**
F-4G	**1978 - 30/3/81**

Red colour noted in styles much like the 562 TFTS. Carried half red fin cap, on F-4E and F-4G. Some aircraft noted trimmed fin cap in white. Squadron assigned to 37 TFW maintaining assets, tail codes and base on 30/3/81, inactivating on 5/10/89. (*Possibly a paper unit between* 1/7/77 *until* 12/7/82.)

F-4G Phantom 69-0304 **WW**, 563 TFS 35 TFW, George AFB, with red fin cap. Photo: Grant Matsuoka, Edwards AFB, 25 January 1979.

TACTICAL AIR COMMAND - CONTINENTAL U.S.

WZ
414 Fighter Weapons Squadron
F-4D   Spring 71 - 1972

57 Fighter Weapons Wing
Nellis AFB, Nevada

A deployment of two special F-4D coded **WZ** called Detachment 1 414 FWS sent to Udorn RTAFB in the Spring of 1971 possibly Wild Weasel role related. The **WZ** tail code also used at Nellis AFB. The squadron also deployed to Udorn RTAFB, between June 1972 and late 1972 under the 432 TRW with unknown tail code (*The 432 TFW history does not reflect this assignment*). (*Squadron standard code WD prior.*)

ZD
436 Tactical Fighter Squadron   10/7/68* - 15/10/70
                                                  15/10/70 - 30/10/70

4531 Tactical Fighter Wing
31 Tactical Fighter Wing
Homestead AFB, Florida

F-4D   10/7/68* - late 1968
F-4E   late 1968 - 30/10/70

The 436 TFS activated within the 31 TFW on 15/10/70 for 15 days before replaced by the 306 TFS maintaining F-4E assets. Assigned to the 479 TFW at George AFB on 30/10/70 non-operationally.

ZD
306 Tactical Fighter Squadron
F-4E   30/10/70 - 15/7/71

31 Tactical Fighter Wing
Homestead AFB, Florida

Squadron previously flew SD tail coded F-100 within the 4403 TFW at England AFB. The 306 TFS assigned to the 31 TFW on 30/10/70 with assets from the inactivating 436 TFS. Squadron F-4E carried a red fin cap until inactivated on 15/7/71 with assets going to form the 307 TFS.

F-4E Phantom 68-0351 **ZD**, 306 TFS 31 TFW, Homestead AFB, with red fin cap. Photo: Tom Brewer, Eglin AFB, 10 May 1971.

ZD
307 Tactical Fighter Squadron
F-4E   15/7/71 - 1972

31 Tactical Fighter Wing
Homestead AFB, Florida

Squadron previously active flying **TJ** tail coded F-4E within the 401 TFW at Torrejon AB, Spain until 15/7/71. Assets assigned from the 306 TFS with **ZD** tail coded F-4E on 14/7/71.

ZE
478 Tactical Fighter Squadron   10/7/68* - 15/10/70
                                                  15/10/70 - 31/10/70*

4531 Tactical Fighter Wing
31 Tactical Fighter Wing
Homestead AFB, Florida

F-4D   10/7/68* - 1968
F-4E   1968 - 31/10/70*

The 478 TFS tail coded F-4E **ZE** within the 4531 TFW in July 1968. The squadron attached to the 354 TFW at Kunsan AB, ROK between 21/5/70 and 15/6/70 and 54 TFW between 15/6/70 and 2/9/70. The 478 TFS reassigned to the 31 TFW on 15/10/70. Squadron F-4E carried a white outlined blue fin cap, containing white arrows. The squadron inactivated on 30/10/70 and replaced by the 309 TFS maintaining assets and tail code.

ZE
309 Tactical Fighter Squadron
F-4E   30/10/70 - 1972

31 Tactical Fighter Wing
Homestead AFB, Florida

Previously active with **SS** tail coded F-100, assigned to the 4403 TFW, at England AFB. Activated with former **ZE** tail code F-4E, maintaining a blue fin cap. Recoded to **ZF** during 1972, under AFM66-1 common wing concept.

TAIL CODE

F-4E Phantom 68-0326 **ZE**, 309 TFS 31 TFW, Homestead AFB, with blue fin cap. Photo: Doug Remington, McChord AFB, 20 August 1971.

ZF
560 Tactical Fighter Squadron   25/9/68 - 15/10/70   **4531 Tactical Fighter Wing**
                                      15/10/70 - 31/10/70   **31 Tactical Fighter Wing**
                                                               Homestead AFB, Florida

F-4D   25/9/68 - late 1968
F-4E   late 1968 - 31/10/70*

The 560 TFS flew the F-105 within the 23 TFW with the assigned tail code of **MC** until transferred on 25/9/68. Initially tail coded **ZF** within the 4531 TFW, the squadron attached to the 354 TFW at Kunsan AB between 23/6/69 and 17/12/69. The F-4E carried a green fin cap. The 560 TFS reassigned to the 31 TFW on 15/10/70 and inactivated on 31/10/70. The 308 TFS activating on the same day maintaining assets and **ZF** tail code. Squadron reactivated flying T-38A as the 560 FTS 12 FTW at Randolph AFB on 1/5/72.

F-4D Phantom 65-0621 **ZF**, 560 TFS 4531 TFW, Homestead AFB, with green and white fin cap and drop tank markings. Photo: Tokanaga, Yokota AB, Japan, September 1969.

ZF
308 Tactical Fighter Squadron   **31 Tactical Fighter Wing**
F-4E   30/10/70 - 1972   **Homestead AFB, Florida**

The 308 TFS previously flew **SM** tail coded F-100D/F until 30/10/70, within the 4403 TFW at England AFB. Reassigned to the 31 TFW with assets and **ZF** tail code from the inactivating 560 TFS.

ZF
31 Tactical Fighter Wing   1972* - 30/3/81
31 Tactical Training Wing   30/3/81 - 1/10/85
31 Tactical Fighter Wing   1/10/85 - 1/12/86*
* *Wing recoded to* **HS**
                                                               Homestead AFB, Florida

306 Tactical Fighter Training Squadron
F-4D   1/7/78 - 11/85
F-16A/B   11/85 - 1/10/86

The 306 TFS previously inactivated within the 31 TFW on 15/7/71 with **ZD** tail code. Redesignated to 306 TFTS on 5/6/78 and reactivated to complete four squadron wing on 1/7/78. Squadron F-4D carried yellow fin cap. Squadron converted to F-16A/B during November 1985. The 306 TFTS inactivated on 30/10/86 with F-16A/B assets assumed by the 308 TFS. Squadron F-16A/B carried a yellow tail stripe.

TACTICAL AIR COMMAND - CONTINENTAL U.S.

F-4D Phantom 66-7476 **ZF**, 306 TFTS 31 TTW, Homestead AFB, with yellow fin cap. Photo: John Sheets, Buckley ANGB, 20 February 1983.

307 Tactical Fighter Squadron	1972* - 1/7/83	
307 Tactical Fighter Training Squadron	1/7/83 - early 1978	
F-4E	1972* - 1981	
F-4D	1981 - early 1987	

The F-4E of 307 TFS recoded from **ZD** to **ZF** under AFM66-1 concept. Attached to the 432 TRW at Udorn RTAFB between 29/7/72 and 28/10/72 replacing the 308 TFS on rotation. Down graded to F-4D along with wing in 1981 and redesignated to 307 TFTS on 1/7/83 while flying red fin capped F-4D. Wing recoded to **HS** on 1/12/86. The 307 TFTS operated both **ZF** and **HS** tail coded F-4D in early 1987.

308 Tactical Fighter Squadron	1972* - 9/10/80	
308 Tactical Fighter Training Squadron	9/10/80 - 1/10/86	
308 Tactical Fighter Squadron	1/10/86 - early 1987	
F-4E	1972* - 1/7/82	
F-4D	1/7/82 - 10/86	
F-16A/B	31/10/86 - early 1987	

The 308 TFS maintained **ZF** tail code under common wing tail code on F-4E. The squadron flew two combat tours in Southeast Asia with F-4E. Initially attached to the 432 TRW at Udorn RTAFB between 9/5/72 and 29/7/72 replaced by the 307 TFS. Attached to the 8 TFW at Ubon RTAFB between 11/12/72 and 11/1/73 for the second tour. Designated 308 TFTS on 9/10/83, with F-4D. Squadron F-4 carried a green fin cap outlined in white. Converted to F-16A/B by October 1986 and again redesignated to 308 TFS, on 1/10/86. Wing and squadron started recoded to **HS** on 1/12/86. Squadron F-16A/B carried white outlined green tail stripe. Flew both **ZF** and **HS** tail coded F-16 during change over period in early 1987.

F-16A Falcon 83-1073 **ZF**, 308 TFS 31 TFW, Homestead AFB, with white outlined green tail stripe. Photo: Carswell AFB, 9 November 1986.

309 Tactical Fighter Squadron	1972* - 1/7/82	
309 Tactical Fighter Training Squadron	1/7/82 - 15/4/86	
309 Tactical Fighter Squadron	15/1/86 -	
F-4E	1972* - 1981	
F-4D	1981 - 1987	
F-16A/B	1986 - early 1987	

The 309 TFS recoded from **ZE** to **ZF** in 1972 converting to F-4D in 1981. Redesignated to 309 TFTS on 1/7/82 and recoded to **HS** on 1/12/86. The 309 TFTS F-4D carried a yellow tail stripe. Replacement F-16A initially carried white outlined blue tail stripe with white "Wild Geese" added by 1987.

ZG

68 Tactical Fighter Squadron	1/10/68 - 15/10/70	**4531 Tactical Fighter Wing**
	15/10/70 - 30/10/70	**31 Tactical Fighter Wing**
		Homestead AFB, Florida
F-4D	1/10/68 - 1970	
F-4E	1970 - 30/10/70	

The 68 TFS reassigned uncoded from the 479 TFW on 1/10/68, at George AFB (*tail code **GA** assigned, but not carried*). Squadron tail coded **ZG** within the 4531 TFW on initially tail code application on 10/7/68. Squadron deployed to Kunsan AB, ROK under the 354 TFW between 20/6/69 and 9/12/69. The 68 TFS reassigned to the 31 TFW on 15/10/70 and further reassigned to the 4403 TFW at England AFB with unknown status on 30/10/70.

Air Force Reserve

Squadron/Code Summary AFRES

BD   AFRES
46 Tactical Fighter Training Squadron   30/9/83 - 1/7/87   917 Tactical Fighter Group/
                                                                                   434 Tactical Fighter Wing
                                               1/7/87 - current 31/12/90   917 Tactical Fighter Wing
A-10A   30/9/83 - current 31/12/90   Barksdale AFB, Louisiana

Squadron previously active as the 46 TFS flying **ID** tail coded A-37 until 1/7/78. Squadron redesignated to 46 TFTS on 16/6/83 and reactivated within AFRES on 30/9/83, with **BD** coded A-10A. Blue squadron colour carried in fin cap form.

47 Tactical Fighter Squadron   917 Tactical Fighter Group/434 Tactical Fighter Wing
A-10A   1/10/80 - current 31/12/90   Barksdale AFB, Louisiana

Squadron completed conversion to **BD** tail coded A-10A from **ES** tail coded A-37B on 1/10/80. The squadron A-10 carried green fin caps. Trim of gold, red or black added during 1987.

A-10A Thunderbolt 79-0136 **BD**, 47 TFS 917 TFG, Barksdale AFB, displaying boar's head on nose with green fin cap. Photo: Doug Remington, McChord AFB, 24 September 1982.

DG   AFRES
700 Tactical Airlift Squadron   1/4/72 - 1/7/72   918 Tactical Airlift Group
                                               1/7/72 - 1/12/74+   918 Tactical Airlift Group/
                                                                                   94 Tactical Airlift Wing
C-7A   1972 - 1/12/74+   Dobbins AFB, Georgia

The squadron converted from the C-124C to C-7A and redesignated 700 TAS on 1/4/72. Tail codes maintained until MAC control on 1/12/74.

DO   AFRES
89 Tactical Fighter Squadron   906 Tactical Fighter Group/302 Tactical Fighter Wing
                                                                                   Wright-Patterson AFB, Ohio
F-4D   1/7/82 - 10/89
F-16A/B   7/89 - current 31/12/90

Designated as 89 TFS on 20/1/82 and activated within AFRES on 1/7/82 with **DO** tail coded F-4D. Equipment changed from F-4D to F-16A/B between July 1989 and October 1989.

AIR FORCE RESERVE

ER   AFRES
704 Tactical Airlift Squadron   **924 Tactical Airlift Group/433 Tactical Airlift Wing**
C-130A   **1/7/72 - 1/12/74+**   **Ellington AFB, Texas**

Squadron completed conversion from the C-119 on 25/3/68 to the initial roman nose C-130A. The **ER** tail code applied in 1972 and then dropped under MAC control in December 1974. Squadron converted to C-130B in post tail code era, then redesignated to 704 TFS on 1/7/81, flying **TX** tail coded F-4D.

ER   AFRES
705 Tactical Airlift Squadron   **924 Tactical Airlift Group/433 Tactical Airlift Wing**
C-130A   **1/7/72 - 1/12/74+**   **Ellington AFB, Texas**

Squadron converted from the C-119 by 25/3/68 and redesignated to 705 TAS on 1/7/72. Roman nose version of the C-130A initially flown. Codes removed under MAC control on 1/12/74.

C-130A Hercules 53-3135 **ER**, 705 TATS 924 TAG, Ellington AFB. Photo: Ben Knowles, Hill AFB, 15 September 1973.

ES   AFRES
78 Special Operations Squadron   **917 Special Operations Group/434 Special Operations Wing**
A-37B   **1972 - 1/10/73**   **Barksdale AFB, Louisiana**

Squadron tail coded A-37 **ES** during 1972. Application of green and yellow fin tips occurred in October 1978. The 78 SOS was replaced by the 47 TFS on 1/10/73.

ES   AFRES
47 Tactical Fighter Squadron   **917 Tactical Fighter Group/434 Tactical Fighter Wing**
A-37B   **1/10/73 - 1/10/80**   **Barksdale AFB, Louisiana**

The 47 TFS formerly flew **FE** tail coded F-4E within the 1 TFW at MacDill AFB. The 47 SOS activated on 1/10/73 within AFRES replacing the 78 SOS. The 47 TFS assumed A-37 assets and **ES** tail code. Green and yellow fin tips noted. On 1/10/80, the 47 TFS converted to **BD** tail coded A-10A.

FM   AFRES
93 Tactical Fighter Squadron   **1/10/78 - 1/4/81**   **915 Tactical Fighter Group**
                                             1/4/81 - current 31/12/90   **482 Tactical Fighter Wing**
                                                                                                   Homestead AFB, Florida

F-4C   **1/10/78 - 1/10/83**
F-4D   **30/9/83 - 4/90**
F-16A/B   **7/89 - current 31/12/90**

The squadron designated 93 TFS on 23/2/78 and activated with **FM** tail coded F-4C on 1/10/78. The majority of F-4D came from the 401 TFW and formerly coded TJ. Green and white noted as the squadron colour. Grey camouflaged F-4 have two tone grey checkered tail stripe.

F-4C Phantom 63-7500 **FM**, 93 TFS 482 TFW, Homestead AFB, with black and white checkered tail stripe and eyes in "OO." Photo: Martin collection, 6 March 1982.

158   TAIL CODE

GP   AFRES
758 Tactical Airlift Squadron   911 Tactical Airlift Group/302 Tactical Airlift Wing
C-123K   1972 - 1/12/74+   Greater Pittsburgh IAP, Pennsylvania

     The squadron converted from C-124 to C-123K and redesignated to 758 TAS on 1/3/72. The 758 TAS applied the **GP** tail code to C-123 until MAC control on 1/12/74.

HF   AFRES
731 Tactical Airlift Squadron   1/10/72 - 1/9/73   901 Tactical Airlift Group/
                                                                                               302 Tactical Airlift Wing
                                                                       Hanscom AFB, Massachusetts
                                                       1/9/73 - 1/4/74   901 Tactical Airlift Group/
                                                                             302 Tactical Airlift Wing
                                                         1/4/74 - 1/12/74+   439 Tactical Airlift Wing
C-123K   1/10/72 - 1/12/74+   Westover AFB, Massachusetts

     The squadron redesignated to 731 TAS and converted from C-124 to C-123K on 1/10/72. The 731 TAS C-123K carried the **HF** tail code. On 1/9/73 the squadron moved from Hanscom AFB to Westover AFB. Tail codes eliminated under MAC control on 1/12/74.

HI   AFRES
466 Tactical Fighter Squadron   1/1/73 - 25/3/73   508 Tactical Fighter Group/
                                                                        301 Tactical Fighter Wing
                                                         25/3/73 - 17/10/75   301 Tactical Fighter Wing
                                                         17/10/75 - 1/10/82   508 Tactical Fighter Group/
                                                                        301 Tactical Fighter Wing
                                                         1/10/82 - current 31/12/90   419 Tactical Fighter Group
                                                                                        Hill AFB, Utah
F-105B   1/1/73 - by 5/81
F-105D,F   5/81 - 25/2/84
F-16A,B   28/1/84 - current 31/12/90

     The 466 TFS activated at Hill AFB on 1/1/73 after redesignating to TFS on 23/6/72. Squadron equipped with **HI** tail coded F-105B. By November 1982 the F-105B assets transferred to the 141 TFS, New Jersey ANG with replacement F-105D arriving from the 465 TFS (ex-**SH** tail code). A black outlined yellow tail stripe carried by squadron F-105. Further conversion to F-16A/B occurred in early 1984. The F-16 carried a black tail stripe containing yellow diamonds.

HM   AFRES
336 Tactical Airlift Squadron   904 Tactical Airlift Group/452 Tactical Airlift Wing
C-130B   5/72 - 1/12/74+   Hamilton AFB, California

     The 336 TAS redesignated from 336 MAS to 336 TAS and converted from C-124 to C-130B on 1/4/72. Tail codes eliminated under MAC control on 1/12/74.

C-130B Hercules 58-0757 **HM**, 336 TAS 904 TAG, Hamilton AFB. Photo: David Davenport, 19 January 1973.

HO   AFRES
71 Special Operations Squadron   25/7/70 - 15/1/71   930 Special Operations Group/
                                                                             403 Composite Wing
                                                            15/1/71 - 15/9/73   930 Special Operations Group/
                                                                            434 Special Operations Wing
71 Tactical Fighter Squadron   15/9/73 - 1/10/73   930 Tactical Fighter Group/
                                                                           434 Special Operations Wing
A-37A   1972 - 1/10/73   Grissom AFB, Indiana

     The 71 SOS formerly assigned to the 1 SOW flying **IC** tail coded AC-119 and AC-130. Uncoded AC-119 also flown within the 14 SOW in Southeast Asia. The 71 SOS returned to uncoded C-119 operations until converting to **HO** tail coded A-37A. Blue trim carried as squadron markings. The 71 SOS redesignated to 71 TFS on 15/9/73. On 1/10/73 the 78 TFS inactivated and replaced by 45 TFS, maintaining **HO** code.

AIR FORCE RESERVE

HO	AFRES		
45 Tactical Fighter Squadron		1/10/73 - 1/7/75	930 Special Operations Group
			434 Tactical Fighter Wing
		1/7/75 - by 3/79	434 Tactical Fighter Wing
A-37B	1/10/73 - by 3/79		Grissom AFB, Indiana

The 45 TFS formerly flew **FB** tail coded F-4E within the 1 TFW at MacDill AFB until 1/7/71. The 45 TFS activated on 1/10/73 as an AFRES unit, assuming assets from the inactivating 71 SOS. Blue and yellow trimmed A-37B noted. Squadron recoded to **IN** by March 1979.

ID	AFRES		
72 Special Operations Squadron			931 Special Operations Group/434 Special Operations Wing
A-37B	1972 - 1/10/73		Grissom AFB, Indiana

The 72 SOS tail coded A-37B **ID** in 1972, with red noted as squadron colour. The 72 SOS replaced by the 46 TFS on 1/10/73.

ID	AFRES		
46 Tactical Fighter Squadron		1/10/73 - 1/7/75	931 Tactical Fighter Group/
			434 Tactical Fighter Wing
		1/7/75 - 1/7/78	434 Tactical Fighter Wing
A-37A	1/10/73 - 1/75		Grissom AFB, Indiana
A-37B	1/75 - 1/7/78		

Formerly flew **FD** tail coded F-4E within the 1 TFW at MacDill AFB as a regular force unit until 1/7/71. Replaced the 72 SOS on 1/10/73, **ID** tail code and A-37A aircraft maintained. Red trim noted on A-37A, yellow on A-37B. Squadron inactivated on 1/7/78. Squadron later reactivated as 46 TFTS at Barksdale AFB on 30/9/83 flying **BD** tail coded A-10A.

IM	AFRES		
357 Tactical Airlift Squadron		1972 - 1/7/72	908 Tactical Airlift Group/
			302 Tactical Airlift Wing
		1/7/72 - 1/12/74+	908 Tactical Airlift Group/
			94 Tactical Fighter Wing
C-7A	1972 - 1/12/74+		Maxwell AFB, Alabama

The 357 TASS 908 TASG redesignated 357 TAS 908 TAG and converted from the uncoded O-2A to C-7A on 15/12/71. The **IM** tail code carried until MAC control on 1/12/74.

C-7A Caribou 63-9757 **IM**, 357 TAS 908 TAG, Maxwell **AFB**. Photo: Remington collection Sheppard AFB, 21 April 1973.

IN	AFRES		
45 Tactical Fighter Squadron		3/79 - 1/6/81	434 Tactical Fighter Wing
		1/6/87 - current 31/12/90	930 Tactical Fighter Group
			Grissom AFB, Indiana
A-37B	3/79 - 1/6/81		
A-10A	1/6/81 - current 31/12/90		

By March 1979 the 45 TFS recoded from **HO** to **IN**. Squadron converting to the A-10A with blue fin caps by mid 1981. Yellow or black trim added blue shadow effect added to **IN** tail code after 1987.

TAIL CODE

A-10A Thunderbolt 77-0181, **IN**, 45 TFS 930 TFG, Grissom **AFB**. Photo: Daniel Soulaine, Mirabel IAP, 30 May 1987.

IY	**AFRES**		
757 Special Operations Squadron		1972 - 1/10/73	910 Special Operations Group/
			434 Special Operations Wing
757 Tactical Fighter Squadron		1/10/73 - 1/4/81	910 Tactical Fighter Group/
			434 Tactical Fighter Wing
		1/4/81 - 1/7/81	910 Tactical Fighter Group/
			459 Tactical Airlift Wing
A-37B	1972 - least 3/79		Youngstown MAP, Ohio

The 757 TASS redesignated 757 SOS on 29/6/71 and reequipped from U-3 to A-37B. The **IY** tail code maintained until squadron reequipped with C-130B on 1/7/81. Maroon noted on some A-37, perhaps as a flight colour.

KC	**AFRES**		
303 Tactical Fighter Squadron			442 Tactical Fighter Group/434 Tactical Fighter Wing
A-10A	2/82 - current 31/12/90		Richards Gebaur AFB, Missouri

Squadron converted from C-130 to **KC** tail coded A-10A occurred between February and September 1982, while redesignating 303 TFS. Markings consist of black fin caps outlined in yellow.

KM	**AFRES**		
303 Tactical Airlift Squadron		10/74 - 1/11/74	935 Tactical Airlift Group/
			442 Tactical Airlift Wing
		1/11/74 - 1/12/74	422 Tactical Airlift Wing
C-130A	10/74 - 5/75+		Richards Gebaur AFB, Missouri

The 303 TAS assigned **KM** tail code tail during October 1974 with the consolidation of 303 TAS and 304 TAS (tail codes **UA** and **UB**). Squadron C-130A noted with **KM** tail code up until May 1975, through MAC control period starting on 1/12/74.

LH	**AFRES**		
302 Special Operations Squadron		1/4/74 - 8/10/76	unknown
		8/10/76 - 1/3/83	10 Air Force
		1/3/83 - 19/9/85	4 Air Force
		19/9/85 - 1/7/87	302 Special Operations Group
CH-3E	1/4/74 - 1/7/87		Luke AFB, Arizona

The 302 SOS activated on 1/4/74 with **LH** tail coded CH-3E. The squadron converted to **LR** tail coded F-16C/D redesignating to 302 TFS 944 TFG 419 TFW on 1/7/87. Assets transferred to the 71 SOS taking some time before removal of all tail codes.

CH-3E 67-14703 **LH**, 302 SOS 10 AF, Luke AFB. Photo: Ben Knowles, 23 August 1974.

AIR FORCE RESERVE

LR   AFRES
302 Tactical Fighter Squadron   944 Tactical Fighter Group/419 Tactical Fighter Wing
F-16C/D   1/7/87 - current 31/12/90   Luke AFB, Arizona

Squadron converted from **LH** tail coded CH-3 operations to F-16C/D on 1/7/87. A yellow tail stripe with a red trident superimposed, carried as squadron markings.

MC   AFRES
314 Tactical Airlift Squadron   940 Tactical Airlift Group/452 Tactical Airlift Wing
                                                                                                  McClellan AFB, California
C-130A   1972 - 1/5/73
C-130B   1/11/72 - 1/12/74+

The 314 MAS redesignated to 314 TAS while converting from C-124 to **MC** tail coded C-130A on 1/4/72. A further equipment change to C-130B occurred in late 1972. Tail codes dropped in December 1974 with MAC control.

MH   AFRES
64 Tactical Airlift Squadron   928 Tactical Airlift Group/
                                                                                            440 Tactical Airlift Wing
C-130A   1/7/72 - 1/12/74+   O'Hare IAP, Chicago, Illinois

The 64 TAS converted from the C-119 to C-130A and reassigned from the 403 TAW to 440 TAW on 17/9/70. Tail codes applies in 1972 and removed starting on 1/12/74 with MAC control of tactical airlift assets.

MI   AFRES
328 Tactical Airlift Squadron   914 Tactical Airlift Group/403 Tactical Airlift Wing
C-130A   1972 - 1/12/74+   Niagara Falls IAP, New York

The 328 TAS converted from the C-119 to C-130A on 12/12/70. The **MI** tail code applied in 1972 and carried until MAC control on 1/12/74.

MK   AFRES
95 Tactical Airlift Squadron   933 Tactical Airlift Group/440 Tactical Airlift Wing
C-130A   8/71 - 1/12/74+   General Mitchell Field, Milwaukee, Wisconsin

The 95 TAS converted from the C-119 to C-130A on 19/1/71. Squadron colours noted as grey, purple and lavender (perhaps flight colours). The tail code of **MK** noted on C-130A by August 1971. Codes dropped under MAC control in December 1974.

MS   AFRES
96 Tactical Airlift Squadron   934 Tactical Airlift Group/440 Tactical Airlift Wing
C-130A   1972 - 1/12/74+   Minneapolis St Paul IAP, Minnesota

The 96 TAS applied the **MS** tail codes, with purple noted as the squadron colour. Under MAC control the **MS** tail codes dropped in December 1974.

NO   AFRES
706 Tactical Airlift Squadron   1972 - 1/7//72   926 Tactical Airlift Group/
                                                                                       446 Tactical Airlift Wing
                                          1/7/72 - 1/4/78   926 Tactical Airlift Group/
                                                                                       442 Tactical Airlift Wing
706 Tactical Fighter Squadron   1/4/78 - current 31/12/90   926 Tactical Fighter Group/
                                                                                       434 Tactical Fighter Wing
                                                                                     New Orleans NAS, Louisiana

C-130A   1972 - 1/11/73
C-130B   1/11/73 - 1/12/74+
A-37B   1/4/78 - 7/82
A-10A   1/82 - current 31/12/90

The squadron converted from C-119 to C-130A on 13/12/69. The **NO** tail code applied in 1972. Further conversion to C-130B completed by 1/11/73. The **NO** tail applied until MAC control of TAS units on 1/12/74. The 706 TAS redesignated to 706 TFS on 1/4/78 and converted to A-37B, maintaining the **NO** tail code. The 706 TFS A-37 carried a red fin cap with a yellow trim. Conversion to A-10A starting in January 1982 and continued markings with white or black trim outlining the red fin caps.

NR   AFRES
327 Tactical Airlift Squadron   91 Tactical Airlift Group/403 Tactical Airlift Wing
C-130A   4/71 - 1/12/74+   Willow Grove NAS, Pennsylvania

Squadron converted from C-119 to roman nose version of the C-130A on 17/9/70. Tail codes eliminated under MAC control in December 1974, after conversion to standard C-130A.

NS   AFRES
355 Tactical Airlift Squadron   906 Tactical Airlift Group/302 Tactical Airlift Wing
C-123K   1/4/73 - 1/12/74+   Lockbourne AFB, Ohio

Conversion from C-119 to C-123K stared in April 1973. Tail codes dropped under MAC control on 1/12/74.

NT   AFRES
1 Tactical Airlift Training Squadron   906 Tactical Airlift Group/302 Tactical Airlift Wing
C-119G/K   1972 - 3/73   Lockbourne AFB, Ohio

TAIL CODE

Initial designated on formation as 1 CCTS. Date of redesignation to 1 TATS is unknown. Squadron operated in the AC-119 training role from Lockbourne AFB between July 1968 and March 1973. Tail code of **NT** reported but not confirmed. Unit inactivated in March 1973.

NT **AFRES**
356 Tactical Airlift Squadron   **907 Tactical Airlift Group/302 Tactical Airlift Wing**
C-123K   1/4/73 - 8/5/74   **Lockbourne AFB, Ohio**

The squadron equipped with C-119 on move to Lockbourne AFB, redesignated to 356 TAS and converted to **NT** tail coded C-123K on 1/4/73. Tail codes removed under MAC control on 1/12/74.

QA **AFRES**
756 Tactical Airlift Squadron   **919 Tactical Airlift Group/459 Tactical Airlift Wing**
C-130A   1972 - 1/12/74+   **Andrews AFB, Maryland**

The squadron converted from C-124 to C-130A and designated to 756 TAS on 29/6/71 with C-130A. The **QA** tail code eliminated when MAC assumed control of all tactical airlift assets on 1/12/74.

C-130B Hercules 58-0746 **QA**, 756 TAS 919 TAG, Andrews AFB. Photo: Frank MacSorley, 17 February 1973.

QB **AFRES**
711 Tactical Airlift Squadron   **919 Tactical Airlift Group/459 Tactical Airlift Wing**
                                                                                                                   Hurlburt Field, Florida
C-130A   1972 - 2/7/73
C-130B   2/7/73 - 1/12/74+

The 711 TAS activated on 30/7/71 with C-130A. Squadron redesignated to 711 SOS and equipped with uncoded AC-130.

C-130A Hercules 57-0522 **QB**, 711 TAS 919 TAG, Hurlburt Field, in rare grey and natural metal finish. Photo: David Davenport, Pope AFB, September 1972.

QC **AFRES**
337 Tactical Airlift Squadron   **905 Tactical Airlift Group/459 Tactical Airlift Wing**
C-130B   6/72 - 1/4/74   **Westover AFB, Massachusetts**

The 337 TAS recoded from **WC** in June 1972. The squadron reassigned to the 439 TAW directly on 1/4/74, and recoding **WX**.

QD **AFRES**
815 Tactical Airlift Squadron   **920 Tactical Airlift Group/459 Tactical Airlift Wing**
C-130B   25/4/73 - 1/12/74+   **Keesler AFB, Mississippi**

AIR FORCE RESERVE

The 815 TAS previously inactivated with **MA** tail coded C-130 within **PACAF**. Squadron reactivated on 25/4/73 with C-130B. Under MAC control on 1/12/74, tail codes removed.

SH	AFRES		
465 Tactical Fighter Squadron		5/73 - 17/10/75	301 Tactical Fighter Wing
		17/10/75 - 1/10/82	507 Tactical Fighter Group/
			301 Tactical Fighter Wing
		1/10/82 - current 31/12/90	507 Tactical Fighter Group/
			419 Tactical Fighter Wing
			Tinker AFB, Oklahoma
F-105D/F		5/73 - 1/10/80	
F-4D		1/10/80 - 8/88	
F-16A/B		by 1/10/88 - current 31/12/90	

In 1973 the 465 TFS recoded from the **UC**. Squadron F-105 carried a blue tail stripe outlined in white. Squadron F-105D assets reassigned to the 466 (**HI** at Hill AFB) and replaced by F-4D. On reequipping with F-16A/B markings changed to a black tail stripe with squadron crest centred.

F-16A Falcon 80-0506 **SH**, 465 TFS 507 TFG, Tinker AFB, with black tail stripe with squadron crest centred. Photo: Martin collection, Tinker AFB, July 1988.

TF	AFRES		
457 Tactical Fighter Squadron			301 Tactical Fighter Wing
F-16C		12/90 - current 31/12/90	Carswell AFB, Texas

Squadron converted from **TH** tail coded F-4E to **TF** tail coded F-16C the end of 1990. Tail code changed to **TF** on change of equipment, after two F-16A carried **TH** tail code.

TH	AFRES		
457 Tactical Fighter Squadron		8/7/72 - 25/3/73	506 Tactical Fighter Group/
			301 Tactical Fighter Wing
		25/3/73 -	301 Tactical Fighter Wing
			Carswell AFB, Texas
C-123B		1973	
F-105D		8/7/72 - 1982	
F-105D T-stick		unknown	
F-4D		least 1981 - 1987	
F-4E		8/87 - 1990	
F-16C		late 1990	

The 457 TFS activated at Carswell AFB on 8/7/72 with **TH** tail coded F-105. The squadron also operated at least one **TH** tail coded C-123 during 1973. Red noted as the squadron colour. Two F-16C carried the **TH** tail code for 3-4 days before switching to the **TF**, as standard. Squadron markings of blue and red, first half of band blue with white star, second with white stripes on red, noted.

TI	AFRES		
68 Tactical Airlift Squadron			922 Tactical Airlift Group/433 Tactical Airlift Wing
C-130B		1972 - 30/6/74	Kelly AFB, Texas

The 68 TAS converted from C-119 operations to C-130B on 31/10/70. The assets combined with the co-based, but inactivating 67 TAS on 30/6/74, carrying the **TK** tail code.

TK	AFRES		
68 Tactical Airlift Squadron		30/6/74 - 1/11/74	921 Tactical Airlift Group/
			433 Tactical Airlift Wing
		1/11/74 - 1/12/74+	433 Tactical Airlift Wing

TAIL CODE

C-130B 30/6/74 - 1/12/74+ Kelly AFB, Texas

The **TI** tail coded 68 TAS combined assets with the co-based 67 TAS on 30/6/74 adopting **TK** tail code. Codes dropped under MAC control.

TK   AFRES
67 Tactical Airlift Squadron 921 Tactical Airlift Group/433 Tactical Airlift Wing
C-130B 1972 - 30/6/74 Kelly AFB, Texas

Converted from C-119 to C-130B on 29/6/71. Combined with 68 TAS on 30/6/74 maintaining the **TK** tail code.

TX   AFRES
704 Tactical Fighter Squadron 924 Tactical Fighter Group/482 Tactical Fighter Wing
Bergstrom AFB, Texas

F-4D 1/7/81 - 4/89
F-4E 1/89 - current 31/12/90

The 704 TAS redesignated to 704 TFS on 1/7/81 and converted from **ER** tail coded C-130B, to **TX** tail coded F-4D. Markings similar to the 457 TFS, with stylized state flag. The 704 TFS converted to F-4E between January and April 1989.

F-4D Phantom 66-8740 **TX**, 704 TFS 924 TFG, Bergstrom AFB, displaying state flag as tail stripe on non-standard two tone grey camouflage. Photo: Patrick Martin, Abbotsford IAP, 6 August 1987.

UA   AFRES
303 Tactical Airlift Squadron 1972 - 1/11/74 935 Tactical Airlift Group/
442 Tactical Airlift Wing
1/11/74 - 1/12/74+ 442 Tactical Airlift Wing
C-130A 1972 - 10/74 Richards Gebaur AFB, Missouri

The squadron designated 303 TAS and converted from C-124 to C-130A on 29/6/71. Red noted as the squadron colour. The former **UB** coded assets from the 304 TFS absorbed on 30/6/74, with all C-130A recoding **KM** in October 1974.

UB   AFRES
304 Tactical Airlift Squadron 936 Tactical Airlift Group/442 Tactical Airlift Wing
C-130A 1972 - 30/6/74 Richards Gebaur AFB, Missouri

The squadron converted from C-124 to C-130A on 27/10/71. The 304 TAS inactivated on 30/6/74, when squadron assets combined with co-based 303 TAS. Blue noted as squadron colour.

C-130A Hercules 57-0522 **UB**, 304 TAS 936 TAG, Richards Gebaur AFB. Photo: David Davenport, 5 June 1974.

AIR FORCE RESERVE

UC   AFRES
465 Tactical Fighter Squadron   20/5/72 - 25/7/72   507 Tactical Fighter Group/
                                                             442 Tactical Airlift Wing
                                     25/7/72 - 25/3/73   507 Tactical Fighter Group/
                                                                  301 Tactical Fighter Wing
                                     25/3/73 - 17/10/75   301 Tactical Fighter Wing
F-105D/F   20/5/72 - 5/73   Tinker AFB, Oklahoma

     The 465 TFS activated on May 1972 with **UC** tail coded F-105D. Squadron temporarily assigned to the 442 TAW pending activation of the 301 TFW. A blue tail stripe carried with a white outline added later. Assignment of the **UC** tail code was primarily on the basis of the **UA** and **UB** tail codes already in usage within the 442 TAW. The 465 TFS recoded F-105 to **SH** during May 1973.

WC   AFRES
337 Tactical Airlift Squadron   905 Tactical Airlift Group/459 Tactical Airlift Wing
C-130B   1972 - 8/72   Westover AFB, Massachusetts

     On 1/4/72 the 337 MAS redesignated to 337 TAS and converted from C-124 to C-130B. The **WC** tail code applied until exchanged for **QC** starting in June 1972.

WX   AFRES
337 Tactical Airlift Squadron   439 Tactical Airlift Wing
C-130B   1/4/74 - 1/12/74+   Westover AFB, Massachusetts

     The 337 TAS recoded WX from **QC** on 1/4/74 with direct assignment to 439 TAW from 905 TAG 439 TAW.

YA   AFRES
63 Tactical Airlift Squadron   927 Tactical Airlift Group/403 Tactical Airlift Wing
C-130A   1972 - 1/12/74+   Selfridge AFB, Michigan

     The squadron converted from U-3A to C-130A and redesignated from 63 TASS to 63 TAS on 29/6/71. Orange noted as squadron colour. Tail code dropped under MAC control starting on 1/12/74.

C-130A Hercules 55-0032 **YA**, 63 TAS 927 TAG, Selfridge ANGB. Photo: David Davenport, Pope AFB, 29 November 1972.

Air National Guard

Squadron/Code Summary ANG

AG   California ANG
195 Tactical Airlift Squadron   **195 Tactical Airlift Group**
C-130A   **4/70 - 1974**   Van Nuys Airport, California

During April 1970 the squadron converted to **AG** tail coded C-130A. The 195 TAS operating along the co-based 115 TAS also flying C-130A. Assets of both the units consolidated into the 115 TAS, with **VG** tail code during 1974.

C-130A Hercules 56-0468 **AG**, 195 TAS 146 TAW, Van Nuys Airport. Photo: Tom Walker, King Salmon, Alaska 20 August 1972.

AL   Alabama ANG
160 Tactical Fighter Squadron   **187 Tactical Fighter Group**
                                                                                               Dannelly ANGB, Montgomery, Alabama

F-4D   1983 - 1988
F-16A/B   1988 - current 31/12/90

The 160 TRS converted from uncoded RF-4C to F-4D and redesignated 160 TFS on 1/7/83. Squadron F-4D carried a red fin cap with two lines and "MONTGOMERY" in grey. With the adoption of grey camouflage the fin cap markings were dropped. The 160 TFS completed F-16A/B conversion on 1/10/88. Squadron F-4D and F-16A/B extended the darker grey camouflage over nose on grey aircraft.

AIR NATIONAL GUARD

F-4D Phantom 66-7591 **AL**, 160 TFS 187 TFG, Alabama ANG, Dannelly ANGB, with toned down grey markings, including extension of dark grey over nose. Photo: Norm Taylor, 10 October 1986.

AZ	Arizona ANG		
162 Tactical Fighter Training Group		3/78 - 24/7/79	
162 Tactical Fighter Group		24/7/79 - current 31/12/90	Tucson IAP, Arizona
152 Tactical Fighter Training Squadron		3/78 - 24/7/79	
152 Tactical Fighter Squadron		24/7/79 - current 31/12/90	
A-7D/K	3/78 - current 31/12/90		
A-7K	1981 - current 31/12/90		

Originally a Rhode Island Air National Guard unit, the squadron reassigned to Arizona in the 1950's due to the unsuitability of previous home base for jet operations. After several types the squadron converted to uncoded A-7D in 1976, adding the **AZ** tail coded in 1978. The A-7 carried a fin cap containing a stylized Arizona flag with a red sunburst, copper star and blue band from state flag. Assigned aircraft pooled with 195 TFTS in 1983.

A-7D Corsair 80-0286 **AZ**, 162 TFG, Arizona ANG, Tucson IAP. Photo: Gary Vincent, March 1982.

195 Tactical Fighter Training Squadron
A-7D   1983 - 1985
A-7K   1983 - 1985

The 195 TFS equipped with the A-7D in 1983 and shared **AZ** tail coded A-7 within the 152 TFS. The squadron converted to uncoded F-16A/B starting on 1/1/85.

BC	Michigan ANG		
172 Tactical Air Support Squadron		- 11/6/71	110 Tactical Air Support Group
OA-37B	11/3/81 - current 31/12/90		Battle Creek ANGB, W.K. Kellogg MAP, Michigan

The squadron previously operated O-2 from May 1971 until 1981 when converted to OA-37B. No special markings noted.

OA-37 Dragonfly 69-6369 **BC**, 172 TASS 110 TASG, Michigan ANG, Kellogg MAP. Photo: John A Sheets, Volk Field, 26 August 1989.

BH   Alabama ANG
106 Tactical Reconnaissance Squadron   **117 Tactical Reconnaissance Wing**
RF-4C   15/5/86 - current 31/12/90   **Birmingham MAP, Alabama**

The 106 TRS flew uncoded RF-4C from since conversion in January 1979. Squadron assigned **BH** tail code during May 1986. Camouflaged aircraft had red, yellow, blue or green fin cap with 4 stars while grey F-4 had 4 red, yellow, blue or green stars. Some RF-4C noted without fin cap with only stars.

CG   North Carolina ANG
156 Tactical Airlift Squadron   **145 Tactical Airlift Group**
C-130B   spring 71 - 1/12/74+   **Douglas MAP Charlotte Airport, North Carolina**

Squadron converted to C-130B from C-124C in spring 1971. The **CG** tail code first noted in the spring of 1971 and lasted until MAC control of tactical airlift assets on 1/12/74.

CO   Colorado ANG
120 Tactical Fighter Squadron   **140 Tactical Fighter Wing**
                                                                                       Buckley ANGB, Aurora, Colorado

A-7D   1981 - current 31/12/90
A-7K   11/83 - current 31/12/90

The 120 TFS originally adopted the **VX** tail code while on active duty with the 35 TFW at Phang Rang AB, RSVN. Squadron returned to Buckley ANGB and converted from F-100 to A-7D in April 1974. Applied the **CO** tail code in 1981 with a waved Colorado flag, of blue and white with yellow "C" centred on tail.

A-7D Corsair 70-1022 **CO**, 120 TFS 140 TFG, Colorado ANG, Buckley ANGB, with Colorado State stylized flag. Photo: McChord AFB, 31 January 1981.

CS   New York ANG
138 Tactical Fighter Squadron   **140 Tactical Fighter Wing**
F-86H   10/7/68* - 8/12/68   **Cannon AFB, New Mexico**

In December 1957 the squadron received F-86H and designated to 138 TFS 107 TFG in 1958. The **CT** tail code carried on F-86H while on Federal Active Duty, (13/5/68 - 20/12/68) before moving to Cannon AFB during the Pueblo Crisis. The 138 TFS assigned to the 140 TFW on 1/6/68 along with 104 TFS (**CT**). Recoded to **NY** later in history with A-37, A-10 and F-16.

CT   Maryland ANG
104 Tactical Fighter Squadron   **140 Tactical Fighter Wing**
F-86H   10/7/68* - 8/12/68   **Cannon AFB, New Mexico**

The squadron converted from F-86E to H models during deployment to Travis AFB. The 104 FIS moved to Glenn L. Martin Airport, Baltimore and redesignated to 104 TFS in November 1968. During the Pueblo Crisis under Federal Active Duty, the 104 TFS activated (13/5/68 -20/12/68) and moved to Cannon AFB on 1/6/68 where tail coded **CT**. Later the 104 TFS flew **MD** tail coded with A-10A.

CT   Connecticut ANG
118 Tactical Fighter Squadron   **103 Tactical Fighter Group**
                                                                                       Bradley IAP, Connecticut

F-100D/F   12/74 - 1979
A-10A   5/79 - current 31/12/90

In April 1971 the squadron converted from F-102 to the F-100 and redesignated to 118 TFS 103 TFG. Conversion to A-10A started in the summer 1979, becoming the first ANG unit to convert.

AIR NATIONAL GUARD

F-86H Sabre 53-1304 **CT**, ex 104 TFS 140 TFW, Maryland ANG, Cannon AFB, with faded tail code. Photo: Martin collection, March AFB Museum, 14 November 1982. Note: 116 FIS/TFS patch.

DC	District of Columbia ANG	
121 Tactical Fighter Squadron		**113 Tactical Fighter Wing**
		Andrews AFB, Maryland

F-4D   1/6/81 - by 1989
F-16A/B   by 11/89 - current 31/12/90

The 121 TFS converted from F-105D to **DC** tail coded F-4C during 1981. A wide red tail stripe carried with four white stars, later adding green trim. Converted to F-16 with grey tail stripe with four white stars in 1989.

F-16B Falcon 79-0430 **DC**, 121 TFS 113 TFW, District of Columbia ANG, Andrews AFB, with grey tail stripe and white stars, plus shadow **DC** tail code. Photo: Tom Kaminski, 27 January 1990.

FS	Arkansas ANG	
184 Tactical Fighter Squadron		**188 Tactical Fighter Group**
F-16A/B	5/88 - current 31/12/90	**Fort Smith MAP, Arkansas**

The 184 TFS previously flew uncoded F-4D until conversion to F-16A/B in mid 1988. In addition to the **FS** tail code, the F-16 carried a red tail stripe with white "ARKANSAS" and outline containing a further thicker blue outline containing white stars.

FW	Indiana ANG	
163 Tactical Fighter Squadron		**122 Tactical Fighter Wing**
		Fort Wayne MAP (Baer Field), Indiana

F-4C   2/4/79 - by mid 86
F-4E   by 7/86 - current 31/12/90

Squadron tail coded F-4C **FW** in 1979. The 163 TFS converted to F-4E in mid 1986. Assigned F-4 carried a blue fin cap and gold trim containing "INDIANA" in gold.

F-4E Phantom 68-0442 **FW**, 163 TFS 122 TFW, Indiana ANG, Fort Wayne MAP, with gold trim on blue fin cap. Photo: Douglas E Slowiak, 8 September 1986.

HA	Iowa ANG	
174 Tactical Fighter Squadron		132 Tactical Fighter Wing
		Sioux City MAP, Iowa

F-100D/F   11/5/69 - 1977
A-7D   12/76 -
A-7K   1983 -

The 174 TFS converted from F-100C to F-100D in 1974. The squadron deployed to Phu Cat AB, RSVN between 14/5/68 and 11/5/69. Tail codes maintained on return to CONUS with conversion to A-7D commencing in 1976. Originally carried a yellow tail stripe, latter added black bat and "Sioux City" to **HA** tail code. Tail stripe dropped with the new two tone grey scheme on A-7.

F-100 Super Sabre 56-2977 "MAGGIE'S MOB" **HA**, 174 TFS 132 TFW, Sioux City MAP, with large round ANG crest normally carried by non tail coded aircraft. Photo: Doug Remington, Langley AFB.

HF	Indiana ANG	
113 Tactical Fighter Squadron		181 Tactical Fighter Group
		Terre Haute Airport, Hulman Field, Indiana

F-100D/F   - 1979
F-4C   7/79 - 7/87
F-4E   7/87 - current 31/12/90

The 113 TFS flew the F-100 since September 1971. Tail codes applied in the late 1970's. Squadron converted from F-100D/F to F-4C in the second half of 1979. A red, white and blue fin band with "INDIANA" centred, carried by F-4.

IA	Iowa ANG	
124 Tactical Fighter Squadron		132 Tactical Fighter Wing
		Des Moines Airport, Iowa

A-7D   1/77 - current 31/12/90
A-7K   1981 - current 31/12/90

Squadron converted from uncoded F-100D/F in January 1977 to **IA** tail coded A-7D. A red and yellow checkered tail stripe carried as squadron markings.

IL	Illinois ANG	
169 Tactical Air Support Squadron		182 Tactical Air Support Group
		Greater Peoria Airport, Illinois

OA-37B   3/81 - current 31/12/90

AIR NATIONAL GUARD

Conversion started from O-2A to OA-37 during March 1981. The 169 TASS applied **IL** tail code in 1981 to OA-37B. Different individual flights carried various colours as fin cap such as blue, white and red.

OA-37B Dragonfly 69-6428 **IL**, 169 TASS 182 TASG, Illinois ANG, Peoria Airport. Note last three of serial repeated on tip tanks. Photo: Patrick Martin, Nellis AFB, 29 June 1984.

JA   Mississippi ANG
183 Tactical Airlift Squadron   **172 Tactical Airlift Group**
C-130E   6/72 - 1/12/74+   Thompson Field Hawkins Field Jackson Airport, Mississippi

The squadron flew C-124C until conversion to the C-130E in May 1972. Redesignated to 183 TAS from 183 ATS at the end of June 1972. Tail codes dropped under MAC control on 1/12/74.

KE   Mississippi ANG
153 Tactical Reconnaissance Squadron   **186 Tactical Reconnaissance Group**
RF-4C   fall 78 - late 1983   Key Field, Meridian), Mississippi

In the fall of 1978 the 153 TRS converted from RF-101 to RF-4C. The last RF-101 departing on 13/1/79. A large green area of tail outlined with gold markings and "MISSISSIPPI" carried on RF-4C.

RF-4C Phantom 66-0428 **KE**, 153 TRS 186 TRG, Arkansas ANG, Gulfport-Biloxi Regional Airport. Note the a large segment of the tail painted green and outlined in yellow. Also note the ANG crest normally carried by non tail coded aircraft. Photo: Geoffrey B Rhodes, 7 February 1982.

KG   West Virginia ANG
167 Tactical Airlift Squadron   **167 Tactical Airlift Group**
C-130A   6/72 - 1/12/74+   Martinsburg Airport, West Virginia

Squadron redesignated from 167 MAS flying the C-121C to 167 TAS flying the C-130A in June 1972. The 167 TAS carried the **KG** tail code for eighteen months.

KY   Kentucky ANG
165 Tactical Reconnaissance Squadron   **123 Tactical Reconnaissance Wing**
RF-4C   by 3/81 - 1989   Standiford Field, Louisville, Kentucky

The 165 TRS RF-101 displayed a small **KY** on the tail (*See entry for* **RG, RB**) of RF-101 in the late 1970's. Squadron converted to RF-4C, which carried full **KY** tail code and a white fin cap with "KENTUCKY" script. Redesignated 165 TAS 123 TAW on 8/1/89 with conversion to the C-130.

MA   Massachusetts ANG
131 Tactical Fighter Squadron   **104 Tactical Fighter Group**
                                                                                                  Barnes MAP, Massachusetts

F-100D/F   12/74 - 1978
A-10A   1978 - current 31/12/90

The 131 TFS operated **MA** tail coded F-100 until converting to A-10A. A red tail stripe with five white stars carried as squadron markings. A thin black line extending through tail stripes also noted.

MD   Maryland ANG
104 Tactical Fighter Squadron   **175 Tactical Fighter Group**
        Warfield ANGB, Glenn Martin State Airport, Maryland

A-37B   1972 - 1979
A-10A   9/79 - current 31/12/90

Flight colours of yellow, orange and white carried on leading edges of A-37. Some carried a white stripe with "MARYLAND" in black script. Squadron started converting to A-10A on 3/10/80. Flight colours of blue, yellow or red flight carried white with five blue stars and "MARYLAND" in black. After some time A-10A carried green and white tail stripes maintaining "MARYLAND" script.

MG   Minnesota ANG
109 Tactical Airlift Squadron   **133 Tactical Airlift Group**
C-130A   20/3/71 - 1/12/74+   Minneapolis St Paul Airport, Minnesota

A former C-97G unit, the 109 ATS converted to C-130A and redesignated to 109 TAS on 20/3/71. Tail codes noted in March 1973 until removed under MAC control.

MI   Michigan ANG
107 Tactical Fighter Squadron   **127 Tactical Fighter Wing**
        Selfridge ANGB, Michigan

A-7D   9-10/78 - 1990
A-7K   by 11/83 - 1990
F-16A   1990 one a/c

The 107 TFS converted from F-100 to A-7 starting in September 1978. The tail coded **MI** applied with a small red and black fin cap. Tail stripe dropped on many Corsairs by 1987. Converted to F-16A/B in 1990 with only one F-16A receiving the **MI** tail code.

A-7D Corsair 70-1047 **MI**, 107 TFS 127 TFW, Michigan ANG. Note red and black checkered fin cap, stylized "Michigan" and red ANG emblem. Photo: John A Sheets, Volk Field, 17 August 1989.

MT   Tennessee ANG
155 Tactical Airlift Squadron   **164 Tactical Airlift Group**
C-130A   1/8/74 - 1/12/74+   Memphis MAP, Tennessee

The squadron converted from C-124C in August 1974 to C-130A. Tail codes officially carried for five months.

C-130A Hercules 56-0498 **MT**, 155 TAS 164 TAG, Tennessee ANG, Nashville Airport. Photo: Doug Remington, McChord AFB, 7 June 1975.

AIR NATIONAL GUARD

NG   Tennessee ANG
105 Tactical Airlift Squadron   **118 Tactical Airlift Group**
C-130A   1/4/72 - 1/12/74+   Nashville Airport, Tennessee

In March 1971 the 105 TAS converted to C-130A from C-124C. Believe codes applied 1/4/72 lasting until removed with MAC control.

NH   New Hampshire ANG
133 Tactical Airlift Squadron   **157 Tactical Airlift Group**
C-130A   spring 71 - 1/12/74+   Pease AFB, New Hampshire

In the spring of 1971 the squadron reequipped from C-97L to C-130A. Tail codes carried until MAC control on 1/12/74.

NJ   New Jersey ANG
150 Tactical Airlift Squadron   **170 Tactical Airlift Group**
C-7A   6/73 - 1/12/74+   McGuire AFB, New Jersey

Formerly a C-121C/G ATS unit, the squadron redesignated to 150 TAS and assigned C-7A in June 1973. The 150 TAS flew until the mission changed to refuelling and C-7 given up for KC-135A.

NJ   New Jersey ANG
141 Tactical Fighter Squadron   **108 Tactical Fighter Group**
    McGuire AFB, New Jersey

F-4D   16/10/81 - 12/85
F-4E   16/7/85 - current 31/12/90

In 1981 the 141 TFS converted from uncoded F-105B to **NJ** tail coded F-4D. Squadron aircraft carried a red tail stripe outlined in black with "NEW JERSEY" in white/black lettering. Converted to F-4E starting in December 1990.

F-4E Phantom 68-0357 **NJ**, 141 TFS 108 TFG, New Jersey ANG, McGuire AFB, with "New Jersey" tail markings and Tiger illustration on nose. Photo: Daniel Soulaine, London IAP, June 1988.

(NM)   New Mexico ANG
188 Tactical Fighter Squadron   **150 Tactical Fighter Group**
    Kirtland AFB, New Mexico

The **NM** tail code assigned to 188 TFS 150 TFG, but not carried on A-7.

NY   New York ANG
138 Tactical Fighter Squadron   late 1970 - 1979   **174 Tactical Fighter Group**
    Syracuse Airport, New York
    1979 - current 31/12/90   **174 Tactical Fighter Wing**
    Hancock Field, New York

A-37B   late 1970 - summer 79
A-10A   summer 79 - least 1/89
F-16A   by mid 88 - current 31/12/90

The 138 TFS tail coded A-37 in late 1970, later adding a blue fin cap. Converted to A-10A in the summer of 1979 carrying black script "BOYS FROM SYRACUSE" on engines. Squadron further converted to the F-16A/B in mid 1988 carrying a grey and white check tail band.

OH   Ohio ANG
112 Tactical Fighter Squadron   **180 Tactical Fighter Group**
    Toledo Express Airport, Ohio

A-7D   5/79 - current 31/12/90
A-7K   7/80 - current 31/12/90

The 112 TFS converted from F-100D to A-7D in the summer of 1979. Squadron A-7D maintained tail stripe of two rows of green checks edged in white. This changed to black with toned down markings during 1980-81. The solid green tail stripe applied around 1987 outlined with white "OHIO" stylized in white.

TAIL CODE

OH   Ohio ANG
162 Tactical Fighter Squadron
                                            178 Tactical Fighter Group
                                                      Springfield Airport, Ohio

A-7D   22/1/78 - current 31/12/90
A-7K   1982 - current 31/12/90

    Squadron started converting from F-100 to A-7D on 22/1/78 and fully converted by 29/6/78. A red tail band carried with white outlined and "OHIO" script. Some aircraft noted with silver outline before switching to a red tail stripe with yellow outline and "OHIO" centred.

OH   Ohio ANG
166 Tactical Fighter Squadron
                                            121 Tactical Fighter Wing
                                                        Rickenbacker AFB, Ohio

A-7D   1974 - current 31/12/90
A-7K   by 11/83 - current 31/12/90

    The 166 TFS converted from F-100 to A-7D in 1974. A blue tail stripe with a white outline and "OHIO" centred carried by most A-7.

OK   Oklahoma ANG
125 Tactical Fighter Squadron
                                            138 Tactical Fighter Group
                                                         Tulsa IAP, Oklahoma

A-7D   4/81 - current 31/12/90
A-7K   by 1983 - current 31/12/90

    The 125 TFS changed tail code change from **TL** to **OK** in early 1981. A red tail stripe outline in white with "OKLAHOMA" centred carried as squadron markings, some aircraft also added "Tulsa."

A-7D Corsair 80-0295 **OK**, 125 TFS 138 TFG, Tulsa IAP. Photo: Martin collection, 27 June 1975.

OK   Oklahoma ANG
185 Tactical Airlift Squadron
C-130A   1/8/74 - 1/12/74+
                                           137 Tactical Airlift Group
                                             Will Rogers Airport, Oklahoma

    After exchanging C-124C for the C-130A in August 1974 the 185 TAS applied the **OK** tail code. By the time conversion was complete in December 1974, MAC control necessitated removal of tail codes.

C-130A Hercules 54-1624 **OK**, 185 TAS 137 TAG, Oklahoma ANG, Will Rogers Airport. Photo: Martin collection, 27 June 1975.

PA   Pennsylvania ANG
193 Tactical Electronic Warfare Squadron   1978 - 10/10/80   **193 Tactical Electronic Warfare Group**
                                                                                       Harrisburg IAP, Middletown, Pennsylvania

EC-130E(rr)   1978 - 1986
EC-130E(ll)   1978 - 1986

    The squadron operated C-121 variants from Pennsylvania and Korat RTAFB, as 193 TEWS 193 TEWG. Redesignated to 193 SOS 193 SOG between April and December 1977. Reverted to 193 TEWS 193 TEWG while converting to EC-130E in late 1977.

AIR NATIONAL GUARD

Redesignated on 10/10/80 to 193 ECS 193 ECG with control passing to MAC on 1/3/83, thus in theory ending tail code. Some **PA** tail coded C-130 noted up until 1986. Unit further redesignated 193 SOS during 1990.

EC-130E Hercules 63-7869 **PA**, 193 TEWS 193 TEWG, Pennsylvania ANG, NAS Willow Grove, with TAC crest (*rarely applied on ANG aircraft*). Photo: Kansau, Nellis AFB, 18 June 1982.

PA	**Pennsylvania ANG**	
103 Tactical Air Support Squadron		**111 Tactical Air Support Group**
		NAS Willow Grove, Pennsylvania

OA-37B   25/3/81 - 1990
OA-10A   by 6/90 - current 31/12/90

The 103 TASS converted from O-2 to OA-37 March 1981 with some A-37B carrying a red fin cap. Squadron converted to OA-10A in 1989, with very few A-10A noted with **PA** tail codes.

PR	**Puerto Rico ANG**	
198 Tactical Fighter Squadron		**156 Tactical Fighter Group**
		Muniz ANGB, San Juan IAP, Puerto Rico

A-7D   summer 1976 - current 31/12/90
A-7K   by 11/83 - current 31/12/90

Converted from F-104C/D to A-7D in July 1975. Assigned A-7 carried white flying star on blue background removed in 1980. In the late 1980's a yellow tail stripe outlined in white containing "Puerto Rico" and the flag Puerto Rico.

PT	**Pennsylvania ANG**	
146 Tactical Fighter Squadron		**112 Tactical Fighter Group**
		Greater Pittsburgh IAP, Caraopolis, Pennsylvania

A-7D   1980 - current 31/12/90
A-7K   spring 1983 - current 31/12/90

The squadron flew uncoded F-102 operational until 31/12/74. The last F-102A left during February 1975 with the first replacement A-7D arriving in April 1975. Tail codes applied in 1980. Black tail stripe with gold outline and "PENNSYLVANIA" centred carried on A-7D.

RB	**Arkansas ANG**	
154 Tactical Reconnaissance Squadron		**123 Tactical Reconnaissance Wing**
RF-101G		**Little Rock AFB, Arkansas**

In 1965 the 154 TRS converted to RF-101G from RB-57A/B as part of the 189 TRG. Called to active duty on 25/1/68 and moved to Itazuke AB, Japan on 27/7/68 (*See* **RB/RG/RJ** *special note*), converted to KC-135A on 1/1/76 and redesignated 154 ARS 189 TRG.

RG	**Kentucky ANG**	
165 Tactical Reconnaissance Squadron		**123 Tactical Reconnaissance Wing**
RF-101H		**Louisville, Kentucky**

The squadron converted from RB-57 in July 1965 to RF-101G/H. Converted to uncoded RF-101C before further equipping with RF-4C in 1976 (*See* **RB/RG/RJ** *special note*), also flew uncoded TF-101F.

RI	**Rhode Island ANG**	
143 Tactical Airlift Squadron		**143 Tactical Airlift Group**
C-130A	10/75 - 1976	**Theodore F Green Airport, Rhode Island**

Converted from C-119 and U-10 in October 1975 and redesignated from 143 SOS 143 SOG. Unit did paint a few C-130A with the **RI** tail code. In theory tail codes should not have adorned aircraft as post 1/12/74. See note under **TN**.

C-130 Hercules 57-0515 **RI**, 143 TAS 143 TAG, T F Green Airport. Photo: Martin collection.

RJ	Nevada ANG	
192 Tactical Reconnaissance Squadron		**123 Tactical Reconnaissance Wing**
RF-101H		**Reno, Nevada**

The squadron designated to 192 TRS 152 TRG with the introduction of the RB-57B early in 1961. The 192 TRS converted to RF-101H in 1965 and activated during the Pueblo crisis on 25/1/68, moving to Richards Gebaur AFB (*see* **RB/RG/RJ** *special note*). In May 1969 the 192 TRS returned to Reno and released from active duty on 9/6/69. Squadron converted to uncoded RF-101B in November 1971 and RF-4C July 1975.

RF-101H Voodoo 56-0018 **RJ**, 192 TRS 123 TRW, Nevada ANG, Richards Gebaur AFB. Photo: Douglas D Olson, McClellan AFB, 28 September 1968.

SA	Texas ANG	
182 Tactical Fighter Squadron		**149 Tactical Fighter Group**
		Kelly AFB, Texas

F-4C	19/9/83 - by 5/86
F-16A/B	5/86 - current 31/12/90

The 182 TFS flew uncoded F-4C until 16/4/86. In 1983 a red and blue tail stripe, with white outline and the inscription "TEXAS" added to **SA** tail code. Converted to F-16A/B in 1986.

SC	South Carolina ANG	
157 Tactical Fighter Squadron		**169 Tactical Fighter Group**
		McEntire ANGB, Columbia, South Carolina

A-7D	1975 - 1983
A-7K	1982 - 1983
F-16A/B	11/4/83 - 10/86

In late 1974 the squadron converted from the F-102 to A-7D. The **SC** tail code adopted on A-7 with a white tail stripe changing to black on low vis painted A-7. The 157 TFS converted to F-16A/B in late 1983 maintaining the **SC** tail code adding a white outlined black tail stripe containing "South Carolina." In October 1986 the 157 TFS exchanged the **SC** tail codes for large "South Carolina" across the tail.

AIR NATIONAL GUARD

F-16A Falcon 79-0289 **SC**, 157 TFS 169 TFG, South Carolina ANG, McEntire ANGB, with black tail stripe with white outline and "South Carolina." Photo: Daniel Soulaine, 26 July 1985.

SD   South Dakota ANG
175 Tactical Fighter Squadron   **114 Tactical Fighter Group**
                                                                                        Sioux Falls Airport, Joe Foss Field, South Dakota

A-7D   1977 - current 31/12/90
A-7K   1982 - current 31/12/90

The 175 TFS converted from F-100D to A-7D in 1977. A red tail stripe with an outline and inscription "SOUTH DAKOTA" in white carried. By 1988 the squadron markings changed to a black tail stripe with white outline and script "SOUTH DAKOTA", all outlined in red. In addition presidential faces on MT Rushmore noted on a black fin cap.

SG   New York ANG
139 Tactical Airlift Squadron   **109 Tactical Airlift Group**
C-130A/D   3/71 - 1/12/74+   Schenectady Airport, New York

In March 1971 the squadron converted from C-97 to C-130A and designated to 139 TAS (*unconfirmed if C-130D ever carried* **SG** *tail code*). Tail code carried until MAC control on 1/12/74.

SI   Illinois ANG
170 Tactical Fighter Squadron   **183 Tactical Fighter Group**
                                                                                                          Capital Airport, Springfield, Illinois

F-4D   24/7/84 - 1/10/89
F-16A   1/10/89 - current 31/12/90

The 170 TFS started receiving uncoded F-4C in January 1972. The assigned F-4C carried a yellow tail stripe outlined in black with "ILLINOIS" and a black star. The **SI** tail code applied during 1984. The first F-16A carried a blue and red tail band outlined in white with "illinois", arrived on 1/10/89. At the base of the fin, a red white and blue banner containing the inscription "fly'n illini" also noted.

SL   Missouri ANG
110 Tactical Fighter Squadron   **131 Tactical Fighter Wing**
                                                                  Robertson ANGB, Lambert-St Louis International Airport, Missouri

F-4C   9/82 - 1985
F-4E   2/85 - current 31/12/90

The **SL** tail code applied to the 110 TFS F-4C during the last week of September in 1982. The 110 TFS F-4 carried white "MISSOURI" inscription on a red fin cap, outlined in white.

SV   Georgia ANG
158 Tactical Airlift Squadron   **165 Tactical Airlift Group**
C-130E   1/8/74 - 1/12/74+   Savannah Airport, Georgia

In August 1974 the squadron converted from C-124C to C-130E. Tail codes applied for a very short period as removed under MAC control on 1/12/74.

TL   Oklahoma ANG
125 Tactical Fighter Squadron   **138 Tactical Fighter Group**
A-7D   7/78 - early 81   Tulsa IAP, Oklahoma

The 125 TFS converted from the F-100D/F to the A-7D in 1978. A red tail stripe with a white outline and centred "OKLAHOMA" carried. Recoded to **OK** early 1981.

A-7D Corsair 70-1039 **TL**, 125 TFS 138 TFG, Oklahoma ANG, Tulsa IAP, with red tail stripe with white outline and "OKLAHOMA" centred. Photo: Ben Knowles, Davis-Monthan AFB, 12 January 1979.

TN   Rhode Island ANG
143 Tactical Airlift Squadron   **143 Tactical Airlift Group**
C-130A   1976 - 1976   Theodore F Green Airport, Rhode Island

The 143 TAS recoded from **RI** to **TN** in 1976 after MAC control date 1/12/74. This was reportedly due to a mix up of regulations.

VA   Virginia ANG
149 Tactical Fighter Squadron   **192 Tactical Fighter Group**
                                                                                       Byrd IAP, Richmond, Virginia
A-7D   1982 - current 31/12/90
A-7K   1982 - current 31/12/90

The 149 TFS converted from the F-105D to the A-7D in 1982. The tail code **VA** previously used by 703 TASS at Shaw AFB. A grey tail stripe outlined in blue "VIRGINIA" inscription carried with three white stars. The forward third of tail stripe is black with three white stars. In 1989 a grey tail stripe carried.

VG   California ANG
115 Tactical Airlift Squadron   **146 Tactical Airlift Group**
                                                                                       Van Nuys Airport, California
C-130A   4/70 - 1/12/74+
C-130B   1973 - 1/12/74+

The squadron converted at Van Nuys Airport from C-97C to C-130A in April 1970. The 115 TAS operating along the co-based 195 TAS, carrying the **AG** tail code. Most C-130A transferred to SVAF and the squadron operated a mix of A and B models during 1973 conversion to B model. Consolidated with 115 TAS - 195 TAG - 146 TAW in 1974 to become 115 TAS - 146 TAW.

VT   Vermont ANG
134 Tactical Fighter Squadron   **158 Tactical Fighter Group**
F-4D   9/10/81 - 1/7/87   Burlington IAP, Vermont

The 134 DSES converted from B-57 to F-4D, and redesignated to 134 TFS. The squadron carried the **VT** tail code until conversion to F-16A started on 1/4/86. A yellow tail stripe with green outlining "green mountain boys also carried. The **VT** tail dropped on redesignation 134 FIS 158 FIG on 1/7/87.

WG   Delaware ANG
142 Tactical Airlift Squadron   **166 Tactical Airlift Group**
C-130A   5/71 - 1/12/74+   Newcastle County, Greater Wilmington Airport, Delaware

In May 1971 the squadron converted from C-97F/G to C-130A. A single C-130D also used although tail code status unknown. The **WG** tail code dropped with MAC control in December 1974.

AIR NATIONAL GUARD

C-130A Hercules 56-0487 **WG**, 142 TAS 166 TAG, Delaware ANG, Greater Wilmington Airport, with unusual serial presentation repeated on upper tail. Photo: David Davenport, Pope, 5 April 1973.

WI	Wisconsin ANG		
176 Tactical Air Support Squadron		1979 - 9/6/1981	
176 Tactical Fighter Squadron		9/6/1981 - current 31/12/90	

128 Tactical Fighter Wing
Dane County Regional Airport, Truax, Wisconsin

OA-37B	late 1979 - 1981
A-10A	9/6/81 - current 31/12/90

The squadron redesignated from FIS to TASS when equipment changed from F-102 to O-2A. Reporting unit changed from 115 TASG to 128 TASW. The 176 TASS converted in late 1979 to the OA-37B. Red markings carried but dropped on conversion to the OA-37B. A non standard size **WI** tail code carried on the tail. The first A-10A arrived June 1981 and the 176 TASS redesignating to 706 TFS.

WY	Wyoming ANG	
187 Tactical Airlift Squadron		
C-130B	4-7/72 - 1/12/74+	

153 Tactical Airlift Group
Cheyenne Airport, Wyoming

The squadron replaced the C-121G with C-130B in April 1972, and also redesignated from 187 ATS to 187 TAS July 1972. Tail codes removed under MAC control.

XA	New Jersey ANG	
119 Tactical Fighter Squadron		
F-100C/F	10/7/68* - 27/5/69	

113 Tactical Fighter Wing
Myrtle Beach AFB, South Carolina

The 119 TFS flew F-100C when activated between 26/1/68 and 17/6/69 moving to Myrtle Beach AFB during the Pueblo crisis. Later the squadron converted to uncoded F-105B and then F-106A/B, redesignated to 119 FIS 177 FIG on 27/1/73.

F-100C Super Sabre 54-1798 **XA**, 119 TFS 113 TFW, New Jersey ANG, Myrtle Beach AFB. Photo: John Buchanan, MacDill AFB, May 1969.

XB	District of Columbia ANG	
121 Tactical Fighter Squadron		
F-100C/F	10/7/68* - 27/5/69	

113 Tactical Fighter Group
Myrtle Beach AFB, South Carolina

Activated between 26/1/68 and 18/6/69 with F-100C/F, moving to Myrtle Beach AFB during the Pueblo crisis. Most crews of the 121 TFS assigned to Phu Cat AB, RSVN. After two years, the squadron reactivated at Andrews AFB, with uncoded F-105B.

XD   District of Columbia ANG
HQ Flight   **113 Tactical Fighter Wing**
F-100C/F   1968 - 5/69   **Myrtle Beach AFB, South Carolina**

    A rather confusing picture exists on this unit. The 119 and 121 TFS activated and deployed Myrtle Beach under the 113 TFW, when squadrons status changed by Federal Active Duty. It appears the 113 TFW Headquarters flight, perhaps remaining at Atlantic City, applied the tail code **XD**.

F-100C Super Sabre 54-1855 **XD** HQ Flight 113 TFW. Photo: Tom Brewer, November 1969.

* Special Note RB/RG/RJ Note

    As part of response to the seizure of USS Pueblo off North Korea, a number of ANG units were federally activated. Three of these units flew RF-101. The 154, 165 and 192 TRS flew RF-101G, G/H and H respectively before activating on 25/1/68. The 165 and 192 TRS deployed to Richards Gebaur AFB on 30/6/68 and 11/7/68. The 154 TRS remained at Little Rock AFB until deployed to Itazuke AB, Japan on 27/7/68 with RF-101G models. While at Itazuke AB, Japan, most missions were flown over Korea. While in the Far East **RB** tail codes applied to some RF-101G.

    The 165 and 192 TRS operated as one organization during this period applying the tail codes **RG** and **RJ** to CONUS operations in July 1968. On 15/11/68 airmen of the 192 TRS replaced the 154 TRS crews Itazuke AB, Japan. The 154 TRS crews deployed to Richards Gebaur on 22/4/69 and were given a mix of RF-101G/H models. The squadron was released from active duty and returned to Little Rock on 9/6/69. The 192 TRS crews replaced the 165 TRS during February 1969 in Japan, the 165 TRS returned with RF-101G to Richards Gebaur on 20/4/69. The 192 TRS returned to Reno in May 1969. During August 1969 a shuffle arranged aircraft to similar pre-activation positions. In this shuffle, all three squadrons flew with **RB**, **RG** and **RH** tail codes.

United States Air Forces Europe

10th Tactical Reconnaissance - Tactical Fighter Wing
20th Tactical Fighter Wing
26th Tactical Reconnaissance Wing
36th Tactical Fighter Wing
32d Tactical Fighter Squadron
48th Tactical Fighter Wing
50th Tactical Fighter Wing
52d Tactical Fighter Wing
66th Electronic Combat Wing
81st Tactical Fighter Wing
86th Tactical Fighter Wing
401st Tactical Fighter Wing

United States Air Forces Europe

Wing Summary USAFE

10th Tactical Reconnaissance Wing
10th Tactical Fighter Wing

The 10 Tactical Reconnaissance Wing moved to RAF Alconbury from Spangdahlem AB, Germany during 1959 flying B-66. The 10 TRW converted to the RF-4C during 1965. The three RF-4C squadrons 1, 30 and 32 TRS, coded **AR**, **AS**, and **AT** in January 1970. Under wing common tail code concept introduced in 1972, all three units recoded to **AR**. The 30 and 32 TRS inactivated in 1976, followed by the 1 TRS in 1987. The 10 TRW redesignated on 20/8/87 to 10 TFW. Two former **WR** tail coded A-10A units, 509 and 511 TFS reassigned from the 81 TFW to the 10 TFW on moving to RAF Alconbury during 1988.

A-10A Thunderbolt 81-0979 **AR**, 10 TFW, RAF Alconbury, Wing Commander's aircraft with both 509 and 510 TFS markings applied, plus shadow tail code and **10 TFW**. Photo: Martin collection, RAF Waddington 1990.

20th Tactical Fighter Wing

The former F-100 equipped 20 Tactical Fighter Wing transferred to RAF Upper Heyford from RAF Weathersfield during April 1970. The three components, 55, 77 and 79 TFS converted to the F-111E, transferred from Cannon AFB starting on 12/9/70. Tail coding of swing-wing fighters began in October 1970 with **US**, **UT** and **UR** tail codes. The **US** tail code was never applied before wing codes changed to **JS**, **JT** and **JR**, due to undesirability of the **US** tail code. A second oddity within the 20 TFW, is the non-numeric assignment of tail codes (*ie* **R**, **S** *and* **T** *for 55, 77 and 79*). Under AFM66-1 concept the 20 TFW adopted the **UH** tail code during July and August 1972.

26th Tactical Reconnaissance Wing

The 26 Tactical Reconnaissance Wing arrived at Ramstein AB, Germany from Toul-Rosieres AB, France in late 1966 flying RF-101. The wing operated a variety of uncoded aircraft such as EB-57, C-47, C-130, F-4, F-102, and UH-1N. The 38 TRS and 526 TFS tail coded assigned RF-4C **RR** and F-4E **RS** in early 1970. Under AFM66-1 concept, the 26 TRW wing recoded to **RS**. (*note 38 TRS only recoded two aircraft due to knowledge of squadron move to Zweibrucken AB*) "Battle Creek", was a series of base and wing switches including the 26 TRW and 86 TFW on 31/1/73. The 38 TRS moved to Zweibrucken AB, Germany with the 26 TRW wing and adopted the **ZR** tail code. The 525 TFS remained at Ramstein AB, Germany, absorbed by the 86 TFW. The 26 TRW absorbed the 17 TRS at Zweibrucken AB, Germany using the **ZR** tail code. The 417 TFS activated flying a single **ZR** coded F-4D in late 1978, lasting less than one month before inactivating.

32d Tactical Fighter Squadron

The 32 Tactical Fighter Squadrons utilized the **CR** tail code initially on F-4E and later on F-15. The 32 TFS reporting directly to the 17 Air Force. Assignment changed on 16/11/89 with the creation of the 32 Tactical Fighter Group.

36th Tactical Fighter Wing

The 36 Tactical Fighter Wing flew uncoded F-84, F-86, F-100, F-105, F-4 and F-102 from Bitburg AB, Germany. In mid 1970 the wing flew F-4D with the 22, 23, 53 TFS, F-4E with the 525 TFS and B-66 with the 39 TEWS, with **BR**, **BS**, **BT**, **BU** and **BV** tail codes assigned. Control of 23 TFS and 39 TEWS, based at Spangdahlem AB, Germany, passed to the newly activated 52 TFW on 31/12/71. The three remaining F-4 units adopted the **BT** tail code under AFM66-1 common wing code concept during 1972. The 22 and 53 TFS converted to F-4E during the 1972 - 1973. All three squadrons further reequipped with F-15A/B during 1977 - 1980 and the more capably F-15C/D during 1980 - 1981.

48th Tactical Fighter Wing

Formerly based at Chaumont AB, France the 48 Tactical Fighter Wing moved to RAF Lakenheath in January 1960 with F-100. The three squadrons, 492, 493 and 494 TFS tail coded F-100 **LR**, **LS**, and **LT** in March 1970. The conversion period to F-4D commenced during 1972 and finished in August 1974. As the conversion commenced close to the wing common code date, F-4D adopted the **LK** tail code. This tail code lasted from early 1972 until July - August 1972 when the 48 TFW further recoded to **LN**. Under operation "Ready Switch" the F-4D assets transferred to the 474 TFW at Nellis AFB. The 474 TFW sent the swing-wing F-111A to Mountain Home AFB while F-111F transferred to RAF Lakenheath in early 1977. A fourth squadron, the 495 TFS activated within the 48 TFW in 1977.

UNITED STATES AIR FORCES EUROPE

50th Tactical Fighter Wing

The 50 Tactical Fighter Wing operated the F-4D since 1966 from Hahn AB, Germany. The two components, 10 and 496 TFS, tail coded F-4D, **HR** and **HS** starting in April 1970. In 1972 the 50 TFW adopted **HR** under AFM66-1 common wing code concept. Both squadrons converted to F-4E and a third squadron, the 313 TFS activated with F-4E in 1976. Operations continued with F-4E, until the 50 TFW converted to the F-16A/B during 1982. Further conversion affected in 1986 to F-16C/D.

F-4E Phantom 68-0532 **HR**, 50 TFW, Hahn AB, with multi coloured fin cap and "E" individual aircraft marking for the 1978 NATO Tactical Air Meet. Photo: Jean-Pierre Hoehn, June 1978.

52d Tactical Fighter Wing

The 52 Tactical Fighter Wing activated within the USAFE to control former 36 TFW units based at Spangdahlem AB, Germany on 31/12/71. The **BS** tail coded F-4D of the 23 TFS and **BV** tail coded B-66 of the 39 TEWS retained the 36 TFW **BV** tail code, until the AFM66-1 common wing coded concept standard of **SP** occurred eight months later. In theory the squadrons should have adopted the **SR** and **SS** tail codes, both tail codes already use (*within the 64 TAW and 31 TFW, CONUS*). The **ZS** tail coded Wild Weasel F-4C, arrived to replace the B-66 operations ceased in late 1972 (*movement achieved through operation "Battle Creek", a reshuffling of USAFE units on and around 15/1/73*). The 480 TFS activated with F-4D during 1976. The 23 TFS and 480 TFS converted to F-4E during early 1980. In 1979 the 81 TFS converting from the Wild Weasel F-4C to the more capable F-4G. In December 1983 a change in policy resulted in all three squadrons flying both F-4E and F-4G, rather than one variant. This equipment remained until 1987, when the wing exchanged the F-4E for the F-16C/D.

66th Electronic Combat Wing

The 66 Electronic Combat Wing activated on 1/6/85 at Sembach AB, Germany. The **SB** tail coded EC-130H assigned to the 43 ECS in May 1987. The wing also controlled the 42 ECS with **UH** tail coded EF-111A, based at RAF Upper Heyford 43 ECS.

81st Tactical Fighter Wing

In January 1970 the 81 Tactical Fighter Wing tail coded resident F-4 in the **W_** range at RAF Bentwaters and RAF Woodbridge. The 78 TFS flew **WR** tail coded F-4D while the 91 and 92 TFS flew F-4C, tail coded **WS** and **WT**. The 81 TFW adopted **WR** the tail code as the common wing code under the AFM66-1 concept in 1972. The 81 TFW started converting to A-10A 24/8/78. Bulk deliveries started in January 1979. Three additional squadrons 509, 510, and 511 TFS activated during 1979 and 1981 to fly further A-10A. The 509 and 511 TFS transferred to the 10 TFW at RAF Alconbury in 1988 recoding to **AR**. The 81 TFW A-10A also operated from forward operating locations at Sembach, Leipheim, Norvenich and Ahlorn in West Germany. The 527 AS formerly flew uncoded F-5E at RAF Alconbury, converting to **WR** tail coded F-16C and joined the 81 TFW in June 1988 at RAF Woodbridge. Until inactivated in early 1990 the 527 AS flew in the aggressor role.

86th Tactical Fighter Wing

The 86 Tactical Fighter Wing operated from Landstuhl (*later Ramstein-Landstuhl*) until 1968, flying various types such as F-100, F-102 and F-104. The 86 TFW established at Zweibrucken AB, Germany, in November 1969 flying F-4. The RF-4C of the 17 TRS tail coded **ZR** and F-4C of 81 TFS **ZS** in 1970. The 81 TFS transferred from the 50 TFW in early 1970. The wing adopted **ZR** as tail code under AFM66-1 concept in 1972. The 81 TFS did not recode due to transfer to the 52 TFW in January 1973, under "Battle Creek." This was a base and unit shuffle between 26 TRW and 86 TFW. Under this move the 17 TRS remained at Zweibrucken AB, Germany, while the 86 TFW absorbed the 526 TFS at Ramstein AB, Germany. This remained the only tail coded component until the 512 TFS activated with **RS** coded F-4E in 1977. All 86 TFW F-4E exchanged for the F-16C/D during 1985 and 1986. The 417 TFS due several times to activate as the third F-16 unit several times.

401st Tactical Fighter Wing

The 401 Tactical Fighter Wing transferred to Torrejon AB, Spain from England AFB. Conversion from F-100 to F-4E occurred during 1970 for the 307, 353 and 613 TFS with **TJ**, **TK**, and **TL** tail codes. In 1971 the 612 TFS replaced the 307 TFS and the 614 TFS the 353 TFS. Each assumed the assets and tail code of the former unit. In mid 1972 the 401 TFW adopted **TJ** as the wing common tail code. The 401 TFW downgraded to the less capable F-4C model in 1973 and upgraded to the F-4D in 1979. As a further upgrade, the first F-16 arrived on 3/2/83, before yet further converting to the F-16C/D in 1989.

Squadron/Code Summary USAFE

AR

1 Tactical Reconnaissance Squadron	10 Tactical Reconnaissance Wing
RF-4C 1/70 - 8-9/72	RAF Alconbury

The 1 TRS received the first RF-4C on 12/5/65 at RAF Alconbury. During January 1970 the **AR** tail code with a blue tail stripe was applied on RF-4C. Squadron maintained the **AR** tail code as wing common code under the AFM66-1 concept.

TAIL CODE

RF-4C Phantom 65-0830 **AR**, 1 TRS 10 TRW, RAF Alconbury, with blue tail stripe. Photo: Denis Hughes, 14 August 1971.

AR
10 Tactical Reconnaissance Wing	6/72 - 28/8/87
10 Tactical Fighter Wing	28/8/87 - current 31/12/90

RAF Alconbury

1 Tactical Reconnaissance Squadron
RF-4C   8-9/72 - 29/5/87

The 1 TRS maintained **AR** as the common wing tail code with a blue stripe until 1979. Many machines did not carry colour markings between 1972 and 1985. A black fin cap introduced in mid 1980 carried until inactivation on 29/5/87. Few RF-4C carried the blue fin cap.

30 Tactical Reconnaissance Squadron
RF-4C   8/72 - 1/4/76

The 30 TRS formerly flew **AS** tail coded RF-4C prior adoption of **AR** wing common tail code in 1972. The squadron inactivated on 1/4/76. The red tail stripe carried.

32 Tactical Reconnaissance Squadron
RF-4C   6/72 - 1/1/76

The 32 TRS flew with **AT** tail coded RF-4C converting to **AR** as wing common code 1972. A yellow tail stripe carried until the 32 TRS inactivation on 1/1/76.

509 Tactical Fighter Squadron
A-10A   15/4/88 - current 31/12/90

The 509 TFS operated A-10A within the 81 TFW with **WR** tail codes until transferred to the 10 TFW in April 1988. Squadron A-10 carried grey bands outlined in white.

511 Tactical Fighter Squadron
A-10A   1/7/88 - current 31/12/90

The 511 TFS operated A-10A within the 81 TFW with **WR** tail codes until transferred to the 10 TFW, on 1/7/88. Aircraft carried black tail bands outlined in white with the inscription "Vultures" in white.

AS
30 Tactical Reconnaissance Squadron   **10 Tactical Reconnaissance Wing**
RF-4C   1/70 - 8/72   **RAF Alconbury**

The 30 TRS operated from RAF Alconbury and coded RF-4C, **AS** in January 1970. The squadron colour red carried as a tail stripe, changed to checkered black and yellow starting in July 1971. Under AFM66-1 concept the 30 TRS recoded to **AR** in August 1972.

F-4C Phantom 64-1006 **AS**, 30 TRS 10 TRW, RAF Alconbury, with red tail stripe. Photo: J Peck, 14 August 1971.

UNITED STATES AIR FORCES EUROPE

AT
32 Tactical Reconnaissance Squadron   **10 Tactical Reconnaissance Wing**
RF-4C   **1/70 - 1972**   **RAF Alconbury**

The 32 TRS tail coded RF-4C **AT** in January 1970. The squadron colour of yellow applied as a fin stripe. Under AFM66-1 concept in June 1972 the 32 TRS recoded **AR**.

RF-4C Phantom 64-1033 **AT**, 32 TRS 10 TRW, RAF Alconbury, with yellow tail stripe. Photo: J Peck, 14 August 1971.

BR
22 Tactical Fighter Squadron   **36 Tactical Fighter Wing**
F-4D   **6/70 - 1/4/72**   **Bitburg AB, West Germany**

The 22 TFS applied the **BR** tail code to F-4D in June 1970 at Bitburg AB. The 22 TFS also applied squadron colours of red and white diagonal stripes as a fin cap. By March 1972 an all red fin carried. Tail code changed to **BT** under AFM66-1 concept in 1972.

F-4D Phantom 66-7560 **BR**, 22 TFS 36 TFW, Bitburg AB, with diagonally divided red and white fin cap. Photo: Lesieutre, Beauvechain, 27 June 1970.

BS
23 Tactical Fighter Squadron   **1957 - 31/12/71**   **36 Tactical Fighter Wing**
                                        31/12/71 - 6-8/72   **52 Tactical Fighter Wing**
F-4D   **5/70 - 6-8/72**   **Spangdahlem AB, West Germany**

The 36 TFW at Bitburg AB controlled the Spangdahlem AB assigned 23 TFS. The **BS** tail code applied on squadron F-4D during May 1970. Blue and red 45 diagonal stripes carried as a fin cap noted as squadron markings. Control of the 23 TFS passed to the activated 52 TFW on 31/12/71. The squadron F-4D carried the **BS** tail code until AFM66-1 concept in June 1972 when recoded **SP**. In theory the 23 TFS ought to have recoded with an **S** range tail code within the 52 TFW and then **SP** in mid 1972 under common wing tail code.

BT
53 Tactical Fighter Squadron   **36 Tactical Fighter Wing**
F-4D   **5/70 - 1972**   **Bitburg AB, West Germany**

As the third squadron within the 36 TFW the 53 TFS adopted the **BT** tail code on F-4D in May 1970. The tiger colours of yellow and black carried diagonally as a fin cap. Between February and August 1972, only yellow capped aircraft noted. The squadron maintained the **BT** tail code after AFM66-1 concept.

BT
36 Tactical Fighter Wing   **1972* - current 31/12/90**   **Bitburg AB, West Germany**

22 Tactical Fighter Squadron
F-4D   **1/4/72 - 8/72**
F-4E   **8/72* - 25/10/76**

F-15A/B	1/7/77 - 5/81
F-15C/D	5/81 - current 31/12/90

On April 1, 1972 under the AFM66-1 concept, the 22 TFS changed assigned tail code from **BR** to **BT** while retaining red fin caps. Squadron converted from F-4D to F-4E after August 1972. The 22 TFS status changed to non-operational between 25/10/76 and 30/6/77 during conversion to F-15A/B (*various sources having different dates*). The final assigned F-4E left Bitburg AB on 26/2/77, with the first F-15 landing on 5/1/77. Conversion to F-15C/D commenced by May 1981. Squadron carried red tail stripes.

53 Tactical Fighter Squadron
F-4D	1972* - 9/73
F-4E	9/73 - 1/2/77
F-15A/B	9/11/77 - 5/81
F-15C/D	5/81 - current 31/12/90

The 53 TFS maintained the **BT** tail code under wing common tail coding in 1972. The 53 TFS added yellow fin caps, changing to red between August 1972 and September 1973 when removed. Conversion to the F-4E completed in September 1973. Conversion to the F-15A/B complete by 9/11/71, carrying a yellow stripe. Further conversion to the F-15C/D under way by May 1981, when a few remaining F-15A noted. The F-15C/D carried yellow stripes, giving way to yellow and black tiger stripes in late 1987.

F-15C Eagle 79-0053 **BT**, 53 TFS 36 TFW, Bitburg AB, with single sided yellow tail stripes. Note the unusual serial presentation of 790053 and "53TFS", plus a black eagle on inner face of tail fins. Photo: Hans Schroder, 16 August 1984.

525 Tactical Fighter Squadron
F-4E	6/72 - 9/3/77
F-15A/B	4/77 - 1/81
F-15C/D	12/80 - current 31/12/90

As per AFM66-1 concept the 525 TFS F-4E adopted the **BT** tail code in June 1972 with a blue fin cap. The 525 TFS converted to F-15A/B in December 1976, deploying back to Bitburg AB from Langley AFB (*conversion period*) in April 1977. Some F-15 noted with blue stripes and later added superimposed white stars. Further conversion to the F-15C/D completed in late 1980. White paw marks noted on tail stripes in late 1987.

F-4E Phantom 68-0508 **BT** 525 TFS 36 TFW, Bitburg AB, with a blue fin cap. Photo: Henk Schakelaar, Florennes, September 1972.

BU   **36 Tactical Fighter Wing**

525 Tactical Fighter Squadron   **Bitburg AB, West Germany**

F-4E   2/70 - 8/72

The squadron operated F-102 in the interceptor role prior to F-4E conversion starting in October 1969. Conversion completed by 1/10/69 with **BU** tail codes applied by February 1970. A blue fin cap added in May 1970. As a component of the 36 TFW the 525 TFS adopted the **BT** wing tail code in June 1972.

UNITED STATES AIR FORCES EUROPE

F-4E Phantom 68-0460 **BU**, 525 TFS 36 TFW, Bitburg AB. Photo: Martin collection.

BV
39 Tactical Electronic Warfare Squadron 1/70 - 31/12/71 36 Tactical Fighter Wing
31/12/71 - 8/72 52 Tactical Fighter Wing
EB-66C/E 1/70 - 8/72 Spangdahlem AB, West Germany

The 39 TEWS activated at Spangdahlem AB on 1/4/69 with EB-66 assigned to the 36 TFW at Bitburg AB on 15/9/69. As the fifth 36 TFW squadron, the tail code **BV** was assigned in January 1970. A green and white diagonally striped fin cap carried until mid 1971, after which the white portion was dropped and an all green fin cap maintained. When the 52 TFW activated at Spangdahlem AB on 31/12/71, the 39 TEWS reassigned from the 36 TFW along with 23 TFS. The 39 TEWS carried the **BV** tail code until August 1972, although in theory a **S** range tail code should have been carried. The result of this was a period (*31/12/71 - 8/72*) of control by the 52 TFW while carrying the 36 TFW range tail code of **BV**. In June 1972 the 39 TEWS recoded to **SP** as 52 TFW wing common code.

EB-66C Destroyer 54-0459 **BV**, 39 TEWS 36 TFW, Spangdahlem AB, with green and white diagonally striped fin cap. Photo: Lindsay Peacock, RAF Bentwaters, August 1970.

CR
32 Tactical Fighter Squadron 5/70 - 16/11/89 17 Air Force
16/11/89 - current 31/12/90 32 Tactical Fighter Group
Soesterberg AB, Netherlands

F-4E 5/70 - end 1979
F-15A/B 15/9/78 - 5/80
F-15C/D 13/6/80 - current 31/12/90

The 32 TFS converted from uncoded F/TF-102A in July 1969 to F-4E and reported directly to the 17 Air Force. The initial letter **C**, for "Camp Amsterdam" used rather than **S** for Soesterberg. In theory the 32 TFS should have coded **SR** under the standard USAFE coding system, which was already in use with the 62 TAS, 64 TAW at Sewart AFB. The squadron F-4 carried an orange tail stripe. Conversion to F-15A/B started on 20/11/78 with maintenance examples. Further conversion to F-15C/D started in June 1980. The 32 TFS used orange and green flight colours, each outlined by the opposite. Squadron known as the "Wolfhounds."

F-15A 77-0081 **CR**, 32 TFS 17 AF, Soesterberg AB, with orange tail stripe. Photo: Pat Martin, Greenham Common 1979.

HR
10 Tactical Fighter Squadron   **50 Tactical Fighter Wing**
F-4D   **4/70 - 7/72**   **Hahn AB, West Germany**

On initial coding the 10 TFS applied the **HR** tail code to F-4D with blue trim. Under wing common tail code concept the **HR** tail code maintained post 1972.

F-4D Phantom 65-0781 and 65-0780 **HR**, 10 TFS 50 TFW, Hahn AB. Note non-standard serial presentation. Photo: Zastrow collection mid 1970.

HR
50 Tactical Fighter Wing   **1972* - current 31/12/90**   **Hahn AB, West Germany**

10 Tactical Fighter Squadron
F-4D	7/72 - 23/9/76
F-4E	16/7/76 - 4/82
F-16A/B	1/82 - 8/86
F-16C/D	16/7/86 - current 31/12/90

The 10 TFS maintained **HR** as the wing common tail code in 1972. From July 1972 until September 1973 F-4D carried a blue or yellow trim. Colour markings later dropped. Squadron converted to F-4E in July 1976 with F-4D transferred to other USAFE users. The blue trim returned after 1978 on F-4E. In April 1982 the F-16A/B replaced the F-4E maintaining a blue tail stripe. These were in turn traded for F-16C/D staring on 16/7/86. The latter carried a blue tail stripe outlined in yellow.

F-4D Phantom 66-7558 **HR**, 10 TFS 50 TFW, Hahn AB, with blue fin cap. Photo: Henk Schakelaar, CFB Baden-Soellingen, 28 May 1974.

313 Tactical Fighter Squadron
F-4E	15/11/76 - 12/81
F-16A/B	12/81 - at least 9/86
F-16C/D	by 7/87 - current 31/12/90

The 313 TFS activated within the 50 TFW on 15/11/76 with **HR** coded F-4E. The squadron declared operational on 27/12/76 adding a white tail stripe in January 1982. By July 1987 the 313 TFS started conversion to F-16C/D and changed tail stripe to orange.

UNITED STATES AIR FORCES EUROPE

F-16A Falcon 80-0542 **HR**, 313 TFS 50 TFW, Hahn AB, with white tail stripe. Photo: John Kuehnert, Hahn, April 1982.

496 Tactical Fighter Squadron
F-4E	least 6/72 - mid 1982
F-16A/B	6/1982 - until at least 9/86
F-16C/D	by 5/86 - current 31/12/90

The 496 TFS formerly applied the **HS** tail code. Squadron recoded to **HR** in mid 1972 as wing common tail code on F-4D. Conversion to F-4E completed by September 1973 with black and white trim exchanged for red trim early in 1973. In 1977 F-4E markings changed again to red and black check fin tips. The Belgian Air Force provided initial the F-16 for ground crew training. A red tail stripe initially carried by F-16A/B switching to yellow with the conversion to F-16C/D in 1986.

HS
496 Tactical Fighter Squadron   **50 Tactical Fighter Wing**
F-4D	5/70 - 10/70	Hahn AB, West Germany
F-4E	15/10/70 - 7/72	

The 496 TFS assigned to 50 TFW on 1/11/68 flying the uncoded F-102. The squadron converted to **HS** tail coded F-4D in January 1970 with black and yellow fin caps added by May 1970. The two flights colours of black and white carried by July 1972. Recoded to **HR** under AFM66-1 concept.

JR
79 Tactical Fighter Squadron   **20 Tactical Fighter Wing**
F-111E	1/71 - 11/72	RAF Upper Heyford

The 79 TFS recoded from **UR** to **JR** in January 1971. The squadron F-111E carried a yellow fin cap and further recoded to **UH** under wing common tail code starting in 1972.

JS
55 Tactical Fighter Squadron   **20 Tactical Fighter Wing**
F-111E	4/71 - 3/73	RAF Upper Heyford

Squadron originally to have F-111E tail coded **US**. Due to the undesirability of **US** as a tail code the wing switched to **J** range codes. The 55 TFS added blue fin caps along with the **JS** tail code. The 55 TFS changed tail codes to **UH** along with 77 and 79 TFS starting in mid 1972.

JT
77 Tactical Fighter Squadron   **20 Tactical Fighter Wing**
F-111E	1/71 - 11/72	RAF Upper Heyford

The third TFS of the 20 TFW recoded in the **J** range in January 1971 from **U** range maintaining red fin cap. The squadron declared operational with F-111E on 27/7/71 the final 20 TFW squadron to do so. Under AFM66-1 common wing tail coded concept, the wing recoded to **UH** starting in July 1972.

F-111E 68-0077 **JT**, 77 TFS 20 TFW, RAF Upper Heyford, with a red fin cap. Photo: Denis Hughes, September 1971.

LK
48 Tactical Fighter Wing 3/72 - 7-8/72 RAF Lakenheath

The 48 Tactical Fighter Wing converted from **LR**, **LS** and **LT** tail codes on F-100 to **LK** coded F-4D in late in 1971 through 1974. Only twenty-seven pooled F-4D carried the **LK** wing code. The **LK** tail code was phased out during 1972, with **LN** code first appearing during July and August 1972. The F-4D carried wing standard fin cap of blue, yellow and red fin tip with wing badge on both intakes. Squadron conversion dates noted as:

492 TFS: 1/10/71 and 31/1/72
493 TFS: 1/12/71 and 4/72
494 TFS: 1/2/72 and 25/7/74

The first F-4D for the wing was coded **WR**, as transferred from the 78 TFS, 81 TFW on 30/12/71, prior to the first 48 TFW marked machine.

F-4D Phantom 66-7563 **LK**, 493 TFS 48 TFW, RAF Lakenheath, displaying the short lived wing common markings of blue, yellow and red. Photo: Dick Powers, 13 April 1972.

LN
48 Tactical Fighter Wing 7-8/72 - current 31/12/90 RAF Lakenheath

*The 48 TFW recoded F-4D operations from **LK** to **LN** during July and August 1972.*

492 Tactical Fighter Squadron
F-4D   7-8/72 - 4/77
F-111F   22/4/77 - current 31/12/90

The squadron converted to F-111F under operation "Ready Switch" between 22/4/77 and 1/7/77. The 492 TFS known as "Bolars", carried blue trim of F-111F.

F-4D Phantom 65-0615 **LN**, 492 TFS 48 TFW, RAF Lakenheath, with blue fin cap. Photo: Bob Archer, 13 August 1976.

493 Tactical Fighter Squadron
F-4D   7-8/72 - 4/77
F-111F   22/4/77 - current 31/12/90

The squadron F-4D carried yellow a fin cap. Conversion to F-111F under "Ready Switch" effected between 22/4/77 and 28/6/77. Yellow trim carried, squadron known as "Roosters."

UNITED STATES AIR FORCES EUROPE

F-111F 70-2375 **LN**, 493 TFS 48 TFW, RAF Lakenheath, with yellow fin cap. Photo: Bob Archer, 17 May 1980.

494 Tactical Fighter Squadron
F-4D   7-8/72 - 4/77
F-111F   22/4/77 - current 31/12/90

Squadron F-4D carried red fin cap until converted to F-111F under "Ready Switch" between 22/4/77 and 31/5/77. Squadron known as "Panthers."

495 Tactical Fighter Squadron
F-111F   1/4/77 - current 31/12/90

On 1/4/77 the 495 TFS activated as the fourth F-111F squadron assigned to the 48 TFW. Became fully operational with F-111F on 29/7/77 flying with green trim. The 494 TFS is also the F-111F RTU.

LR
492 Tactical Fighter Squadron   **48 Tactical Fighter Wing**
F-100D/F   3/70 - 3/72   **RAF Lakenheath**

The 492 TFS tail coded F-100D/F during March 1970 adding a light blue fin cap. The squadron converted to F-4D starting on 1/10/71. By March 1972 under AFM66-1 concept the squadron applied the **LK** tail code.

F-100D Super Sabre 56-3213 **LR**, 492 TFS 48 TFW, RAF Lakenheath, with light blue fin cap. Photo: Denis Hughes, 6 June 1970.

LS
493 Tactical Fighter Squadron   **48 Tactical Fighter Wing**
F-100D/F   3/70 - 3/72   **RAF Lakenheath**

The F-100D/F of the 493 TFS applied the **LS** tail code during March 1970 and carried a yellow fin cap. In January the squadron received the first F-4D for wing conversion and by March 1972 carried the wing common code of **LK** carried on F-4D.

LT
494 Tactical Fighter Squadron   **48 Tactical Fighter Wing**
F-100D/F   3/70 - 3/72   **RAF Lakenheath**

The 494 TFS applied the **LT** tail code to F-100D/F during March 1970. Squadron converted to F-4D between 1/2/72 and 25/7/74. By March 1972 the 494 TFS carried the AFM66-1 wing tail code of **LK** on F-4D.

RR
38 Tactical Reconnaissance Squadron   **26 Tactical Reconnaissance Wing**
RF-4C   1/4/70 - 1/73   **Ramstein AB, West Germany**

The 38 TRS arrived at Ramstein AB assigned to the 26 TRW flying RF-4C on 1/1/66. The **RR** tail code applied starting on 1/4/70. A very large green and white fin cap supplemented an all green fin cap as squadron markings. Under common wing tail code concept the 38 TRS adopted the **RS** tail code (*Only two aircraft noted with the* **RS** *tail code, due to knowledge of the "Battle Creek" move to Zweibrucken on 31/3/73*).

TAIL CODE

RF-4C Phantom 65-0873 **RR**, 38 TFS 26 TRW, Ramstein AB, with green and white checkered fin cap. Note the variety of 'zaps' forward of the intake. Photo: Denis Hughes, 7 June 1971.

RS

526 Tactical Fighter Squadron		26 Tactical Reconnaissance Wing
F-4E	1/4/70 - 1972	Ramstein AB, West Germany

The 526 TFS formerly flew F-102A until converting to the F-4E on 1/4/70. The squadron was assigned the **RS** tail code as the second squadron under the **R - R, S, T, U** and **V** theory. Squadron F-4E carried red fin cap and **RS** tail code maintained as wing common tail code of the 26 TRW in 1972.

RS
26 Tactical Reconnaissance Wing   1972* - 31/1/73   Ramstein AB, West Germany

38 Tactical Reconnaissance Squadron
RF-4C   1972* - 31/1/73

Under AFM66-1 concept the 38 TRS should have adopted the 86 TFW tail code of **RS** during 1972, recoding from **RR**. Only two aircraft tail coded **RS** as further recoding delayed due to knowledge of the "Battle Creek" move to Zweibrucken on 31/1/73. Under "Battle Creek" (*post June 1972*) the 26 TRW and the 86 TFW switched bases, generally gaining each others components.

526 Tactical Fighter Squadron
F-4E   1972* - 31/1/73

Under the common wing tail code concept the **RS** tail code maintained on 526 TFS F-4E as part of the 26 TRW. The reporting unit changed to 86 TFW on 31/1/73 under "Battle Creek" movement of tactical air assets.

RS
86 Tactical Fighter Wing   31/1/73 - current 31/12/90   Ramstein AB, West Germany

512 Tactical Fighter Squadron
F-4E   3/77 - 12/85
F-16C/D   20/9/85 - current 31/12/90

The 512 TFS activated within the 86 TFW with **RS** tail coded F-4E carrying a yellow fin cap. By 1981 markings changed to yellow and black checks. When converting to F-16C/D the squadron colours changed with a large green band with black diagonal stripes applied. The 512 TFS received the first F-16C on 20/9/85.

F-4E Phantom 68-0475 **RS**, 512 TFS 86 TFW, Ramstein AB, with yellow fin cap. Photo: P Balkhoven.

526 Tactical Fighter Squadron
F-4E   31/1/73 - 7/86
F-16C/D   6/86 - current 31/12/90

Through "Battle Creek" the 526 TFS remained at Ramstein AB but switched reporting wings to the 86 TFW on 31/1/73. Squadron F-4E displayed red fin caps until changed in late 1981 to red and black checkered markings adopted. Converted to F-16C/D summer of 1986 with final F-4E leaving Ramstein AB on 1/7/86. Red diagonal stripes in a black tail band, carried on F-16C/D.

SB
66 Electronic Combat Wing   3/3/87 - current 31/12/90   Sembach AB, West Germany

UNITED STATES AIR FORCES EUROPE

43 Electronic Combat Squadron*
EC-130H   5/87 - current 31/12/90*
   The 43 ECS activated with EC-130H Hercules in May 1987 at Sembach AB. Tail code assigned to squadron on 3/3/87.

EC-130H Hercules 73-1584 **SB**, 43 ECS 66 ECW, Sembach AB. Photo: Christoph Kugler, RAF Alconbury 13 August 1990.

SP
52 Tactical Fighter Wing   1972* - current 31/12/90   Spangdahlem AB, West Germany

39 Tactical Electronic Warfare Squadron
EB-66C/E   8/72 - 1/1/73
   The 39 TEWS was based at Spangdahlem AB under the 36 TFW with **BV** tail codes as the fifth squadron assigned. Control transferred to the 52 TFW on activation of wing on 31/12/71. Some time after August 1972 the tail code change to **SP**. Status changed to non-operational on 5/12/72 and squadron inactivated on 15/1/73. Replaced in electronic warfare role by the 81 TFS flying Wild Weasel F-4C (ww).

EB-66E Destroyer 55-0531 **SP**, 39 TEWS 52 TFW, Spangdahlem AB, with a yellow tail stripe. Photo: Martin collection, Bitburg AB, 26 August 1972.

23 Tactical Fighter Squadron
F-4D   8/72 - 4/82
F-4E   4/80 - late 1987
F-4G   12/83 - current 31/12/90
F-16C/D   10/87 - current 31/12/90
   The 23 TFS maintained the **SP** tail code after AFM66-1 concept. Squadron F-4 continued to carry a blue fin cap (*some noted with black*). In 1981 squadron converted to F-4E 1981 carrying a white trimmed blue tail stripe (*white trim dropped in 1989*). Several F-4E carried a black fin cap with a blue stripe outlined in white, while further F-4 omitted the outline. The 81 TFS operated all F-4G until December 1983 when all three squadrons shared F-4E and G. By October 1987 the F-16C/D started to replace the F-4E.

81 Tactical Fighter Squadron
F-4C (ww)   15/1/73 - 7/79
F-4E   5/84 - late 1987
F-4G   4/1979 - current 31/12/90
F-16C/D   10/87 - current 31/12/90
   The 81 TFS flew **ZS** tail coded F-4C with the 86 TFW through the common wing tail code period, even after it should have recoded **ZR**. On 15/1/73 the squadron moved to Spangdahlem AB under "Battle Creek" prior to the 26 TRW and 86 TFW base switch. The **SP** tail coded Wild Weasel F-4C continued as 81 TFS mounts, carrying yellow fin caps until replaced by F-4G in April 1979. The 52 TFW F-4G operated solely by 81 TFS until December 1983, then all three squadrons shared both F-4E and F-4G. By October 1987 the F-16C/D carrying a yellow tail stripe with white trim received to replace the F-4E. The F-4G carried a yellow fin cap then switching to a yellow tail stripe.

480 Tactical Fighter Squadron
F-4D   15/11/76 - 3/80

F-4E	3/80 - 1987
F-4G	12/83 - current 31/12/90
F-16C/D	9/87 - current 31/12/90

The 480 TFS activated with the 52 TFW on 15/11/76. Previously activate with **HK** tail coded F-4D within the 12 TFW at Phu Cat AB, RSVN. Squadron operated ex-Hahn and Bentwaters F-4D with red fin caps. Conversion to F-4E complete by March 1980 with red trim outlined in white. A change to red and black markings started in November 1983. The 52 TFW F-4G operated by 81 TFS until December 1983 when F-4E/G operated by all three squadrons. The 480 TFS F-4G carried a red fin cap. By October 1987 the F-4E started to give way to F-16C/D.

F-4G Phantom 69-0250 **SP**, 480 TFS, 52 TFW, Spangdahlem AB, with a red tail stripe. Photo: Jan Jorgensen, Husum Germany, 19 April 1989.

F-16C Falcon 85-1552 **SP**, 480 TFS 52 TFW, Spangdahlem AB, with red tail stripe outlined in white. Note shadowed tail code and non-standard serial presentation to include "52" TFW. Photo: Martin collection.

TJ
307 Tactical Fighter Squadron   **401 Tactical Fighter Wing**
F-4E   5/70 - 15/7/71   **Torrejon AB, Spain**

The 307 TFS coded F-4E **TJ** in May 1970 and carried blue trim. Under one year later the 307 TFS was replaced by the 612 TFS and transferred to the 31 TFW at Homestead AFB.

TJ
612 Tactical Fighter Squadron   **401 Tactical Fighter Wing**

F-4E   15/7/71 - 6/72   **Torrejon AB, Spain**
When the 307 TFS returning to CONUS assets were taken over by 612 TFS transferring from the 35 TFW flying **VS** tail coded F-100, at Phan Rang AB, RSVN. The 35 TFW records claim the actual date is 31/7/71. Under the AFM66-1 concept the 612 TFS continued to carry **TJ** tail codes.

TJ
401 Tactical Fighter Wing   1972* - current 31/12/90   **Torrejon AB, Spain**
                                                                                                       612 Tactical Fighter Squadron
F-4E   1972* - 9/73
F-4C   9/73 - 1978-79
F-4D   1978-79 - 1983
F-16A/B   24/1/83 - 1989
F-16C/D   least 2/89 - current 31/12/90

Under AFM66-1 the 401 TFW used the **TJ** tail code for all components. During October 1973 F-4E traded for the less capable F-4C. Both F-4E and F-4C carried black and white checked fin caps. In 1979 the F-4D introduced with a blue fin cap. The F-16A/B added on 24/1/83 and may have carried blue trim changing to black and white check fin cap by June 1985. The F-16C/D received in 1983 and carried blue and white markings.

613 Tactical Fighter Squadron
F-4E   6/72 - 9/73
F-4C   9/73 - 1978-79
F-4D   1978-79 - 1983
F-16A/B   1983 - 1989
F-16C/D   early 1989 - current 31/12/90

By June 1972 the 613 TFS recoded F-4E from **TL** to **TJ**. The squadron F-4E continued carrying black and white check markings until conversion to F-4C by September 1973. Further converted to F-4D model during 1979. The F-4D equipment remained until F-16A/B conversion by 1983, carrying black and white check pattern. This changed to the yellow and black check by August 1984. During early 1989 conversion took place to the more capable F-16C/D.

614 Tactical Fighter Squadron
F-4E   6/72 - 9/73
F-4C   9/73 - 1978-79
F-4D   1978-79 - mid 1983
F-16A/B   by 19/5/83 - least 2/90
F-16C/D   2/90 - current 31/12/90

The 614 TFS adopted the wing tail code of **TJ** in June 1972 and changing squadron markings to black and white check. The 614 TFS changed equipment from the F-4E to the F-4C during September 1973 and F-4D during 1979 with red fin caps. Squadron converted to F-16A/B in 1983, adding red and black checkered band by July 1987. Further converted to F-16C/D with red black markings by February 1990.

F-4D Phantom 66-7768 **TJ**, 614 TFS 401 TFW, Torrejon AB, with a red fin cap and tips on horizontal stabilizers. Photo: Martin collection, Ramstein AB, October 1979.

TAIL CODE

F-16A Falcon 82-0922 **TJ**, 614 TFS 401 TFW, Torrejon AB, with red tail stripe. Note the non standard white outlined Falcon and nose art. Photo: Martin collection.

TK
353 Tactical Fighter Squadron   **401 Tactical Fighter Wing**
F-4E   6/70 - 15/7/71   Torrejon AB, Spain

The 353 TFS activated with the 401 TFW on 27/4/66 and was replaced by the 614 TFS on 15/7/71. Squadron F-4E carried a red fin cap with black diamonds. The 353 TFS transferred to the 354 TFW flying A-7D with **MR** tail codes.

TK
614 Tactical Fighter Squadron   **401 Tactical Fighter Wing**
F-4E   15/7/71 - 6/72   Torrejon AB, Spain

The 614 TFS reassigned from the 35 TFW at Phan Rang AB, RSVN (**VP**) to the 401 TFW on 15/7/71, assuming assets of the 353 TFS. The 35 TFW records claim the actual date is 31/7/71. The **TK** tail code carried until the AFM66-1 concept tail code **TJ** applied in June 1972. By June 1972 black and white check markings replaced the red and black. Some F-4E noted with red fin caps containing black diamonds.

TL
613 Tactical Fighter Squadron   **401 Tactical Fighter Wing**
F-4E   6/70 - 6/72   Torrejon AB, Spain

The 613 TFS served with 401 TFW since 1957 with various aircraft types. The wing converted to F-4E from F-100 in 1970 and applied the **TL** tail code in June 1970. A yellow fin cap displayed with ten black stars added by late 1970. A further change occurred by mid 1971 with two black horizontal lightning flashes added. In 1972 tail code changed to **TJ** as wing common tail code.

F-4E Phantom 69-7264 **TL**, 613 TFS 401 TFW, Torrejon AB, with a yellow fin cap. Photo: N Kropfl, Jagel, 2 August 1970.

UH
20 Tactical Fighter Wing   1972* - current 31/12/90   RAF Upper Heyford

42 Electronic Combat Squadron (*66 Electronic Combat Wing*)
EF-111A   3/2/84 - current 31/12/90

The 42 ECS activated in early 1984 and based with the 20 TFW tail coding **UH**. Controlled by the 20 TFW until 1986 when the 66 ECW assumed control for several years. Squadron EF-111A carried a 20 TFW badge on the starboard and the 66 ECW on port with a grey lightning bolt carried on fin.

55 Tactical Fighter Squadron
F-111E   7-8/72 - current 31/12/90

The 55 TFS recoded from **JS** between July and August 1972, under the AFM66-1 concept. Squadron F-111E continued to a carry blue fin cap until March - April 1985 when replaced by blue and white checked fin cap.

77 Tactical Fighter Squadron
F-111E   7/72 - current 31/12/90

The 77 TFS recoded from **JT** to wing common tail code of **UH** in July 1972, maintaining a red fin cap.

UNITED STATES AIR FORCES EUROPE

F-111E 68-0068 **UH**, 77 TFS 20 TFW, RAF Upper Heyford, with a red fin cap. Photo: Patrick Martin, Nellis AFB, 29 June 1984

79 Tactical Fighter Squadron
F-111E   **7-8/72 - current 31/12/90**

The common wing coding of **UH** introduced to the 79 TFS during July and August 1972. Sometime between 1981 and 1983 black and yellow tiger stripes amended yellow fin caps.

UR
79 Tactical Fighter Squadron   **20 Tactical Fighter Wing**
F-111E   **10/70 - 1/71**   **RAF Upper Heyford**

The 79 TFS changed equipment from F-100 to F-111E prior to tail code introduction. The F-111E were a combination of new builds and transfers from the 27 TFW, at Cannon AFB. The 79 TFS tail coded **UR** in October 1970, with yellow tips noted. In January 1971 the squadron recoded to **JR**.

(US)
55 Tactical Fighter Squadron   **20 Tactical Fighter Wing**
                                                                                                                  RAF Upper Heyford

The 55 TFS reequipped from F-100 to F-111E prior to tail code application. The wing started coding **UR**, **US** and **UT**. The **UR** and **UT** appeared briefly before the wing changed to **JR**, **JS** and **JT**. The 55 TFS tail code **US** not applied, due to the undesirability of **US** as a tail code. (*United States or Un-Serviceable*)

UT
77 Tactical Fighter Squadron   **20 Tactical Fighter Wing**
F-111E   **12/70 - 1/71**   **RAF Upper Heyford**

The 77 TFS was one of three 20 TFW F-100 squadrons to transition to the F-111E. The 77 TFS coded F-111E **UR** in December 1970, with red fin caps. The squadron recoded to **JT** in January 1971, due to 55 TRS non-usage of the **US** tail code.

WR
78 Tactical Fighter Squadron   **81 Tactical Fighter Wing**
F-4D   **2/70 - 1972**   **RAF Woodbridge**

The 78 TFS was the first 81 TFW squadron to code F-4D February 1970. Squadron F-4D carried a fin cap. Preserved the **WR** tail code as wing common tail code 1972. The 78 TFS known as the "Bushmasters."

WR
81 Tactical Fighter Wing   **1972* - current 31/12/90**   **RAF Woodbridge/Bentwaters**

78 Tactical Fighter Squadron
F-4D   **1972* - by 9/1979**
A-10A   **by 9/1979 - current 31/12/90**

The RAF Woodbridge based 78 TFS maintained the **WR** tail code after wing adoption of code. In January 1973 red fin caps dropped and reintroduced again by November 1976. The A-10A introduced in 1979 and carried red bands containing a white Indian head motif. By 1987 evolved to red bands thickly outlined in white.

F-4D Phantom 65-0738 **WR**, 78 TFS 81 TFW, RAF Woodbridge, with a red fin cap. Photo: Jean-Pierre Hoehn, Florennes Belgium, September 1972.

91 Tactical Fighter Squadron

F-4C	1972* - 9/73
F-4D	9/73 - by 9/1979
A-10A	by 9/1979 - current 31/12/90

The 91 TFS F-4C adopted the **WR** wing tail code under the AFM66-1 concept, changing from **WS**. The F-4C carried blue trim until early in 1973 when removed. The F-4D replaced F-4C in September 1973 and reapplied the blue trim markings. Conversion to the A-10A occurred 1979. These RAF Woodbridge aircraft originally carried blue bands with a white Indian head. This evolved into a white lightning bolt. By 1985 squadron outlined bands in white adding a white lightning bolt.

A-10A Thunderbolt 81-0991 **WR**, 91 TFS 81 TFW, RAF Bentwaters, with single sided blue tail bands outlined in white and lightning flash. Photo: Patrick Martin, Nellis AFB 7 June 1985.

92 Tactical Fighter Squadron

F-4C	7-8/72 - 9/73
F-4D	9/73 - 1979
A-10A	1/79 - current 31/12/90

During July and August 1972 the 92 TFS based at RAF Bentwaters and recoded assigned F-4C to the wing standard code **WR** from **WT**. Yellow trim gave way to black, before trim eliminated at the end of September 1973. The F-4D replaced F-4C in September 1973 and yellow trim applied again. Further conversion to A-10A started by the end of 1978. The squadron machines ferried to RAF Bentwaters on 25/1/79 with several variations of markings noted. Yellow bands with or without a white Indian head motif noted followed by yellow checker marks, later with white outlines added. One scheme supplemented the yellow tail stripe with black skull emitting lightning bolts.

509 Tactical Fighter Squadron

A-10A	1/10/79 - 15/9/88

The 509 TFS was previously activate with **PK** tail coded F-102 as the 509 FIS 405 FW at Clark AB, Philippines. The 509 TFS activated within the 81 TFW on 1/10/79 to operate **WR** tail coded A-10A at RAF Bentwaters carrying grey bands with a white Indian head. Later markings changed to grey bands outlined in white, and yet a further change contained the inscription "Pirates" in black. The 509 TFS reassigned to the 10 TFW at RAF Alconbury on 15/9/88 and recoding **AR**.

510 Tactical Fighter Squadron

A-10A	1/10/78 - current 31/12/90

Formerly flew **CE** tail coded F-100D/F from Bien Hoa AB, RSVN within the 3 TFW. The 510 TFS activated within the 81 TFW on 1/10/78 with **WR** tail coded A-10A. Squadron based at RAF Bentwaters carrying purple bands with a white Indian head. The latter amended with the addition of white bands and switched to a fish motif by 1987.

511 Tactical Fighter Squadron

A-10A	1/80 - 7/88

Previously active within the 354 TFW at Myrtle Beach AFB, flying **MR** tail coded A-7D. The 511 TFS activated within the 81 TFW operating **WR** tail coded A-10A. The RAF Bentwaters based 509 TFS carried black bands with a white stylized Indian head. All black bands introduced in 1985 and by 1986 inscription "Vultures" added in white. In 1987 white outlines added to bands. Squadron reassigned to the 10 TFW at RAF Alconbury on 7/7/88 and recoding to **AR**.

F-16C Falcon 86-0229 **WR**, 525 AS 81 TFW, RAF Bentwaters, with a red tail stripe and outlined in yellow. The same colours applied to "04" individual aircraft marking. Photo: Christoph Kugler, 16 July 1989.

UNITED STATES AIR FORCES EUROPE

527 Aggressor Squadron
F-16C **14/6/88 - 1/3/90**

The 527 AS transferred to RAF Bentwaters after flying uncoded F-5E, under the 10 TRW at RAF Alconbury since 1/4/76. Squadron assets originated from other F-16C USAFE units in June 1988. After only eight months of operating **WR** tail coded F-16C the 527 AS inactivated with assets distributed to USAFE users.

WS
91 Tactical Fighter Squadron   **81 Tactical Fighter Wing**
F-4C **2/70 - 5/72**   **RAF Bentwaters**

The 91 TFS operated F-4C, with pale blue fin caps, from RAF Bentwaters. In February 1970 squadron adopted the **WS** tail code. It is possible the squadron also flew with red fins caps in mid 1972 prior to recoding to AFM66-1 common wing code of **WR**.

F-4C Phantom 63-7638 **WS**, 91 TFS 81 TFW, RAF Bentwaters, with pale blue fin cap. Photo: Henk Schakelaar, Soesterberg, 9 July 1971.

WT
92 Tactical Fighter Squadron   **81 Tactical Fighter Wing**
F-4C **2/70 - 7-8/72**   **RAF Bentwaters**

The 92 TFS coded assigned F-4C **WT** in February 1970 with and applied yellow fins caps introduced in the same period. In July and August 1972 the wing tail code **WR** applied.

ZR
17 Tactical Reconnaissance Squadron   **86 Tactical Fighter Wing**
RF-4C **12/1/70 - 6/72**   **Zweibrucken AB, West Germany**

The 17 TRS flew RF-4C at Zweibrucken AB when tail codes first applied on USAFE aircraft in the winter of 1969 - 1970. Under initial coding practice applied the **ZR** tail code. On adoption of the AFM66-1 concept in June 1972, the 17 TRS maintained **ZR** as the 86 TFW tail code.

ZR
86 Tactical Fighter Wing **1972* - 31/1/73** Zweibrucken AB, West Germany

17 Tactical Reconnaissance Squadron
RF-4C **1972* - 31/1/73**

Under AFM66-1 concept the 17 TRS RF-4C maintained the 86 TFW common tail code **ZR**, until the 86 TFW and 26 TRW switched bases on 31/1/73. The 26 TRW assumed **ZR** tail code on that date.

ZR
26 Tactical Fighter Wing **31/1/73 - current 31/12/90** Zweibrucken AB, West Germany

17 Tactical Reconnaissance Squadron
RF-4C **31/1/73 - 13/12/78**

Under "Battle Creek" the 17 TRS, RF-4C remained at Zweibrucken AB, but switched reporting wing to the 26 TRW on 31/1/73, with the tail code remaining as **ZR**. The 17 TRS continued flying operations until 15/11/78, inactivating on 20/11/78 (*final RF-4C flown out on 13/12/78*). The RF-4C carried red fin cap.

RF-4C Phantom 68-0553 **ZR**, 17 TRS 26 TRW, Zweibrucken AB, with a very faded red fin cap. Photo: Denis Hughes, Florennes Belgium, July 1973.

TAIL CODE

38 Tactical Reconnaissance Squadron
RF-4C   31/1/73 - current 31/12/90
F-4D   1980

On arrival at Zweibrucken AB on 31/1/73 from Ramstein AB (*where coded* **RS**) the 38 TRS adopted the wing tail code **ZR** as per the AFM66-1 concept. Black fin caps noted during 1982 - 1983 changing to a green and white diamond checked fin cap in 1985. In early 1980 the 38 TRS also operated five F-4D. While individual F-4D are known, no photographic proof of this tail code usage exist.

RF-4C Phantom 69-0350 **ZR**, 38 TRS 26 TRW, Zweibrucken AB, with a green and white checkered fin cap. Photo: Martin collection, September 1979.

417 Tactical Fighter Squadron   **26 Tactical Reconnaissance Wing**
F-4D   12/10/78 - 6/11/78   **Zweibrucken AB, West Germany**

The 417 TFS activated on 1/10/78 and assigned to the 26 TRW. A single F-4D arrived on 12/10/78 from Spangdahlem AB, and tail coded **ZR**. The F-4D return to source on 6/11/78. A personnel strength of seven aircrew and nine enlisted personnel noted on inactivation on 1/11/70, due to "poor munitions storage."

ZS

81 Tactical Fighter Squadron   **86 Tactical Fighter Wing**
F-4C   12/6/71 - 15/1/73   **Zweibrucken AB, West Germany**

The 81 TFS assigned to the 50 TFW since 1957 and should have tail coded while at Hahn AB, in 1970 but did not. Coding of F-4C held off until attachment to the 86 TFW at Zweibrucken AB on 12/6/71 and assigned on 15/1/71. The code **ZS** assigned as per the current USAFE **R**, **S**, **T**, **U**, and **V** coding practice. A yellow fin cap carried on Wild Weasel F-4C. The 81 TFS should have recoded to **ZR** under the AFM66-1 concept, but did not due to knowledge of "Battle Creek" movement and assignment to the 52 TFW at Spangdahlem AB. The squadron reassigned on 15/1/73 and recoded **SP**. Reassigned **ZS** F-4C were noted with other units as late as 22/1/73.

Air Training Command

Squadron/Code Summary ATC

CM
50 Flying Training Squadron   **14 Flying Training Wing**
T-38A   **3/3/86 - least 3/87**   **Columbus AFB, Mississippi**
    In March 1986 the 50 FTS applied the **CM** tail code on T-38A. The T-38A were painted in a blue and white scheme.

LL
86 Flying Training Squadron   **47 Flying Training Wing**
T-38A   **1986 - 1989**   **Laughlin AFB, Texas**
    A few 86 FTS T-38A carried the **LL** tail code on the blue and white horizontal split fuselage T-38A scheme.

NT
454 Flying Training Squadron   **323 Flying Training Wing**
T-43A   **17/10/88 - current 31/12/90**   **Mather AFB, California**
    The 454 FTS carried the only Air Training Command recognized tail code of **NT**, which the squadron applied to T-43A during 1988.

T-43A Boeing (737-253) 73-1155 **NT**, 454 FTS 323 FTW, Mather AFB, displaying Air Training Command crest. Photo: Patrick Martin, Abbotsford IAP, 10 August 1990.

OK
71 Flying Training Wing   **Vance AFB, Oklahoma**

8 Flying Training Squadron
25 Flying Training Squadron
T-37, T-38A   **1986 - current 31/12/90**
    The **OK** tail code not presented in normal Air Training Command method. A small stylized **OK** carried on fin. As A-7 of the 125 TFS, Oklahoma ANG, originally assigned the **OK** tail code, the 71 TFW presentation is non standard.

TAIL CODE

T-37B Tweety Bird 58-1901 **OK**, 8 FTS 71 FTW, Vance AFB, with stylized tail code. Photo: Martin collection, 1989.

RA
12 Flying Training Wing   11/85 - current 31/12/90   **Randolph AFB, Texas**

559 Flying Training Squadron
T-37   11/85 - current 31/12/90
560 Flying Training Squadron
T-38A   11/85 - current 31/12/90

The **RA** tail codes applied on blue and white painted T-38A by at least November 1985. Tail coded aircraft have been painted in light blue and white wrap camouflage with black tail codes. The more common T-38A have a blue and white horizontal split fuselage, white wings, with tail code and serial in red. The T-38A noted in the latter scheme until at least November 1986. Tail codes also seen on T-37B with a similar painted scheme.

T-37B 66-7982 Tweety Bird **RA**, 559 FTS 12 FTW, Randolph AFB, with red codes. Photo: Brian Rogers, Carswell AFB, 30 August 1986.

T-38A Talon 67-14846 **RA**, 12 FTW, Randolph AFB, with red tail code. Photo: Doug Remington, McChord AFB, 16 August 1986.

AIR TRAINING COMMAND

(RE)
64 Flying Training Wing   Reese AFB, Texas

35 Flying Training Squadron
54 Flying Training Squadron
Assigned on 3/3/86 but not carried on T-37B of 35 FTS and T-38A of 54 FTS.

VN
25 Flying Training Squadron   **71 Flying Training Wing**
T-38A   3/3/86 - 1990   Vance AFB, Oklahoma
Wing historian states "the test T-38 aircraft did have the code **VN**, and the aircraft are still located at Vance AFB, Oklahoma. When the aircraft is due its scheduled painting, it will be changed back to the **OK** code." Last noted on 20/8/90.

WF
90 Flying Training Squadron   **80 Flying Training Wing**
T-38A   3/3/86 - current 31/12/90   Sheppard AFB, Texas
A red tail code and serial presented on blue and white horizontal split fuselage, with white wings. Effective May 1986, also listed as 3/3/86.

WL
82 Flying Training Wing   Williams AFB, Arizona

97 Flying Training Squadron
99 Flying Training Squadron
T-38A   3/3/86 - current 31/12/90*
Red tail code and serial presented on blue and white horizontal split fuselage with white wings.

T-38A Talon 63-8221 **WL**, 97 FTS 82 FTW, Williams AFB, with red tail code. Photo: Douglas Slowiak, 30 August 1986.

XL
47 Flying Training Wing   23/6/86 - current 31/12/90   Laughlin AFB, Texas

85 Flying Training Squadron
T-37   23/6/86 - current 31/12/90
86 Flying Training Squadron
T-38A   23/6/86 - current 31/12/90
The **XL** tail code carried on blue and white scheme aircraft only after June 1986.

Air Force Logistics Command

Squadron/Code Summary AFLC

RG
Warner Robins Air Logistics Center   **Robins AFB, Georgia**
F-15A, F-105   2/78 - 78
F-15A, F-105   7/82 - current 31/12/90

    The Air Logistics Center is responsible for the overhaul and management of C-130, C-141 and F-15 aircraft. A single F-15A arrived for center use early 1978 from the 49 TFW at Holloman AFB. The **HO** tail code replaced by **RG** tail code with the WRALC badge replacing the TAC Badge. This tail code lasted several months until the aircraft recoded **WR**. In July 1982 the aircraft again recoded to **RG**, with an indian head feature added early in 1985.

    Several F-105B arrived in October 1980 and went to the combat battle damage area in late November and December, applying the **WR** tail code. The **RG** tail code applied replacing the **WR** in the same time period as the F-15. The conversion back to **RG** occurred in the same time period as the F-15. The assigned F-105 are no longer current.

F-15A Eagle 77-0068 **RG**, WRALC Robins AFB, over head sun gives the impression of a tail stripe. Photo: Martin collection, 26 March 1985.

WR
Warner Robins Air Logistics Center   **Robins AFB, Georgia**
F-15A, F-105   78 - 7/82
See RG for details

F-15A Eagle 77-0068 **WR**, WRALC Robins AFB, with a single sided non-standard red, white and blue tail bands plus a large eagle on the nose. Photo: Robert J Leavite, 12 September 1980.

Air Force Systems Command

Squadron/Code Summary AFSC

AD
3247 Test Squadron   **3246 Test Wing**
Various   late 1982 - 1/10/89   **Eglin AFB, Florida**

The 3247 Test Squadron operated a large variety of **AD** tail coded aircraft. The unit started adding tail codes in late 1982 maintaining a white tail stripe containing a row of red diamonds. The following types all reported tail coding within the 3246 TESTS; A-10A, YA-10B, F-4C/D/E, RF-4C, F-15A/B/D, F-16A/B, F-111E, HH-1H, UH-1N, T-38A and CT-39A. The abbreviation for the 3246 changed from TS to TESTS on 30/6/86. The 3247 TESTS recoded to **ET** starting on 1/10/89.

F-4C Phantom 64-0817 **AD**, 3247 TS 3246 TW, in ADC overall grey scheme with red diamonds on a white tail stripe. Photo: Doug Remington, McChord AFB, 28 January 1983.

ED
6512 Test Squadron   **6510 Test Wing**
Various   1983 - current 31/12/90   **Edwards AFB**

The 6512 Test Squadron, 6510 Test Wing applied the **ED** tail code during 1983 to most tactical aircraft assigned. The 6512 TS operated numerous types, including several single example types. Several types, such as YA-10B did not carry tail codes. A large variety of non coded aircraft are also operated from Edwards AFB with contractors and on special projects. Some aircraft remained in tactical paint schemes others adopting specialized test schemes. Several long serving types such as A-7, F-4 and UH-1 adopting an overall white scheme, embellished with high visibility red areas. The following types have been noted with the **ED** tail code; A-7D, YA-7D, A-10A, A-37B, OA-37B, MC-130H, F-4C/D/E, RF-4C, F-15A/B/C/D/E, F-16A/B/C/D and F-111A/D/E. Most types also carried a white outlined blue tail stripe containing white "X"s.

F-4D Phantom 66-7438 **ED**, 6512 TS 6510 TW, Edwards AFB, in an overall white scheme containing large red patches, with a blue tail stripe and white "X"s. Photo: Geoff Lebaron, McGuire AFB, October 1985.

A-7D Corsair 67-14582 **ED**, 6512 TS, 6510 TW, Edwards AFB, in a grey and light grey scheme containing large red patches, with a blue tail stripe and white "X"s. Note unusual serial presentation. Photo: Patrick Martin, 1 December 1983.

A-7D Corsair 68-8222 **ED**, 6512 TS, 6510 TW, Edwards AFB, in an overall white scheme containing large red patches, with blue tail stripe with white "X"s. Photo: Patrick Martin, CFB Comox, 3 August 1986.

ED
4485 Test Squadron

Tactical Air Warfare Center/
Armament Development and Test Center
Eglin AFB, Florida

F-4D   12/78 - early 1982

The Eglin based 4485 TS recoded to **EG**, in common with like based 33 TFW in October 1978. In December 1978, the 4485 TS recoded assigned F-4D to **ED**. The squadron recoded to **ET** between 1988 - 1989. The **ED** tail code taken up by Edwards AFB assigned 6152 TESTS.

EG
4485 Test Squadron

Tactical Air Warfare Center
Eglin AFB, Florida

F-4D	12/4/71 - 12/78
RF-4C	slide 5/71 - least 11/72
F-4C	unknown
F-4E	least 11/71 - least 6/74

On 12/4/71, the 4485 TS replaced the inactivated 4453 TTS(T), 33 TFW. The 4485 TS assigned to the Tactical Air Warfare Center at Eglin AFB. The squadron operated a pair of **EG** tail coded F-4D, a RF-4C and a loaned F-4E in late 1977. The 4485 TS recoded to **ED** prior to December 1978. A yellow fin cap noted for squadron markings on some aircraft.

AIR FORCE SYSTEMS COMMAND

RF-4C Phantom 68-0594 **EG**, 4485 TS TAWC, Eglin AFB. Photo: Tom Brewer, 4 May 1971.

ET
3247 Test Squadron   **3246 Test Wing**
Various   **1/10/89 - current 31/12/90**   **Eglin AFB, Florida**

The 3247 TESTS recoded from **AD** to **ET** starting on 1/10/89. Aircraft types noted with the **ET** tail code include; A-10A, YA-10B, F-4E, F-15A/B/D, F-16A/B/C, F-111E, HH-1H, UH-1N and T-38A. Markings of a white stipe containing red diamonds maintained.

F-4E Phantom 72-0126 **ET**, 3247 TESTS, with red diamonds on a white tail stripe. Photo: Jerry Geer, McConnell AFB, March 1990.

OT
4485 Test Squadron   **Tactical Air Warfare Center or**
                                                                    Armament Development and Test Center
Various   **Eglin AFB, Florida**

The 4485 Test Squadron recoded from **ED** to **OT** in 1982. The 4485 Test Squadron adopted the **OT** tail code in early 1982. Numerous tactical aircraft types used in the armament development role. These include A-10A, RF-4C, F-4E, F-15A/B/C, F-16A/B/C and possibly EF-111A. The squadron also assigned F-4G under Detachment 5 at George AFB. Later the F-4G also carried the **OT** tail code. Detachment 5 reported to have coded **WW** for a short period starting in 1987, before returning to **OT** in 1989. Squadron markings consist of a black and white checkered tail stripe, while F-4G carried a grey checkered fin cap.

A-10A Thunderbolt 78-0599 **OT**, 4485 TS TAWC, Eglin AFB, with twin double sided black and white checkered tail stripes. Photo: Charles B. Mayer, Minneapolis-St Paul IAP, 20 October 1984.

TAIL CODE

F-4E Phantom 66-0306 **OT** 4485 TS TAWC, Eglin AFB, with black and white checkered tail stripe. Photo: Doug Remington, McChord AFB, 29 September 1982.

F-4G Phantom 69-7235 **OT**, Detachment 5 - 4485 TESTS TAWC, George AFB, with a grey checkered fin cap, shadow tail code and "**Det 23 5**." Photo: Mick Roth, October 1989.

F-16 Falcon 79-0326 **OT**, 4485 TS TAWC, Eglin AFB, with black and white checkered tail stripe. Photo: Douglas E Slowiak, unknown location, 22 September 1984.

WW
4485 TESTS Detachment 5   **Tactical Air Warfare Center**
F-4G   1987 - current 31/12/90   **George AFB, California**

Detachment 5, 4485 TESTS reported established at George AFB with the **OT** tail code. Reported recoded to 35 TFW code **WW** in 1987, but unconfirmed. Reverted to controlling squadron 4485 TESTS tail code of **OT** in 1989. Squadron markings of blue and grey fin cap carried.

CONCLUSION

The years 1991-94 have provided an abundance of changes to Tail Code usage within the USAF. The unwillingness of the Soviet Union to use force to reign in the former Warsaw Pact countries as they peeled away, started a chain of events that would see massive reductions in United States Forces. Following the reduction of these threats, along with the relatively short and somewhat one-sided Gulf War (and follow-on events) provided the impetus for major changes within USAF units and associated markings.

While air power alone cannot win a war, it can and did shorten the ground phase to 100 hours, making for what some call an uncompetitive conflict. This in contrast to Vietnam, where it could not win but did force an end. The Gulf War saw the assignment of units from most commands deployed to the Gulf States, most under the jurisdictions of activated provisional wings.

F-15C Eagle 82-0046 **FF**, 27 TFS 1TFW, Dhabran IAP. Photo: Martin collection, 1990.

F-15C Eagle 79-0025 **BT**, 525 TFS 36 TFW, immediately on its return from the gulf conflict to Bitburg AB, Germany. Photo: Martin collection

For the United States the timing of the Gulf War came at an opportune time. If events had occurred two years later the forces committed would have represented a much larger portion of existing air power. It had been nearly twenty years since the last massive use of USAF air power in which a credible opposition was present for airpower. Most units added art work to aircraft while maintaining regular squadron markings. While mild in comparison to British standards, some noted and very talented art work lasted until "official-dum" ordered the removal in June 1991. The only full wing to return from the Gulf without emblazed "war paint" was the 35 TFW from George.

To some, the swiftness and completeness of the aerial campaign along with USN, USMC, British, French, Canadian, Italian and Arab allies, was proof that all the current inventory was not necessary.

F-16C Falcon 86-0287 **SP**, 23 FS 52 FW, Spangdahlem AB, arriving back at Incirlik AB from a combat air patrol over Iraq during operation "Provide Comfort". Photo: Martin collection, July 1992.

On return from combat, the down-sizing (or right-sizing, depending on budget or political opinions) began with major organizational and strength reductions. The first major change in USAF "code-ology" came on October 1, 1991 when the majority of units dropped the word Tactical from designations. The same effect was felt at the Wing and Group level on the same date. Few units that were slated for deactivation maintained the former titles for a short while.

The similar name changes followed on March 15, 1992 for the ANG and AFRES. These changes did not effect all commands equally. For example, the TASS designation remained in PACAF (this avoided two 19 FS designations) until 1993 when several units were redesignated to solve the number problem.

Many long serving units disappeared completely like the 67 TRW at Bergstrom along with 50 TFW at Hahn and 56 TFW at MacDill. Serveral others have found non-flying redesignated roles such as the former 35 TFW now at Iceland and 36 FW at Anderson, Guam.

Serveral units moved around "bumping" other wing titles. With the closure of bases in the Philippines, the former 3 TFW moved to Alaska replacing the 21 FW. The long time A-10A operator 354 FW, after closing out at Myrtle-beach, also moved to Alaska replacing the 343 FW. The 20 TFW, which served so long with the USAFE is to replace the 363 FW at Shaw.

On June 1, 1992 Tactical Air Command passed into history and was replaced by Air Combat Command. Serveral wing structures were altered to provide "composite" forces of several types based together. The 366 W at Mountain Home operates F-15, F-16, KC-135 and B-52 based at Castle but coded **MO** like other 366 W units. Pope based 23 W flies a variety of types with the **FT** tail code. Because of the T.O. 1-1-4 directive allowing the 23 W to apply teeth to assigned aircraft, the C-130E make an impressive sight.

C-130E Hercules 63-7846 **FT**, 41 ALS 23 W, Pope AFB, attending Fairchild AFB open house, 7 August 1993. Photo: Patrick Martin.

The former TAC assets have seen reductions in the order of 30 percent. Numerous wings have folded under budget cuts and re-alignments. In a very short time serveral types have faded into history.

The legendary Phantom, after serving in the hundreds in each theatre is now reduced to the specialized anti-SAM role at Nellis. The replacing F-16, is the only type seen in the large numbers, of the past years. The A-7D, long time mount of the ANG has been replaced again by the Lawn Dart (alias F-16). The Eagle continuing to be the premier air defense fighter for the USAF. Even the high-tech F-111 is now reduced to one hive of activity with the F-15E Beagle standing in elsewhere in the precision air to ground role of mud moving. The A-10 started to fade from fashion, when the Gulf War made it a star performer. Two years on, most were reassigned to the ANG and AFRES.

CONCLUSION

A-10A Thunderbolt 79-0188 **TC**, 354 FS 355 FW, McChord AFB, showing the newer all light grey scheme. This squadron is based at McChord AFB while the parent wing, the 355 FW is based at Davis-Monthan AFB. Photo: Patrick Martin, 27 August 1993.

The three main tactical types, A-10, F-15, F-16 are to be around for many years to come. The F-117A stealth fighter, while no longer in production, will only serve in one wing and moved from its hide-away at Tonopah, to Holloman pushing out F-15 and AT-38. The AT-38B advanced fighter lead-in trainer role was all but eliminated with budget cuts.

At Nellis, the self professed "Home of the Fighter Pilot" the most advanced versions of all the fighter types continue to apply their trade. The aggressor role, while on a reduced scale with the 414 CTS, continues to roam to places like CFB Cold Lake. Combat rescue forces assigned to the newly designated RQS have applied tail codes to types such as UH-IN and HH-60G with regular force and AFRES.

F-16C Falcon 86-0272 **WA**, 4450 FTTG 57 FWW, Nellis AFB, in aggressor colours. Photo: Patrick Martin, 15 June 1991.

Strategic Air Command also phased out with assets passing to Air Combat Command. This set the stage for a massive influx of new tail codes to be applied to such types as B-1, B-52, C-135, T-37 and U-2.

Unit titles changed back and forth between "Wing" and "Bomber Wing". The same went for the squadrons and Reconnaissance Wings. The training flights of T-37 added numerous codes, some like the heavier stable mates did not last long. As 1993 drew to a close many of these former SAC units had inactivated taking with them a variety of the short lived codes.

B-52H Stratofortress 61-0003 **FC**, 325 BS 92 BW, Fairchild AFB, with red and black check tail stripe. Photo: Patrick Martin, NAS Whidbey Island, 16 July 1993.

Space Command also appeared in July 1993 and was assigned the former SAC Missile Wings. The units had recently acquired tail codes for Rescue Flights, mainly based on location such as **MN** (Malmstrom) and **WM** (Whitman). Several of these duplicated codes were already in use with major former SAC bases like **EL** (Ellsworth) and **FC** (Fairchild).

Air Training Command has evolved into Air Education & Training Command with an abundance of tail codes now assigned. Codes such as **AU** and **EN** on a variety of types.

T-38A Talon 65-10407 **LB**, 64 FTW, Reese AFB, at the bi-annual trade show at Abbotsford, Canada. Photo: Patrick Martin, 5 August 1993.

The originating command of tail codes, PACAF has been reduced to Alaska which used to be a separate command of its own. This geographic area had been the only location not to see wholesale reductions in strength.

F-16D Falcon 89-2172 **AK**, 18 FS 3 W, Eielson AFB, arriving at CFB Comox for the bi-annual airshow. Photo: Patrick Martin, 31 July 1992.

The USAFE has been cut from 31 combat role units to 9 by the end of 1994. While re-equipment has taken place, it is now only 25 percent of the strength from just four years ago. This all happening just when "in place" may be more necessary for a different foe.

F-15C Eagles 84-0021 & 84-0019 **BT**, 53 TFS 36 FW, Bitburg AB, arriving at the 1991 Tiger meet at RAF Fairford. Photo: Patrick Martin, 16 July 1991.

CONCLUSION

Test squadrons are using tail codes on more types than ever before. Even prototypes such as the C-17 and UC-130 are now carrying tail codes.

F-111F 70-2416 **LN**, 494 TFS 48 TFW, RAF Lakenheath, this aircraft participated against Libya, and the Gulf War. Photo: Patrick Martin, 29 July 1991.

The tactical transport role, once massed at major transport hubs like Dyess, Little Rock, and Pope, have been passed to ANG and AFRES units. These units long devoid of codes once again got the nod to add the big letters some twenty years after their removal.

RF-4C 65-0900 **BH**, 106 RS 117 RW arriving back from the mass fly past at the 1993 Phantom convention at Birmingham MAP. Photo: Patrick Martin, 24 October 1993.

F-16B 82-1030 **PR**, 198 FS FG, Muniz ANGB, Puerto Rico. Photo: Daniel Soulaine, 3 November 1993.

F-16C 88-0503 **NM**, 188 FS 150 FG, Kirtland AFB, Photo: Ben Knowles, August 1993.

RF-4C 68-0589 **ZR**, ex 38 TRS 26 TRW Zweibrucken AB, Germany. After participating in the Gulf War, this Phantom like hundreds of others now resides at the great bone-yard of D-M. Note the Iraqi flag and Kodak missions. Photo: Martin collection, June 1991.

APPENDIX A

Tail Code Summary

Code	Command	Unit	Wing	Aircraft	Dates
A_	PACAF	389 TFS	366 TFW	F-4C	late 66/mid 1967- 1/68
				F-4D	1/68 - 24/6/69
AA	TAC	7 SOF/Det 1	1 SOW	C-47	1/7/69 - 1/4/70
				UC-123K	1/7/69 - 31/5/72
				U-10B	1/7/69 - 1971
AB	TAC	Det 2	1 SOW	C-130E	15/7/69 - 15/11/71
AB	TAC	318 SOS	1 SOW	C-130E	15/11/71 - 1/6/74
AC	PACAF	12 TRS	460 TRW	RF-4C	1968 - 31/8/71
AD	TAC	4407 CCTS	4410 CCTW/1 SOW	A-1E/G/H	10/7/68 - 1972
				T-28D	1969 - 1972
AD	AFSC	3246 TW	3247 TS	various	late 1982 - 1/10/89
AE	PACAF	16 TRS	460 TRW	RF-4C	1967 - 15/3/70
AF	TAC	603 SOS	1 SOW	A-26	15/7/69 - 15/5/71
				A-37B	15/7/69 - 15/5/71
AG	TAC	319 SOS	1 SOW	C-123K	30/7/69 - 15/1/72
AG	ANG	195 TAS	195 TAG	C-130A	4/70 - 1974
AH	PACAF	45 TRS	460 TRW	RF-101C	1968 - 31/12/70
AH	TAC	415 SOTS	1 SOW	AC-119G	15/7/71 - pre 1972
				AC-119K	15/7/71 - 1972
				AC-130A	15/7/71 - 1972
AH	TAC	1 SOW/834 TCW/1 SOW	8 SOS	C-130E	1/3/74 - by 1980
			16 SOS	AC-130H	12/12/75 - by 1980
			20 SOS	UH-1N	1/1/76 - by 1980
				CH-3E	1/1/76 - by 1980
			317 SOS	C-123K	1972 - 1973
				UH-1N/P	1972 - 24/6/71
				A-1E/G/H	1972 - 26/10/72
				T-28D	1972 - 30/4/74
				CH-3E	1972 - 4/74
			415 SOTS	AC-119K	1972 - 26/10/72
				AC-130A	1972 - 30/6/75
			547 TASTS	U-10	1972 - 30/4/75
			549 TASTS	UH-1F/P	1972 - 15/12/75
			603 SOTS	C-47	1/7/73 - 1/7/74
			4407 CCTS	A-1E/G/H	1972 - 30/4/73
				AT/T-28D	1972 - 30/4/73
			7 SOF	UH-1N	1972 - 31/5/72
AJ	PACAF	360 TEWS	460 TRW/483 TAW/377 ABW	EC-47N/P/Q	1968 - 24/11/72
AK	AAC	343 CW/TFW	18 TFS	A-10A	1/10/81 - current 31/12/90
			25 TASS	OV-10A	1986 - 1989
			43 TFS	F-15A/B	1/3/82 - 12/8/88
				F-15C/D	1987 - current 31/12/90
AK	AAC	21 CW/21 TFW	54 TFS	F-15C/D	8/5/87 - current 31/12/90
AL	PACAF	361 TEWS	460 TRW/483 TAW/unknown/56 SOW	EC-47N/P/Q	1968 - 30/6/74
AL	ANG	160 TFS	187 TFG	F-4D	1983 - 1988
				F-16A/B	1988 - current 31/12/90
AN	PACAF	362 TEWS	460 TRW/483 TAW/366 TFW	EC-47N/P/Q C-47H	1968 - 27/6/72
AO	TAC	4408 CCTS	4410 CCTW/1 SOW	C-123K	10/7/68 - 22/9/69
AO	TAC	317 SOS	1 SOW	C-123K	15/4/70 - 1972
				UH-1N/P	15/4/70 - 1972
				A-1E	15/4/70 - 1972
				U-10D	15/4/70 - 1972
AP	TAC	4409 CCTS	4410 CCTW/1 SOW	UH-1F/P	10/7/68 - 15/10/69
AP	TAC	549 TASTS	1 SOW	UH-1F/P	15/10/69 - 1972
AQ	TAC	4410 CCTS	4410 CCTW/1 SOW	UH-1F/P	10/7/68 - 15/10/69
AQ	TAC	1 SOW	547 SOTS/TASTS	U-10	15/10/69 - 1972
AR	USAFE	1 TRS	10 TRW	RF-4C	1/70 - 8/9/72
AR	USAFE	10 TRW	1 TRS	RF-4C	6/72 - 29/5/87
			30 TRS	RF-4C	8/72 - 1/4/76
			32 TRS	RF-4C	6/72 - 1/1/76
		10 TFW	509 TFS	A-10A	4/88 - current 31/12/90
			511 TFS	A-10A	1/7/88 - current 31/12/90
AS	USAFE	30 TRS	10 TRW	RF-4C	1/70 - 8/72
AT	USAFE	32 TRS	10 TRW	RF-4C	1/70 - 1972
AZ	ANG	162 TFTG/TFG	152 TFTS/TFS	A-7D	3/78 - current 31/12/90
				A-7K	1981 - current 31/12/90
			195 TFTS	A-7D/K	1983 - 1985
B_	PACAF	390 TFS	366 TFW	F-4C	mid 1967 - 1/68

TAIL CODE

Code	Command	Unit	Wing	Aircraft	Dates
BA	TAC	91 TRS	75/67 TRW	F-4D	1/68 - 1969
BA	TAC	67 TRW	12 TRS	RF-4C	10/7/68 - 1972
			45 TRS	RF-4C	1972- current 31/12/90
			62 TRTS	RF-4C	1972- 31/10/75
			91 TRS	RF-4C	1972- 31/12/89
BB	TAC	4 TRS	75/67 TRW	RF-4C	1972- current 31/12/90
BB	TAC	45 TRS	67 TRW	RF-4C	10/7/68 - 15/10/71
BC	TAC	9 TRS	75/67 TRW	RF-4C	15/10/71 - 1972
BC	TAC	12 TRS	67 TRW	RF-4C	10/7/68- 31/8/71
BC	ANG	172 TASS	110 TASG - 172 TASG	RF-4C	31/8/71 - 1972
BD	AFRES	46 TFTS	917 TFG - 434 TFW/917 TFW	OA-37B	1/3/81 -current 31/12/90
		47 TFS	917 TFG - 434 TFW	A-10A	30/9/83 - current 31/12/90
BH	ANG	106 TRS	117 TRW	A-10A	1/10/80 -current 31/12/90
BO	PACAF	166 TFS	354 TFW	RF-4C	15/5/86 - current 31/12/90
BP	PACAF	127 TFS	354 TFW	F-100C/F	5/7/68- 10/6/69 Ohio ANG
BR	USAFE	22 TFS	36 TFW	F-100C/F	5/7/68- 10/6/69 Kansas ANG
BS	USAFE	23 TFS	36/52 TFW	F-4D	6/70 - 1/4/72
BT	USAFE	53 TFS	36 TFW	F-4D	5/70 - 6/8/72
BT	USAFE	36 TFW	22 TFS	F-4D	5/70 - 1972
				F-4D	1/4/72 - 8/72
				F-4E	8/72 - 25/10/76
				F-15A/B	1/7/77 - 5/81
				F-15C/D	5/81 - current 31/12/90
			53 TFS	F-4D	1972 - 9/73
				F-4E	9/73 - 1/2/77
				F-15A/B	9/11/77 - 5/81
				F-15C/D	5/81 - current 31/12/90
			525 TFS	F-4E	6/72 - 9/3/77
				F-15A/B	4/77 - 1/81
				F-15C/D	12/80 - current 31/12/90
BU	USAFE	525 TFS	36 TFW	F-4E	2/70 - 8/72
BV	USAFE	39 TEWS	36/52 TFW	EB-66C/E	1/70 - 8/72
C_	PACAF	480 TFS	366 TFW	F-4C	mid 1967- 1/68
				F-4D	1/68 - 15/4/69
CA	TAC	481 TFS	27 TFW	F-100D/F	10/7/68- 27/10/71
				F-111E	30/9/69 - by 7/71
				F-111A	10/69 - 11/71
CB	PACAF	90 TFS	3 TFW	F-100D/F	1967- 11/69
CC	TAC	522 TFS	27 TFW	F-100D/F	10/7/68- 19/7/72
				F-111E	10/71 - 11/71
				F-111A	1971
				F-111D	5/72 - 1972
CC	TAC	27 TFW	481 TFS	F-111D	1972- 31/8/73
				F-111D	15/1/76 - 8/7/80
			522 TFS	F-100D/F	1972 - 19/7/72
				F-111D	5/72 - current 31/12/90
			523 TFS	F-111D	31/8/73 - current 31/12/90
			524 TFS	F-100D/F	1972- 19/7/72
				F-111D	1972- current 31/12/90
			4427 TFRS	F-111D	8/72 - 15/1/76
			428 TFTS	F-111G	1/6/90 - current 31/12/90
CC	TAC	Det 2	57 FWW	F-111	1/10/70 - 1/5/72
CD	TAC	524 TFS	27 TFW	F-100D/F	10/7/68- 19/7/72
				F-111A	- 1972
				F-111E	- 7/71
				F-111D	27/10/71 - 1972
CE	TAC	4427 TFRS	27 TFW	F-111D	1/10/71 - 1972
CE	PACAF	510 TFS	3 TFW	F-100D/F	1967- 15/11/69
CF	PACAF	8 AS	3 TFW	A-37B	15/11/69 - 30/9/70
		8 SOS	35 TFW/215 TAW/377 ABW	"	30/9/70 -15/12/72
CG	PACAF	90 AS	3 TFW	A-37B	11/69 - 31/10/70
		90 SOS	14 SOW/483 TAW	"	31/10/70 - 15/4/72
CG	ANG	156 TAS	156 TAG	C-130B	spring 71 - 1/12/74+
CK	PACAF	604 ACS	unknown & 14 ACW	A-37A/B	late 1967- 1/8/68
		604 SOS	3 TFW	"	1/8/68 - 30/9/70
CM	ATC	50 FTS	14 TFW	T-38A	3/3/86 - least 3/87
CO	ANG	120 TFS	140 TFW	A-7D	1981 - current 31/12/90
				A-7K	11/83 - current 31/12/90
CP	PACAF	531 TFS	3 TFW	F-100D/F	1967- 6/7/70
CR	USAFE	32 TFS	17 AF/32 TFG	F-4E	5/70 - end 1979
				F-15A/B	15/9/78 - 5/80
				F-15C/D	13/6/80 - current 31/12/90
CS	ANG	138 TFS	140 TFW	F-86H	10/7/68 - 8/12/68
CT	ANG	104 TFS	140 TFW	F-86H	10/7/68 - 8/12/68
CT	ANG	118 TFS	103 TFG	F-100D/F	12/74 - 1979
				A-10A	5/79 - current 31/12/90
DA	TAC	354 TFS	355 TFW	A-7D	1/7/71 - 1972
DB	TAC	346 TATS	516 TAW	C-130E	10/7/68- 15/3/69
DB	TAC	463 TAW	18 TATS	C-7A	1/6/72- 25/8/72
			47 TAS	C-130E	6/7/73 - 1/8/73
			772 TAS	C-130E	1/6/72 - 1/12/74+

APPENDIX A

			773 TAS	C-130E	1/6/72 - 1/12/74+
			774 TAS	C-130E	1/8/73 - 1/12/74+
DC	TAC	357 TFS	355 TFW	A-7D	1/7/71 - 1972
DC	ANG	121 TFS	113 TFW	F-4D	1/6/81 - 6/89
				F-16A/B	by 11/89 - current 31/12/90
DD	TAC	40 TFS	355 TFW	A-7D	1/10/71 - 1/6/72
DE	PACAF	50 TAS	314/374 TAW	C-130E	1968 - 8/2/73
DF	TAC	11 TDS	355 TFW	DC-130A	1/7/71 - 1972
DG	AFRES	700 TAS	918 TAG/918 TAG - 94 TAW	C-7A	1972 -1/7/72
DH	PACAF	345 TAS	314/374 TAW	C-130E	1968 -1/12/74+
DL	PACAF	776 TAS	314/374 TAW	C-130E	1968 -1/12/74+
DM	TAC	4453 CCTW	4454 CCTS	F-4C/D	10/7/68 - 16/8/71
			4455 CCTS	F-4C	10/7/68 - 8/10/71
			4456 CCTS	F-4C/D	10/7/68 - 30/7/71
			4472 CCTS/SS(SPA)	DC-130A	10/7/68 -1/7/71
DM	TAC	333 TFTS	355 TFW	A-7D	16/7/71 - 1972
DM	TAC	355 TFW/TTW	11 TDS	DC-130A	1972 - 1/7/76
			333 TFTS	A-7D	1972 - 1976
				A-10A	3/76 - 15/2/90
			354 TFS	A-7D	1972 - 1/4/79
			357 TFS/TFTS	A-7D	20/11/72 - 1/7/76
				A-10A	1/7/76 - current 31/12/90
			358 TFS	A-7D	1972 - mid 1978
				A-10A	1978 - current 31/12/90
			4455 CCTS	F-4C	1/10/71 - 8/10/71
DM	TAC	Det 1	57 FWW	A-7D	15/7/71 - 1/7/72
DM	TAC	41 ECS	28 AD	EC-130H	19/3/82 - least 4/87
DO	AFRES	89 TFS	906 TFG - 302 TFW	F-4D	1/7/82 -10/89
				F-16A/B	7/89 - current 31/12/90
DS	PACAF	1 TS	405 FW	F-4	between 30/4/70 - 1972
DY	TAC	516 TAS	516 TAW	C-130E	10/7/68 - 1/6/72
DY	PACAF	346 TAS	314 TAW	C-130E	15/3/69 - 31/5/71
DY	PACAF	21 TAS	374 TAW	C-130E	31/5/71 -1/12/74+
DZ	TAC	348 TAS	516 TAW	C-130E	10/7/68 - 1/6/72
EA	PACAF	16 SOS	8 TFW	AC-130A	late 1967 - 4/69
EB	TAC	4 TFS	33 TFS	F-4E	10/7/68 - 12/4/69
EC	PACAF	1 ACS	14 ACW	A-1E	1967- 20/12/67
ED	TAC	16 TFS	33 TFW	F-4E	10/7/68- 9/70
ED	TAC	58 TFS	33 TFW	F-4E	1/9/70 - 1972
ED	TAC	33 TFW	58 TFS	F-4E	1972- 10/78
			59 TFS	F-4E	1973 - 10/78
ED	AFSC	4485 TS	TAWC	F-4D	12/4/71 - 12/78
				RF-4C	5/71 - least 11/72
				F-4C	unknown
				F-4E	11/71 - least 6/74
ED	AFSC	6512 TESTW	6512 TESTS	various	1983 - current 31/12/90
EE	TAC	40 TFS	33 TFW	F-4E	10/7/68- 7/5/69
EG	TAC	4533 TFS(T)	33 TFW	F-4D	10/7/68- 12/4/71
				F-4E	10/7/68- 12/4/71
				RF-4C	- 12/4/71
EG	TAC	33 TFW	58 TFS	F-4E	10/78 - 3/79
				F-15A/B	1/79 - 1984
				F-15C/D	10/84 - current 31/12/90
			59 TFS	F-4E	10/78 - 3/79
				F-15A/B	3/79 - 1984
				F-15C/D	1984 - current 31/12/90
			60 TFS	F-15A/B	early 1979 - 10/84
				F-15C/D	10/84 - current 31/12/90
EL	TAC	23 TFW	74 TFS	A-7D	1/7/72 - 1980-81
				A-10A	1980 - current 31/12/90
			75 TFS	A-7D	1/7/72 - 1980-81
				A-10A	1980 - current 31/12/90
			76 TFS	A-7D	1/10/72 - 11/6/81
				A-10A	1981 - current 31/12/90
EL	PACAF	3 ACS/SOS	14 ACW/SOW	AC-47D	1/5/68 - 15/9/69
EN	PACAF	4 ACS/SOS	14 ACW/SOW	AC-47D	1967 -15/12/69
EO	PACAF	5 ACS/SOS	14 ACW/SOW	A/SC-47D, U-10A	1968- 15/10/69
ER	PACAF	9 ACS/SOS	14 ACW/SOW/315 TAW	AC-47D	1967- 29/2/72
ER	AFRES	704 TFS	924 TAG - 433 TAW	C-130A	1/7/72 - 1/12/74+
ER	AFRES	705 TFS	924 TAG - 433 TAW	C-130A	1/7/72 - 1/12/74+
ES	AFRES	78 SOS	917 SOG - 434 SOW	A-37B	1972-1/10/73
ES	AFRES	47 SOS	917 TFG - 434 TFW	A-37B	1/10/73 - 1/10/80
ET	PACAF	6 ACS/SOS	14 ACW/SOW/633 SOW	A-1E/H	29/2/68 - 15/3/69
ET	AFSC	3246 TESTW	3247 TESTS	various	1/10/89 - current 31/12/90
FA	PACAF	25 TFS	8 TFW	F-4D	28/5/68- 1/73
FB	TAC	43 TFS	15 TFW	F-4E	10/7/68- 23/6/70
FB	TAC	45 TFS	15/1 TFW	F-4E	6/70 - 1/7/71
FB	TAC	71 TFS	1 TFW	F-4E	1/7/71 - 1972
FB	TAC	47 TAS	313 TAW	C-130E	10/7/68- 1972
FB	TAC	313 TAW	47 TAS	C-130E	1972- 6/7/73
			48 TAS	C-130E	1972- 6/8/73

TAIL CODE

Code	Command	Unit	Wing	Aircraft	Dates
FC	TAC	45 TFS	15 TFW	F-4E	10/7/68- 6/70
FC	AAC	43 TFS	21 CW	F-4E	23/6/70 - 1972
FC	AAC	21 CW/TFW	18 TFS	F-4E	15/11/77 - late 1982
			43 TFS	F-4E	1972- 1/3/82
FD	TAC	46 TFS	15/1 TFW	F-4E	10/7/68- 1/7/71
FD	TAC	27 TFS	1 TFW	F-4E	1/7/71 - 1972
FE	TAC	47 TFS	15/1 TFW	F-4E	10/7/68 - 1/7/71
FE	TAC	94 TFS	1 TFW	F-4E	1/7/71 - 1972
FF	TAC	4530 TFTS	1 TFW	F-4E	10/7/68- 1/10/71
FF	TAC	4501 TFRS	1 TFW	F-4E	1/10/71 - 1972
FF	TAC	1 TFW	27 TFS	F-4E	1972- 30/6/75
				F-15A/B	30/6/76 - 4/11/82
				F-15C/D	11/81 - current 31/12/90
			71 TFS	F-4E	1972- 30/6/75
				F-15A/B	1/76 - 11/81
				F-15C/D	11/81 - current 31/12/90
			94 TFS	F-4E	1972- 30/6/75
				F-15A/B	30/6/75 - 4/11/81
				F-15C/D	4/11/81 - current 31/12/90
			4501 TFRS	F-4E	1972- 30/6/75
FG	PACAF	433 TFS	8 TFW	F-4C	early 1967- least 10/67
				F-4D	7/67 - 1/73
FH	TAC	38 TAS	313 TAW	C-130E	1/10/69 - 15/11/71
FH	TAC	48 TAS	313 TAW	C-130E	15/11/71 - 1972
FK	PACAF	13 BS	8 TFW	B-57G	late 1970 -12/4/72
FL	TAC	549 TASTS	549 TASTG - 1 SOW	OV-10A/OT-37B	15/12/75 - 11/3/87
FM	AFRES	93 TFS	915 TFG	482 TFW F-4C	1/10/78 -1/10/83
				F-4D	30/9/83 - 4/90
				F-16A	7/89 - current 31/12/90
FO	PACAF	435 TFS	8 TFW	F-4D	25/7/67- 1/73
FP	PACAF	497 TFS	8 TFW	F-4C	early 1967- 11/67
				F-4D	11/67 - 1/73
FS	TAC	4424 CCTS	15/1 TFW	B-57C	15/10/68 - 30/6/72
				B-57E	1971 - 1972
				B-57G	late 1971 - 30/6/72
FS	TAC	13 BS	15 TFW	B-57G	8/2/69 - 15/9/70
FS	PACAF	13 BS	8 TFW	B-57G	15/9/70 - late 1970
FS	ANG	184 TFS	188 TFG	F-16A/B	12/88 - current 31/12/90
FT	PACAF	16 SOS	8 TFW	AC-130A	4/69 - 5/74
				AC-130E/H	7/73 - 5/74
FW	ANG	163 TFS	122 TFW	F-4C	2/4/79 - by mid 1986
				F-4E	by 7/86 - current 31/12/90
FY	PACAF	555 TFS	8 TFW	F-4C	1967- least 12/6/67
				F-4D	28/5/67 - 1/6/68
(GA)	TAC	68 TFS	479 TFW	F-4D	25/9/68 - 8/69
GA	TAC	4535 CCTS	479 TFW	F-4E	5/69 - 5/70
			35 TFW	F-4C	2/70 - 1972
GA	TAC	35 TFW/TTW/TFW	20 TFTS	F-4C	1/7/72 - by 1981
				F-4E	by 1981 - current 31/12/90
				F-4F	1972 - 1975
			21 TFTS/TFS/TFTS	F-4C	1/12/72 - by 1981
				F-4E	1/12/72 - current 31/12/90
			39 TFTS	F-4C	1/7/77 - by 6/6/79
				F-4C (ww)	1/7/77 - by 6/6/79
				F-4E	least 22/11/80 - 11/5/84
			431 TFTS	F-4E	15/1/76 - 1/1/78
			434 TFTS	F-4D	- 1972
				F-4E	1972- 1/1/77
			561 TFS	F-105F/G	15/7/73 - 12/7/80
				F-4E	- 30/3/81
			562 TFS	F-105F/G	31/10/74 - 12/7/80
				F-4E	- 30/3/81
			563 TFTS/TFS	F-105F/G	31/7/75 - 1/7/77
				F-4E	- 30/3/81
			4435 TFRS	F-4C	1972- 15/1/76
				F-4E	1972- 1/12/72
			4535 CCTS	F-4C	1972- 1/12/72
			4452 CCTS	F-4D	1972- 1/12/72
				F-4E	1972- 10/72
			35 OMS	UH-1P	late 1972- pre 1988
GB	TAC	479 TFW	431 TFS	F-4D	10/7/68- 1/1/69
				F-4D	1/3/69 - 6/69
				F-4E	by June 1969 - 31/5/70
GB	TAC	4546 TTS	479 TFW	F-4E	31/5/70 - 2/71
				F-4C	1971 - 1/10/71
GB	TAC	4435 TFRS	35 TFW	F-4C	1/10/71 - 1972
GC	TAC	434 TFS	479 TFW	F-4D	10/7/68 - 9/68
GC	TAC	4452 CCTS	479/35 TFW	F-4E	5/69 - 8/70
				F-4C	2/70 - 10/70

APPENDIX A

Code	Command	Squadron	Wing	Aircraft	Dates
(GD)	TAC	4535 CCTS	479 TFW	F-4D	3/72 - 1972
GD	TAC	434 TFS	479/35 TFW	F-4D	9/68 - 5/69
				F-4E	5/69 - 1972
(GE)	TAC	4452 CCTS	479 TFW		
GE	TAC	35 OMS	479/35 TFW	UH-1P	unknown - late 1972
GG	PACAF	35 TFS	347 TFW	F-4C	1968- 15/3/71
GL	PACAF	36 TFS	347 TFW	F-4C	1968- 15/5/71
GP	AFRES	758 TAS	911 TAG - 302 TAW	C-123K	1972 -1/12/74+
GR	PACAF	80 TFS	347 TFW	F-105D	1968- 2/68
				F-4C	2/68 - 15/3/71
GT	PACAF	556 RS	347 TFW/6100 ABW	EB-57E	1/7/68-15/12/72
				RC-130B-ii	1971
			475 TFW	EB-57E	1/11/71 - 30/6/72
GT	PACAF	1 SOS	18 TFW	EB-57E	15/12/72 - 1973
GU	PACAF	497 TFS	51 TFW	F-4E	7/9/84 - 1/10/89
GU	PACAF	15 TRS	460 TRG	RF-4C	1/10/89 - late 1990
HA	PACAF	174 TFS	37 TFW	F-100C/F	14/5/68- 11/5/69 Iowa ANG
HA	TAC	417 TFS	49 TFW	F-4D	15/11/70 - 1970
HA	ANG	174 TFS	132 TFW	F-100D/F	11/5/69 - 1977
				A-7D	12/76 - current 31/12/90
				A-7K	1983 - current 31/12/90
HB	TAC	7 TFS	49 TFW	F-4D	15/7/68 - 1972
HB	PACAF	389 TFS	37 TFW/12 TFW	F-4D	15/6/69 -15/10/71
HC	TAC	8 TFS	49 TFW	F-4D	10/7/68 - 1972
HD	TAC	9 TFS	49 TFW	F-4D	10/7/68 - 1972
HE	TAC	417 TFS	49 TFW	F-4D	mid 1971 - 1972
HE	PACAF	416 TFS	37 TFW	F-100D/F	1968- 27/5/69
HF	AFRES	731 TAS	901 TAG - 302 TAW/439 TAW	C-123K	1/10/72 - 1/12/74+
HF	ANG	113 TFS	181 TFG	F-100D/F	- 1979
				F-4C	7/79 - 7/87
				F-4E	7/87 - current 31/12/90
HG	PACAF	347 TFW	428 TFS	F-111A	30/7/73 - 30/6/75
			429 TFS	F-111A	30/7/73 - 30/6/75
HI	AFRES	466 TFS	508 TFG - 301 TFW/301 TFW/ 508 TFG - 301 TFW/419 TFW	F-105B	1/1/73 - by 5/81
				F-105D/F	5/81 - 25/2/84
				F-16A/B	28/1/84 - current 31/12/90
HK	PACAF	480 TFS	37/12 TFW	F-4D	15/4/69 - 17/11/71
HL	TAC	388 TFW	4 TFS	F-4D	23/12/75 - by 9/79
				F-16A/B	1/79 - least 5/89
				F-16C/D	by 5/90 - current 31/12/90
			16 TFTS/TFS	F-16A/B	1/79 - 30/6/86
			34 TFS	F-4D	23/12/75 - 1/79
				F-16A/B	1/79 - 5/89
				F-16C/D	5/89 - current 31/12/90
			421 TFS	F-4D	23/12/75 - 1979
				F-16A/B	1979 - by 5/90
				F-16C/D	by 5/90 - current 31/12/90
HL	TAC	Det 16	57 FWW	F-16A/B	late 1979 - unknown
HM	AFRES	336 TAS	904 TAG - 452 TAW	C-130B	1972 -1/12/74+
HM	TAC	479 TTW	416 TFTS	AT-38A	14/3/79 - 1/9/83
			433 TFTS	AT-38B	1/9/83 - current 31/12/90
			434 TFTS	AT-38B	1/1/77 - current 31/12/90
			435 TFTS	AT-38B	1/1/77 - current 31/12/90
			436 TFTS	AT-38B	1/1/77 - current 31/12/90
HO	TAC	49 TFW	7 TFS	F-4D	1972- early 1978
				F-15A/B	10/77 - current 31/12/90
			8 TFS	F-4D	1972- late 1978
				F-15A/B	late 1978 - current 31/12/90
			9 TFS	F-4D	1972- late 1978
				F-15A/B	late 1978 - current 31/12/90
			417 TFS	F-4D	1972- 31/3/77
HO	AFRES	71 SOS/TFS	930 SOG - 403 CW/930 SOG - 434 SOW	A-37A	1972 - 1/10/73
				A-37B	1/10/73 - by 3/79
HO	AFRES	45 TFS	930 SOG - 434 SOW/434 TFW		
HP	PACAF	355 TFS	37 TFW	F-100D/F	1968- 15/5/69
HR	USAFE	10 TFS	50 TFW	F-4D	4/70 - 7/72
HR	USAFE	50 TFW	10 TFS	F-4D	7/72 - 23/9/76
				F-4E	16/7/76 - 1982
				F-16A/B	1/82 - least 5/86
				F-16C/D	16/7/86 - current 31/12/90
			313 TFS	F-4E	15/11/76 - 12/81
				F-16A/B	by 1/82 - least 9/86
				F-16C/D	by 7/87 - current 31/12/90
			496 TFS	F-4E	least 6/72 - mid 1982
				F-16A/B	6/82 - least 9/86
				F-16C/D	by 5/86 - current 31/12/90
HS	PACAF	612 TFS Det 1	37 TFW	F-100D/F	1968- 13/4/69
HS	TAC	31 TFW	307 TFTS/TFS	F-4D	1/12/86 - least 5/88

TAIL CODE

Code	Command	Unit	Wing	Aircraft	Dates
				F-16A/B	1988 - by 11/89
		308 TFS		F-4D	1/12/86 - least 10/87
				F-16A/B	least 10/87 - 1990
				F-16C/D	by 10/90 - current 31/12/90
		309 TFS		F-4D	1/12/86 - 1987
				F-16A/B	1/12/86 - current 31/12/90
				F-16C/D	8/12/90 - current 31/12/90
HS	USAFE	496 TFS	10 TFW	F-4D	5/70 - 10/70
				F-4E	15/10/70 - 10/72
HW	TAC	24 SOS	24 CW	A-37	- 1/2/87
				UH-1N	- 1990
IA	TAC	Det 1	1 SOW	C-123K	10/7/68- 1/7/69
				C-47	10/7/68- 1/7/69
IA	ANG	124 TFS	132 TFW	A-7D	1/77 - current 31/12/90
				A-7K	1981 - current 31/12/90
IB	TAC	Det 2	1 SOW	C-130E	10/7/68- 1/11/69
IC	TAC	71 TAS	1 SOW	AC-119G/AC-130A	10/7/68- 16/12/68
ID	TAC	317 ACS	1 SO/4410 CCTW	EC-47P/Q	10/7/68- 15/4/70
ID	AFRES	72 SOS	931 SOG - 434 SOW	A-37B	1972 -1/10/73
ID	AFRES	46 TFS	931 TFG - 434 TFW/434 TFW	A-37A/B	1/10/73 - 1/7/78
IE	TAC	319 ACS	1 SOW/4410 CCTW	UC-123B, C-123K	10/7/68- 30/7/69
IF	TAC	603 ACS S/RS	1 SOW	A-37	10/7/68- 15/7/69
IG	TAC	4412 CCTS	1 SOW/4410 CCTW/SOTG	AC-47D C-47D	10/7/68- by 6/72
IH	TAC	4413 CCTS	1 SOW/4410 CCTW	AC-119G	10/7/68-1/7/70
				AC-119K	8/11/68 - 1/7/70
				AC-130A	6/8/68 - 1/7/70
IH	TAC	415 SOTS	4410 CCTW/SOTG	AC-119G	1/7/70 - 15/7/71
				AC-119K	1/7/70 - 28/6/71
				AC-130A	1/7/70 - 9/3/71
II	TAC	4532 CCTS	1 SOW/4410 CCTW	A-37A/B	10/7/68-28/7/70
IJ	TAC	4406 CCTS	1 SOW/4410 CCTW	A-37B	1/10/68 - 1/7/70
IJ	TAC	427 SOTS	4410 CCTW/SOTG	A-37B	1/7/70 - 15/7/72
IJ	TAC	6 SOTS	1 SOW/23 TFW	A-37B	31/3/73 - 15/9/74
IK	TAC	514 AS	4410 CCTW	A-37B	15/7/69 - 8/1/70
IK	TAC	6 SOS	4410 CCTW	A-37B	15/4/70 - 31/7/73
		6 SOTS	4410 SOTG		
IL	ANG	169 TASS	182 TASG	OA-37B	3/81 - current 31/12/90
IM	AFRES	357 TAS	908 TAG 302 TAW/	C-7A	1972 - 1/12/74+
			908 TAG 94 TFW		
IN	AFRES	45 TFS	434 TFW/930 TFG	A-37B	3/79 -1/6/81
				A-10A	1/6/81 - current 31/12/90
IS	ADTAC	57 FIS	1 AF	F-15C/D	2/7/85 - current 31/12/90
IY	AFRES	757 SOS/TFS	910 SOG/TFG - 434 SOW/	A-37B	1972 - least 3/79
			TFW/459 TAW		
JA	ANG	183 TAS	172 TAG	C-130E	6/72 - 1/12/74+
JB	PACAF	17 WWS	388 TFW	F-105G	1/12/71 -29/10/74
JC	PACAF	7 ACCS	388 TFW/374 TAW	EC-130E	30/4/72 - 31/3/75
JE	PACAF	44 TFS	388 TFW	F-105D/F	1968- 10/10/69
JH	PACAF	3 TFS	388 TFW	A-7D	15/3/73 - 22/12/75
JJ	PACAF	34 TFS	388 TFW	F-105D/F	1/68- 7/5/69
				F-4E	7/5/69 - 1/10/74
				F-4D	1/10/74 - 23/12/75
JK	TAC	4414 CCTS	363 TRW	RF-101A/C	10/7/68- 15/10/69
JK	TAC	31 TRTS	363 TRW	RF-101A/C	15/10/69 - 18/2/71
JL	TAC	4415 CCTS	363 TRW	RF-4C	10/7/68- 15/10/69
JL	TAC	33 TRTS	363 TRW	RF-4C	15/10/69 - 1972
(JM)	TAC	4416 TES	363 TRW		
JM	TAC	16 TRS	363 TRW	RF-4C	15/2/71 - 1972
JN	TAC	4417 CCTS	363 TRW	RB-66B/E	10/7/68- 15/10/69
JN	TAC	39 TRTS/TEWTS	363 TRW	EB-66B/C/E	15/10/69 -15/3/74
JO	TAC	29 TRS	363 TRW	RF-101A/C	10/7/68- 24/1/71
JO	TAC	22 TRS	363 TRW	RF-4C	15/7/71 - 15/10/71
				B-57E	1971 - 15/10/71
JO	TAC	62 TRS	363 TRW	RF-4C	15/10/71 - 1/7/83
JO	TAC	363 TRW/TFW	16 TRS	RF-4C	1972- 3/2/83
				B-57E	1972- 9/74
			18 TRS	RF-4C	1972- 30/9/79
			33 TRTS	RF-4C	1972- 1/10/82
			62 TRS	RF-4C	1972- 1/7/82
JP	TAC	18 TRS	363 TRW	RF-101A/C	30/1/70 - late 1970
				RF-4C	30/11/70 - 1972
JR	USAFE	79 TFS	20 TFW	F-111E	1/71 - 11/72
JS	USAFE	55 TFS	20 TFW	F-111E	4/71 - 3/73
JT	USAFE	77 TFS	20 TFW	F-111E	1/71 - 11/72
JV	PACAF	469 TFS	388 TFW	F-105D/F	1968- 11/69
				F-4E	11/69 - 31/10/72
JW	PACAF	42 TEWS	388 TFW	EB-66C/E	23/9/70 - 17/1/74
KA	PACAF	457 TAS	483 TAW	C-7A	1968- 30/3/72
KB	TAC	417 TFS	67 TRW	F-4D	15/7/68 - 15/11/70
KC	PACAF	458 TAS	483 TAW	C-7A	1968- 1/3/72

APPENDIX A

Code	Command	Unit	Wing/Group	Aircraft	Dates
KC	AFRES	303 TFS	442 TFG - 434 TFW	A-10A	2/82 -current 31/12/90
KE	PACAF	459 TAS	483 TAW	C-7A	1968- 1/6/70
KE	ANG	153 TRS	186 TRG	RF-4C	fall 1978 - late 1983
KG	ANG	167 TAS	167 TAG	C-130A	6/72 - 1/12/74+
KH	PACAF	535 TAS	483 TAW	C-7A	1968- 24/1/72
KL	PACAF	536 TAS	483 TAW	C-7A	1968- 15/10/71
KM	AFRES	303 TAS	935 TAG - 442 TAW/422 TAW	C-130A	10/74 - 5/75+
KN	PACAF	537 TAS	483 TAW	C-7A	1968- 1/6/70
KR	TAC	10 TRS	67 TRW	RF-4C	10/7/68- 30/6/71
KS	TAC	22 TFS	67 TRW	RF-4C	10/7/68- 15/7/71
KS	TAC	1 ACCS	522 AW & CW/28 AD	EC-130E/H	20/7/83 - least 9/87
KT	TAC	7 TRS	67 TRW	RF-4C	10/7/68- 15/10/71
KY	ANG	165 TRS	123 TRW	RF-4C	by 3/81 - 1989
LA	PACAF	4 TFS	366 TFW/432 TRW	F-4E	12/4/69 -8/73
LA	TAC	4510 CCTW/58 TFTW/TTW/TFTW	310 TFTS	A-7D	15/12/69 -31/7/71
				F-4C	7/5/71 - 4/11/83
			311 TFTS	F-100D	18/1/70 - 21/8/71
				F-4C	21/8/71 - 4/11/83
			425 TFTS	F-5B	1974 - 8/79 or 5/85
				F-5E	6/4/73 - 1/8/89
				F-5F	1985 - 1/8/89
			426 TFTS	F-100D	18/1/70 - 21/8/71
				F-4C	21/8/71 - 12/80
				F-15A/B	1/1/81 - 29/11/90
				F-15D	by 1989 - 29/11/90
			461 TFTS	F-15A/B	1/7/77 - 3/3/88
				F-15D	1/83 - late 1990
				F-15E	18/7/88 - current 31/12/90
			550 TFTS	F-4C	18/1/70 - 8/77
				F-15A/B	by 8/77 - 2/89
				F-15E	15/5/89 - current 31/12/90
			555 TFTS	F-15A/B	14/11/74 - current 31/12/90
				F-15D	by 10/82 - current 31/12/90
			4461 CCTS	F-15A/B	23/6/76 - 1/7/77
			4511 CCTS	F-100D/F	10/7/68- 18/1/70
			4514 CCTS	F-100D/F	10/7/68- 15/12/69
			4515 CCTS	F-100D/F	10/7/68- 18/1/70
			4517 CCTS	F-100D/F	10/7/68- 18/1/70
			50 OMS/Base flight	UH-1F/P	1983 - 1987
LA	TAC	Det 1	57 FWW	A-7D	15/10/69 - 15/7/71
LA	TAC	Det 1	TFWC	F-15	1/7/74 - unknown
LC	PACAF	421 TFS	475/366 TFW/unknown/432 TRW	F-4E	23/4/69 - 8/73
LF	PACAF	390 TFS	366 TFW	F-4D	1969 - 30/6/72
LF	TAC	58 TTW	310 TFTS	F-16A/B	6/12/82 - 6/89
				F-16C/D	5/89 - current 31/12/90
			311 TFTS	F-16A/B	4/83 - current 31/12/90
			312 TFTS	F-16C/D	5/11/84 - current 31/12/90
			314 TFTS	F-16C/D	1984 - current 31/12/90
LF	TAC	Det 1	57 FWW	F-16C	1/4/85 - 1990
LH	AFRES	302 SOS	unknown/10/4 AF/302 SOG	CH-3E	1/4/74 - 1/7/87
LK	TAC	314 TAW	16 TATS	C-130E	1972- 1/12/74+
			32 TAS	C-130E	1/9/73 - 1/12/74+
			48 TAS	C-130E	6/8/73 - 1/9/73
			50 TAS	C-130E	15/9/73 - 1/12/74+
			61 TAS	C-130E	1972- 1/12/74+
			62 TAS	C-130E	1972- 1/12/74
LK	USAFE	48 TFW	492 TFS	F-4D	3/72 - 7-8/72
			493 TFS	F-4D	3/72 - 7-8/72
			494 TFS	F-4D	3/72 - 7-8/72
LL	ATC	86 FTS	47 FTW	T-38A	1986 - 1989
LM	TAC	36 TAS	316 TAW	C-130E	10/7/68- 1972
LM	TAC	316 TAW	36 TAS	C-130E	1972- 1/12/74+
		37 TAS	C-130E		1972- 1/12/74+
			38 TAS	C-130E	1972- 1/12/74+
LN	TAC	37 TAS	316 TAW	C-130E	10/7/68- 1972
LN	USAFE	48 TFW	492 TFS	F-4D	7-8/72 - 4/77
				F-111F	22/4/77 - current 31/12/90
			493 TFS	F-4D	7-8/72 - 4/77
				F-111F	22/4/77 - current 31/12/90
			494 TFS	F-4D	7-8/72 - 4/77
				F-111F	22/4/77 - current 31/12/90
			495 TFS	F-111F	1/4/77 - current 31/12/90
LO	TAC	38 TAS	316 TAS	C-130E	10/7/68- 1/7/69
LO	TAC	38 TAS	316 TAS	C-130E	15/11/71 - 1972
LR	USAFE	492 TFS	48 TFW	F-100D/F	3/70 - 3/72
LR	AFRES	302 TFS	944 TFG - 419 TFW	F-16C/D	1/7/87 - current 31/12/90
LS	USAFE	493 TFS	48 TFW	F-100D/F	3/70 - 3/72
LT	USAFE	494 TFS	48 TFW	F-100D/F	3/70 - 3/72
LV	TAC	4451 TS	4450 TG	A-7D	11/84 - 1988
				A-7K	11/84 - 1988

TAIL CODE

Code	Command	Unit	Wing/Group	Aircraft	Dates
LY	ADTAC	48 FIS	23/24 AD	F-15A/B	1987 - current 31/12/90
LZ	TAC	4441 CCTS	4510 CCTW	F-5A/B/C	10/7/68- 15/10/69
LZ	TAC	425 TFS	58 TFTW	F-5A	15/10/69 - 1973
				F-5B	15/10/69 - 1974
MA	PACAF	815 TAS	315 AD/374 TAW	C-130A	1968-19/10/69
MA	ANG	131 TFS	104 TFG	F-100D/F	12/74 - 1978
				A-10A	1978 - current 31/12/90
MB	TAC	355 TFS	354 TFW	A-7D	1/11/70 - 1972
MB	TAC	354 TFW	353 TFS	A-7D	1972- 1976
				A-10A	1976 - current 31/12/90
			355 TFS	A-7D	1972- 1977
				A-10A	1977 - current 31/12/90
			356 TFS	A-7D	1972- 1977
				A-10A	1977 - current 31/12/90
			4554 TFRS	A-7D	15/2/72 - 15/10/75
MC	TAC	560 TFS	23 TFW	F-105D/F	10/7/68- 25/9/68
MC	AFRES	314 TAS	940 TAG - 452 TAW	C-130A	1972 -1/5/73
				C-130B	1/11/72 - 1/12/74+
MC	TAC	56 TFW	13 TFTS	F-4E	13/1/76 - 25/8/78
		56 TTW		F-4D	25/8/78 - 30/6/82
			61 TFS/TFTS	F-4E	30/6/75 - 30/4/78
				F-4D	30/4/78 - 19/11/79
				F-16A/B	4/80 - 4-6/89
				F-16C/D	4-6/89 - current 31/12/90
			62 TFS/TFTS	F-4E	30/6/75 - 4/2/78
				F-4D	4/2/78 - 14/11/80
				F-16A/B	15/10/80 - 6/89
				F-16C/D	6/89 - current 31/12/90
			63 TFS/TFTS	F-4E	30/6/75 - 26/5/78
				F-4D	26/5/78 - 1/10/81
				F-16A/B	1/10/81 - 6/89
				F-16C/D	6/89 - current 31/12/90
			72 TFTS	F-16A/B	1/7/82 - 3/90
				F-16C/D	11/3/90 - current 31/12/90
			4501 TFRS	F-4E	30/6/75 - 15/1/76
MD	TAC	561 TFS	23 TFW	F-105D/F	10/7/68- 1/7/72
				F-105G	9/6/70 - 1/7/72
MD	PACAF	Det 561 TFS	23 TFW	F-105F/G	7/4/72 - 1/7/72
MD	ANG	104 TFS	175 TFG	A-37B	1972 - 1979
				A-10A	9/79 - current 31/12/90
ME	TAC	562 TFS	23 TFW	F-105D	10/7/68- 1/7/72
				F-105F	1/7/72 - 31/7/72
MF	TAC	563 TFS	23 TFW	F-105B	1970
				F-105D	10/7/68- 1/7/72
				F-105D T-Stick	unknown
				F-105F	- 1/7/72
MG	TAC	4519 CCTS	23 TFW	F-105B/D	10/7/68- 16/10/69
				F-105F	1968 - 16/10/69
				F-105G	1969 - 16/10/69
MG	TAC	419 TFTS	23 TFW	F-105B/D/F	15/10/69 - 8/5/71
MG	ANG	109 TAS	133 TFG	C-130A	20/3/71 - 1/12/74+
MH	AFRES	64 TAS	928 TAG - 440 TAW	C-130A	1/7/72 - 1/12/74+
MI	AFRES	328 TAS	914 TAG - 403 TAW	C-130A	1972 -1/12/74+
MI	ANG	107 TFS	127 TFW	A-7D	9-10/78 - 1990
				A-7K	by 11/83 - 1990
				F-16A	1990
MJ	PACAF	432 TFW	13 TFS	F-16A/B	4/7/85 - 27/2/87
				F-16C/D	31/7/86 - current 31/12/90
			14 TFS	F-16C/D	1/4/87 - current 31/12/90
MK	AFRES	95 TAS	933 TAG - 440 TAW	C-130A	8/71 -1/12/74+
MN	TAC	356 TFS	354 TFW	A-7D	15/5/71 - 1972
MO	TAC	391 TFS	347 TFW	F-111F	30/6/71 - 1972
MO	TAC	347 TFW	388 TFTS	F-111A	1/7/77 - 1981
		366 TFW	388 ECS	EF-111A	5/11/81 - 28/3/84
			389 TFS	F-111F	1972- 1977
			389 TFTS	F-111A	1977 - current 31/12/90
			390 TFS	F-111F	1972- 1977
			390 ECS	F-111A	1977 - 28/3/84
				EF-111A	28/3/84 - current 31/12/90
			391 TFS	F-111F	1972- 1977
				F-111A	1977 - current 31/12/90
MO	TAC	Det 2	57 FWW	F-111A	1/7/77 - 30/12/81
MO	TAC	Det 3	57 FWW	F-111F	15/8/71 - 1/5/72
MO	TAC	FWS Det 1	57 FWW	F-111	30/12/81 -
(MP)	TAC	4589 TFS	347 TFW	F-111F	1/9/71 - 15/10/71
(MP)	TAC	389 TFS	347 TFW	F-111F	15/10/71 - 1972
(MQ)	TAC	4590 TFS	347 TFW	F-111F	1/1/72 - 30/6/72
(MQ)	TAC	390 TFS	347 TFW	F-111F	30/6/72 - 1972
MR	TAC	511 TFS	354 TFW	A-7D	15/6/70 - 15/7/71
MR	TAC	353 TFS	354 TFW	A-7D	15/7/71 - 1972

APPENDIX A

Code	Command	Unit	Wing/Group	Aircraft	Dates
MS	AFRES	96 TAS	934 TAG - 440 TAW	C-130A	1972 -1/12/74+
MT	ANG	155 TAS	164 TFG	C-130A	1/8/74 - 1/12/74
MY	TAC	347 TFW	68 TFS	F-4E	30/9/75 - 1/1/88
				F-16A/B	1/1/88 - by 31/12/90
				F-16C/D	1990 - current 31/12/90
			69 TFS	F-4E	1/9/83 - 1/1/88
				F-16A/B	1/1/88 - by 10/90
				F-16C/D	by 7/90 - current 31/12/90
			70 TFS	F-4E	30/9/75 - 1/4/88
				F-16A/B	1/4/88 - by 10/90
				F-16C/D	by 10/90 - current 31/12/90
			339 TFS	F-4E	30/9/75 - 1/9/83
NA	TAC	428 TFS	474 TFW	F-111A	10/7/68- 1972
NA	TAC	474 TFW	428 TFS	F-111A	1972- 30/7/73
				F-111A	15/6/75 - by 8/77
				F-4D	by 8/77 - 1982
				F-16A/B	1982 - 1/8/89
			429 TFS	F-111A	1972- 30/7/73
				F-111A	21/6/75 - by 8/77
				F-4D	by 8/77 - 1982
				F-16A/B	1982 - 1/8/89
			430 TFS	F-111A	1971- by 8/77
				F-4D	by 8/77 - 1982
				F-16A/B	1982 - 1/8/89
NB	TAC	429 TFS	474 TFW	F-111A	10/7/68- 1972
NC	TAC	430 TFS	474 TFW	F-111A	10/7/68- 1972
ND	TAC	4527 CCTS	474 TFW	F-111A	10/7/68- 15/10/69
NF	TAC	602 TAIRCW	22 TASTS	OV-10A	14/10/88 - current 31/12/90
				OA-10A	15/6/88 - current 31/12/90
			23 TASS	OA-37B	2/5/81 - 4/3/88
				OA-10A	1/10/87 - current 31/12/90
NG	ANG	105 TAS	118 TAG	C-130A	1/4/72 - 1/12/74+
NH	ANG	133 TAS	157TAG	C-130A	spring 1971 - 1/12/74+
NJ	ANG	150 TAS	170 TAG	C-7A	6/73 - 1/12/74+
NJ	ANG	141 TFS	108 TFG	F-4D	16/10/81 - 12/85
				F-4E	16/7/85 - current 31/12/90
(NM)	ANG	188 TFS	150 TFG		
NO	AFRES	706 TAS	926 TAG - 446 TAW/442 TAW	C-130A	1972 - 1/11/73
				C-130B	1/11/73 - 1/12/74+
		706 TFS	926 TFG - 434 TFW	A-37B	1/4/78 -7/82
				A-10A	1/82 - current 31/12/90
NR	AFRES	327 TAS	913 TAG - 403 TAW	C-130A	4/71 -1/12/74+
NS	AFRES	355 TAS	906 TAG - 302 TAW	C-123K	1/4/73 - 1/12/74+
NT	AFRES	1 TATS	907 TAG - 302 TAW	C-119G/K	1972 - 3/73
NT	AFRES	356 TAS	907 TAG - 302 TAW	C-123K	1/4/73 - 8/5/74
NT	ATC	454 FTS	323 FTW	T-43A	17/10/88 - current 31/12/90
NV	PACAF	82 FIS	51 FIW	T/F-102A	1968- 31/5/71
NY	ANG	138 TFS	174 TFG	A-37B	late 1970 - summer 1979
				A-10A	summer 1979 - least 1/89
				F-16A/B	by mid 1988 - current 31/12/90
OA	TAC	39 TAS	317 TAW	C-130A	10/7/68- 30/6/71
OB	TAC	40 TAS	317 TAW	C-130A	10/7/68- 31/8/71
				AC-130A	14/7/70 - 31/8/71
OC	PACAF	13 TFS	432 TRW	F-4C	9/67- 10/67
				F-4D	21/10/67 - 8/73
OD	TAC	4408 CCTS	317 TAW	C-123K	22/9/69 - 15/8/71
OH	ANG	112 TFS	180 TFG	A-7D	5/79 - current 31/12/90
				A-7K	7/80 - current 31/12/90
OH	ANG	162 TFS	178 TFG	A-7D	22/1/78 - current 31/12/90
				A-7K	1982 - current 31/12/90
OH	ANG	166 TFS	121 TFW	A-7D	1974 - current 31/12/90
				A-7K	by 11/83 - current 31/12/90
OK	ANG	125 TFS	138 TFG	A-7D	4/81 - current 31/12/90
				A-7K	by 1983 - current 31/12/90
OK	ANG	185 TAS	137 TAG	C-130A	1/8/74 - 1/12/74+
OK	ATC	71 TFW	8 FTS	T-37	1986 - current 31/12/90
			25 FTS	T-38A	1986 - current 31/12/90
OO	PACAF	11 TRS	432 TRW	RF-4C	1968- 10/1170
OS	PACAF	4 SOS	unknown/432 TRW/TFW	AC-47D	10/69 - 29/10/70
OS	PACAF	51 ABW/CW T/51 TFW	19 TASS	OV-10A	least 11/75 - 1983
				OA-37B	least 5/83 - late 1985
				OV-10A	mid 1985 - 1990
				OA-10A	mid 1990 - current 31/12/90
			25 TFS	A-10A	1/82 - 1/1/84
				A-10A	1990 - current 31/12/90
			36 TFS	F-4E	30/9/74 - by 6/1/89
				F-16C/D	by 6/1/89 - current 31/12/90
			497 TFS	F-4E	1/1/82 - 7/9/84
OT	AFSC	TAWC	4485 TS	various	1982 - current 31/12/90
OY	PACAF	555 TFS	432 TRW	F-4D	1/6/68- 8/73

TAIL CODE

Code	Command	Unit	Wing	Aircraft	Dates
OZ	PACAF	14 TRS	432 TRW	RF-4C	1968- 8/73
PA	PACAF	1 TS	405 FW	F-4C	30/4/70 - 1973
PA	ANG	193 TEWS	193 TEWG	EC-130E	1978 - 1986
PA	ANG	103 TASS	111 TASG	OA-37B	25/3/81 - 1990
				OA-10A	by 6/90 - current 31/12/90
PB	TAC	777 TAS	464 TAW	C-130E	10/7/68- 31/8/71
PB	TAC	39 TAS	317 TAW	C-130E	31/8/71 - 1972
PB	TAC	317 TAW	39 TAS	C-130E	1972- 1/12/74+
		40 TAS		C-130E	1972- 1/12/74+
			41 TAS	C-130E	1972- 1/12/74+
PE	PACAF	64 FIS	405 FW	T/F-102A	1968- 12/5/69
PF	TAC	549 TASTS	549 TASTG - 1 SOW	OV-10A/OT-37B	11/3/87 - 1988
PG	TAC	778 TAS	464 TAW	C-130E	10/7/68- 31/8/71
PG	TAC	40 TAS	317 TAW	C-130E	31/8/71 - 1972
PK	PACAF	509 FIS	405 FW	F/TF-102A	1968- 17/7/70
PN	PACAF	523 TFS	405 FW	F-100D	1968- by 1970
				F-4C/D	by 1970 - 1972
PN	PACAF	405 FW/3 TFW	1 TS	F-4C/D	1972 - 1/80
			3 TFS	F-4E	15/12/75 - current 31/12/90
			90 TFS	F-4D	15/12/72 - 1973
				F-4E	1973 - current 31/12/90
				F-4G	1/7/79 - current 31/12/90
			523 TFS	F-4D	1972- 31/8/73
PR	TAC	779 TAS	464 TAW	C-130E	10/7/68- 31/8/71
PR	TAC	41 TAS	317 TAW	C-130E	31/8/71 - 1972
PR	ANG	198 TFS	156 TFG	A-7D	summer 1976 - current 31/12/90
				A-7K	by 11/83 - current 31/12/90
PQ	PACAF	8 BS	35 TFW	B-57B/C/E	1967- 15/11/69
PT	ANG	146 TFS	112 TFG	A-7D	1980 - current 31/12/90
				A-7K	spring 1983 - current 31/12/90
PV	PACAF	13 BS	405 FW	B-57B/C/E	1967- 15/1/68
QA	AFRES	756 TAS	919 TAG - 459 TAW	C-130A	1972 -1/12/74+
QB	PACAF	29 TAS	463 TAW	C-130A	1968- 1/7/70
QB	AFRES	711 TAS	919 TAG - 459 TAW	C-130A	1972 -2/7/73
				C-130B	2/7/73 - 1/12/74+
QC	AFRES	337 TAS	905 TAG - 459 TAW	C-130B	6/72 -1/4/74
QD	AFRES	815 TAS	920 TAG - 459 TAW	C-130B	24/4/73 - 1/12/74+
QF	PACAF	772 TAS	463 TAW	C-130B	1968- 1/6/71
QG	PACAF	773 TAS	463 TAW	C-130B	15/7/68-15/10/71
QW	PACAF	774 TAS	463 TAW/405 FW	C-130B	1968-2/9/72
RA	ATC	12 FTW	559 FTS	T-37	11/85 - least 1986
			560 FTS	T-38A	11/85 - least 1086
RB	PACAF	7 AF	154 TRS	RF-101G	27/7/68 - 15/11/68 Ark ANG
			165 TRS	RF-101G	2/69 - 20/4/69 Kentucky ANG
			192 TRS	RF-101G	15/11/68 - 2/69 Nevada ANG
RB	ANG	154 TRS	123 TRW	RF-101G	see special note
RC	PACAF	41 TEWS	355 TFW	EB-66B/C	1968- 31/10/69
RE	PACAF	44 TFS	355 TFW	F-105D/F	15/10/69 - 10/12/70
(RE)	ATC	64 FTW	35/54 FTS		
RG	ANG	165 TRS	123 TRW	RF-101H	see special note Kentucky ANG
RG	AFLC	WRALC		F-15A, F-105	2/78 - 1978
				F-15A, F-105	7/82 - current 31/12/90
RH	PACAF	42 TEWS	355 TFW	EB-66B/C/E	1968- 23/9/70
RI	ANG	143 TAS	143 TAG	C-130A	10/75 - 1976
RJ	ANG	192 TRS	123 TRW	RF-101H	see special note Nevada ANG
RK	PACAF	333 TFS	355 TFW	F-105D/F	3/68- 10/12/70
RM	PACAF	354 TFS	355 TFW	F-105D/F	2/68- 10/12/70
RR	USAFE	38 TRS	26 TRW	RF-4C	1/4/70 - 1/73
RS	USAFE	526 TFS	26 TRW	F-4E	1/4/70 - 1972
RS	USAFE	26 TRW	38 TRS	RF-4C	1972- 31/1/73
			526 TFS	F-4E	1972- 31/3/73
RS	USAFE	86 TFW	512 TFS	F-4E	3/77 - 12/85
				F-16C/D	20/9/85 - current 31/12/90
			526 TFS	F-4E	31/1/73 - 7/86
				F-16C/D	7/86 - current 31/12/90
RU	PACAF	357 TFS	355 TFW	F-105D/F	3/68- 10/12/70
SA	TAC	334 TFS	4 TFW	F-4D	10/7/68- by mid 1970
				F-4E	7/70 - 1972
SA	ANG	182 TFS	149 TFG	F-4C	19/9/83 - by 5/86
				F-16A/B	5/86 - current 31/12/90
SB	TAC	335 TFS	4 TFW	F-4D	10/7/68- late 1970
				F-4E	10/70 - 1972
SB	USAFE	43 ECS	66 ECW	EC-130H	5/87 - current 31/12/90
SC	TAC	336 TFS	4 TFW	F-4D	10/7/68- 7/70
				F-4E	16/4/70 - 1972
SC	ANG	157 TFS	169 TFG	A-7D	1975 - 1983
				A-7K	1982 - 1983
				F-16A/B	11/4/83 - 10/86
SD	PACAF	306 TFS	31 TFW	F-100D/F	1968- 28/9/70
SD	TAC	306 TFS	4403 TFW	F-100D/F	28/9/70 - 30/10/70

APPENDIX A

Code	Command	Unit	Wing	Aircraft	Dates
SD	ANG	175 TFS	114 TFG	A-7D	1977 - current 31/12/90
				A-7K	1982 - current 31/12/90
SE	PACAF	416 TFS	31 TFW	F-100D/F	28/5/69 - 28/9/70
SE	TAC	416 TFS	4403 TFW	F-100D/F	28/9/70 - 1/4/72
SG	PACAF	136 TFS	31 TFW	F-100C	1968- 25/5/69 N.Y. ANG
SG	ANG	139 TAS	109 TAG	C-130A/D	3/71 - 1/12/74+
SH	AFRES	465 TFS	301 TFW/507 TFG - 301 TFW	F-105D/F	25/3/73 - 1/10/80
				F-4D	1/10/80 - 8/88
			507 TFG - 419 TFW	F-4D	1/10/82 - 8/88
				F-16A/B	by 1/10/88 - current 31/12/90
SI	ANG	170 TFS	183 TFG	F-4D	24/7/84 - 10/89
				F-16A/B	
SJ	TAC	4 TFW	334 TFS	F-4E	1972- current 31/12/90
				F-15E	1990 - current 31/12/90
			335 TFS	F-4E	1972- early 1990
				F-15E	1/3/90 - current 31/12/90
			336 TFS	F-4E	1972- least 1/10/89
				F-15E	20/4/89 - current 31/12/90
			337 TFS	F-4E	1/4/82 - 1/7/85
SK	PACAF	188 TFS	31 TFW	F-100C/F	14/6/68- 18/5/69 N.M.ANG
SL	ANG	110 TFS	131 TFW	F-4C	9/82 - 1985
				F-4E	2/85 - current 31/12/90
SM	PACAF	308 TFS	31 TFW	F-100D/F	1968- 5/10/70
SM	TAC	308 TFS	4403 TFW	F-100D/F	5/10/70 - 30/10/70
SP	PACAF	355 TFS	31 TFW	F-100D/F	15/5/69 - 30/9/70
SP	USAFE	52 TFW	39 TEWS	EB-66C/E	8/72 - 1/1/73
			23 TFS	F-4D	8/72 - 4/82
				F-4E	4/80 - late 1987
				F-4G	12/83 - current 31/12/90
				F-16C/D	10/87 - current 31/12/90
			81 TFS	F-4C (ww)	15/1/73 - 7/79
				F-4E	5/84 - late 1987
				F-4G	4/79 - current 31/12/90
				F-16C/D	10/87 - current 31/12/90
			480 TFS	F-4D	15/11/76 - 3/80
				F-4E	3/80 - 1987
				F-4G	12/83 - current 31/12/90
				F-16C/D	9/87 - current 31/12/90
SR	TAC	62 TAS	64/314 TAW	C-130E	10/7/68-1972
SR	TAC	703 TASS	507 TACW	CH-3E	9/4/85 - 28/4/85
SR	TAC	507 TACW	20 TASS	OV-10A	1/4/90 - current 31/12/90
				OT-37B	17/3/86 - 1988
			21 TASS	OV-10A	10/88 - current 31/12/90
SS	PACAF	309 TFS	31 TFW	F-100D/F	1968- 5/10/70
SS	TAC	309 TFS	4403 TFW	F-100D/F	5/10/70 - 30/10/70
ST	TAC	61 TAS	64/314 TAW	C-130E	10/7/68-1972
SU	PACAF	25 TFS	51 TFW	A-10A	1/1/84 - 1990
SV	ANG	158 TAS	165 TAG	C-130E	1/8/74 - 1/12/74+
SW	TAC	363 TFW	16 TRS	RF-4C	1/10/82 - 15/9/85
			17 TFS	F-16A/B	1/7/82 - late 1985
				F-16C/D	12/9/85 - current 31/12/90
			19 TFS	F-16A/B	1/4/82 - mid 1985
				F-16C/D	27/6/85 - current 31/12/90
			33 TFS	F-16C/D	8/3/85 - current 31/12/90
TA	PACAF	609 ACS/SOS	56 ACW/SOW	A-26A/K	1967-1/12/69
				T-28D	1967- 1969
TC	PACAF	1 ACS/SOS	56 ACW/SOW	A-1E/G/H/J	20/12/67- 15/12/72
TC	ADTAC	318 FIS	25 AD	F-15A/B	by 2/88 - 7/12/89
TD	TAC	4449 CCTS	516 TAW	C-7A	27/8/69 - 15/10/69
TD	TAC	18 TATS	516 TAW	C-7A	15/10/69 - 1/6/72
TE	TAC	16 TATS	314 TAW	C-130E	9/3/70 - 1972
TF	AFRES	457 TFS	301 TFW	F-16C	12/90 - current 31/12/90
TH	AFRES	457 TFS	506 TFG - 301 TFW	F-105D	8/7/72 - 25/3/73
				C-123B	1973
			301 TFW	F-105D	25/3/73 - 1982
				F-105D T-Stick	unknown
				F-4D	least 1981 - by 1987
				F-4E	8/87 - end 1990
				F-16C	late 1990 - current 31/12/91
TI	AFRES	68 TAS	922 TAG - 433 TAW	C-130B	1972 -30/6/74
TK	AFRES	68 TAS	921 TAG - 433 TAW/433 TAW	C-130B	30/6/74 - 1/12/74+
TK	AFRES	67 TAS	921 TAG - 433 TAW	C-130B	1972 -30/6/74
TJ	USAFE	307 TFS	401 TFW	F-4E	5/70 - 15/7/71
TJ	USAFE	612 TFS	401 TFW	F-4E	15/7/71 - 6/72
TJ	USAFE	401 TFW	612 TFS	F-4E	1972- 9/73
				F-4C	9/73 - 1978/79
				F-4D	1978/79 - gone by 24/1/83
				F-16A/B	least 24/1/83 - 1989
				F-16C/D	least 2/89 - current 31/12/90
			613 TFS	F-4E	6/72 - 9/73

TAIL CODE

Code	Command	Squadron	Wing	Unit	Aircraft	Dates
					F-4C	9/73 - 1978/79
					F-4D	1978/79 - least 24/1/83
					F-16A/B	3-4/85 - 1989
					F-16C/D	early 1989 - current 31/12/90
				614 TFS	F-4E	6/72 - 9/73
					F-4C	9/73 - 1978/79
					F-4D	1978/79 - mid 1983
					F-16A/B	around 19/5/83 - least 2/90
					F-16C/D	least 2/90 - current 31/12/90
TK	USAFE	353 TFS	401 TFW		F-4E	6/70 - 15/7/71
TK	USAFE	614 TFS	401 TFW		F-4E	15/7/71 - 6/72
TL	USAFE	613 TFS	401 TFW		F-4E	6/70 - 6/72
TL	ANG	125 TFS	138 TFG		A-7D	7/78 - early 1981
TN	ANG	143 TAS	143 TAG		C-130A	1976
TO	PACAF	606 ACS/SOS	56 ACW/SOW		T-28D	1967-15/6/71
					C-123B	1968 - 15/6/71
TR	TAC	37 TFW		415 TFS	F-117A	5/10/89 - current 31/12/90
				416 TFS	F-117A	5/10/89 - current 31/12/90
				417 TFTS	F-117A	5/10/89 - current 31/12/90
					AT-38B	5/10/89 - current 31/12/90
ST	TAC	4442 CCTW		4446 CCTS	C-130E	10/7/68- 9/3/70
				4447 CCTS	C-130E	10/7/68- 1/3/69
				4448 CCTS	C-130E	10/7/68- 1/8/71
				4449 CCTS	C-130E	10/7/68- 27/8/69
TS	PACAF	22 SOS	56 SOW		A-1E/G/H/J	25/10/68 -18/7/70
TT	PACAF	602 ACS/SOS	56 ACW/SOW		A-1E/H/J	1968-20/12/70
TX	AFRES	704 TFS	924 TAG - 482 TAW		F-4D	1/7/81 -4/88
					F-4E	1/89 - current 31/12/90
TY	TAC	325 TTW		1 TFTS	F-15A/B	27/4/84 - current 31/12/90
				2 TFTS	F-15A/B	1/10/83 - current 31/12/90
				95 TFTS	F-15A/B	1/4/84 - current 31/12/90
UA	AFRES	303 TAS	935 TAG - 422 TAW/442 TAW		C-130A	1972 - 10/74
UB	AFRES	304 TAS	936 TAG - 442 TAW		C-130A	1972 -30/6/74
UC	AFRES	465 TFS	507 TFG - 422 TAW/			
			507 TFG - 301 TFW/301 TFW		F-105D/F	20/5/72 - 5/73
UD	PACAF	391 TFS	475 TFW		F-4C/D	22/7/68-28/2/71
UD	PACAF	432 TRW/TFW		4 TFS	F-4E	8/73 - 23/12/75
				13 TFS	F-4D	8/73 - 30/6/75
				14 TRS	RF-4C	8/73 - 30/6/75
		25 TFS	F-4D			5/7/74 - 18/12/75
				421 TFS	F-4E	8/73 - 23/12/75
				555 TFS	F-4D	8/73 - 5/7/74
UD	PACAF	80 TFS	3 TFW		F-4D	15/3/71 - by 16/9/74
					F-4E	8/7/74 - 16/9/74
UE	PACAF	16 TRS	475 TFW		RF-4C	16/3/70 -15/2/71
UH	USAFE	20 TFW		55 TFS	F-111E	7-8/72 - current 31/12/90
				77 TFS	F-111E	7-8/72 - current 31/12/90
				79 TFS	F-111E	7-8/72 - current 31/12/90
UH	USAFE	43 ECS	66 ECW/20 TFW		EF-111A	3/2/84 -current 31/12/90
UK	PACAF	356 TFS	475 TFW		F-4C/D	1968- 15/3/71
UK	PACAF	36 TFS	3 TFW		F-4D	15/5/71 - 28/1/73
					F-4E	12/71 - 16/9/74
UP	PACAF	67 TFS	475 TFW		F-4D	1968- 15/3/71
UP	PACAF	35 TFS	3 TFW		F-4D	15/3/71 - by 1974
					F-4E	8/7/74 - 16/9/74
UR	USAFE	79 TFS	20 TFW		F-111E	10/70 - 1/71
(US)	USAFE	55 TFS	20 TFW			
UT	USAFE	77 TFS	20 TFW		F-111E	12/70 - 1/71
VA	TAC	68/TAS6/507	70350S/TASS		CH-53E	6/3/70 - 15/11/71
					CH-3E	1973 - 9/4/85
VA	ANG	149 TFS	192 TFG		A-7D	1982 - current 31/12/90
					A-7K	1982 - current 31/12/90
VG	ANG	115 TAS	146 TAG		C-130A	4/70 - 1/12/74+
VM	PACAF	352 TFS	35 TFW		F-100D/F	1968- 31/7/71
VN	ATC	25 FTS	71 FTW		T-38A	3/3/86 - 1990
VP	PACAF	614 TFS	35 TFW		F-100D/F	1968- 18/7/71
VS	PACAF	120 TFS	35 TFW		F-100C/F	4/67- 18/4/69 Colorado ANG
VS	PACAF	612 TFS	35 TFW		F-100D/F	14/4/69 - 31/7/71
VT	ANG	134 TFS	158 TFG		F-4D	9/10/81 - 1/7/87
VV	TAC	602 TACW	27 TASS		OV-10A	15/5/84 - 8/6/90
VZ	PACAF	615 TFS	35 TFW		F-100D/F	14/4/69 - 31/7/71
WA	TAC	4525 FWW	Det 1		A-7D	16/9/69 - 15/10/69
WA	TAC	57 FWW/TTW/FWW	64 FWS/TFAS/AS		F-5E	spring 1987 -early 1989
					F-16C/D	by 7/4/89 - 5/10/90
			65 FWS/TFAS		A-7D	23/6/72 - 8/75
					F-5E	spring 1987 - 7/4/89
			66 FWS		F-105D/F/G	1/10/71 - 7/75
					F-4C (ww)	9/71 - 7/75
					A-10A	1/10/77 - 1/6/81
			414 FWS		F-4C	1/10/71 - 1972

APPENDIX A

				F-4D	1/10/71 - least 1972
				F-4E	1/10/71 - 1/6/81
			422 FWS/TES	F-111A	1/10/71 - least 1/73
			422 TES	F-111E	1973 - 1987
				F-111D	- by 1988
				F-111F	- 1988
				F-16A/B	- by 1989
				F-16C/D	by 22/7/87 - current 31/12/90
				F-16/ADV	1989 - current 31/12/90
				F-16C	22/7/87 - current 31/12/90
				F-16D	20/6/87 - current 31/12/90
				F-4E	least 1980 - 1985
				F-15A/B	post 30/12/81 - by 1990
				F-15C/D	by 1989 - current 31/12/90
				F-15E	post 30/12/81 - current 31/12/90
				A-10A	post 30/12/81 - current 31/12/90
			431 FWS	F-111A	1/10/80 - current 31/12/90
				F-111D	- least 4/89
				F-111E	by 1981 - current 31/12/90
				F-111F	by 1981 - current 31/12/90
			433 FWS	F-15A/B	1/11/76 - 1/6/81
			Det 3	F-111	1/8/77 - 15/8/77
				F-111	15/8/77 - 1/10/80
			A-10 Division	A-10A	1/6/81 - current 31/12/90
			F-4 Division	F-4E	1/6/81 - 8/85
			F-15 Division	F-15A/B	1/6/81 - 1983
				F-15C/D	1/7/83 - current 31/12/90
			F-16 Division	F-16A/B	1/10/81 - 1987
				F-16C/D	1/7/83 - current 31/12/90
			4440 TFTG	F-16C/D	5/10/90 - current 31/12/90
WB	TAC	4535 CCTS	4525 CCTW	F-100D/F	10/7/68- 15/10/69
WB	TAC	65 FWS	57 FWW	F-100D/F	15/10/69 - 31/12/69
WC	TAC	4537 CCTS	4525 CCTW	F-100D/F	10/7/68- 15/10/69
WC	TAC	66 FWS	57 FWW	F-100D/F	15/10/69 - 1/10/71
WC	AFRES	337 TAS	905 TAG - 459 TAW	C-130B	1972 -8/72
WD	TAC	4538 CCTS	4525 FWW	F-1C/D/E	10/7/68- 15/10/69
WD	TAC	414 FWS	57 FWW	F-4C/D	15/10/69 - 1/10/71
				F-4C(ww)	- 9/71
				F-4E	10/6/72
WD	TAC	66 FWS	57 FWW	F-4C(ww)	9/71 - 1/10/71
WE	PACAF	19 ACS/SOS/TAS	315 ACW/SOW/TAWC-123B		1967-1968
				C-123K	1967- 1/5/71
WF	TAC	4539 CCTS	4525 FWW	F-111A	10/7/68- 15/10/69
WF	TAC	422 FWS	57 FWW	F-111A	15/10/69 - by 1972
				F-111E	by 10/70 - by 1972
				F-111D	- by 1972
				F-111F	- 1/10/71
WF	ATC	80 FTW	90 FTS	T-38A	3/3/86 - current 31/12/90
WG	ANG	142 TAS	166 TAG	C-130A	5/71 - 1/12/74+
WH	PACAF	309 ACS/SOS/TAW	315 ACW/SOW/TAS	C-123B	1967- 1968
				C-123K	1968- 31/7/70
WH	PACAF	22 TASS	326 AD	OV-10A	early 1984 - 11/9/88
WI	ANG	176 TFS	128 TFW	OA-37B	late 1979 - 6/81
				A-10A	9/6/81 - current 31/12/90
WL	ATC	82 FTW	97 FTS	T-38A	3/3/86 - current 31/12/90
			99 FTS	T-38A	3/3/86 - current 31/12/90
WM	PACAF	310 ACS/SOS/TAS	315 ACW/SOW/TAW	C-123B, K	1967- 26/1/72
WP	PACAF	8 TFW	16 SOS	AC-130A/H	5/74 - 8/12/74
			25 TFS	F-4D	1/73 - 5/7/74
			35 TFS	F-4D	16/9/74 - 11/81
				F-16A/B	14/9/81 - 1988
				F-16C/D	5/88 - current 31/12/90
			80 TFS	F-4D	16/9/74 - 11/81
				F-16A/B	14/9/81 - 1988
				F-16C/D	5/88 - current 31/12/90
			433 TFS	F-4D	1/73 - 23/7/74
			435 TFS	F-4D	1/73 - 8/8/74
			497 TFS	F-4D	1/73 - 16/9/74
			497 TFS	F-4D	11/78 - 1/1/82
WR	USAFE	78 TFS	81 TFW	F-4D	2/70 - 1972
WR	USAFE	81 TFW	78 TFS	F-4D	1972- by 9/79
				A-10A	by 9/79 - current 31/12/90
			91 TFS	F-4C	1972- 9/73
				F-4D	9/73 - by 9/79
				A-10A	by 9/79 - current 31/12/90
			92 TFS	F-4C	7-8/72 - 9/73
				F-4D	9/73 - 1979
				A-10A	1/79 - current 31/12/90
			509 TFS	A-10A	1981 - 15/9/88
			510 TFS	A-10A	by 9/79 - current 31/12/90

TAIL CODE

Code	Command	Unit	Wing	Aircraft	Dates
			511 TFS	A-10A	1/79 - 7/88
			527 AS	F-16C	14/6/88 - 2/90
WR	AFLC	WRALC		F-15A, F-105	1978 - 7/82
WS	USAFE	91 TFS	81 TFW	F-4C	2/70 - 5/72
WT	USAFE	92 TFS	81 TFW	F-4C	2/70 - 7-8/72
WV	PACAF	311 ACS/SOS/TAS	315 ACW/SOW/TAW	C-123B	1967- 1968
				C-123K	1968 - 5/10/71
WW	PACAF	Det 1 561 TFS	388 TFW	F-105G	1/2/73 - 5/9/73
WW	TAC	35 TFW/37 TFW/35 TFW	39 TFTS/TFS	F-4E	9/10/90 -11/5/84
				F-4G	1979 - 1981
			561 TFS	F-105G	1978 - 12/7/80
				F-4E	1981 - current 31/12/90
				F-4G	1978 - current 31/12/90
			562 TFTS	F-105G	1978 - 12/7/80
				F-4E	1981 - current 31/12/90
				F-4G	1978 - current 31/12/90
			563 TFS	F-4E	1978 - 30/3/81
				F-4G	1981 - 30/3/81
WW	AFSC	TAWC	4485 TESTS Det 5	F-4G	1987 - current 31/12/90
WX	AFRES	337 TAS	439 TAW	C-130B	1/4/74 - 1/12/74+
WY	ANG	187 TAS	153 TAG	C-130B	4-7/72 - 1/12/74
WZ	TAC	414 FWS	(57 FWW)	F-4D	Spring 71 - 1972
XL	ATC	47 FTW	85 FTS	T-37	3/3/86 - current 31/12/90
			86 FTS	T-38A	3/3/86 - current 31/12/90
YA	AFRES	63 TAS	927 TAG - 403 TAW	C-130A	1972 -1/12/74+
XA	ANG	119 TFS	113 TFW	F-100C/F	10/7/68 - 27/5/69
XB	ANG	121 TFS	113 TFW	F-100C/F	10/7/68 - 27/5/69
XC	PACAF	557 TFS	12 TFW	F-4C	1966- 31/3/70
XD	PACAF	558 TFS	12 TFW	F-4C	1966- 22/7/68
XD	PACAF	391 TFS	12 TFW	F-4C	22/7/68 - 22/7/68
XD	ANG	HQ Flight	113 TFW	F-100C/F	1968 - 5/69
XL	ATC	47 FTW	85 FTS	T-37	23/6/86 - current 31/12/90
			86 FTS	T-38A	23/6/86 - current 31/12/90
XN	PACAF	559 TFS	12 TFW	F-4C	1966- 31/3/70
XT	PACAF	391 TFS	12 TFW	F-4C	1966- 22/7/68
XT	PACAF	558 TFS	12 TFW	F-4C	22/7/68 - 31/3/71
YD	PACAF	21 TAS	374 TAW	C-130A	1968- 27/4/71
				AC-130A	1970 - 1971
YJ	PACAF	35 TAS	374 TAW	C-130A	1968- 24/3/71
YP	PACAF	41 TAS	374 TAW	C-130A	1968- 21/2/71
YU	PACAF	817 TAS	374 TAW	C-130A	1968- 27/4/70
ZA	PACAF	12 TFS	18 TFW	F-105D/F	9/67- 15/6/72
ZB	PACAF	Det 1 12 TFS	18 TFW	F-105F/G	24/9/70 - 1/11/70
ZB	PACAF	6010 WWS	388 TFW	F-105F/G	1/11/70 - 1/12/71
ZD	TAC	436 TFS	4531/31 TFW	F-4D	10/7/68- late 1968
				F-4E	10/7/68-30/10/70
ZD	TAC	306 TFS	31 TFW	F-4E	30/10/70 - 15/7/71
ZD	TAC	307 TFS	31 TFW	F-4E	15/7/71 - 1972
ZE	TAC	478 TFW	4531/31 TFW	F-4D	10/7/68- 1968
				F-4E	1968 - 31/10/70
ZE	TAC	309 TFS	31 TFW	F-4E	30/10/70 - 1972
ZF	TAC	560 TFS	4531/31 TFW	F-4D	10/7/68- late 1968
				F-4E	late 1968 - 31/10/70
ZF	TAC	308 TFS	31 TFW	F-4E	30/10/70 - 1972
ZF	TAC	31 TFW/TTW	306 TFTS/TFS	F-4D	1/7/78 - 11/85
				F-16A/B	11/85 - 1/10/86
			307 TFS/TFTS	F-4E	1972- 1981
				F-4D	1981 - early 1987
			308 TFS/TFTS/TFS	F-4E	1972- 1/7/82
				F-4D	1/7/82 - 10/86
				F-16A/B	31/10/86 - early 1987
			309 TFS/TFTS/TFS	F-4E	1972- 1981
				F-4D	1981 - 1987
				F-16A/B	1986 - early 1987
ZG	PACAF	67 TFS	18 TFW	F-4C	15/3/71 - 10/73
				F-4C (ww)	15/3/71 - 10/73
ZG	TAC	68 TFS	4531/31 TFW	F-4D	1/10/68 - 1970
				F-4E	1970 - 30/10/70
ZL	PACAF	44 TFS	18 TFW	F-4C	15/3/71 - 12/72
ZR	USAFE	17 TRS	86 TFW	RF-4C	12/1/70 - 6/72
ZR	USAFE	86 TFW	17 TRS	RF-4C	1972- 31/1/73
ZR	USAFE	26 TRW	17 TRS	RF-4C	31/1/73 -13/12/78
			38 TRS	RF-4C	31/1/73 - current 31/12/90
				F-4D	-
			417 TFS	F-4D	12/10/78 - 6/11/78
ZS	USAFE	81 TFS	86 TFW	F-4C	15/1/71 - 15/1/73
ZT	PACAF	19 TEWS	18 TFW	EB-66E	31/12/68 -30/10/70
ZZ	PACAF	15 TRS	18 TFW	RF-4C	1967- 6/72
ZZ	PACAF	18 TFW	12 TFS	F-4D	29/11/75 - least 5/79
				F-15C/D	1/80 - current 31/12/90

APPENDIX A

			25 TFS	F-4D	19/12/75 - 22/8/80
			44 TFS	F-4C	post 10/73 - 6/75
				F-4D	6/75 - 1979
				F-15C/D	29/9/79 - current 31/12/90
			67 TFS	F-4C	post 10/73 - 1/9/80
				F-15C/D	7/79 - current 31/12/90
			15 TRS	RF-4C	1972 - 1/10/89
6T	PACAF	6 SOS	14 SOW	A-1E/H	1968 - 1969

APPENDIX B
Tail Coded Unit
Base List USA

Alabama
Dannelly Field Montgomery
Maxwell AFB
Smith ANGB, Birmingham MAP

Alaska
Eielson AFB
Elmendorf AFB

Arizona
Davis-Monthan AFB
Luke AFB
Tucson IAP
Williams AFB

Arkansas
Ebing ANGB Fort Smith MAP
Little Rock AFB

California
Edwards AFB
George AFB
Hamilton AFB
McClellan AFB
Mather AFB
Van Nuys ANGB

Colorado
Buckley ANGB

Connecticut
Bradley ANGB Bradley IAP

Delaware
Greater Wilmington AP

Florida
Eglin AFB
Homestead AFB
Hurlburt Field
MacDill AFB
Patrick AFB
Tyndall AFB

Georgia
Dobbins AFB
Moody AFB
Robins AFB
Savannah AP

Hawaii
Wheeler AFB

Idaho
Mountain Home AFB

Illinois
Capital AP Springfield
Chicago O'Hare IAP
Greater Peoria AP

Indiana
Baer Field Fort Wayne MAP
Grissom AFB
Hulman Regional AP, Terre Haute

Iowa
Des Moines MAP
Sioux City MAP

Kansas
McConnell AFB
Forbes Field ANGB

Kentucky
Standiford Field, Louisville

Louisiana
Barksdale AFB
England AFB
New Orleans NAS

Maryland
Andrews AFB
Glenn L Martin State AP, Baltimore

Massachusetts
Barnes MAP Westfield
Otis AFB
Westover AFB

Michigan
W.K. Kellogg Regional AP, Battle Creek
Selfridge AFB

Minnesota
Minneapolis St Paul IAP

Mississippi
Allen C Thompson Field V Jackson
Columbus AFB
Keesler AFB
Key Field, Meridian

Missouri
Lambert Field, St Louis IAP
Richards Gebaur AFB

Nevada
Indian Springs AFAF
Nellis AFB
May ANGB, Reno-Cannon IAP
Tonopah Test Range

New Jersey
McGuire AFB

New Hampshire
Pease AFB

New Mexico
Cannon AFB
Holloman AFB
Kirtland AFB

New York
Hancock Field, Syracuse
Niagara Falls IAP
Schenectady County AP

North Carolina
Douglas MAP Charlotte AP
Seymour Johnson AFB
Pope AFB

APPENDIX B

Ohio
Mansfield Lahm AP
Rickenbacker AFB *(former Lockbourne AFB)*
Springfield MAP
Toledo Express AP
Wright-Patterson AFB
Youngstown MAP

Oklahoma
Tinker AFB
Tulsa IAP
Vance AFB
Will Rogers World AP, Oklahoma City

Panama
Howard AFB
Albrook AFB

Pennsylvania
Greater Pittsburgh IAP
Olmsted Field, Harrisburg IAP
NAS Willow Grove

Puerto Rico
Muniz ANGB, San Juan IAP

Rhode Island
Theodore F Green AP

South Carolina
Shaw AFB
McEntire ANGB
Myrtle Beach AFB

South Dakota
Joe Foss Field, Sioux Falls

Tennessee
Nashville Metropolitan AP
Memphis IAP
Sewart AFB

Texas
Bergstrom AFB
Carswell AFB
Dyess AFB
Ellington AFB
Kelly AFB
Laughlin AFB
Randolf AFB
Reese AFB
Sheppard AFB

Utah
Hill AFB

Vermont
Burlington IAP

Virginia
Admiral Byrd IAP, Richmond
Langley AFB

Washington
McChard AFB

West Virginia
Martinsburg MAP

Wisconsin
General B Mitchell Field, Milwaukee
Truax Field Dane County Regional AP

Wyoming
Cheyenne Map

Base List Europe

Germany
Bitburg AB
Hahn AB
Ramstein AB
Sembach AB
Spangdahlem AB
Zweibrucken AB

Iceland
Keflavik NAS

Netherlands
Soesterberg AB, Camp New Amsterdam

Spain
Torrejon AB

United Kingdom
Alconbury, RAF
Bentwaters, RAF
Lakenheath, RAF
Upper Heyford, RAF
Woodbridge, RAF

Basic List Asia

Japan
Itazuke AB
Misawa AB
Tachikawa AB
Yokota AB

Korea, Republic of; (ROK)
Kunsan AB
Osan AB
Suwon AB
Taegu AB

Okinawa
Naha AB
Kadena AB

Philippines
Clark AB

Taiwan
Ching Chaun Kang AB
Tainan

Thailand
Korat RTAFB
Nakhon Phanom ARAFB
Takhli RTAFB
Ubon RTAFB
Udorn RTAFB
Don Muang AP

South Vietnam, Republic of; (RSVN)
Bien Hoa AB
Bien Thuy AB
Cam Ranh Bay AB
Da Nang AB
Tan Son Nhut AB
Nha Trang AB
Phan Rang AB
Phu Cat AB
Pleiku AB
Tuy Hoa AB
Vung Tau AB

APPENDIX C
Tail coded aircraft types

Designation	Name	Manufacturer
A-1 E/G/H/J	Skyraider	Douglas
A-7 D/K	Corsair	LTV
A-10A	Thunderbolt	Fairchild
OA-10A	Thunderbolt	Fairchild
A-26 A/K	Invader	Douglas
A-37 A/B	Dragonfly	Cessna
OT-37B	Dragonfly	Cessna
OA-37B	Dragonfly	Cessna
EB-57E	Canberra	Martin
B-57 B/C/E/G	Canberra	Martin
EB-66 B/C/E	Destroyer	Douglas
C-7 A/B	Caribou	DeHavilland Canada
C-47 D/H	Skytrain	Douglas
AC-47D	Skytrain	Douglas
EC-47 N/P/G	Skytrain	Douglas
SC-47D	Skytrain	Douglas
AC-119 G/K	Flying Boxcar	Fairchild
C-123 B/K	Provider	Fairchild
UC-123K	Provider	Fairchild
C-130 A/B/E/H	Hercules	Lockheed
AC-130 A/E/H	Hercules	Lockheed
DC-130A	Hercules	Lockheed
EC-130 E/E(rr)/E(ll)/H	Hercules	Lockheed
MC-130H	Hercules	Lockheed
RC-130	Hercules	Lockheed
F-4 C/C (ww)/D/E/G	Phantom	McDonnell-Douglas
RF-4C	Phantom	McDonnell-Douglas
F-5 E/F	Tiger	Northrop
F-15 (TF-A)A/B/C/D/E	Eagle	McDonnell-Douglas
F-16 A/B/C/D/ADV	Falcon	General Dynamics
F-86H	Sabre	North American
F-100 C/D/F	Super Sabre	North American
RF-101 C/G/H	Voodoo	McDonnell
T/F-102A	Delta Dagger	Convair
F-105 B/D/F/G	Thunderchief	Republic
F-105D T-stick	Thunderchief	Republic
F-111 A/D/E/F	Aardvark	General Dynamics
EF-111A	Sparkvark, Raven	General Dynamics
F-117A	Stealth Fighter	Lockheed
UH-1 F/P	Huey	Bell
HH-1H	Huey	Bell
UH-lN	Twin Huey	Bell
C/HH-3E	Jolly Green Giant	Sikorsky
CH-53C	Jolly Green Giant	Sikorsky
A/T-28D	Trojan	North American
T-37	Tweety Bird	Cessna
T-38A	Talon	Northrop
AT-38B	Talon	Northrop
T-43A	737-253	Boeing
U-10A/B	Courier	Helio
OV-10A	Bronco	North American

APPENDIX D
T.O. 1-1-4

The following pages are excerpts from T.O. 1-1-4. Tail code placement drawings are followed by four illustrations which demonstrate camouflage patterns for tactical aircraft.

Typical tail code stencil used by 35 TFW for painting F-4E of 35 TFW. Photo: Patrick Martin, George AFB, 14 May 1991.

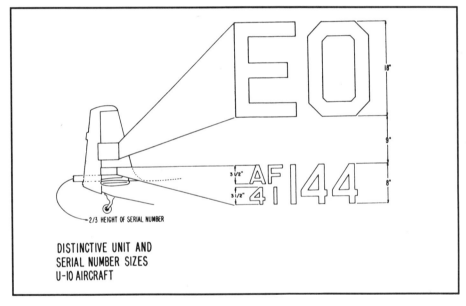

DISTINCTIVE UNIT AND SERIAL NUMBER SIZES
U-10 AIRCRAFT

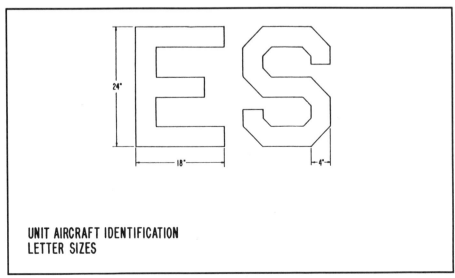

UNIT AIRCRAFT IDENTIFICATION LETTER SIZES

TAIL CODE

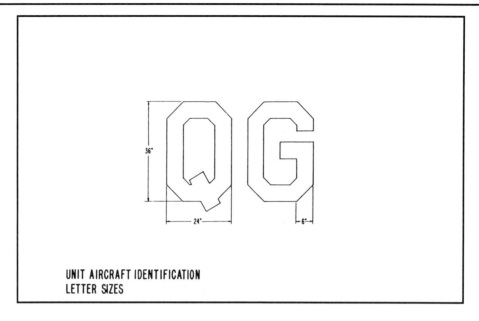

UNIT AIRCRAFT IDENTIFICATION LETTER SIZES

AIRCRAFT SERIAL NUMBER SIZES

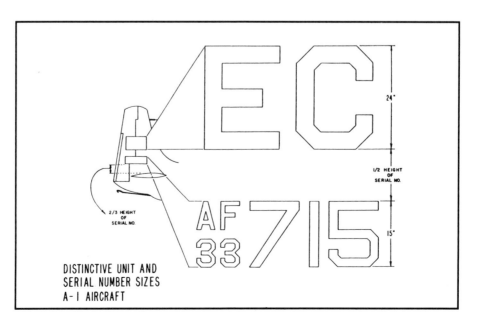

DISTINCTIVE UNIT AND SERIAL NUMBER SIZES A-1 AIRCRAFT

APPENDIX D

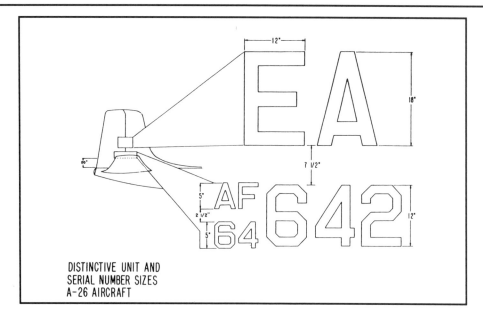

DISTINCTIVE UNIT AND
SERIAL NUMBER SIZES
A-26 AIRCRAFT

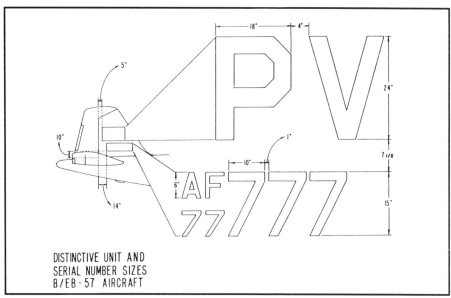

DISTINCTIVE UNIT AND
SERIAL NUMBER SIZES
B/EB-57 AIRCRAFT

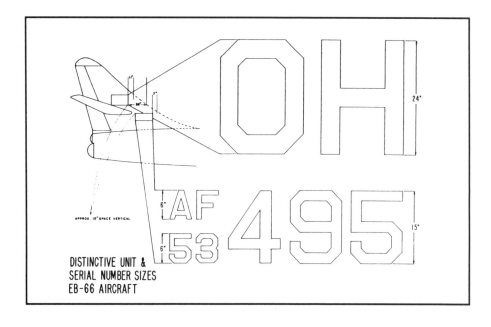

DISTINCTIVE UNIT &
SERIAL NUMBER SIZES
EB-66 AIRCRAFT

TAIL CODE

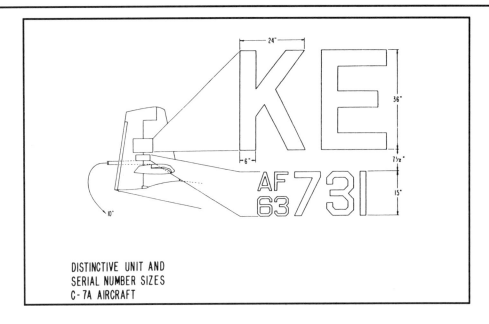

DISTINCTIVE UNIT AND
SERIAL NUMBER SIZES
C-7A AIRCRAFT

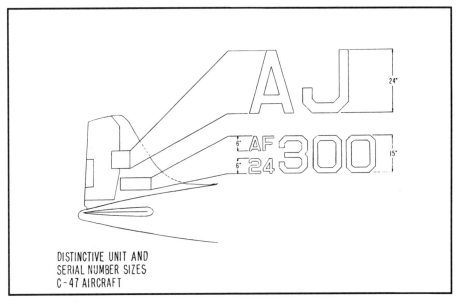

DISTINCTIVE UNIT AND
SERIAL NUMBER SIZES
C-47 AIRCRAFT

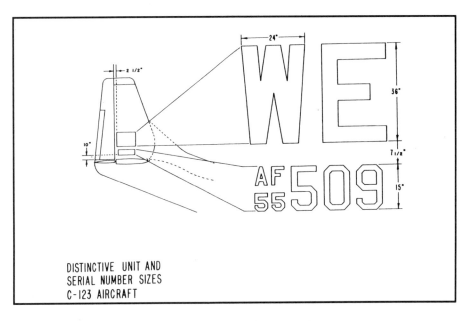

DISTINCTIVE UNIT AND
SERIAL NUMBER SIZES
C-123 AIRCRAFT

APPENDIX D

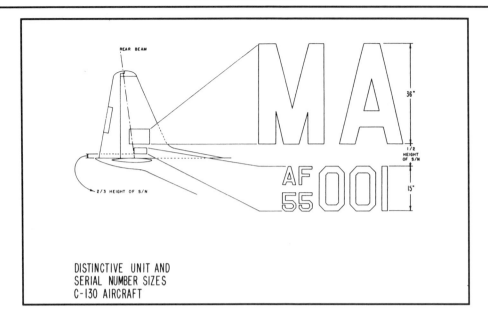

DISTINCTIVE UNIT AND
SERIAL NUMBER SIZES
C-130 AIRCRAFT

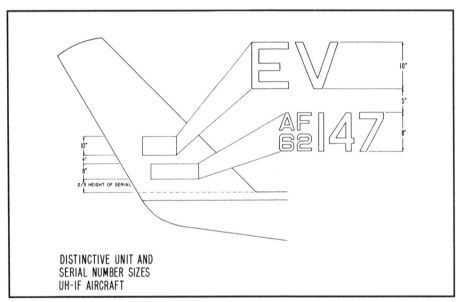

DISTINCTIVE UNIT AND
SERIAL NUMBER SIZES
UH-IF AIRCRAFT

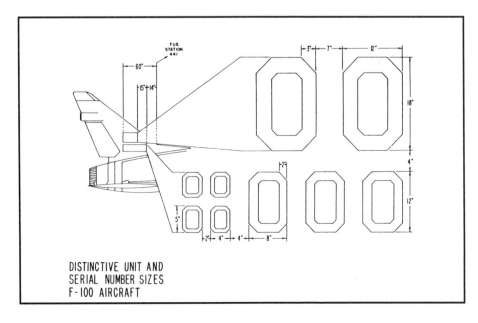

DISTINCTIVE UNIT AND
SERIAL NUMBER SIZES
F-100 AIRCRAFT

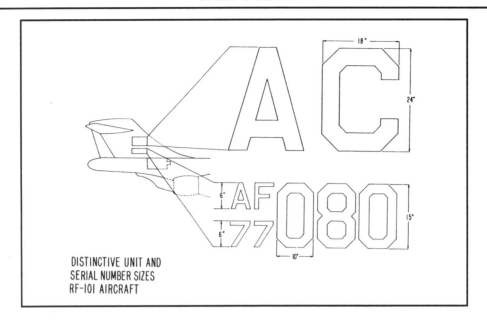

DISTINCTIVE UNIT AND
SERIAL NUMBER SIZES
RF-101 AIRCRAFT

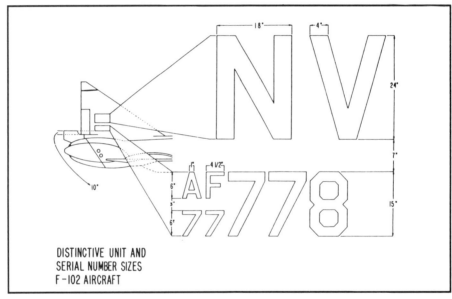

DISTINCTIVE UNIT AND
SERIAL NUMBER SIZES
F-102 AIRCRAFT

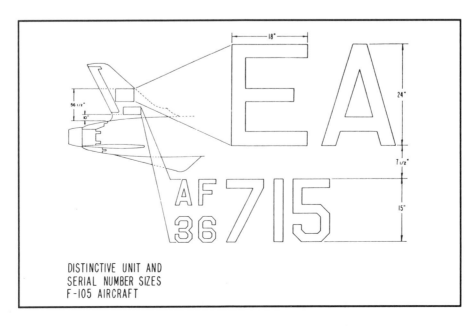

DISTINCTIVE UNIT AND
SERIAL NUMBER SIZES
F-105 AIRCRAFT

APPENDIX D

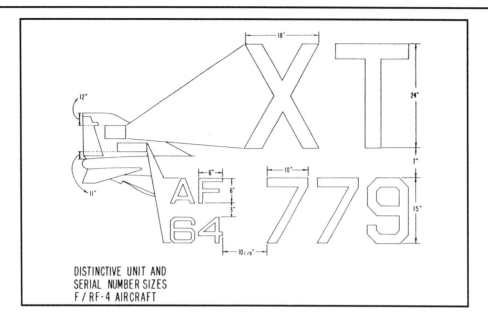

DISTINCTIVE UNIT AND
SERIAL NUMBER SIZES
F/RF-4 AIRCRAFT

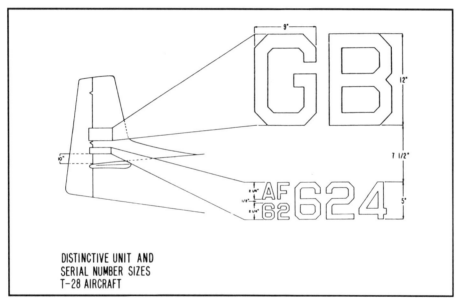

DISTINCTIVE UNIT AND
SERIAL NUMBER SIZES
T-28 AIRCRAFT

TAIL CODE

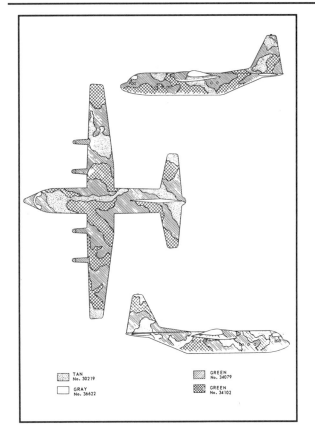

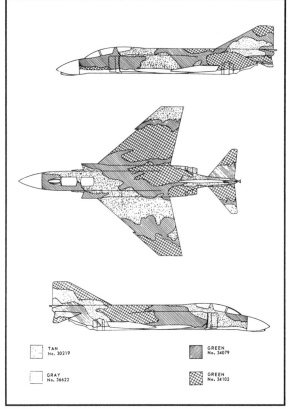

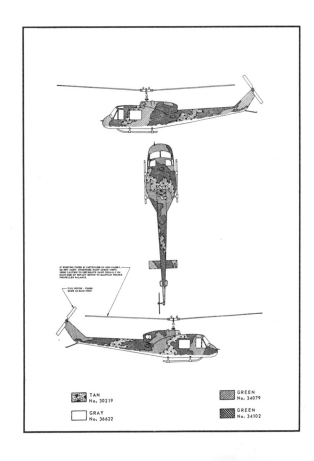

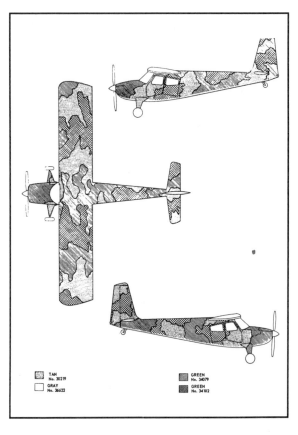

APPENDIX E
United States Air Force
Tail Codes 31 December 1990

Code	Command	Parent Unit	Squadron	Aircraft Type	Colour	Base
AK	PACAF	343 TFW	18 TFS	A-10A	bl	Eielson AFB, Alaska
AK	PACAF	21 TFW	43 TFS	F-15C/D	bl	
			54 TFS	F-15C/D	ye	Elmendorf AFB, Alaska
AL	ANG	187 TFG	160 TFS	F-16A/B	var.	Dannelly Field, Alabama
AR	USAFE	10 TFW	509 TFS	A-10A	gy	RAF Alconbury
			511 TFS	A-10A	bk	RAF Alconbury
AZ	ANG	162 TFG	152 TFS	A-7D	multi.	Tucson IAP, Arizona
BA	TAC	67 TRW	12 TRS	RF-4C	or	Bergstrom AFB, Texas
			91 TRS	RF-4C	rd	Bergstrom AFB, Texas
BC	ANG	110 TASG	172 TASS	OA-37B	—	Battle Creek ANGB, Michigan
BD	AFRES	917 TFW	46 TFTS	A-10A	bl	Barksdale AFB, Louisiana
			47 TFS	A-10A	gr	Barksdale AFB, Louisiana
BH	ANG	117 TRW	106 TRS	RF-4C	var.	Birmingham MAP, Alabama
BT	USAFE	36 TFW	22 TFS	F-15C/D	rd	Bitburg AB, Germany
			53 TFS	F-15C/D	bk/ye	Bitburg AB, Germany
			525 TFS	F-15C/D	bl	Bitburg AB, Germany
CC	TAC	27 TFW	522 TFS	F-111D	rd	Cannon AFB, New Mexico
			523 TFS	F-111D	bl	Cannon AFB, New Mexico
			524 TFTS	F-111D	ye	Cannon AFB, New Mexico
			428 TFTS	F-111G		Cannon AFB, New Mexico
CO	ANG	140 TFW	120 TFS	A-7D/K	bl/wh	Buckley ANGB, Colorado
CR	USAFE	32 TFG	32 TFS	F-15C/D	or-gr	Soesterberg AB, Netherlands
CT	ANG	103 TFG	118 TFS	A-10A	—	Bradley ANGB, Connecticut
DC	ANG	113 TFW	121 TFS	F-16A/B	rd/wh	Andrews AFB, Maryland
DM	TAC	355 TFW	357 TFTS	A-10A	ye	Davis-Monthan AFB, Arizona
			358 TFTS	A-10A	gr	Davis-Monthan AFB, Arizona
DO	AFRES	906 TFG	89 TFS	F-16A/B	or/bk	Wright-Patterson AFB, Ohio
ED	AFSC	6510 TESTW	6512 TESTS	Various		Edwards AFB, California
EG	TAC	33 TFW	58 TFS	F-15C/D	bl	Eglin AFB, Florida
			59 TFS	F-15C/D	ye	Eglin AFB, Florida
			60 TFS	F-15C/D	rd	Eglin AFB, Florida
EL	TAC	23 TFW	74 TFS	A-10A	bl	England AFB, Louisiana
			75 TFS	A-10A	bk/wh	England AFB, Louisiana
			76 TFS	A-10A	rd	England AFB, Louisiana
ET	AFSC	3246 TW	3247 TESTS	Various	wh/rd	Eglin AFB, Florida
FF	TAC	1 TFW	27 TFS	F-15C/D	ye	Langley AFB, Virginia
			71 TFS	F-15C/D	rd	Langley AFB, Virginia
			94 TFS	F-15C/D	bl	Langley AFB, Virginia
FM	AFRES	482 TFW	93 TFS	F-16A/B	bk/wh	Homestead AFB, Florida
FS	ANG	188 TFW	184 TFS	F-16A/B		Fort Smith MAP, Arkansas
FW	ANG	122 TFW	163 TFS	F-4E	bl	Fort Wayne MAP, Indiana
GA	TAC	35 TFW	20 TFTS	F-4E	si	George AFB, California
			21 TFTS	F-4E	bk	George AFB, California
HA	ANG	185 TFG	174 TFS	A-7D/K	ye	Sioux City, Iowa
HF	ANG	181 TFG	113 TFS	F-4E	rd/wh/bl	Hulman RAP, Indiana
HI	AFRES	419 TFW	466 TFS	F-16A/B	ye	Hill AFB, Utah
HL	TAC	388 TFW	4 TFS	F-16C/D	ye	Hill AFB, Utah
			34 TFS	F-16C/D	rd	Hill AFB, Utah
			421 TFS	F-16C/D	bk	Hill AFB, Utah
HM	TAC	479 TTW	433 TFTS	AT-38B	gr	Holloman AFB, New Mexico
			434 TFTS	AT-38B	rd	Holloman AFB, New Mexico
			435 TFTS	AT-38B	bl	Holloman AFB, New Mexico
			436 TFTS	AT-38B	ye	Holloman AFB, New Mexico
HO	TAC	49 TFW	7 TFS	F-15A/B	bl	Holloman AFB, New Mexico
			8 TFS	F-15A/B	ye	Holloman AFB, New Mexico
			9 TFS	F-15A/B	rd	Holloman AFB, New Mexico
HR	USAFE	50 TFW	10 TFS	F-16C/D	bl	Hahn AB, Germany
			313 TFS	F-16C/D	or	Hahn AB, Germany
			496 TFS	F-16C/D	ye	Hahn AB, Germany
HS	TAC	31 TFW	307 TFS	F-16C/D	rd	Homestead AFB, Florida
			308 TFS	F-16C/D	gr	Homestead AFB, Florida
			309 TFS	F-16C/D	bl	Homestead AFB, Florida

TAIL CODE

Code	Command	Wing	Squadron	Aircraft	Color	Base
IA	ANG	132 TFW	124 TFS	A-7D/K	rd/ye cb	Des Moines MAP, Iowa
IL	ANG	182 TASG	169 TASS	OA-37B	var.	Grt. Peoria Arpt, Illinois
IN	AFRES	930 TFG	45 TFS	A-10A	bl	Grissom AFB, Indiana
IS	TAC	1 AF	57 FIS	F-15C/D	bk/wh	NAS Keflavik, Iceland
KC	AFRES	442 TFW	303 TFS	A-10A	bk	Richards-Gebaur AFB, Montana
LA	TAC	405 TTW	461 TFTS	F-15E	ye/bk	Luke AFB, Arizona
			550 TFTS	F-15E	bk/si	Luke AFB, Arizona
			555 TFTS	F-15A/B/D	gr	Luke AFB, Arizona
LF	TAC	58 TTW	310 TFTS	F-16C/D	gr	Luke AFB, Arizona
			311 TFTS	F-16A/B	bl	Luke AFB, Arizona
			312 TFTS	F-16C/D	bk	Luke AFB, Arizona
			314 TFTS	F-16C/D	ye/bk	Luke AFB, Arizona
LN	USAFE	48 TFW	492 TFS	F-111F	bl	RAF Lakenheath
			493 TFS	F-111F	ye	RAF Lakenheath
			494 TFS	F-111F	rd	RAF Lakenheath
			495 TFS	F-111F	gr	RAF Lakenheath
LR	AFRES	944 TFG	302 TFS	F-16C/D	—	Luke AFB, Arizona
LY	TAC	24 AD	48 FIS	F-15A/B		Langley AFB, Virginia
MA	ANG	104 TFG	131 TFS	A-10A	rd	Barnes MAP, Massachusetts
MB	TAC	354 TFW	353 TFS	A-10A	rd	Myrtle Beach AFB, South Carolina
			355 TFS	A-10A	bl	Myrtle Beach AFB, South Carolina
			356 TFS	A-10A	gr	Myrtle Beach AFB, South Carolina
MC	TAC	56 TTW	61 TFTS	F-16C/D	ye	MacDill AFB, Florida
			62 TFTS	F-16C/D	bl	MacDill AFB, Florida
			63 TFTS	F-16C/D	rd	MacDill AFB, Florida
			72 TFTS	F-16C/D	bk	MacDill AFB, Florida
MD	TAC	175 TFG	104 TFS	A-10A	var.	Martin Apt, Maryland
MJ	PACAF	432 TFW	13 TFS	F-16C/D	bk/wh	Misawa AB, Japan
			14 TFS	F-16C/D	bk/ye	Misawa AB, Japan
MO	TAC	366 TFW	389 TFTS	F-111A	ye	Mountain Home AFB, Idaho
			390 ECS	EF-111A	—	Mountain Home AFB, Idaho
			391 TFS	F-111A	bl	Mountain Home AFB, Idaho
			34 BS	B-52G		Castle AFB, California
MY	TAC	347 TFW	68 TFS	F-16C/D	rd	Moody AFB, Georgia
			69 TFS	F-16C/D	bk	Moody AFB, Georgia
			70 TFS	F-16C/D	bk/wh	Moody AFB, Georgia
NF	TAC	602 TACW	22 TASTS	OV/OA-10A	ye	Davis-Monthan AFB, Arizona
			23 TASS	OA-10A		Davis-Monthan AFB, Arizona
NJ	ANG	108 TFG	141 TFS	F-4E	—	McGuire AFB, New Jersey
NO	AFRES	926 TFG	706 TFS	A-10A	rd	New Orleans, Louisiana
NT	ATC	323 TFW	455 FTS	T-37B, T-43A		Mather AFB, California
NY	ANG	174 TFW	138 TFS	F-16A/B	—	Hancock Field, New York
OH	ANG	121 TFW	162 TFS	A-7D/K	rd	Springfield MAP, Ohio
			112 TFS	A-7D/K	gr/bk	Toledo Exp. Apt, Ohio
			166 TFS	A-7D/K	bk	Rickenbacker AFB, Ohio
OK	ANG	138 TFG	125 TFS	A-7D/K	rd	Tulsa IAP Oklahoma
OK	ATC	71 FTS	8 FTS	T-37B		
			25 FTS	T-38A		Vance AFB, Oklahoma
OS	PACAF	51 TFW	25 TFS	A-10A		Osan AB, ROK
			36 TFS	F-16C/D	rd	Osan AB, ROK
			19 TASS	OA-10A	bl	Osan AB, ROK
OT	AFSC	TAWC	4485 TESTS	Various	bk/wh	Eglin AFB, Florida
PA	ANG	111 TASG	103 TASS	OA-10A		Willow Grove ARFF, Pa.
PN	PACAF	3 TFW	3 TFS	F-4E	bl	Clark AB, Philippines
			90 TFS	F-4E/G	rd	Clark AB, Philippines
PR	ANG	156 TFG	198 TFS	A-7D/K	bl/rd/wh	Muniz ANGB, Puerto Rico
PT	ANG	112 TFG	146 TFS	A-7D/K	bk	Greater Pittsburgh IAP, Pa.
RA	ATC	12 TFW	559 FTS	T-37		Randolph AFB, Texas
			560 FTS	T-38A		Randolph AFB, Texas
RG	AFLC	Warner Robins	ALC	F-15B		Robins AFB, Georgia
RS	USAFE	86 TFW	512 TFS	F-16C/D	gr/bk	Ramstein AB, Germany
			526 TFS	F-16C/D	rd/bk	Ramstein AB, Germany
SA	ANG	149 TFG	182 TFS	F-16A/B	rd/wh	Kelly AFB, Texas
SB	USAFE	66 ECW	43 ECS	EC-130H		Sembach AB, West Germany
SD	ANG	114 TFG	175 TFS	A-7D/K	bk	Joe Foss Field, South Dakota
SH	AFRES	507 TFG	465 TFS	F-16A/B	bl	Tinker AFB, Oklahoma
SI	ANG	183 TFG	170 TFS	F-16A/B	ye	Springfield Airport, Illinois
SJ	TAC	4 TFW	334 TFS	F-15E, F-4E	bl	Seymour Johnson AFB, N.Carolina
			335 TFS	F-15E	gr	Seymour Johnson AFB, N.Carolina
			336 TFS	F-15E	ye	Seymour Johnson AFB, N.Carolina
SL	ANG	131 TFW	110 TFS	F-4E	rd	Lambert St Louis, Missouri

APPENDIX E

SP	USAFE	52 TFW	23 TFS	F-4G F-16C/D	bl/wh	Spangdahlem AB, Germany
			81 TFS	F-4G F-16C/D	ye/wh	Spangdahlem AB, Germany
			480 TFS	F-4G F-16C/D	rd/wh	Spangdahlem AB, Germany
SR	TAC	507 TACW	20 TASS	OV-10A		Shaw AFB, South Carolina
			21 TASS	OV-10A		Shaw AFB, South Carolina
SW	TAC	363 TFW	17 TFS	F-16C/D	wh	Shaw AFB, South Carolina
			19 TFS	F-16C/D	yl	Shaw AFB, South Carolina
			33 TFS	F-16C/D	bk	Shaw AFB, South Carolina
TF	AFRES	301 TFW	457 TFS	F-16C/D		Carswell AFB, Texas
TJ	USAFE	401 TFW	612 TFS	F-16C/D	bl/wh	Torrejon AB, Spain
			613 TFS	F-16C/D	ye/bl	Torrejon AB, Spain
			614 TFS	F-16C/D	rd/bl	Torrejon AB, Spain
TR	TAC	37 TFS	415 TFS	F-117A	rd	Tonopah Test Range, Nevada
			416 TFS	F-117A	bl	Tonopah Test Range, Nevada
			417 TFTS	F-117A	ye	Tonopah Test Range, Nevada
				AT-38B	bk	Tonopah Test Range, Nevada
TX	AFRES	924 TFG	704 TFS	F-4E	bl/rd	Bergstrom AFB, Texas
TY	TAC	325 TTW	1 TFTS	F-15A/B	rd	Tyndall AFB, Florida
			2 TFTS	F-15A/B	ye	Tyndall AFB, Florida
			95 TFTS	F-15A/B	bl	Tyndall AFB, Florida
UH	USAFE	20 TFW	42 ECS	EF-111A	gy	RAF Upper Heyford
			55 TFS	F-111E	bl/wh cb	RAF Upper Heyford
			77 TFS	F-111E	rd	RAF Upper Heyford
			79 TFS	F-111E	ye/bk	RAF Upper Heyford
VA	ANG	192 TFG	149 TFS	A-7D/K	—	Byrd Field, Virginia
WA	TAC	57 FWW	FWS	A-10A	ye/bk cb	Nellis AFB, Nevada
			FWS	F-16C/D	ye/bk cb	Nellis AFB, Nevada
			FWS	F-15C/D	ye/bk cb	Nellis AFB, Nevada
			422 TES	A-10A,F-15C/D/E,F-16C/D/ADF		
					ye/bk cb	Nellis AFB, Nevada
			431 FWS	F-111A/E	ye/bk	McClellan AFB, California
		FWS	A-10 Division	A-10A		Nellis AFB, Nevada
		FWS	F-15 Division	F-15C/D		Nellis AFB, Nevada
	FWS		F-16 Division	F-16C/D		Nellis AFB, Nevada
WF	ATC	80 FTW	90 FTS	T-38A		Sheppard AFB, Texas
WI	ANG	128 TFW	176 TFS	A-10A	—	Traux ANGB, Wisconsin
WL	FTC	82 TFW	97 FTS	T-38A		Williams AFB, Arizona
			99 FTS	T-38A		Williams AFB, Arizona
WP	PACAF	8 TFW	35 TFS	F-16C/D	bl	Kunsan AB, Korea
			80 TFS	F-16C/D	ye	Kunsan AB, Korea
WR	USAFE	81 TFW	78 TFS	A-10A	rd/wh	RAF Woodbridge
			91 TFS	A-10A	bl/wh	RAF Woodbridge
			92 TFS	A-10A	ye/wh	RAF Bentwaters
			510 TFS	A-10A	pu/wh	RAF Bentwaters
WW	TAC	35 TFW	561 TFS	F-4E/G	ye	George AFB, California
			562 TFS	F-4E/G	bl	George AFB, California
WW	AFSC	TAWC	4485 TESTS	F-4G		George AFB, California
XL	ATC	47 FTW	85 FTS	T-37		Laughlin AFB, Texas
			96 FTS	T-38		Laughlin AFB, Texas
ZR	USAFE	26 TRW	38 TRS	RF-4C	gr/wh	Zweibrucken AB, Germany
ZZ	PACAF	18 TFW	12 TFS	F-15C/D	ye	Kadena AB, Okinawa
			44 TFS	F-15C/D	bl	Kadena AB, Okinawa
			67 TFS	F-15C/D	rd	Kadena AB, Okinawa

244 TAIL CODE

F-4E Phantom 73-1160 **SJ,** 334 TFS 4 TFW, Seymour-Johnson AFB, with blue tail stripe. Photo: Patrick Martin, Washington State Air Fair, Paine Field, 16 August 1990.

F-100D Super Sabre 56-3395 marked as 56-3298 **WB**, 4536 CCTS/65 FWS 4525 FWW/57 FWW, Nellis AFB, on the pole at Nellis. Photo: Patrick Martin 21 August 1989.

Also from the publisher

PHANTOM IN COMBAT
Walter J. Boyne

Size: 8 1/2" x 11"   192 pages, hard cover, over 300 b/w and color photographs, charts, diagrams
ISBN: 0-88740-599-1 $35.00

BOEING B-52
A Documentary History
Walter J. Boyne

Size: 8 1/2" x 11"   160 pages, hard cover, over 200 b/w photographs, cutaway drawings, charts, diagrams
ISBN: 0-88740-600-9 $29.95

DOUGLAS A-1 SKYRAIDER
A Photo Chronicle
Frederick A. Johnsen

Size: 8 1/2" x 11"   128 pages, soft cover, over 100 b/w photographs, line drawings
ISBN: 0-88740-512-6-9 $19.95